DEFENDING THE NATIONAL INTEREST

Written under the auspices of
the Center for International Affairs,
Harvard University

A list of other Center publications
of related interest appears at the back
of this book

DEFENDING THE NATIONAL INTEREST

Raw Materials Investments and U.S. Foreign Policy

STEPHEN D. KRASNER

PRINCETON UNIVERSITY PRESS
Princeton, New Jersey

Published by Princeton University Press, Princeton, New Jersey
In the United Kingdom: Princeton University Press,
Guildford, Surrey

Library of Congress Cataloging in Publication Data will be
found on the last printed page of this book

This book has been composed in VIP Times Roman

Clothbound editions of Princeton University Press books
are printed on acid-free paper, and binding materials are
chosen for strength and durability

Printed in the United States of America by Princeton
University Press, Princeton, New Jersey

For my family

Table of Contents

List of Tables and Figure

Preface and Acknowledgments

There was a period when I thought that if a question could be clearly formulated, it could be easily answered. I have learned that it isn't so. The basic question that informs this study was one that plagued me for many years, and the answer was hard in coming. The question can be put in many ways, but the most immediate (at least for the graduate student I was when I first began pondering these issues) is something like the following: why are so many social scientists so anxious to give advice to policymakers when there is nothing in their theories that would suggest that it would do any good? This is not because their theories are necessarily inadequate, or because government officials are thick-headed, but because academic explanations have treated government behavior as the outcome of a series of pressures that emanate from the society. The state has been seen not as an autonomous actor, but rather as a mirror reflecting particularistic societal interests. Yet, given all the time that social scientists spend on planes to Washington, their own behavior seemed to belie their theoretical positions. If a piece of advice in the ear of a decision-maker could change things, the image of politics underlying most contemporary analyses could hardly be adequate.

Only over the course of several years did I come to the conclusion that most of what has passed for political science in recent years, at least in the United States, has really been political sociology. It has dealt with the impact of the society on the government, not with the impact of the state on the society. The lines between the state and the society have become blurred. "Although the problems of state and sovereignty are occasionally discussed," writes Frederick Watkins in the most recent edition of the *International Encyclopedia of the Social Sciences* (Vol. 15, p. 155), "they are rarely regarded as central to the discipline [of political science]." Similarly, Ralph Miliband, who reflects a very different theoretical orientation, notes on the first page of *The State in Capitalist Society* that "the state itself, as a subject of political study, has long been very unfashionable."

Happily, in my estimation, concern with the state seems to be returning. This trend is very explicit in Marxist writings, where the work of Poulantzas, Miliband, Habermas, O'Connor, and others has led to lively debate. It is also reflected in the new-found popularity of policy studies. (Of course, there was a period when what we now call policy studies was the central concern of political science.) In comparative politics, the most recent volume of the Social Science Research Council's influential series on political development—*The Formation of National States in Western Europe* edited by Charles Tilly—deals explicitly with the question of state building, and recent work on corporatism also gives the state a central role. In international politics, the concept of the state as an autonomous actor was never displaced from the stage, although bureaucratic and transnational conceptualizations have been trying to elbow it into the wings. The theoretical orientation offered in this book, it is hoped, will be part of a general movement to take the state seriously again, to recognize that even in democratic politics it is not merely a passive reactor, but rather a creator, in some measure, of its own social environment.

In the course of writing this book I have accumulated many debts. Financial support came from the faculty research fund at UCLA, the Washington Center of Foreign Policy Research of the Johns Hopkins School of Advanced International Studies, and, most importantly, the Center for International Affairs at Harvard University. While working at the Center, I had the benefit of extensive contact with Samuel P. Huntington and Joseph S. Nye, both gentlemen and scholars. My intellectual development was also greatly facilitated by a truly extraordinary group of colleagues at the Center, including James Kurth, Peter Gourevitch, Thomas Horst, Robert Jervis, Peter Katzenstein, Peter Lange, Samuel Popkin, and Martin Shefter.

Few authors can work in a vacuum; we all become too entranced with our own ideas. There is only one real check on this tendency—effective criticism from colleagues. I have benefitted more than most. Robert Gilpin, Peter Gourevitch, Robert Jervis, Peter Katzenstein, Robert Keohane, Robert W. Tucker, and Kenneth Waltz all subjected themselves to earlier versions of this study. Since I know what went into the garbage pail, I realize how important their comments have been. Although I expect that many of them will still disagree with some of the central arguments in the following pages, their remarks forced me to make a less opaque presentation and to think through my own position. Sanford Thatcher has been an extraordinarily responsive and helpful editor. Finally, I want to thank my wife Joan for preparing the index and for accepting, with varying degrees of grace, the reply, "I can't, I have to work," to many requests.

DEFENDING THE NATIONAL INTEREST

PART ONE

CHAPTER I

A Statist Approach to the Study of Foreign Policy

This is a study of the aims of central decision-makers and their relationship with private corporations. Its basic analytic assumption is that there is a distinction between the state and the society. While this might seem straightforward, it is very much at variance with the way in which Americans have recently studied domestic, and increasingly international, politics. The governing liberal paradigm does not view the state as an independent entity. At best it is seen as a referee among competing social groups, at worst as a cipher. Studies of international politics and foreign policy have been less affected by this interest-group or liberal perspective. But even here recent work associated with the notion of bureaucratic politics has raised serious questions about the analytic utility of the concept of the state. Marxist writers have also challenged analyses that do not begin from the perspective of the society. For them the policy of the state reflects either the preferences of the bourgeoisie or the structural needs of a capitalist system. Both liberal and Marxist perspectives explain the action of public officials in terms of private pressures or needs. The fundamental problem for political analysis is to identify the underlying social structure and the political mechanisms through which particular societal groups determine the government's behavior. It is meaningless from these perspectives to use terms like "national interest" or "reason of state." The state does not have objectives that cannot ultimately be understood in terms of societal wants or needs.

This book tries to demonstrate the superiority of an alternative approach, a statist image of foreign policy, by undertaking two central analytic tasks. The first is to elaborate a statist or state-centric approach. A statist paradigm views the state as an autonomous actor. The objectives sought by the state cannot be reduced to some summation of private desires. These objectives can be called appropriately the national interest. For a statist approach explanation and description involve (a) demonstrating empirically that American central decision-makers have sought a consistent set of goals—for this study, in the area of foreign raw materials investments—and (b) defining the conditions under which they have been able to attain their goals in the face of international and, more importantly, domestic constraints.

The second central analytic task of this study is to defend a statist approach against its most important rivals—interest-group liberalism and Marxism. For variants of these approaches that see the state as the handmaiden of particular powerful private actors, the defense is not very difficult: many of the cases in the following chapters show a clear divergence between private and public goals. However, distinguishing a statist argument from a structural Marxist approach, which views the state as acting to preserve the coherence of capitalist society as a whole, is a much more difficult task. The most powerful evidence I can offer in defense of a theoretical perspective that denies that state actions can be reduced to societal needs, even very general ones like preserving the coherence of capitalist structures, is that the behavior of the United States when it extended itself to the utmost—when it was prepared to use overt or covert force—must ultimately be understood not in terms of economic or strategic objectives, but in terms of ideological ones.

The Empirical Evidence

The Cases

The conclusions of this study are drawn primarily from a number of detailed case studies concerning international raw materials investments. These are presented in Chapters IV, VI, VII, and VIII. For some issues, such as the explicit official sanctioning of a specific new investment (as described in Chapter IV) it was possible to cover almost the whole universe of events. For others, such as the protection of foreign investment through diplomacy and economic pressure after World War II (examined in Chapter

VII), it was only possible to look at a small sample; there have been literally hundreds of takeovers since 1950. Here I have selected four cases that illustrate the range of American response, two of which—the reaction to Peru's nationalizations beginning in the 1960s and to the oil crisis of the mid-1970s—were the subject of much public attention.

I cannot defend the cases presented here as a scientific sample. They have been chosen primarily because they have attracted both public and scholarly attention, rather than through some process of random selection. However, they are not systematically biased in favor of a statist argument. American raw materials policy is not an area where a coherent and persistent set of public initiatives would necessarily be expected. First, central decision-makers in the United States do not have as much control over domestic actors as their counterparts in other industrialized market economy countries, such as France or Japan, or in Leninist political systems. (This argument is elaborated in Chapter III.) Second, raw materials industries involve very large and politically powerful private actors. This is particularly true of the petroleum sector: five out of the ten largest American industrial corporations are oil companies. If the efficacy of a statist paradigm can be demonstrated in explaining the raw materials policy of the United States, it should apply with even greater force to most other political systems (at least those of developed countries) and to other policy issues.

Furthermore, the possibilities of systematic bias are vitiated by the number of cases presented. The use of case studies is now an established scholarly tradition for foreign policy analysis. Most investigations have concentrated on a single case, albeit a carefully chosen one. The conclusions of this study are drawn from some fifteen cases. They encompass the beginning and end of a period when private corporations structured international markets for unprocessed commodities. They also impinge on many of the major issues of U.S. foreign policy in the twentieth century, including engagement in the First and Second World Wars as well as intervention in the Third World after 1945.

Chronologically, the first case investigated is the American reaction to Mexican pressures during the Mexican Revolution,

1910-1920. Mexico was the first major area of foreign investment for American raw materials companies. Policies adopted by Mexican leaders after 1910 were the earliest systematic threat to U.S. investors, although several instances of capricious takeovers stemming from local political feuds or personal cupidity had taken place earlier. The last case presented is the oil crisis of the 1970s. In terms of economic impact, it is by far the most significant conflict involving American foreign raw materials investment.

Although this book concludes with recent events, the mid-1970s are not just a chronologically necessary stopping point. A fundamental change is taking place in international commodity markets: the central role played by private multinational corporations is being undermined by the growing power of host-country governments. Virtually all major raw materials companies have been formally nationalized. But nationalization has not necessarily meant full control for host-country governments. In the petroleum industry, in particular, a symbiotic relationship has continued between oil-exporting countries and the international companies. Nevertheless, there is an undeniable thrust toward less autonomy for private firms. Though their discretion over pricing and allocation has not disappeared, it is waning. An era is coming to an end.

The Actors

From the first decade of this century until the mid-1970s controversies about foreign raw materials investments involved three sets of actors: large private corporations, American central decision-makers, and foreign governments. Each had different goals and different capabilities.

The discovery, exploitation, transportation, processing, and marketing of raw materials has usually been carried out by large private firms operating in oligopolistic market structures. In the early 1950s the Paley Commission, appointed by the President to study the needs of the United States for raw materials, described the situation in the following terms: "The risk, size and length of term of investment tend to concentrate United States investment in petroleum and minerals development abroad in relatively few corporate hands. Nearly all United States private investment in resource development abroad has been made by a few large companies, which have been in operation for many years and have large property holdings and ample reserves."[1] These companies had large economic commitments in foreign areas. They wanted to ensure their long-term profit and growth. Their control over vast economic, and at times political, resources provided them with power that state actors could not easily ignore.

Foreign raw materials investments have always been of some concern to American government officials for both political and economic reasons. Such activities obviously involve interaction with other states. Typically, when U.S. firms have developed foreign sources, they have signed formal concession agreements with host-country governments. International resource exploitation has, moreover, sometimes involved the United States in conflicts with other industrial countries. Economic concerns have also led to official involvement in foreign raw materials investments. Periodically U.S. policy-makers have been seized with the fear of impending shortages. The United States is still relatively self-sufficient in consumption of minerals compared with other industrial market economies. In the mid-1970s the United States was dependent on foreign sources for only 15 percent of its supply of critical nonfuel minerals while Western Europe and Japan had to import, repectively, 75 and 90 percent of their supplies.[2] However, as the following table shows, the importance of foreign

TABLE I-1

Imports as a Percentage of U.S. Consumption (by value)

	All Minerals	*Fuels*	*Nonmetals*	*Metals*
1900	11	1	8	48
1930	11	6	8	44
1950	17	9	11	48
1969	21	17	12	51

Source: Derived from figures in U.S. Dept. of Commerce, Bureau of the Census, *Historical Statistics*, pp. 584-85.

[1] U.S., Paley Commission Report, Vol. I, p. 63.

[2] U.S., Council on International Economic Policy, *Critical Imported Materials*, p. 4.

sources has been growing. A final reason for official interest in foreign raw materials investments is that such activities have occasionally impinged on general foreign policy questions, including the formation of alliances during the First and Second World Wars and relations with the Communist Bloc and the Third World since 1945.

Lastly, raw materials investments have been of great concern to a third group of actors—host-country governments. Often foreign corporations were the largest economic enterprises in particular less developed countries. They were the major source of foreign exchange. Their activities sometimes accounted for a large part of a country's aggregate national product. In many countries they were the largest employer. The exploitation of natural resources offered both economic promise and political dangers to regimes in host countries.

In sum, direct foreign investments in the exploitation of raw materials have involved powerful societal actors and a wide range of governmental institutions and have touched upon issues of major importance to the state.

The Analytic Framework

This historical material is used to illuminate and demonstrate the descriptive and explanatory utility of a statist image of politics. This approach makes a critical assumption: that it is useful to conceive of a state as a set of roles and institutions having peculiar drives, compulsions, and aims of their own that are separate and distinct from the interests of any particular societal roup. These goals are associated either with general material objectives or with ambitious ideological goals related to beliefs about how societies should be ordered. They can be labelled the national interest. In striving to further the national interest, the state may confront internal as well as external resistance. Central decision-makers may be frustrated not only by other states but also by their inability to overcome resistance from within their own society. This study is premised upon an intellectual vision that sees the state autonomously formulating goals that it then attempts to implement against resistance from international and domestic actors. The ability of the state to overcome domestic resistance depends upon the instruments of control that it can exercise over groups within its own society.

For U.S. foreign policy the central state actors are the President and the Secretary of State, and the most important institutions are the White House and the State Department. What distinguishes these roles and agencies is their high degree of insulation from specific societal pressures and a set of formal and informal obligations that charge them with furthering the nation's general interests. After being transferred from the Pentagon to the White House, one correspondent for a major television network complained: "I could walk right into the Army Chief of Staff's office, but here you've got that guard out in the hallway to the West Wing, with a gun to prevent you from going down the hall to see the lowliest White House Assistant."[3] Many other governmental agencies, including the Defense, Treasury, Agriculture, and Commerce Departments as well as the CIA, the FBI, the Internal Revenue Service, and the Antitrust Division of the Justice Department, have affected foreign policy decisions involving international raw materials investments. I do not mean to imply that each and every one of them should be thought of as part of the state. Their behavior has varied. At some times they have acted to promote collective goals, at others to further specific societal and bureaucratic interests.[4] Furthermore, I am not trying to reify the state. In the United States, at least in the realm of foreign affairs, the White House and the State Department are the pivot of the state.

I also do not mean to imply that a state's objectives are unrelated to the needs of its society; in a democracy the two are inextricably bound together. Friedrich Meinecke, one of the great expostulators of the power theory of the state, wrote that the ruler "must also serve the interests of the subjects in some way, because the existence of the whole power-system depends on them; a satisfied people, willing and able to fulfill the demands made on it, is a source of power."[5] At the same time, however, it is a fun-

[3] Quoted in the *Los Angeles Times*, May 15, 1977, v, 2:3.

[4] Nettl, "The State as a Conceptual Variable."

[5] *Machiavellism*, pp. 10-11.

damental error to identify the goals of the state with some summation of the desires of specific individuals or groups. In *A Treatise on General Sociology* Vilfredo Pareto makes a distinction between what he calls the utility *of* the community and the utility *for* the community. Utility *for* the community involves summing the preferences of individual members of a community. The utility *of* the community involves making a judgment about the well-being of the community as a whole. If some members of a community can be made better off without making others worse off, as determined by each individual's judgment of his own well-being, then utility *for* the community can be increased. But once it is necessary to make some worse off to make others better off (for instance, by sending burglars to jail), we are involved in a problem that requires some arbitrary standard for comparing individual preferences. This problem cannot be resolved, as Bentham tries to do, by summing individual utilities, or as Rousseau tries to do, by identifying individual well-being with the general will.[6] The summation of individual utilities and the collective well-being of the society are not the same thing. The choice between a wealthy community with large income inequalities and a poor one with relatively equal income distribution depends, in Pareto's words, "upon the coefficients that are used in making the heterogeneous utilities of the various social classes homogeneous."[7] That is, it depends on the values that are assigned to various objectives. This is a political and ethical problem, not an economic one. Values are assigned by the state. State objectives refer in this study to the utility *of* the community and will be called a nation's general or national interest. The national interest is defined as the goals that are sought by the state.[8]

In sum, this study begins with, and ultimately attempts to defend, the basic premise underlying what has become known as the state-centric or realist paradigm: namely, that states (defined as central decision-making institutions and roles) can be treated as unified actors pursuing aims understood in terms of the national

[6] Finer, "Introduction" to Pareto, *Sociological Writings*, p. 85.

[7] *A Treatise on General Sociology*, p. 1472 (para. 2135).

[8] *Ibid.*, pp. 1456-74 (paras. 2105-39) for a discussion of utility.

interest.[9] However, because this book deals with a problem of foreign policy rather than international politics, it takes a somewhat different tack than most of the recent work associated with this paradigm. This is not a study of billiard balls, of the way in which individual countries treated as unified wholes interact in the international system. On the contrary, the approach used here explicitly recognizes the need to examine the policy-making process within a country when dealing with questions involving foreign policy. A state must deal with private actors in its own society as well as with other actors in the international arena.

From an analytic perspective that treats the state as an autonomous actor, but one constrained by domestic as well as international structures, there are two central problems for foreign policy analysis: identifying the objectives of central decision-makers, and analyzing their ability to accomplish these aims.

Policy Objectives

The notion of national interest has been subject to much abuse in recent years. It is a term that has been used in many different ways. Most studies of international relations from a realist perspective have treated the national interest as a basic *assumption* in constructing a logical-deductive model of international politics. More precisely, they have assumed that states will act to protect their territorial and political integrity. From this assumption it is possible to derive propositions about how states will behave given the distribution of power in the international system (hegemonic, bipolar, multipolar, etc.) and the position of the individual state in that system.

This book uses the concept in a different way. Here the national interest is defined inductively as the preferences of American central decision-makers. Such a set of objectives must be related to general societal goals, persist over time, and have a consistent ranking of importance in order to justify using the term "national interest." For any issue it is not difficult to make a list of aims

[9] The most important writers associated with this school of thought include E. H. Carr, Robert Gilpin, Hans Morgenthau, Robert W. Tucker, Kenneth Waltz, and Arnold Wolfers.

desired by political leaders. These range from satisfying psychological needs to increasing wealth, weakening opponents, capturing territory, and establishing justice. The second chapter of this study lays out such a list for international raw materials policies. It is gleaned from laws, official studies, public statements, and the general historical outlines of U.S. raw materials policy. The analytic problem is to arrange these objectives according to their importance for the state. If there is no consistent ranking over time, it will not be possible to specify a national interest inductively. A transitive ordering will not be found in public documents; these typically list a variety of unranked objectives. But an ordering can be established by examining the actual behavior of policy-makers. Faced with a choice between one objective and another, which do they choose? How much effort is given to accomplish different aims: when are states willing to use force, when will they merely make diplomatic protests? One purpose of the case studies in Chapters IV, VI, VII, and VIII is to rank, in order of importance, the objectives that are suggested by the public record examined in Chapter II.

The findings of this exercise can be briefly summarized. American officials had three basic aims in international raw materials markets: increasing competitive economic behavior, insuring security of supply, and furthering broader foreign policy objectives. In order of increasing importance, they consistently ranked them in the following way: 1) increase competition; 2) insure security of supply; 3) promote broad foreign policy objectives.

In daring to call this list a specification of American national interest (the aims sought by American leaders), it is necessary to demonstrate that the ordering persisted over time. For any single decision it is possible to impute a rank-order of objectives, but if this changes from day to day or even from year to year, it would be misleading to use the term "national interest." One would better look to bureaucratic preferences or societal pressures to understand the actions taken by central decision-makers. However, the case studies do reveal that the order of priorities given above has been followed over a long period of time.

One amendment must be noted. Broader foreign policy objectives have involved two distinctly different kinds of preferences for American leaders. With the exception of the administration of Woodrow Wilson, the period before the Second World War was one in which American actions can best be understood in terms of interests, that is, aims that had some identifiable material benefit for American society as a whole. These included both enhancing strategic security and furthering economic well-being by increasing competition or promoting security of supply. After the Second World War, and between 1912 and 1920, broader foreign policy aims primarily involved ideological objectives. During these periods American leaders were moved by a vision of what the global order should be like that was derived from American values and the American experience—Lockean liberalism and a nonrevolutionary, democratic, and prosperous historical evolution. They were more concerned with structuring the international system and the domestic polities of other countries than with pursuing readily identifiable economic and strategic interests. The shift from interest-oriented to ideological goals was the result of the growth of America's global power position. Woodrow Wilson could not overcome domestic resistance to his ambitious international program. However, by the end of the Second World War, American central decision-makers commanded a set of power resources unprecedented in modern times. These resources allowed them to turn toward projecting America's vision of a properly ordered society into the international system. They were freed from specific strategic and economic concerns. The distribution of power in the international system is the critical variable in determining the broad foreign policy goals sought by American central decision-makers.

Furthermore, the pursuit of ideological objectives had a component that is crucial for distinguishing the argument in this book from a structural Marxist position. Not only did American central decision-makers try to change the basic political structures of other countries, but they did so in a nonlogical way. Here, again, I resort to a distinction made by Pareto. Pareto refers to logical or rational actions as those in which means-ends relationships for the performer and for an experienced outside observer are the same.

Nonlogical behavior occurs where there is divergence between the two.[10] For the purposes of this study, nonlogical behavior was manifest in American policy directed toward ideological goals in one, or both, of two ways. First, American leaders misperceived the external situation. More specifically, they persistently exaggerated the importance of communist elements in foreign countries. Second, they sometimes made no clear calculations about means and ends. Their ideological objective of defeating communism assumed a millennial coloration. It often appeared that there were no limits to the costs they were willing to incur to achieve this goal.

Such behavior can be understood from a statist perspective, but it violates the basic epistemological premises of materialist formulations. In its most flexible version, Marxism sees the state striving to act rationally to preserve the coherence of capitalist society as a whole, even if the preferences of individual corporations are ignored. The state, according to a structural Marxist perspective, may not always succeed: it may be unable to overcome fundamental contradictions. This scheme does not fit American behavior after the Second World War, however, for in their pursuit of an ideological foreign policy U.S. leaders undermined the coherence of American society; and it is difficult to associate the actions of American policy-makers, particularly in Vietnam, with contradictory pressures emanating from capitalist societal structures. On the contrary, it was the ability of American leaders to free themselves from societal constraints (reflecting America's hegemonic position in the international system) that allowed them to define and pursue ideological goals in a nonlogical manner, even though this activity weakened the fabric of American society.

In sum, an ideological foreign policy manifest in (a) the pursuit of goals directly related to the basic political structures of foreign

[10] Pareto, *Treatise*, pp. 75-79 (paras. 145-54). Nonlogical behavior should be distinguished from irrational behavior. Irrational behavior occurs when a decision-maker is influenced by factors that he is unaware of, and that he would regard as illegitimate if he were aware of them. Various psychological needs are the most obvious example. For a discussion see Verba, "Assumptions of Rationality and Non-Rationality." What Verba terms nonrational I have here called irrational. Verba's definition of nonrationality is very different from Pareto's.

regimes and (b) misperception, or an absence of means-ends calculations, offers strong evidence in support of a statist paradigm.

Policy Implementation

Establishing the objectives of central decision-makers answers only one of the two basic analytic questions involved in explicating a statist paradigm. The other has to do not with policy objectives (the national interest), but with policy implementation—the ability of the state to carry out its aims. In foreign affairs the nature of the international system, its inherent anarchy, places many restraints on the freedom of action of any given state. This study does not treat these in any great depth. It examines instead internal constraints, those imposed by the domestic society upon the state. To deal with foreign raw materials investments from this standpoint means examining the relationship between large multinational corporations and central decision-makers. This is a book about foreign policy, not international politics.

Each of the major aims of the state—increased competition, greater security of supply, and broader foreign policy objectives (general material interests or ideological goals)—presents a different potential range of conflict between the desires of central decison-makers and those of corporate managers. The drive for security of supply has usually coincided with private goals. American policy-makers have seen security enhanced by extending the control of American corporations; corporations generally have seen such expansion increasing their sales, profits, and market control. Under such circumstances there will be little antagonism between the state and the private sector.

However, both the drive to increase competition and broader foreign policy goals can generate antagonism between public and private actors. While American corporations might welcome efforts to dismantle foreign cartels, they will resist those designed to undermine their own oligopolistic practices. Greater competition would enhance at least static collective welfare by reducing prices, but would force firms into more uncertain environments. Since private American investors are often at odds with host-country governments, the desire of central decision-makers to strengthen ties with such countries (or at least to prevent them from deteriorating) in order to enhance the territorial and political security of the United States can bring conflict between American officials and corporate executives. Conflict can also arise when central decision-makers seek ideological goals aimed at establishing a global order. Here public resources may be expended in ways that threaten not only specific corporations but also the material well-being of the society as a whole.

For analyzing policy implementation, the areas of potential conflict provide the significant cases. Can central decision-makers institute policies to increase competition and achieve broader foreign policy objectives over the opposition of private groups? The answer depends upon the structure of the political system within which public officials act. One basic characteristic of that system is the internal strength of the state, the ability of central decision-makers to change the behavior of private groups within their own society. America has a weak state. Political power is fragmented and dispersed. There are many points of access to the decision-making process. Political leaders must struggle to maintain control when they confront opposition from large private corporations lest public purposes be overwhelmed by private ones, or public instruments of power be used to promote corporate but not national interests.

In the United States the ability of state actors to implement their aims, or at least to prevent public resources from being squandered, depends primarily upon the arena in which a decision is made. In raw materials policy such arenas range from the prorationing boards of individual states, such as the Texas Railroad Commission, to the National Security Council and the President. Most of the issues arising from disputes over foreign raw materials investments have been decided in the White House and the State Department, which are relatively insulated from corporate power. In practice, as a consequence, public officials have usually been able to resist private pressures to take actions that were not perceived as furthering the national interest. Central decision-makers have been able to carry out their own policies over the opposition of private corporations, providing that policy implementation only required resources that were under the control of the executive branch. However, when central decision-makers were forced to seek authorization from Congress, or required the cooperation of private companies, they were frustrated or were forced to compromise some of their aims

Aside from the decision-making arena, another determinant of the ability of central decision-makers to implement their objectives is leadership. Leadership in issues concerning international raw materials investments has involved either playing upon divisions within the private sector or taking advantage of situations in which corporate managers have been unable to determine what policy would maximize their own interests. In many of the cases examined in this book there have been divisions among different corporations, or between multinational firms and domestic pressure groups. Private conflicts have muted Congressional opposition or opened the possibility of a symbiotic relationship between particular firms and the state. If public leaders have exploited these opportunities, it has been easier for them to overcome resistance or to carry out positive policies.

Playing upon the confusion of private actors has required greater skills but has offered higher rewards. It is often assumed that private managers know what they want but public actors do not. The complexities that firms can encounter are ignored. It is not difficult for the owner of a small company, producing a single product in one country and operating in a competitive market, to decide what kinds of government policies are economically beneficial. But it may be very difficult for the managers of a large oligopolistic company producing many products in several countries, within a vertically integrated structure, to specify what policy will maximize their firm's objectives. In such situations state actors have an opportunity to remake, albeit in a modest way, the society they confront. They can affect the preferences of firms by presenting a coherent view of the situation, which private actors have not been able to develop themselves. Such an exercise of leadership by central decision-makers goes beyond overcoming the opposition of private actors; it can transform potential opposition into passive acceptance or even active support.

In disputes involving international raw materials investments there have been many examples of effective leadership. These have most often arisen from divisions within the private sector.

Less frequently, state actors have been able to manipulate the behavior of corporate managers, although in recent years the escalating demands of economic nationalists have confronted corporate officials with such a confusing environment that central decision-makers have often been able to influence private preferences.

However, even though decisions about raw materials investments have usually been made in the White House and the State Department, and effective leadership frequently exercised, one central conclusion that emerges from the case studies is that no institution in the United States, public or private, has the power to compel others to act, but many can effectively veto initiatives that they oppose. Private corporations have not been able to force public officials to adopt policies that would make raw materials supplies more unstable or insecure, or would undermine more general foreign policy aims. Conversely, public officials have, at times, been unable to change private behavior, much less alter the fundamental structure of raw materials industries, even when major public objectives were threatened by corporate action. In the American political system negative power prevails: one actor can block the initiative of another but cannot carry through its own preferences.

Two Alternative Perspectives: Marxism and Liberalism

The basic approach taken in this study can better be understood by contrasting its assumptions with those of two other prominent perspectives on the political process: Marxism and liberalism. These paradigms involve different arguments about policy-making and the objectives of official action.

Marxism

Scholars in the Marxist tradition have presented the most extensive analysis of foreign economic policy. Marx himself was primarily concerned with developments within national economies, although he did not entirely ignore international problems. With Lenin's *Imperialism* the international aspects of capitalism assumed a place of first importance for Marxist scholars. The analytic assumptions of this paradigm differ in a number of fundamental ways from the state-centric approach of this study.

Marxist theories can be divided into two basic types: instrumental and structural.[11] Instrumental Marxist theories view governmental behavior as the product of direct societal pressure. In its most primitive form, this kind of argument emphasizes personal ties between leading capitalists and public officials.[12] In its more sophisticated form, instrumental Marxist arguments analyze the general ties between the capitalist sector and public officials. Ralph Miliband is the leading recent exponent of this kind of argument. He maintains that there is a cohesive capitalist class. This class controls the state because public officials are heavily drawn from the middle and upper classes, are in frequent contact with businessmen, and depend on the cooperation of private firms to carry out public policy. In addition, cultural institutions such as the media and churches reflect the dominant conservative ideology. Harold Laski took a very similar position, arguing that "historically, we always find that any system of government is dominated by those who at the time wield economic power; and what they mean by 'good' is, for the most part, the preservation of their own interests."[13] From an instrumental Marxist perspective, the state is the executive committee of the bourgeoisie.[14]

Structural Marxist arguments take a different tack. They do not

[11] Gold, Lo, and Wright, "Recent Developments in Marxist Theories of the Capitalist State." This excellent essay also discusses a third approach, Marxist Hegelianism. A similar distinction is made in Wolfe, "New Directions in the Marxist Theory of Politics," pp. 133-36. Nicos Poulantzas, who is generally described as one of the leading proponents of the structuralist position, has argued that the distinction does not make sense. However, Poulantzas defines structuralism as either the view that does "not grant sufficient importance to the role of concrete individuals . . ." or the view that "neglects the importance and weight of the class struggle in history. . . ." See his essay "The Capitalist State," pp. 70 and 71. This is hardly what those who have described Poulantzas as a structuralist have in mind. Poulantzas dismisses his American Marxist critics with the statement that "the academic and ideologico-political conjuncture in the United States" is responsible for their misreading (p. 76).

[12] For examples of such reasoning in the area of raw materials see Engler, *Brotherhood of Oil*; Goff and Locker, "The Violence of Domination"; and the much more sophisticated argument of Lipson, "Corporate Preferences and Public Choices."

[13] *Foundations of Sovereignty*, p. 289, and *The State in Theory and Practice*.

[14] See Kolko, *Roots of American Foreign Policy*, and Miliband, *The State in Capitalist Society*, for applications of instrumental Marxism to the concerns of this study. Recently, Miliband has taken a more structuralist position.

attempt to trace the behavior of the state to the influence of particular capitalists or the capitalist class. Instead, they see the state playing an independent role within the overall structure of a capitalist system. Its task is to maintain the cohesion of the system as a whole. At particular times this may require adopting policies opposed by the bourgeoisie, but generally official action and the preferences of leading elements in the capitalist class will coincide.

For structural Marxism, the behavior of the state involves an effort to deal with economic and political contradictions that are inherent in a capitalist system. Economically, capitalism is not seen as a self-sustaining system tending toward equilibrium. Rather, over the long-term profit rates decline because capitalists can only secure profit through the exploitation of labor, but technological innovation reduces the long-term equilibrium ratio of labor to capital. This process also leads to underconsumption: the system produces more goods than its members can consume. It promotes concentration because weaker firms are driven out of the market. Excess capital is accumulated because there is no market for the goods that would be produced by more investment.

Politically, concentration—what Marxists call the increased socialization of the production process—produces tensions. As societies develop, they become more complex and interdependent. However, control is increasingly concentrated in the hands of an ever smaller group of the owners or managers of capital. At the same time, the working class grows and workers come into more intimate and constant contact with each other. The increased socialization of the production process itself and the continued private appropriation of power and profit produce political and social tensions that threaten the stability of the system.

From a structural Marxist perspective, policy analysis can be viewed as a catalogue of state efforts to cope with these tensions. In the area of foreign economic policy the major conclusion is that the state must follow an expansionary, an imperialist, foreign policy. Early Marxist writers elaborated the relationship between colonialism and expanded opportunities for trade and investment. The opening of new areas could help alleviate underconsumption because capitalists could find new markets by eliminating local artisans. Colonies also offered opportunities for surplus capital. This is the major argument presented by Lenin. These contentions have not been sustained by empirical investigations, however. Even in the heyday of empire only a small proportion of goods and capital moved from the mother country to colonial areas.[15] Recent radical analyses have suggested somewhat different motivations for expansion, including protection of the oligopolistic position of large firms, militarism, and the quest for raw materials.

The relationship between advanced capitalist societies, giant firms, and foreign activity has been emphasized by two recent Marxist analysts, Harry Magdoff and James O'Connor. Using arguments from the behavioral theory of the firm, Magdoff suggests that corporations are systems of power. Each firm strives to control its own market. This objective could not be realized during the early stages of capitalism because the level of competition was too high. As concentration increases, however, "the exercise of controlling power becomes not only possible but increasingly essential for the security of the firm and its assets."[16] Businesses seek to maximize control over actual and potential sources of raw materials and over foreign markets. Foreign investment is a particularly effective device for guaranteeing such control, although trading opportunities are not ignored. If control is lost, either to competitors or to socialist regimes, the oligopoly can be destroyed. Since these corporations are the foundation of the American capitalist system, their political power is great, and their collapse would precipitate a deep economic crisis. There are impelling reasons for the United States, the world's leading capitalist nation, to maintain an international economic system with minimum constraints on the operations of giant multinational firms.[17]

James O'Connor has taken an even more classical Marxist position. He maintains that the monopoly sector in modern capitalist systems is the most important source of profits. However, there is

[15] Barratt Brown, "A Critique of Marxist Theories of Imperialism," p. 44; Fieldhouse, "Imperialism"; Cohen, *The Question of Imperialism*, Ch. 2.

[16] "Imperialism Without Colonies," p. 157.

[17] *Age of Imperialism*, pp. 34-35 and Ch. 5.

an inherent tendency for the productive capacity of the monopoly sector to expand more quickly than demand or employment. This leads to pressure for an aggressive foreign economic policy. Overseas activity can increase sales and profit, and offer opportunities for new investment. The purpose of foreign assistance and more direct military intervention is to keep foreign client states within the capitalist order.

Magdoff, O'Connor, and other structural Marxist analysts have also postulated an intimate relationship between the economic needs of the capitalist system, military expenditure, and imperialism. Military expenditures are a primary source of revenue for some major firms in the monopoly sector. Such expenditures help maintain the stability of the system because they are not subject to the rational calculations of profit and loss that are an inherent part of the capitalist ideology. Finally, militarism is important in a direct sense because the use of force may be necessary to keep foreign areas open to trade and investment.[18]

An argument directly related to the empirical concerns of this study, which has received new emphasis from Marxists, is that capitalists must have foreign raw materials. This aim was not ignored by classical Marxist writers. Lenin stated that capitalists were driven to control ever increasing amounts of even apparently worthless land because it might contain some unknown material that could lead to economic disaster if it were to fall into the hands of a competitor. Cheap raw materials also contributed to staving off the inevitable tendency toward declining rates of profits: new and rich discoveries could, at least temporarily, provide high profits. Magdoff has maintained that the search for raw materials is part of the general quest of giant corporations for security and oligopolistic profits. Only through vertical integration from mine to final sale can these firms assure themselves of tight market control. Furthermore, the United States and other capitalist states are seen as being vitally dependent on foreign sources for some commodities that are essential for industrial operations and advanced military equipment.[19] One author has argued that all American foreign policy can be explained by the need "to insure that the

[18] O'Connor, *Fiscal Crisis*, Ch. 6.

[19] Lenin, *Imperialism*, pp. 83-84; Magdoff, *Age of Imperialism*, pp. 52, 156; Kolko, *Roots of American Foreign Policy*, pp. 50-54.

flow of raw materials from the Third World is never interrupted."[20]

While Marxist writers have dropped some arguments, modified others, and found new ones, there is a central thread that runs through their position. Foreign economic expansion is a necessity. It is not a matter of the preferences of particular enterprises. It is not a policy that has a marginal effect on profits. It is an issue that touches the very core of capitalism's continued viability. Cut off from the rest of the world, the economies of advanced capitalist states would confront problems of great severity. "For Marxism," Tom Kemp avers, "imperialism is not a political or ideological phenomenon but expresses the imperative necessities of advanced capitalism."[21]

For structural Marxists, the state can be treated as having autonomy, not from the needs of the system as a whole, but from direct political pressure from the capitalist class. Indeed, such autonomy is necessary because internal divisions preclude effective bourgeois political organization. To maintain cohesion the state must mitigate the social and political pressures arising from the increasing socialization of the production process coupled with the continuing private appropriation of profits and control. Carrying out this task requires it to pose as a representative of all the people. To appear to follow the explicit preferences of powerful capitalists too slavishly would weaken the stability of the whole system. Compromises, such as the recognition of unions and higher social welfare payments, are essential, even if they are opposed by the capitalist class. Such policies protect the existing structure of economic relationships by disarming and disuniting potential opposition from the oppressed.[22]

The analytic assumptions of Marxist theories, whether of the

[20] Dean, "Scarce Resources," p. 149.

[21] "The Marxist Theory of Imperialism," p. 17. See also Mack, "Comparing Theories of Economic Imperialism," p. 40.

[22] Poulantzas, *Political Power and Social Classes*; O'Connor, *Fiscal Crisis*, esp. Ch. 1; Poulantzas, "The Capitalist State," p. 73; and Gough, "State Expenditure in Advanced Capitalism," pp. 64-65. It is not my purpose here to critique a structural Marxist position, but it is important to note that granting the state the kind of autonomy imputed to it by this approach weakens any dialectical analysis of capitalism. The state appears to be so independent and prescient that it can save capitalism from its own infirmities.

instrumental or structural variety, differ from the statist approach of this study in at least three ways. First, the notion of national interest is rejected by Marxists. The aims pursued by the state mirror the preferences of the capitalist class or some of its elements, or the needs of the system as a whole. State behavior does not reflect either autonomous power drives or the general well-being of the society. Second, the behavior of the state is taken by them to be intimately related to economic goals; other objectives are instrumental, not consummatory. In particular, ideological objectives cannot be independent of economic considerations. Ideology is a mask that hides the reality of exploitation and thus helps mislead and mollify those who have no real power. Third, even though structural Marxists may view the state as relatively autonomous, they do not believe that it can really be understood outside of its societal context. The state has peculiar tasks within the structure of a capitalist system, but they are ultimately associated with the interests of a particular class.

Liberalism

A statist argument can also be highlighted by contrasting it with another major paradigm—liberalism. Liberal, interest-group, or pluralist theories constitute the most prevalent approach to the study of politics in the United States. They are apparent not only in the analytic framework used by most political scientists but also in the rhetorical expressions of American political leaders.

Analytically, liberalism, like Marxism, begins with the society. Its basic unit of analysis is the group. Politics is viewed as a competition among organized interests. Government policy is understood to be the "resultant of effective access by various interests. . . ."[23] In its most simplified and schematic form, interest-group theories view politics as a vector diagram in which a series of pressures are brought to bear on the state, which then moves in the direction it is pushed by the strongest societal forces. Pluralist analysis differs from instrumental Marxism not in the basic structure of its argument (both view formal government institutions as relatively passive recipients of societal pressure), but in its judgment of the kinds of societal formations that have political influ-

[23] Truman, *The Governmental Process*, p. 507.

ence. For Marxists, power is basically in the hands of the capitalist class; for pluralists, it may be exercised by individuals motivated by any interest that is salient enough to affect behavior.

Studies using a pluralist perspective have been most frequently concerned with local government. Since the Second World War most American investigations of foreign policy have been concerned with national security and have been written from a conventional state-centric perspective. However, during the last decade a new approach, the bureaucratic politics paradigm, has been offered as an alternative to conventional views. Bureaucratic politics applies the logic of pluralism to policy-making within government. Societal groups are replaced by government bureaus. Official policy is viewed as the outcome of bargaining among competing administrative units. Each of these units is motivated by its own interests. Though the President may formally make the final determination of policy, his action is explained by pressures and information that have come to him from the bureaucracy. Like governmental institutions in pluralist analyses of urban politics, the Presidency is basically a passive reactor to external forces.[24]

Interest-group theory can be applied to foreign policy questions in a more direct way when economic issues are at stake. Here it is not difficult to establish a relationship between official policy and the preferences of particular groups. Unlike national security, which has a relatively undifferentiated impact on all political groups, economic policy benefits some more than others. Commercial arrangements or foreign investment usually have a very salient impact on particular actors and a diffuse effect on the society as a whole. In such situations interest-group theory suggests that public policy will be very strongly affected by specific interests: it is very likely that governmental activity will reflect the demands of particular social groups. Probably the most well-known application of this line of reasoning is E. E. Schatt-

[24] For examples see Allison, *Essence of Decision*, and Halperin, *Bureaucratic Politics*. For a study from this perspective dealing with the problems of this book see Einhorn, *Expropriation Politics*. For critiques see Krasner, "Are Bureaucracies Important?" and Art, "Bureaucratic Politics and American Foreign Policy." Art makes a critical distinction between first- and second-wave bureaucratic theorists and their treatment of the President.

schneider's *Politics, Pressures and the Tariff*. This study explains the Smoot-Hawley Tariff of 1930 as a product of the desires of a multiplicity of private economic actors. Each wanted protection for itself and was willing to accept protection for others. Government policy was simply a summation of private goals.

Analysts adopting a liberal or pluralist perspective have been very critical of the concept of the national interest. An inescapable implication of their position is that government policy is a reflection of whatever groups have power in the society. The concept of the public interest slips away. David Truman argues that in a complex modern nation "we do not need to account for a totally inclusive interest, because one does not exist."[25] Stephen Bailey writes that there "is perhaps no better example in all language of the utility of myth than the phrase 'the public interest.' "[26] Robert Dahl states that "if one rejects the notion that public interest is some amalgamation of private interests, there is little philosophical mileage to be gained from using the concept at all."[27] In respect to substance, from a liberal perspective, the public or national interest can only mean some summation of private interests.[28]

Liberal conceptions of politics also have little use for the notion of the state as an autonomous actor motivated by drives associated with its own need for power or with the well-being of the society as a whole. Governmental institutions merely process inputs and outputs. The state is seen as a set of formal structures, not an autonomous actor. There is no cohesive center of decision-making. The locus of power may move from one bureau to another, or from one branch of government to another, depending on the interests and power resources associated with particular issues.[29] At best, from a pluralist perspective, governmental institutions become but one interest group among many; at worst, public policy is corrupted by the influence of particular private actors.[30]

[25] *Governmental Process*, p. 51. [26] "The Public Interest," p. 97.

[27] Quoted in Colm, "The Public Interest," pp. 116-17.

[28] This argument is developed in Flathman, *The Public Interest*, pp. 21ff.

[29] Truman, p. 508. For a critique see Nettl, p. 569.

[30] Truman, at least, is keenly aware of this problem. He argues that the worst is not likely to happen because of cross-cutting cleavages and the existence of what

If the state has any active role to play, from a liberal perspective, it is to maintain the basic rules of the game: to make sure that all groups have an equal opportunity to compete. Government activity must be characterized by fairness. It must create an order within which individuals can express their own needs and wants and within which, one may hope, they can learn to exercise higher human virtues. Indeed, some liberal thinkers have argued that the public interest can be understood essentially in these procedural terms.[31]

In the area of foreign economic policy, liberalism's ultimate concern with the well-being of the individual, with creating a situation in which private actors can most fully exercise their own potential, has been manifest in the persistent rhetorical endorsement of an open economic order by American statesmen. In its most extreme form, liberalism prescribes the complete absence of state interference in global markets regardless of economic or political provocation. This position, which is most closely associated with the nineteenth-century Manchester school, has been of no practical significance. American statesmen, who became the leading advocates of free trade in the twentieth century, have taken a more activist stance: the economy could not be left to work on its own; state intervention is necessary to stifle noncompetitive practices. Internally, this philosophy is reflected in the Sherman, Wilson, and Clayton Acts. Externally, it implies that the state should strive for an international economic order free of restraints on the movement of goods and capital. The purpose of government intervention is not to defend particular traders or investors, but to create a setting in which each firm has equal access to an unrestrained market.

Woodrow Wilson was the first leading American political figure to adopt a policy of active laissez-faire. Wilson believed that government regulation was necessary to "set business free . . . to follow its own right laws."[32] His vision of the ideal global

he calls latent groups that reflect widespread adherence to certain basic values such as civil liberties.

[31] For a discussion of Smith and Ricardo see Flathman, p. 57; Billet, "The Just Economy"; and O'Leary, "Systems Theory and Regional Integration."

[32] Quoted in Diamond, *The Economic Thought of Woodrow Wilson*, p. 109.

order had an important economic component succinctly summarized in the Fourteen Points. Point Three stated that the United States sought "the removal, so far as possible, of all economic barriers and the establishment of an equality of trade conditions among all the nations consenting to the peace and associating themselves for its maintenance." Point Two called for freedom of the seas. Wilson also favored low tariffs, which dovetailed with his desire to stimulate domestic competition, since he believed barriers to trade fostered and protected monopolies.[33]

During World War II the fourth point of the Atlantic Charter stated that the signatories "will endeavor, with due respect for their existing obligations, to further the enjoyment by all states great or small, victor or vanquished, of access, on equal terms, to the trade and to *the raw materials of the world* which are needed for their economic prosperity" (my italics). In the mid-1940s the United States supported the creation of international economic institutions—the International Monetary Fund, the International Bank for Reconstruction and Development, the General Agreement on Tariffs and Trade—that were designed to create a liberal order, one that facilitated the activities of private firms. For instance, one of the five basic purposes of the Bank listed in its Articles of Agreement is "to promote private foreign investment by means of guarantees or participation in loans and other investments made by private investors; and when private capital is not available on reasonable terms, to supplement private investment . . ." (Article 1. ii).

The differences between the analytic assumptions of this study and those of a liberal perspective are very sharp. First, a pluralist perspective rejects the utility of treating the state as an autonomous actor whose motivations and resources are qualitatively different from those of any other institution in the society. Second, it rejects the concept of a national interest that transcends the individual interests of members of the society. Third, insofar as the government has any substantive role to play, it is identified with creating a structure within which individuals can freely exercise their own preferences, rather than striving toward protecting the power resources of the state and the well-being of the society.

[33] *Ibid.*, p. 98.

A Preliminary Defense of Statism

Having outlined a statist approach for the study of foreign policy and contrasted it with two alternatives, liberalism and Marxism, we can briefly review the empirical findings that bear on the macro-analytic task of this book—distinguishing among these three paradigms. The cases presented in Chapters IV, VI, VII, and VIII do indicate that American policy-makers have pursued a transitively ordered set of preferences that has persisted for a long period of time. Furthermore, they show that their primary objectives were associated with broad political goals and not with the desires of American firms. This finding is not compatible with a pluralist argument for three reasons. First, an interest-group theory has difficulty explaining situations in which policy-makers pursue aims that are not actively articulated by domestic pressure groups. Group theory looks at politics from the bottom up. Official decision-makers take their cues from societal interests. It is difficult for such an approach to account for the pursuit of objectives that are not supported by particular pressure groups. Second, several of the cases discussed in this book involve conflict between large corporations and state actors. Under such circumstances a pluralist perspective would predict that private interests would prevail. David Truman's concept of a latent group, which is triggered if public policy violates widely accepted norms, is too amorphous to explain away such situations. It is not clear how the influence of a latent group could become manifest, at least in circumstances that are unlikely to attract widespread public attention. Third, from a more normative standpoint, the goals pursued by American central decision-makers were not those suggested by liberal theory. Despite the rhetorical emphasis on a free market, this objective was consistently given a low priority by U.S. leaders. When there was a clash between more general political aims or security of supply and creation of a more open international order in which individual initiative could flourish, it was the latter that was sacrificed.

In dealing with the extent to which the empirical evidence in this volume challenges radical interpretations, a distinction must be made between instrumental and structural approaches. Instrumental Marxist arguments can be questioned for reasons similar to those that challenge a liberal approach. Central decision-makers did not always follow the preferences of private corporations. U.S. leaders have been more concerned with general political objectives than with specific economic ones. They often ignored the positions taken by large private corporations.

It is far more difficult to distinguish empirically between a statist paradigm and a structural Marxist one. One man's foreign policy goal is another's long-term preservation of capitalism. Yet it is possible to look for strains in either argument, for cases that require convoluted rationalizations. Cases involving general societal interests, such as the maximization of growth or protection of territorial integrity, cannot offer any test: what is good for the society as a whole will be good for its leading economic institutions. Charles Wilson was not wrong about that. Few opportunities for testing are offered by cases involving security of raw materials supply: both statist concerns with maximizing general utility and structural Marxism's focus on preserving the long-term economic interests of the society, particularly its leading firms, predict that this goal would be an important part of public policy. Nevertheless, there is one case dealing with supply that does offer support for a statist position. During World War II American political leaders seriously attempted to force Texaco and Standard Oil of California to sell their oil concession in Saudi Arabia. Although this effort ultimately failed, a policy that violated the fundamental tenet of capitalism—private ownership—in a situation where there were no compelling societal pressures does not fit easily within a materialist interpretation of American behavior.

The most important cases for sorting out a statist from a structural Marxist interpretation involve the use of covert and overt force. The kinds of instruments that a state is willing to use to further certain objectives are an indication of their importance, and force is the most potent instrument of all. Chapter VIII discusses a number of cases occurring after the Second World War in which the United States used force. One point that is indisputable is that American central decision-makers resorted to this alternative only to oppose communist regimes in less developed countries; that is, the use of force was directly related to an ideological goal. Such objectives can be assimilated into a statist framework as a manifestation of the values of central decision-makers. But how does a Marxist position deal with ideology? Basically, it interpolates it into a materialist scheme by arguing that ideology is one mechanism used by the state to increase social coherence; ideology masks the underlying patterns of exploitation that exist in capitalist society. In many cases this is a compelling argument. However, it becomes less convincing if actions directed toward ideological goals undermine the domestic social structure, as did the Vietnam War, which contributed to rising prices, a declining stock market, the demise of Bretton Woods, tensions with allies, and unrest at home. A structural Marxist argument is also strained by the nonlogical character of several cases in which American central decision-makers were prepared to use overt or covert force. Although Vietnam is the most extreme example, there are other instances in which U.S. leaders either misperceived the significance of the communist threat or showed little evidence of calculating the costs of using force to affect the domestic political structure of foreign countries.

The basic aim of this book, then, is to demonstrate the power of a statist approach to foreign policy. This approach begins with the assumption that the state can be treated as an autonomous actor pursuing goals associated with power and the general interests of the society. At any given point in time state behavior can be viewed as the actions of individuals occupying certain positions in the central government. In the United States the most important such positions are the Presidency and some cabinet offices, particularly the Secretary of State. Central decision-makers may be frustrated in their efforts to further the national interest by opposition not only from external actors but from domestic ones as well. The ability of state actors to deal with their own societies depends upon the political system in which they must act—more precisely, on the resources at the disposal of the state to overcome private resistance. This approach to the study of politics can be contrasted with two other major theoretical paradigms—Marxism and liberalism. Both focus on the society and view official behavior as a manifestation of societal interests or needs. They both reject the concept of the national interest. Much of the empirical evidence presented in this book is incompatible with liberal and instrumental Marxist approaches. Although it is much more difficult to distinguish structural Marxist arguments from a statist paradigm, the importance that American central decision-makers have at times attributed to ideological as opposed to economic or strategic aims is more compatible with the theoretical image that guides this study than with any materialist interpretation.

CHAPTER II

The National Interest and Raw Materials

A statist approach must begin by defining the goals sought by central decision-makers. These goals can be called the national interest. There are two basic ways to study the national interest: logical-deductive and empirical-inductive. A logical-deductive formulation *assumes* that states will pursue certain objectives—in particular, preserving territorial and political integrity. This approach is very powerful, but limited in the range of issues that it can deal with. It does not provide a clear prediction of behavior for a hegemonic state (whose political and territorial integrity is completely secure), or for foreign policy questions that are not directly associated with core objectives. Many issues of foreign economic policy, including some raised by cases discussed in this book, fall into the latter category.

An alternative way to define the national interest is by following an empirical-inductive route. Here the national interest is induced from the statements and behavior of central decision-makers. If their preferences meet two basic criteria, they can be called the national interest. First, the actions of leaders must be related to general objectives, not to the preferences or needs of any particular group or class, or to the private power drives of officeholders. Second, the ordering of preferences must persist over time. One of the central tasks of this study is to demonstrate empirically that it is possible to talk sensibly about the national interest, even where core objectives are not at stake. An investigation of the preferences of American central decision-makers, revealed by their actual behavior toward foreign raw materials investments, suggests that their most important goals have been related to broad foreign policy objectives, their next most important to insuring security of supply, and their least important to increasing competition and reducing prices. The choices and tradeoffs made by U.S. leaders are revealed in the case studies presented in Chapters IV, VI, VII, and VIII. Here an effort is made to show how the concept of the national interest can be used analytically and to get a preliminary indication of its possible content by examining some of the general lines of policy and statements related to raw materials that have been followed by the American government.

The notion of the public interest, and its international analog the national interest, has fallen on hard times. Glendon Schubert writes that there is "no public-interest theory worthy of the name" and goes on to argue that it may fulfill a "hair-shirt" function or it may be "nothing more than a label attached indiscriminately to a miscellany of particular compromise of the moment."[1] Frank Sorauf maintains that the term "public interest" confuses political as well as intellectual discussions. It may be, he argues, merely a rationalization for particular group interests.[2] In the article on national interest in the most recent edition of the *International Encyclopedia of the Social Sciences*, James Rosenau concludes that "despite the claims made for the concept and notwithstanding its apparent utility, the national interest has never fulfilled its early promise as an analytic tool."[3]

It is undeniable that "public interest" or "national interest" has been used in a wide variety of ways. For liberals, it has meant either some aggregation of individual group interests or the maintenance of a set of governmental procedures that permit equal access to groups or individuals and an accurate assessment of their preferences. For Marxists, the term, if it has been used at all, has referred to the interests of a particular class. Both liberal and Marxist perspectives reject any substantive definition of the national interest that cannot be reduced to societal preferences or needs.

A Deductive Approach

Even from a statist perspective, the concept has been used in a

[1] "Is There A Public Interest Theory?" p. 175.

[2] "The Conceptual Muddle," pp. 187-88.

[3] Vol. 11, p. 36.

variety of ways. Most prominently, the national interest has been an analytic assumption for deductive theorizing about the behavior of states. This kind of reasoning was apparent in European discussions of the balance of power throughout the period from the sixteenth to the eighteenth century. It begins with the fundamental assumption that states must strive to protect their independence while they interact in an interdependent but anarchical system. It leads to predictions or prescriptions for action such as: resist the efforts of any single state that attempts to gain a dominant position; do not destroy an opponent if its demise will lead to permanent disequilibrium, thereby threatening the independence of other states; be prepared to change allies to preserve balance in the system.[4] The most prominent modern articulation of this kind of reasoning is Hans Morgenthau's dictum that "statesmen think and act in terms of interest defined as power. . . ."[5] The logic of this framework is identical to that used in neo-classical economic theory where it is assumed that firms act to maximize profit. The value of this assertion does not rest on a survey of shop owners to see if, indeed, they do think that they act to maximize profit; it hinges on the ability to derive a set of propositions that can be used to explain and predict, if only in a probabilistic fashion, their actual behavior.[6]

It is possible to draw some implications from a logical-deductive approach for international economic policies. Indeed, this was done in the seventeenth and eighteenth centuries by a group of writers that Adam Smith later labelled mercantilists. The mercantilists were concerned with the underlying power capabilities of states. They assumed that larger and more economically developed states would have more leverage in the international political system. They treated wealth not as a problem of ethics and theology, but as one of power. They brought Machiavelli from the

[4] For a discussion of the historical development of balance of power doctrines see Butterfield, "The Balance of Power." For an elaboration see Kaplan, *System and Process*, pp. 22-36.

[5] *Politics Among Nations*, p. 5. For a superlative discussion of structural reasoning see Waltz, "Theory of International Relations."

[6] There is an underlying logic to the assumptions of both profit maximization and power maximization. If firms do not act to maximize profits, they go out of business, at least in a competitive market. If states do not guard their power, they too may go out of business, by being conquered.

political to the economic arena. *Raîson d'état*—acceptance of the claim that the needs of the state must precede all other considerations—was the basic assumption of their work. The central problem of political life was order, and order could only be established by state power.

Mercantilist writers developed a more or less coherent set of policies to secure their objectives. Some of their specific prescriptions now appear quaint, particularly their desire to accumulate specie, based on the belief that gold and silver were the essence of wealth. But though bullionism is no longer of any practical significance, the ultimate aims of mercantilist policy remain as vital today as they were three hundred years ago. The accumulation of specie was for the mercantilists not an end in itself, but a manifestation of two broad policy concerns associated with maximizing the power of the state. First, they wanted to deflect economic activity toward specific political, particularly military, needs. Second, they sought to create a reservoir of national economic strength that could be drawn upon to further political aims. The first approach led to the accumulation of specific goods, the second to increasing the general level of economic activity in the society.[7]

What do mercantilist prescriptions look like in modern garb? The distinction between policies designed specifically to maintain the sinews of war and those related to achieving general foreign policy goals and maintaining general economic activity remains useful. Policies for securing military power are fairly straightforward. The state must not become dependent on unreliable sources of supply for raw materials that are necessary for the conduct of war. *Ceteris paribus*, this implies that the state should maximize self-sufficiency through stockpiling, government purchase guarantees, subsidies, tariff protection for domestic industries, and similar devices.

When self-sufficiency is impossible, because of the absence of natural deposits, inadequate technical knowledge, or prohibitive costs, the state should attempt to diversify its sources of supply. The state should develop relations with areas that are, for one reason or another, dependent on it. Sources of supply are more secure if the opportunity costs of ending trade are higher for the ex-

[7] Heckscher, *Mercantilism*, Vol. 2, p. 35; Viner, "Power versus Plenty."

porting than for the importing state.[8] A state might, for instance, pay higher prices to particular producers so that foreign suppliers would commit themselves to cost structures and production levels that would make it impossible to shift to other markets if favorable trade terms were withdrawn.

In addition, the state should try to maximize its control over foreign sources of raw materials by promoting the investment activities of its own corporations. In a capitalist society policymakers will rarely have dictatorial power over private firms. Indeed, it may be very difficult for them to exercise any influence at all. But having one's own firms control valuable sources of foreign deposits through ownership or concession agreements does have important advantages. The state has levers of control over the domestic activities of these companies. Public officials can make decisions about taxation or antitrust policy that can influence corporate behavior. They can appeal to corporate managers as citizens (and patriots).

Security of supply is important not just for military reasons but for more general economic and political ones as well. For a peacetime economy, price *stability* is also a matter of concern. Unstable supplies and prices can upset the general functioning of the economy and strain the political system. From a mercantilist perspective—that is, one that focusses on the needs of the state—it is preferable to have higher stable prices than fluctuating ones that are on average lower.

This desideratum follows from the one attribute of raw materials that sets them as a group apart from other commodities: they are a factor in the production of all goods, but their cost is usually only a small percentage of the final selling price. Petroleum is the only important exception. In the early 1970s crude oil accounted for 85 percent of the total selling price of heavy oil, 55 percent of that of home heating oil, and 40 percent of that of gasoline; but wheat accounted for only 18 percent of the price of bread, iron ore for only 9 percent of the cost of steel, and bauxite for only 7 percent of the cost of aluminum.[9] Minimizing prices, particularly for

[8] For a discussion of relative opportunity costs see Hirschman, *National Power*, and Waltz, "The Myth of National Interdependence."

[9] U.S., Council on International Economic Policy, *Critical Imported Materials*, p. 25.

imported goods, can have some economic benefits, but only if this can be done without threatening market stability.

It is the unexpected shortages of raw materials that can have the most serious effect on the economy. Although advanced industrial states can adjust production techniques when prices escalate sharply, such efforts usually take time. Artificial chocolate can be substituted for cocoa rather quickly, but changing generating plants from oil to coal takes longer, and developing new coal mines longer still. Furthermore, the price fluctuations that accompany unexpected supply shortages are inherently inflationary in advanced capitalist economies because there is more resistance to lowering prices than to raising them. It may be very difficult for policy-makers to deal with such inflationary pressures without depressing the economy. Fluctuating prices may also discourage private investment, since they increase uncertainty.[10]

If we turn from the economy to the political system, another set of reasons for seeking stability in international raw materials markets becomes apparent. Economic dislocations caused by abrupt price increases can create local or even national political discontent, whereas greater well-being resulting from lower prices is not likely to engender an equally strong positive response. The dissatisfaction caused by a decline of utility is usually greater than the satisfaction resulting from an unexpected improvement. Politicians are more likely to maximize their support by establishing a stable pattern of earnings, even if over the full course of the business cycle an unstable pattern would give private groups higher total incomes.[11]

I have no basic quarrel with this logical-deductive approach to the problem of specifying the national interest. Despite the criticism to which it has been subject, this kind of reasoning has provided the most powerful theoretical orientation toward the study of international politics. It does have major limitations, however. It is more applicable to states in some situations than to others.

[10] Cooper and Lawrence, "The 1972-1975 Commodity Boom," pp. 707-9; and U.S., Paley Commission Report, Vol. I, p. 83.

[11] A number of studies have pointed to the asymmetrical political effects of gains and losses. See, e.g., Bloom and Price, "Voter Response to Short-Run Economic Conditions."

Both the strength and weakness of Morgenthau's dictum is that it lacks specific content. Power for what is always the puzzling question. The clearest answer is: power to protect the core objectives of the state, its territorial and political integrity. When these goals are threatened, the theory does give fairly precise explanations and predictions about state behavior.

This approach is less potent, however, in dealing with situations in which core objectives are not at stake, either because of a country's position in the international system or because there is only a tenuous connection between core objectives and a particular policy problem. A logical-deductive approach to the problem of the national interest is not of much use when dealing with a hegemonic or imperial state whose territorial and political integrity is completely secure. Even if a realist theory suggests that such a state will be expansionary, it does not indicate the forms such external thrusts will take. Will a hegemonic state move to military conquest, or will it be satisfied with informal control? Will it try to impose its own system of political and social values on subordinate areas, or will it simply engage in economic exploitation?

The second problem with a logical-deductive approach is that it does not provide much explanatory or predictive power when dealing with policy issues that are not related to protecting the territorial and political integrity of the state. This problem is most apparent in domestic politics. There are very few noninternational issues that strike at the core of a political system's coherence and stability, at least for most countries of the northern hemisphere. Perhaps this is why the concept of the public interest (generally applied to domestic affairs) has fallen into even deeper disrepute than that of the national interest. However, even in international affairs it may be difficult to apply a logical-deductive mode of reasoning, particularly to economic matters. Many economic questions are only remotely related to a state's political and territorial integrity. The mercantilists could write forcefully about economic questions because they were giving advice to rulers whose positions were in jeopardy. In the modern world things may be equally clear-cut if a state is threatened with invasion. Usually, however, foreign policy questions, particularly in the economic arena, involve complicated calculations about tradeoffs among various aims that may be only tangentially related to protecting territorial and political integrity.

An Inductive Approach

Although the logical-deductive approach may be very powerful under certain circumstances, it must be supplemented by an alternative statist interpretation of the national interest—one that is inductive and empirical rather than *a priori*. A second way of apprehending the national interest is to examine what state actors say and do. In some ways this is the most straightforward way of dealing with the concept. Samuel Huntington resolves the problem of the public interest by defining it "in terms of the concrete interests of the governing institutions."[12] Max Weber took a similar tack. He states in *Economy and Society* that "the particular content of social action [pursued by a political association], beyond the forcible domination of territory and inhabitants, is conceptually irrelevant. It may vary greatly according to whether we deal with a 'robber state,' a 'welfare state,' a 'constitutional,' or a 'cultural' state. Owing to the drastic nature of its means of control, the political association is particularly capable of arrogating to itself all the possible values toward which associational conduct might be oriented; there is probably nothing in the world which at one time or another has not been an object of social action on the part of some political association."[13]

There are two problems with taking such a simple shortcut, however. First, a Marxist might assert that these expressed preferences are not peculiar to the state at all, but merely reflect the needs or preferences of the leading economic class. This problem is brought home by noting that Charles Beard, who does not share the more statist orientation of Weber or Huntington, offers a very similar definition of the national interest. In his book *The Idea of National Interest* he suggests that "the question—what is national interest?—can be answered, if at all, only by exploring the use of

[12] *Political Order in Changing Societies*, p. 24.

[13] *Economy and Society*, p. 902.

the formula by responsible statesmen and publicists and by discovering the things and patterns of conduct—public and private—embraced within the scope of the formula."[14]

The second problem is that defining the national interest purely by reference to the preferences of state actors violates common usage that associates this concept with the enduring general goals of the society. It would be odd to identify the Watergate coverup with the national interest even though it was endorsed by the President. At least in Weber's "constitutional" state, the notion of an empirically induced public or national interest must not include actions whose sole purpose it is to keep a particular leader in power.

The statements and preferences of central decision-makers can nevertheless be used to define the national interest if two conditions are met: these preferences do not consistently benefit a particular class or group, and they last over an extended period of time. A public act of the state is one that affects the whole community.[15] This is not to say that all citizens will be affected in precisely the same way. However, if there are gains from a policy, these must not always accrue only to a particular group or class. If there are losses, these must not always fall on a particular group or class. Furthermore, the preferences of central decision-makers must not be directed solely to their own personal interests, if they are to be termed the national interest.

Most calculations of gains and losses will be very complicated because the consequences of a policy may be a matter of dispute and the resources at stake may vary for different actors in the system. Some may get additional wealth, others power, others prestige. Some may lose in any one policy area, while others gain. In making such calculations the state is bound to play a critical role. The public interest can never be adequately defined by even the most responsible citizenry without the input of public authority. In complex and interdependent societies only central decision-makers can make adequate calculations about the effect of policies, not only because the state may enforce its decisions against

[14] *The Idea of National Interest*, p. 26.

[15] Barry, "The Use and Abuse of the 'Public Interest'," p. 195.

recalcitrant groups but also because it is the only institution that has the resources needed to make the necessary prudential judgments.[16] Furthermore, as Pareto points out, it is impossible to arrive at the utility of the community (the national interest) by summing the preferences of individuals or groups. Utility *for* the community viewed as a collection of individuals is not the same as the utility *of* the community taken as a collective whole. If a decision cannot make some individuals or groups better off without making others worse off, a Benthamite calculus collapses in the absence of some basis for making interpersonal utility comparisons. The agency in the society that implicitly assigns such values is the state.[17] Thus, an inductively based conceptualization of the national interest can only be operationalized in terms of the preferences of central decision-makers, that is, the state.

A second condition that must be met if the preferences of political leaders are to conform to common usage, when they are called the national interest, is that the ordering of goals must persist over time. For any particular decision it would not be very difficult to impute a set of objectives to central decision-makers. But one decision does not the national interest make. When confronted with a similar problem at a different time, leaders might choose another ordering of goals. It might be that preferences change from one administration to another. Such behavior would not be consistent with an assertion that the United States has a national interest, because this concept is generally viewed as embodying certain lasting values. One need not argue that these values are immutable; but if they reflect certain basic and underlying characteristics of a particular polity, they must change slowly. To demonstrate inductively that the United States has a national interest, it is necessary to show that its leaders have had a transitively ordered set of preferences that has persisted over an extended period of time.

If the goals of central decision-makers are transitory, shifting in importance from one case to another, a bureaucratic-politics or group-oriented approach would be more appropriate. These models predict vacillations in the preferences of governmental actors

[16] This argument is developed in Flathman, *The Public Interest*, pp. 47-48.

[17] Pareto, *Sociological Writings*, pp. 254-55.

because the influence of different bureaus or societal groups changes from one issue to another.

In sum, an inductive statist approach asserts that the national interest consists of a set of transitively ordered state preferences concerned to promote the general well-being of the society that persists over a long period of time.

One of the central aims of this study is to demonstrate, through an examination of the reaction of U.S. central decision-makers to issues involving foreign raw materials investments, that it is possible to talk sensibly about the existence of an American national interest defined in this way. One place to start is with the actual policy statements made by U.S. leaders about raw materials. Such statements can only be a beginning. Central decision-makers are not wont to make hard choices among different goals when they are making rhetorical proclamations or issuing reports. A transitively ordered set of preferences can only be established by examining specific cases. Only such an investigation can reveal what tradeoffs state actors have made among objectives and what kind of resources they have used to defend one aim as opposed to another. Chapters IV, VI, VII, and VIII present some fifteen cases. But looking at general policy statements and the broad historical development of materials policy provides a starting point, a checklist, of the goals sought by the state.

The Profusion of Laws and Bureaus

There is no denying that raw materials policies initially present a confusing picture, one apparently more in conformity with a pluralist approach than a statist or Marxist one. Such policies have touched upon a very wide variety of economic activities, because all products are made from some resource base. There are few initiatives that a government can take that do not impinge in some way upon the exploitation, processing, transportation, or marketing of unprocessed materials. The number of formal governmental rules pertaining to this issue area is very large. A 1972 study prepared for the National Commission on Materials Policy (established under the authority of the National Materials Policy

Act of 1970) identified 265 legal stipulations related to raw materials policy. These included several articles and amendments of the Constitution, numerous international treaties, and twenty-six groups of laws or individual laws "whose policies, purposes, or operations appear to affect significantly the implementation of a national materials policy."[18] Within this last category were twenty-one provisions dealing with foreign commerce. Ten involved import regulations and had the stated purpose of protecting or stimulating domestic production. Eleven of the laws concerned exports, including the Trade Expansion Act of 1962, the International Wheat Agreement Act of 1949, and the Foreign Assistance Act of 1961.[19] This study for the National Commission does not even deal with the topic examined in this book, foreign raw materials investments. Here a whole new spectrum of legal considerations becomes relevant, such as bilateral treaties of friendship, trade, and commerce, laws governing international monetary arrangements, and sanctions against countries that expropriate U.S. firms.

The implementation of these laws has involved the American government in a wide variety of activities. The United States has accumulated large stockpiles of many strategic raw materials. It has imposed quotas for petroleum, sugar, and zinc. It has promoted domestic development through tariffs, special tax incentives, and guaranteed purchase programs. It has limited the export of materials to enhance domestic supplies. It has directly invested in some raw materials industries. It has signed international commodity agreements for wheat, coffee, tin, and sugar. It has promoted and protected foreign raw materials investments.

These activities have spawned a commensurate bureaucratic apparatus. A 1954 Congressional report found fifty-four different boards or agencies dealing with the stockpile program alone. A 1969 study by the Congressional Research Service identified forty-seven different governmental entities involved with various aspects of materials policy. These included four from the Department of Defense, nine from Interior, seven from Agriculture, four

[18] U.S., National Commission on Materials Policy, "National Materials Policies," p. 23.

[19] *Ibid.*, pp. 69-71.

from Commerce, one from Treasury, two from Justice, two from HEW, three from Transportation, one from HUD, six from the White House, and six that were independent. This listing was described as being "a first cut." Three years later the authors of a study commissioned by the National Commission on Materials Policy read the U.S. Government Organization Manual even more closely and identified 136 different agencies associated with raw materials policy.[20]

The Evolution of U.S. Materials Policy

Laws, treaties, and other legal provisions, as well as the bureaucratic involvements they have spawned, are the accretion of a lengthy historical process. One way to begin to sort out the central goals of American raw materials policy is to look at changes in emphasis that have taken place over time. Concerns about natural resources have mirrored the general problems of American society at different stages of its development. Before 1900 materials shortages were of little moment. Vast stretches of territory, much of it owned by the federal government, were untouched. Natural resources were thought to be limitless. Policy was primarily directed toward developing these resources. The government engaged in various surveying and mapping activities. Water control projects were undertaken. Laws, such as the Homestead Act, facilitated the transfer of land from public to private ownership. Mineral land was sold outright to private parties. During the last quarter of the nineteenth century virtually all known public coal lands passed into private hands. Grazing and lumbering were not regulated.[21]

Forests were the first resource to attract public concern. Apprehension about despoilation began during the last quarter of the nineteenth century. Wood was a major resource not only for building material but also for fuel. In 1876 the Department of Agriculture appointed a special agent to study forests. In 1881 a Forestry Division, which later became the Forest Service, was es-

[20] *Ibid.*, Appendix B, p. 2; Percy W. Bidwell, *Raw Materials*, p. 42; U.S. Senate, Committee on Public Works, *Toward a National Materials Policy*, pp. 86-87.

[21] U.S., National Resources Committee, *Energy Resources and National Policy*, p. 383.

tablished. In 1897 the government began to set aside National Forests. However, the commitment to controlled development was not firm until the adminstration of Theodore Roosevelt; McKinley vitiated many of the controls that had been instituted by Cleveland.[22]

Under Theodore Roosevelt and Woodrow Wilson resource development within the United States was controlled more closely. Before 1908 new activity on coal and oil land was stopped so that regulations could be promulgated. Roosevelt appointed the Conservation Commission in 1908; part of its charge was to draw up an inventory of the nation's resources. The Bureau of Mines was established to promote safety and investigate ways to utilize mineral resources more efficiently. In 1914 the Alaska Coal Leasing Act was passed, for the first time changing the disposition of public lands from sales to leases. It was followed by the General Leasing Act of 1920, which covered mineral development on federal lands within the continental United States.[23]

The First World War brought fears of extensive materials shortages. The war sharply increased demand. There was little preparation before the United States became a belligerent. Planning boards were thrown together haphazardly, generally by bringing industrialists into government planning operations. Their attention was fixed on generating materials for the war effort. Had Britain and France not been able to supply American troops, they would probably not have been able to enter battle before the spring of 1919.[24]

World War I also indicated the potential importance of *foreign* raw materials investments for the first time. American entrepreneurs had begun operations in several countries of the western hemisphere around the turn of the century. By 1914 Mexico had become a substantial oil producer as a result of American and British investments. Although this output was not of much importance for the United States, it was a significant source of crude for

[22] *Ibid.*, pp. 379-82; Harbaugh, *Power and Responsibility*, p. 320.

[23] U.S., National Resources Committee, *Energy Resources and National Policy*, pp. 382-84.

[24] Huddle, "The Evolving National Policy for Materials," p. 654; Thatcher, *Planning for Industrial Mobilization, 1920-1940*, pp. 2-4.

the British. During World War I American oil men specifically related their activities in Mexico to national defense. There were also fears, first within the government and later the industry, that the United States was exhausting its domestic reserves while foreign sources were being monopolized by the British. As we shall see in Chapter IV, these worries prompted active government promotion of American oil investment in Latin America and the Middle East during the mid-1920s. At the same time, Secretary of Commerce Herbert Hoover spearheaded a drive against foreign resource cartels in coffee, potash, rubber, and other commodities, which he saw draining the American economy of many millions of dollars.

But by the late 1920s the problem of scarcity was largely forgotten. Prices by that time were already declining, at least in part because of new discoveries. During the depression the government's materials policy, like its activities in other areas, was designed to raise prices and stimulate the economy. In April 1934 Roosevelt appointed a Planning Committee for Mineral Policy. The Committee focussed its attention on "waste" stemming from excess capacity, overproduction, and ruinous competition. The Committee sought greater regulation of the market and government assistance that would, it was hoped, raise prices and spur recovery.[25] During the depression various production controls were promulgated, such as the Connally Hot Oil Act of 1935, which prohibited the interstate movement of crude oil produced in violation of state prorationing regulations. There was little concern with the foreign activities of American corporations. The problem was not too little, but too much. Resource policy was a manifestation of the general preoccupation with the economic crisis.

World War II brought another swing of the pendulum. Again materials were in scant supply. Intervention in the market was more extensive than it had ever been. Price controls and production quotas were imposed. A National Stockpiling Act was passed in 1939 enabling the government to purchase materials that were needed for the national defense. Commodity agreements were

[25] U.S., National Resources Board, *A Report on National Planning*, pp. 2-5, 31-32.

signed with foreign states, such as the Inter-American Coffee Agreement. The United States bought Bolivian tin and Cuban sugar at prices that encouraged more output. New production and mining facilities, including some overseas such as the Nicaro nickel mine in Cuba and an oil pipeline in northern Canada, were built with government funds. Public officials carefully watched over U.S. oil investments in the Middle East and in 1943 and 1944 actually made an effort to purchase the Arabian fields from Standard Oil of California and Texaco. In Venezuela the State Department urged Standard of New Jersey and other American companies to accept Venezuelan demands for higher tax payments. Security of supply was the overriding public concern.

Although the preoccupation with immediate military victory ended in 1945, the fixation with defense and security persisted. The Cold War brought a sense of intense struggle to the United States, in materials policy as in other walks of life. The Korean War led to a sharp increase in commodity prices. In 1951 President Truman appointed a commission to study raw materials, headed by William Paley. The Paley Commission report of 1952 entitled *Resources for Freedom* was the most important and extensive examination of materials undertaken by the American government to that date. The following statement appears on its first page:

> The United States, once criticized as the creator of a crassly materialistic order of things, is today throwing its might into the task of keeping alive the spirit of Man and helping beat back from the frontiers of the free world everywhere the threats of force and of a new Dark Age which rise from the Communist nations. In defeating this barbarous violence moral values will count most, but they must be supported by an ample materials base.

The Commission's report expressed alarm about potential shortages and exhaustion of supply. It recommended more information, conservation, technical substitutes, and closer government monitoring of materials problems.[26] However, when the Korean

[26] U.S., Paley Commission Report, Vol. I, *passim*; and Huddle, p. 655 for a summary.

War concluded, prices stabilized, and most of the recommendations of the Commission were ignored.

In October 1953 Eisenhower appointed a special cabinet committee to study minerals policy. Its basic recommendations were an increase in the size of the stockpile, particularly for zinc and lead, which were then experiencing depressed prices, and greater government support for domestic production. The recommendations for higher levels of stockpiling were implemented even though the Joint Chiefs said they were not needed.[27]

As the Cold War thawed, concern about national security waned. In areas directly related to minerals policy it was replaced by an emphasis on the environment. The National Materials Policy Act of 1970 emphasized environmental quality and materials conservation. It mandated the creation of a National Commission on Materials Policy, the first major group to study natural resources since the Paley Commission nearly twenty years before. The final report of this group was entitled *Material Need and the Environment Today and Tomorrow*. It barely mentioned national security. The late 1960s and early 1970s also saw the passage of many other laws, such as the Environmental Protection Act, which directly affected the development of mineral resources within the United States.

In the mid-1970s policy took another twist. The Arab oil embargo, and the unprecedented increase in commodity prices between 1972 and 1975, brought new awareness of the problem of shortages. Such developments had never before occurred during peacetime. Rising commodity prices, particularly for crude oil, contributed to double-digit inflation and higher unemployment rates in all of the major industrial countries. Economic performance became a major focus of public concern. Materials supply shortages led Senator Mansfield to initiate legislation creating the National Commission on Supplies and Shortages. Its charge was to make a one-year study of ways to provide the government with more information to anticipate, and policy options to deal with, future periods of scarcity. The Commission's conclusions were not particularly alarmist. Nevertheless, its report recognized that

[27] Huddle, pp. 655-56; and U.S., President's Cabinet Committee on Minerals Policy, *Report*.

market imperfections suggested a greater role for the government. The Commission recommended an international convention on export controls, measures to reduce the risk of foreign investment, a stockpiling program for economic as opposed to strategic purposes, improved recycling programs, and additional government capability for gathering and analyzing data.[28]

Some General Themes

While policies specifically related to raw materials have reflected overall economic concerns at different times, there are certain themes that have been present in all periods, albeit with differing emphasis. First, policy-makers have always paid attention to the relationship between materials and the effective functioning of the economy. This has usually been manifested in efforts to insure adequate supplies for industrial production, although during periods of economic depression it has been reflected in efforts to control output. Second, raw materials policy has been related to the well-being of individual citizens as opposed to the overall functioning of the economy. American laws and statements have emphasized the importance of minimizing prices to enhance material well-being. Finally, raw materials policy has been intimately connected with national defense—at the very least, the felt need for sources of supply adequate to meet military needs during national emergencies.[29]

These three goals—security of supply, minimization of price, and national security—are reflected in official statements that are meant to sum up American policy. The report of the Paley Commission states:

> The over-all objective of a national materials policy for the United States should be to insure an adequate and dependable flow of materials at the lowest cost consistent with national security and with the welfare of friendly nations.[30]

[28] U.S., National Commission on Supplies and Shortages, *Government and the Nation's Resources*, pp. xi-xviii.

[29] Environmental protection has been another persistent theme, but has been limited to domestic materials activity and is not relevant for the concerns of this study.

[30] U.S., Paley Commission Report, Vol. I, p. 3.

A 1969 study by the Bureau of Mines concluded that the "underlying goals" of U.S. materials policy as embodied in existing laws were

> . . . to assure an adequate supply of metals and minerals, sufficient for the Nation's continued economic growth and dependable under emergency and nonemergency conditions.[31]

A report prepared for the Committee on Public Works in the same year by an outside group of businessmen and academicians concludes:

> In summary, materials—their availability, use and disposal—are significantly related to national goals of physical health and well-being, economic health and prosperity, national defense and security.[32]

This short review of laws, official reports, and general policy statements suggests, then, that foreign raw materials policy is concerned with 1) minimizing costs for the American consumer, 2) insuring security of supply for the American economy, and 3) furthering broad foreign policy objectives.

In summary, a statist approach to the study of foreign policy must begin by identifying the national interest. This it can do in either a logical-deductive or an empirical-inductive way. This study follows the latter course. The preferences of central decision-makers can be called the national interest if they meet two desiderata: first, they are concerned with the general interests of the society (they do not persistently benefit some groups or classes and harm others); second, they maintain the same transitive ordering over time. In the area of raw materials an examination of general statements and the broad historical outline of policy offers a beginning point for identifying the national interest. U.S. leaders have emphasized general foreign policy goals, security of supply, and lower prices as the basic objectives of policy. This inductively derived list is quite similar to the kind implied by the more deductive arguments presented by mercantilist writers in the

[31] U.S. Senate, *Toward a National Materials Policy*, p. 37.

[32] *Ibid.*, p. 6.

seventeenth and eighteenth centuries. There is no contradiction between the empirical approach used in this study and more conventional deductive reasoning as far as the actual substance of policy in the area of raw materials is concerned. Having established this list does not, however, reveal what American national interest, defined in terms of the preferences of policy-makers, actually has been.[33] This can only be done by examining the choices that have been made in actual cases. Only such an investigation can demonstrate that American leaders had a consistent set of preferences over time that were related to the general well-being of the society rather than to the needs of particular elements within it. An assessment of actual behavior begins in Chapter IV. First, however, it is necessary to present a framework for analyzing the relationship between the state and its own society.

[33] This approach to the national interest, it should be noted, has no normative component. Policy-makers may define the national interest in ways that most observers would find abhorrent or stupid.

CHAPTER III

Policy-making in a Weak State

Establishing a set of transitively ordered preferences that persist over time and are related to general societal goals defines the national interest. The existence of such a set of goals does not imply that they will be implemented. Realist approaches to international relations have focussed on the ways in which other actors in the international system may frustrate state leaders. The analysis of this study, while sharing the same basic assumptions, emphasizes the domestic constraints that are imposed on the state. In structural approaches to international relations the state is a billiard ball whose internal components are impervious to foreign pressures; here the state is a set of central decision-making institutions and roles that must confront internal as well as external opponents. The central analytic characteristic that determines the ability of a state to overcome domestic resistance is its strength in relation to its own society.[1]

Strong and Weak States

The strength of the state in relationship to its own society can be envisioned along a continuum ranging from weak to strong.[2]

[1] In developing this analysis I have benefitted greatly from the work of Peter Katzenstein. See especially his "International Relations and Domestic Structures," and his "Introduction" and "Conclusion" in the Autumn 1977 issue of *International Organization*.

[2] The concept of strength as it is used here is distinct from the increasing scope of governmental activities that has taken place in all countries. The two are related: an increase in scope is likely to mean an increase in state power. However, this is not a logical necessity. For instance, the "capture" thesis of regulatory agencies in the United States contends that increasing scope has enhanced private penetration of public institutions rather than the state's ability to control the private sector. In Britain, where the scope of state activity is greater than in the United States, government agencies still engage in negotiating and conflict resolving rather than au-

The weakest kind of state is one that is completely permeated by pressure groups. Central government institutions serve specific interests within the country, rather than the general aims of the citizenry as a whole. Lebanon before the civil war of 1975-1976 can be thought of as such a state: public functions and positions were divided between Moslems and Christians; there was little or no agreement on what would constitute the general good or the collective interest of the country. The logical terminus of the weak end of the spectrum is civil war and the complete disintegration of the state.

At the other extreme from a state completely permeated by political pressure groups is one that is able to remake the society and culture in which it exists—that is, to change economic institutions, values, and patterns of interaction among private groups. Such extraordinarily powerful states have only existed immediately after major revolutions. It is not that the state is so strong during such periods, but that the society is weak because existing patterns of behavior have been shattered. The clearest examples are the Soviet Union after 1917 and China after 1949. Both countries had suffered many years of war. In China, the old regime had been falling apart for a century, unable to cope with pressures from the West. In Russia, the First World War had devastated the country and demonstrated the incompetence of the Czarist government. In both countries the regimes that seized power made fundamental changes in economic, cultural, and even familial relationships.

Obviously, most states are neither as weak as Lebanon nor as strong as post-revolutionary communist regimes. Usually the state is able to maintain some autonomy from the society, but at the same time it cannot impose rapid and dramatic structural transformations on the economic or cultural systems. In capitalist or market-economy countries, where there is some autonomy between private and public institutions, three *ideal-typical* relationships between the state and society can be envisioned.

First, the state may be able to resist societal pressure, but un-

---

tonomously initiating activity. On this last point see Nettl, "The State as a Conceptual Variable," p. 583.

able to change the behavior of private actors. For instance, central decision-makers may be able to ignore appeals from large corporations, but unable to make corporations follow policies that would further the state's goals or create alternative institutions, such as state-owned businesses.

Second, the state may be able to resist private pressure and to persuade private groups to follow policies that are perceived as furthering the national interest, but be unable to impose structural transformation on its domestic environment. Here public officials have positive power, the ability to change private behavior so that the public interest is better served, and not simply negative power, the ability to prevent the private sector from using public resources to protect private prerogatives. Still, the state must work with existing social structures. In economic affairs these structures can be defined in terms of the juridical nature of the institutions controlling economic activities (for instance, government versus privately owned corporations), the distribution of activity among sectors, and the place of particular firms within sectors.

Finally, a state may have the power to change the behavior of existing private actors and also, over a period of time, the economic structure itself. The state could create new kinds of economic actors. It could build up certain sectors of the economy through credits, tax relief, or other forms of support. It could favor companies whose activities were perceived as serving the national interest. These possibilities are summed up in the following table.

TABLE III-1

Power of the State vis-à-vis Its Domestic Society

	Resist Private Pressure		*Change Private Behavior*		*Change Social Structure*	
	Yes	No	Yes	No	Yes	No
Nonexistent		x		x		x
Weak	x			x		x
Moderate	x		x			x
Strong	x		x		x (but slowly)	
Dominant	x		x		x	

It is important to recognize that the "weak," "moderate," "strong," and "dominant" categories all assume a view of politics that is incompatible with either a liberal or instrumental Marxist approach. All four of these ideal-types imply that the state has some autonomy from its own society even if this autonomy is limited, as in the case of "weak" states, to preventing societal pressure groups from using the instruments of public power for private purposes. "Moderate," "strong," and "dominant" states can alter the societal environment in which they act, a phenomenon that is difficult to capture from either a pluralist or instrumental Marxist perspective.

It is very unlikely that any state will fit neatly into one of the classifications, but an ideal-typical taxonomy helps highlight critical distinctions. The "weak," "moderate," and "strong" types are the most relevant for polities in advanced market-economy countries. In such countries, states may be strong in some issue areas and weak in others. There is no reason to assume *a priori* that the pattern of strength and weakness will be the same for all policies. One state may be unable to alter the structure of its medical system but be able to construct an efficient transportation network, while another can deal relatively easily with getting its citizens around but cannot get their illnesses cured. States in developed capitalist countries are most likely to fit the "moderate" pattern of power shown in Table III-1 in some issue areas and the "weak" pattern in others. None of these states falls into the "nonexistent" or the "dominant" pattern, and only some are "strong" even in a relatively limited number of issue areas.

Despite variations among issue areas within countries, there are modal differences in the power of the state among the advanced market-economy countries. France and Japan probably have the strongest states. Even in periods of rapidly changing governments, such as the Fourth Republic, the French central administration could exercise public control over private actors. The administrative elite has been able to choose those interest groups that it has preferred to deal with, favoring associations whose views coincided with its preferences. The French state has had a fairly wide range of policy instruments to alter the behavior of private actors. The most potent has probably been the control of credit.

Because the ratio of self-financing for French firms is low, they must look to the capital market for loans. This market is heavily influenced by the state. The largest bank in France is publicly owned. The French government has very close ties with some private banks. Special funds have been set up to make investments in areas that are perceived as being in the national interest. Such funds have been controlled by the bureaucrats in charge of implementing French economic plans and have been insulated from the legislature. In addition, planning officials have signed contracts with individual companies: the private sector has promised to meet certain economic goals, such as production targets and prices; the government has offered tax breaks, changes in import duties, social security payment rebates, favorable provision of capital, guaranteed government purchases, subsidized research, and even free advertising on the government-owned television network. Such arrangements made indicative planning more effective during the 1950s and 1960s.

The French government has also created mixed or wholly government-owned enterprises in certain critical economic sectors such as power generation, nuclear energy, railroads, and airlines. In petroleum the French government became a part owner of the Compagnie Française des Pétroles (CFP) in 1929. After the Second World War intervention in the oil industry was extended. In 1965 the government amalgamated a number of smaller firms to form a second French exploration and development company, ERAP. Oil imports have been closely regulated. Special funds have been provided for oil exploration. Tax rebates have been granted for petroleum development in France or the franc zone. By the 1970s these policies had led to a substantial decline in the amount of oil refined and distributed in France by non-French companies.[3]

The pattern of relationships between the state and the economy in Japan has many similarities with that in France. Intervention at the level of the economic sector or the firm (as opposed to the economy as a whole) has been facilitated by the wide range of

[3] Suleiman, *Politics, Power and Bureaucracy in France*, Ch. 12; Shonfield, *Modern Capitalism*, pp. 129-31; Vernon, "Enterprise and Government in Western Europe," pp. 12-14; Katzenstein, "International Relations," pp. 36-37.

policy instruments possessed by the Japanese bureaucracy, particularly the Ministry of International Trade and Industry (MITI) and the Ministry of Finance. MITI has actively coordinated behavior in certain industries by setting goals for output and unit costs. It has been able to grant tax allowances through accelerated depreciation. It has established a system of advisory councils. During the 1950s MITI acted to develop and rationalize the Japanese steel, petrochemical, heavy machinery, automobile, electronics, synthetic rubber, and airplane industries. In dealing with the international economy, Japan has imposed tighter controls than any other advanced capitalist state: through the 1950s the allocation of foreign exchange gave MITI a powerful lever of control over the domestic economy; and MITI has developed close relationships with major trading companies that handle 50-60 percent of Japanese exports. The Ministry of Finance has pursued a policy of keeping interest rates below levels needed to clear the market. Credit has been allocated through institutional controls. Discrimination among borrowers, rationing, and subsidies have been the rule. The Ministry of Finance's decisions about capital have been used to bolster specific sectors and firms.[4]

In France and Japan, the exercise of state power has been facilitated by political culture. In both countries an activist role for the state is widely accepted. In France, prices and patterns of production are not taken as a given, but are regarded as variables that are subject to official control. In Japan, a high regard for private enterprise is coupled with a belief that the government should act as a well-intentioned guide. In both countries the bureaucracy is respected. The best graduates from the most elite universities are likely to choose the central adminstration over the private sector.[5]

This is not to say that in either France or Japan the state always wins, while the private sector plays a merely passive and servile role. Even public ownership has not meant automatic subservience to state preferences in France. The French have recognized

[4] See the articles on trade, industrial organization, and finance in Patrick and Rosovsky, eds., *Asia's New Giant*.

[5] Suleiman, pp. 18-19; Michalet, "France," p. 107; Patrick and Rosovsky "Japan's Economic Performance: An Overview," in *Asia's New Giant*, p. 53; and Kaplan, *Japan*, p. 10.

that such enterprises must have some autonomy. Firms can bargain with decision-makers, and even reject official policy. In recent years, as France has become more immeshed in the international economy, precise control has become more difficult. In Japan, the Ministry of Finance and MITI have also played a less directive role in recent years, at least in part because of greater exposure to the rest of the world. In at least one dramatic case the Japanese government failed to secure the support of the private sector: in 1969 and 1970 Prime Minister Sato was unable to persuade the Japanese textile industry to accept a secret arrangement with the United States for limiting man-made textile exports, which the Nixon administration had linked with the reversion of Okinawa to Japan.[6] However, in comparison with the United States, the state in France and Japan has more power over its own society. In the terms of Table III-1, these two countries fall into either the "moderate" or the "strong" category for most issue areas.

The American Political System

America has a strong society but a weak state. Within little more than a century after becoming independent, the United States had become the world's largest market and leading source of technological innovation. By the end of the Second World War, the United States had achieved a position of global dominance unmatched in previous human history.

Through all of this, the political system remained weak. The central feature of American politics is the fragmentation and dispersion of power and authority. This has been recognized by pluralists such as Dahl, Polsby, and Truman who tend to emphasize the system's virtues, as well as by writers such as Huntington, Lowi, McConnell, and Burnham who see the American polity as gravely flawed. Polsby argues that the different branches of the American government were designed so that they "would be captured by different interests."[7] Truman notes that the

[6] See Destler et al., *Managing an Alliance*, for a discussion of the Okinawa case, and Zysman, *Political Strategies for Industrial Order*, for French difficulties with the electronics industry.

[7] Polsby, *Congress and the Presidency*, pp. 140-41.

"diffusion of leadership and disintegration of policy are not hallucinations."[8] Huntington summarizes the situation as one in which there is a "fusion of functions and division of power."[9] Burnham argues that the political system has been "in domestic matters at any rate—dispersive and fragmented . . . dedicated to the defeat, except temporarily and under the direct pressure of overwhelming crisis, of any attempt to generate domestic sovereignty. . . ."[10]

The Constitution is a document more concerned with limiting than enhancing the power of the state. The Founding Fathers were wary of power; they sought to limit its temptations by dividing power within the government and among societal groups. They preserved the states, gave Congress specific, not unlimited legal powers, established a bicameral legislature, gave the President specific, not unlimited powers, and created an independent judiciary. Although the concept of dividing power among societal groups is not explicitly reflected in the Constitution, it was voiced by Madison at the Convention and clearly explicated in *Federalist No. 10*.[11]

The American state—the President and those bureaus relatively insulated from societal pressures, which are the only institutions capable of formulating the national interest—must always struggle against an inherent tendency for power and control to be dissipated and dispersed. They must operate in a political culture that views the activist state with great suspicion. This is particularly true of the business sector. American capitalists have a more negative reaction to public economic activity than their counterparts in other advanced market economies.[12] American central decision-makers do not command the policy instruments that are important in countries like France and Japan. It is not clear in the United States where sovereignty rests, if indeed it rests anywhere at all.[13] The jurisdictional boundaries of institutions are unclear.

[8] *The Governmental Process*, p. 529.

[9] *Political Order*, p. 110.

[10] Burnham, *Critical Elections*, p. 176.

[11] Dahl, *Pluralist Democracy*, p. 39.

[12] Vogel, "Why Businessmen Distrust Their State."

[13] In *Political Order* Huntington argues that one of the characteristics of the American polity is the persistence of the sixteenth-century notion that the law is above the lawmakers—that is, that the state lacks sovereign power.

"Dispersed leadership and multiple points of control within one branch reflect and reinforce similar patterns in the other."[14] In trying to promote the national interest, the American state often confronts dissident bureaus, a recalcitrant Congress, and powerful private actors.

Within the executive branch it cannot be assumed that the President can control all bureaus. Even here the state must struggle against the legislature and the private sector. Many presidential appointments are subject to ratification by the Senate. Budgets require legislative approval. The legal structures of many agencies reflect the desire of Congressional committees to maintain some formal control. Some agencies can get support from Congress against the preferences of the President.[15] Particular public bureaucracies have ties with the private sector. Many federal regulatory agencies are controlled by the groups that they are supposed to regulate. McConnell argues that "a substantial part of government in the United States has come under the influence or control of narrowly based autonomous elites."[16] Agency heads may appeal to societal constituencies. Truman's hesitancy in removing MacArthur during the Korean War can in large part be explained by the General's political popularity and his ties with the right wing of the Republican Party.[17]

More important, for the empirical problems dealt with in this study, is the impact of the Congress on the ability of central decision-makers to implement their preferences. Congress presents an inherent problem for two reasons. First, the political needs and constituencies of Congressmen are different from those of the President. Second, power within the Congress itself is fragmented and dispersed, offering many points of access for societal groups.

Because Congressmen represent geographically specific areas,

[14] Truman, p. 436.

[15] Seidman, *Politics, Position and Power*, pp. 42-47.

[16] McConnell, *Private Power and American Democracy*, p. 339.

[17] For a discussion of this episode see Neustadt, *Presidential Power*. Neustadt's analysis of bureaucratic politics, with its emphasis on presidential control, is much closer to the perspective of this study than later works from the bureaucratic politics school, which view the President as one actor among many. Even Neustadt tends to exaggerate the autonomous power of the bureaucracy by underemphasizing Congressional and societal sources of bureaucratic power.

they are bound to have different concerns from the President's. While the President can be held accountable for the broad effect of policy, rarely can members of the legislature. To get reelected, members of Congress must serve relatively narrow constituencies. They are likely to prefer particularized legislation that allows them to take credit for rendering service to those whose support they need to stay in office. The general tendency in Congress is to appoint members to committees related to the interests of their constituents. Congressmen will service organized groups with disposable political resources. Such groups often keep a close watch on committee activities. Congressmen will try to protect their own bureaucratic clientele from presidential intervention. Cleavages between Congress and the President have often been more salient than those between political parties.[18]

The problems that Congress presents for the implementation of the preferences of central decision-makers are exacerbated by the absence of cohesion and centralization in the Congress itself. The American legislature does not confront the President as a unified force. American central decision-makers may have to bargain with a number of specific Congressional institutions each capable of blocking state initiatives.

In 1885 Woodrow Wilson wrote about Congress that "power is nowhere concentrated; it is rather deliberately and of set policy scattered amongst many small chiefs."[19] During the twentieth century the dispersal of power in the legislative branch has increased. In both Houses the position of the leader of the majority party, the natural focus of centralized authority, has been persistently undermined. From the attack on Speaker Cannon in the House in 1910 until the legislative reforms of the mid-1970s, the key element in this trend was the seniority system, which deprived the leadership of the right to select committee chairmen. The Legislative Reorganization Act of 1946 strengthened the position of standing committees and limited the discretion that the leadership could exercise in allocating bills among committees. The Legislative Reform Act of 1970 dispersed power still further by strengthening committee chairmen. Reforms in the Congress

[18] This argument is developed in Mayhew, *Congress*.

[19] Quoted in Seidman, p. 38.

from 1970 to 1973 were largely directed at reducing the power of chairmen; in some cases heads of subcommittees have assumed a more prominent role.[20] While recent changes have lessened the importance of seniority, they have not restored any centralized control over individual committees.

The growth of Congressional staff and resources since the Second World War has also made it more difficult to achieve coherence. The number of committee staff members increased from 400 in 1946 to 2,000 in 1974. The number of staff assistants for individual members of the Congress had reached 9,000 by 1974. Support institutions such as the General Accounting Office, the Congressional Research Service, the Office of Technology Assessment, and the Congressional Budget Office have all been expanded or created during the last few decades. Congressional perquisites such as franking privileges have been increased. All of these developments have reduced the power of party leaders in the House and the Senate.[21]

Harvey Mansfield has summed up the situation in the following terms: "Dispersion is a formula for producing and encouraging a cadre of miners and sappers like Senator Proxmire and Congressman Les Aspin, skilled in tunneling and penetrating hidden recesses and placing explosive charges in the executive branch—the military-industrial complex, the CIA, Watergate, and domestic surveillance; missionaries like Congressman Drinan seeking converts to their causes; entrepreneurs and brokers putting together the elements of a conglomerate bill that can pass; broken-field runners and players to the grandstand; and, in the Senate, aspirants to the presidency."[22]

The fragmentation of power means that legislation can be blocked at any one of a number of decision-making nodes. In the House these include subcommittees, full committees, the Rules

[20] Huntington, "Congressional Responses," pp. 23-25, and Mansfield, "Dispersion of Authority in Congress," p. 18. Speaker of the House Thomas P. O'Neill did demonstrate effective leadership in ushering the administration's energy bill through the House in 1977. Whether this heralds a new trend remains to be seen, for the program's treatment in the Senate and in the conference committee was a classic example of the ineffectuality resulting from the fragmentation of power.

[21] Mansfield, "Dispersion of Authority," pp. 14-16.

[22] *Ibid.*, p. 18.

Committee, the full House, the Rules Committee again for a bill going to a conference committee, and the conference committee itself. The situation is similar in the Senate except that there is no direct parallel with the Rules Committee. The Appropriations Committees of both branches can change programs by not approving funds or by issuing reports that tell agencies precisely what to do. Although these reports are not legally binding, an agency jeopardizes its relations with the Committees if such instructions are ignored. The jurisdictional authority of individual committees is often not clearly differentiated: the Appropriations and Government Operations Committees, the House Rules Committee, and the Joint Economic Committee all have virtually universal scope in the matters they can consider. There is usually little cooperation between committees with the same jurisdiction in the two Houses.[23]

Causes of a Weak Political System

The weakness of the American polity is deeply embedded in the country's history. America has never needed a strong state. The political, social, and economic imperatives that have enhanced the role of the state in Japan and continental Europe have been much less compelling in the United States. First, with one minor exception (the War of 1812), the United States has never been confronted with foreign invasion. Second, American society has been unusually cohesive, and dominant social values have been congruent with the needs of a modern economy. Third, the American economy has performed extraordinarily well without much direct government intervention, and the abundance generated by economic success has mitigated the demands placed upon the state.

America has not, until recently, confronted a serious external threat to its territorial and political integrity. On the European continent the great impetus to the centralization of political authority during the sixteenth and seventeenth centuries was the constant threat of war. Fledgling states could not defend themselves without a standing army. To raise and maintain such

[23] See the articles by Fenno and Huitt in Truman, ed., *Congress and America's Future*, and Seidman, pp. 49-50.

forces, it was necessary to strengthen the political system.[24] The United States, on the other hand, enjoyed the protection of Britain's maritime dominance during the nineteenth century. By the time America was thrown upon the world scene in the twentieth century, its size and mastery of technology made it possible to create the world's most formidable military force even with a weak government. Curiously, the very weapons that have, for the first time, made the territorial integrity of the United States vulnerable may also, because of their capital intensity, allow the state to maintain its defenses with a weak political structure. The burdens imposed upon the domestic population by hardened missile sites and nuclear submarines are less than those resulting from large standing armies and extensive reserve corps.

A second reason why a strong state has not developed in America is because dominant social values did not have to be changed to ensure societal cohesion or economic development. America, born modern, did not have to be made modern. Early Americans were favorably disposed to change and to social status based upon achievement rather than ascription. Commitment to social classes was weak. There was never an aristocratic class, or feudal institutions, that stood in the way of rapid social and economic development. Immigrants absorbed the values held by those who had come before them.[25] Huntington argues that "in Europe the opposition to modernization within society forced the modernization of the political system. In America, the ease of modernization within society precluded the modernization of political institutions."[26] The Founding Fathers' desire to decentralize power led to a viable political system only because their view of American society was wrong. It was not riven with dissension. On the contrary, it was exceptionally cohesive. Checks and balances have offered a workable formula only because the society has been able to perform the kind of integrating functions that fell to the state in most European countries.[27]

Finally, there is a set of economic factors that help explain why

[24] Huntington, *Political Order*, pp. 122ff.

[25] *Ibid.*, p. 126; Burnham, p. 176; and Hartz, *The Liberal Tradition*.

[26] Huntington, *Political Order*, p. 129.

[27] See Packenham, *Liberal America and the Third World*, pp. 154-55, and Nettl, for a general argument along these lines.

the state has been weak in America. Alexander Gerschenkron has pointed to a syndrome associated with the sequence of industrialization. Those countries that underwent the industrial revolution at an earlier period, notably the United States and Great Britain, industrialized more slowly; the scale of industry was smaller; there was less direct intervention from the state because private actors could mobilize their own resources; and slower development did not mean that the country's security would be threatened. Late modernizers—France, Germany, Japan, and Russia—experienced more rapid rates of growth. They relied more on large capital-intensive projects. The state played a direct role in moving the economy from a mercantile and agricultural base to an industrial one, particularly by mobilizing resources and dispensing investment funds.[28]

Furthermore, America has been almost from its inception a relatively wealthy country. It was well endowed with natural resources—most importantly during its formative period, a large amount of land. In terms of per capita income it surpassed Britain in the middle of the nineteenth century, then fell back as a result of immigration and other factors, but regained its global lead by the outbreak of the First World War and held it at least through the 1960s. Abundance and rapid growth facilitated equal opportunity and the belief that things would always improve. Social problems were often solved by technological and economic changes rather than political initiatives. All of this good fortune reinforced the myth of social equality and mobility. It was possible to believe that things would always get better, because they usually did for most people. Pressures on the political system were usually relatively modest because the level of social dissatisfaction was mitigated by economic growth. A weak political system could exist because politics was less necessary for a citizenry that perceived itself dividing an expanding rather than stagnant national product. In the words of David Potter, "economic abundance is conducive to political democracy"[29] and, one might add, a democratic system that diffused rather than concentrated power and authority.

Before proceeding, it is well to note, if only briefly, some of

[28] Gerschenkron, *Economic Backwardness*, Ch. 1.

[29] *People of Plenty*, p. 112.

the normative consequences of an analytic framework focussing on the strength and weakness of the state. There is an obvious implication that it is better to have a strong state than a weak one: a weak state may be unable to pursue the general interest because it is frustrated by particular societal actors. However, this does not imply that an authoritarian regime is desirable. Democracy is not incompatible with a strong state. The ability to vote political leaders out of office is the critical check on abuse of power. The stalemate system that can frustrate efforts by American central decision-makers to take action that would enhance collective societal goals should not be confused with democracy. The ability of individual pressure groups to block government initiatives is not the same as the ability of the citizenry to remove a central decision-maker from office. The former makes it difficult for the state to fulfill its purpose of protecting the collective interests of the society; the latter is protection against authoritarianism.

Judgments about the merits of weak and strong political systems cannot be made in an empirical vacuum. America has had a weak state because it has not needed a strong one. And weakness does have its advantages. It probably increases the individual citizen's sense of efficacy, even if attempts to actually influence the government are rare.[30] In addition, as Kenneth Waltz has argued in *Foreign Policy and Democratic Politics*, a political system with many seats of power may enhance debate and ultimately lead to clearer and more responsive policies. A weak state may also offer greater flexibility in the economic sphere. When technology is changing rapidly, flexibility may be critical for economic development, because central decision-making institutions rarely, if ever, have the capacity to direct such change effectively.[31] Hence, in examining a country's collective economic well-being, any judgment about the relative merits of weak and strong states depends upon the situation the state confronts. Despite the difficulty American central decision-makers have in implementing their preferences, American society has still fared extraordinarily well

[30] See Almond and Verba, *The Civic Culture*, for a discussion of participation and perceptions of efficacy.

[31] On the Soviet Union see Leonhard, "The Domestic Politics of the New Soviet Foreign Policy"; on France see Zysman.

because, on the whole, the private sector has been able to operate with great efficiency. Whether this pattern will continue is a question to which we shall return in the conclusion of this study.

If one looks to critics, supporters, or apologists for the American political system, then, a common thread runs through all of their arguments: in America political power is dispersed and fragmented. This structure rests upon a socio-economic foundation characterized by shared values, the absence of external threat, internal harmony, equality, and abundance. The implication that some draw, although others ignore, is that the state is weak: it cannot easily penetrate and transform the society. There is an endemic tendency toward ignoring general goals. The system makes obstruction easy, positive action difficult.

State Leadership and Societal Constraints

The diffusion of power has not, however, had a uniform impact across all political issues. In particular, it has not presented severe problems for defending the core goals of foreign policy, territorial and political integrity. Even those analysts most critical of the American political system have been reluctant to include this issue area in their argument.[32] The protection of the territorial and political integrity of the state does not usually lead to disagreements among societal groups. Political elites may argue about how these aims should be secured, but the state rarely has to contend with conflicting interest groups. A state that is weak in relation to its own society can act effectively in the strategic arena because its preferences are not likely to diverge from those of individual societal groups.

There is, however, no reason to assume that foreign economic policy-making is identical with foreign political policy-making. Any economic decision is likely to affect groups within the society differentially, creating the potential for societal conflict. For this reason it is questionable to assume that policy can be understood solely by examining the motivations and perceptions of central decision-makers. In a political system where state power is

[32] Lowi, "American Business and Public Policy," and Burnham, p. 176.

weak and fragmented, foreign as well as domestic economic policy can be influenced or even determined by societal groups.

Private Political Resources

International raw materials policy is an area where the potential for societal frustration of the national interest is great because the major private actors command substantial political resources. The American corporations involved in the international movement of almost all raw materials are very large, especially the oil companies. Table III-2 lists those handling particular commodities and their rank by sales among all U.S. firms for the year 1976.

In addition, the corporations involved in raw materials industries generally operate in fairly concentrated markets at the national and even the global level. Table III-3 shows levels of concentration for a number of markets within the United States.

Even at the global level many markets have been governed by a relatively small number of firms until recent years, when the influence of host-country governments has risen sharply. Seven companies (five American, one British, one British-Dutch) have dominated the world oil market, three (two Canadian, one French) the nickel market, six (three American, one Canadian, one French, one Swiss) the aluminum market, three (all American) the banana market. In the iron ore industry 30 percent of ore traded in 1968 moved within a vertically integrated structure. Although levels of concentration have declined in several markets since 1950, including aluminum, petroleum, lead, and copper, the structure of almost all raw materials industries, even at the global level, has been oligopolistic.[33]

Such large economic units acting in concentrated markets are likely to possess the attributes that confer political power in

[33] IBRD, Economic Staff Working Paper, No. 15, "The Nickel Outlook Reassessed," Aug. 31, 1972 (mimeo), pp. 2, 4; UNCTAD, Committee on Commodities, "The Marketing and Distribution System for Bananas," TD/B/C.1/162, Dec. 24, 1975 (mimeo); Charles River Associates, "Economic Issues Underlying Supply Access Agreements: A General Analysis and Prospects in Ten Mineral Markets," July 1975 (mimeo), Appendix, pp. 1-2; IBRD, Bank Staff Working Paper No. 160, "The International Market for Iron Ore: Review and Outlook," Aug. 1973 (mimeo), p. 11; Vernon, *Storm Over the Multinationals*, p. 81.

Table III-2

Size of U.S. Raw Materials Firms: Rank by Sales, 1976

Petroleum		*Ferrous Metals*		*Nonferrous Metals*		*Tropical Foodstuffs*		*Rubber*	
Company	Rank	Company	Rank	Company	Rank	Company	Rank	Company	Rank
Exxon	1	U.S. Steel	14	Alcoa	72	Procter and Gamble	19	Goodyear	23
Texaco	4	Bethlehem	33	Reynolds	108	General Foods	44	Uniroyal	95
Mobil	5	Armco	63	Anaconda	151	United Brands	99	General Tire	111
Socal	6	National	76	AMAX	191	Standard Brands	126	Goodrich	112
Gulf	7	Republic	86	Kennecott	234	Castle and Cook	250		
				Phelps Dodge	240	Hershey	328		
				St. Joe's	251				
				Revere	374				

Source: *Fortune* 95 (May 1977).

TABLE III-3

Levels of Concentration:
Percent of Industrial Shipments, 1972

Product	*Four Largest Companies*	*Eight Largest Companies*
Primary Copper	72	98 (1970)
Primary Lead	93	99
Primary Zinc	66	90 (1970)
Primary Aluminum	79	.92
Roasted Coffee	65	79
Petroleum Refinery Products	31	56
Raw Cane Sugar	44	62
Beet Sugar	66	92
Chocolate and Cocoa	74	88

Source: U.S., Department of Commerce, Bureau of the Census, *Concentration Ratios in Manufacturing.*

America. They are usually well represented in Washington through individual lobbyists, law firms, and trade associations. They have large amounts of money. They hold information that public officials cannot procure through other channels. They are competently directed.

Perhaps more than any other societal actor, large corporations are able to appeal to public institutions through all three forms of representation present in the American government: geographic, functional, and national. Because they often employ large numbers of people in geographically specific areas, they are important to particular Congressmen. Because they dominate large areas of the economy, they are important to the functional agencies of the executive branch. Because at least some of them are vital for the economy as a whole, they are important to the White House. All of these attributes combine to give most large American corporations direct access to Congressional committees, executive departments, and often the White House itself.[34]

In some raw materials markets political pressure can come from

[34] For a discussion of the attributes of business and other pressure groups see Schattschneider, *Politics, Pressures and the Tariff*, p. 287; Schattschneider, *Semisovereign People*, p. 31; Wilson, *Political Organizations*, pp. 165-66; Truman, pp. 333-34, 506-7; and Huntington, "Congressional Responses," p. 20.

another source—geographically concentrated groups of domestic owners and workers. Here again the oil industry stands out. In the mid-1960s the value of petroleum and natural gas production accounted for 45 percent of total personal income in Wyoming, 39 percent in Louisiana, 22 percent in New Mexico, 17 percent in Texas, and 15 percent in Oklahoma.[35] Additional sources of energy, especially coal, provide a livelihood for substantial numbers of people in other states. The large membership of such groups can make them particularly telling in influencing Congress, because of its geographic system of representation.

In sum, American decision-makers face serious constraints in formulating international raw materials policy. The American political system diffuses and fragments power. In most raw materials markets they confront societal actors, including large corporations and concentrated groups of domestic producers, that possess substantial political resources. Even when private groups are in disagreement, public initiatives may be frustrated. Political structure and societal interests establish the parameters within which American central decision-makers must operate. Yet it would be a mistake to assume that they rigidly determine final outcomes.

Leadership and Decision Arenas

The weakness of the political system and the political resources of private actors do not always lead to frustration for American leaders in their effort to implement the national interest. Obviously, the preferences of societal groups and those of central decision-makers may converge without any effort by either side to influence the other. Beyond this analytically simple (but practically important) category, the impediments that a fragmented system imposes on central decision-makers can be mitigated in two ways. First, the state can exercise political leadership. In the area of international raw materials investment the most important manifestations of leadership have involved altering private preferences and exploiting divisions among societal groups. Second, the preferences of political leaders are more likely to be adopted

[35] Percentages for individual states are derived from data in U.S., Bureau of Mines, *Mineral Yearbook*, 1967, Vol. III.

and implemented if decisions are taken by central state institutions such as the White House and the State Department rather than by the Congress or executive bureaus that serve specific domestic interest groups. The arena in which decisions are taken is a function of the way in which an issue is defined, and this definition too can sometimes be altered by political leadership. Both leadership and the ability to make decisions within central state institutions involve situations in which the American polity resembles the "moderate" pattern of state power described in Table III-1 rather than the "weak" one, which is the more typical pattern for the United States.

LEADERSHIP AND CONVERGING PREFERENCES

The preferences of public and private actors may converge for a variety of reasons. The most obvious is that the clearly identified needs of the state can coincide with the economic interests of the firm. In raw materials markets the state's desire for secure and stable supplies may lead to policies that further the profits, growth, or market control of the firm. In addition, private and public preferences may converge because the state can modify the perceptions of societal actors. One way that central decision-makers can bring this sort of change about is by offering a compelling interpretation of events that corporate managers are unable to make sense of on their own. By providing a coherent frame of reference the state can alter the way in which private managers define their own interest. Less obviously, preferences may also converge when the state supports policies that have an ambiguous or even moderately negative effect on private actors, because central decision-makers can exploit the nonpecuniary motives of corporate officials. This is a much more likely possibility when the state confronts oligopolistic, diversified corporations than when it must deal with sectors composed of large numbers of small owner-operated producing units. Recent developments in the theory of the firm suggest why this should be so.

Classical economic theory expects firms to act as if they were maximizing profits. It assumes perfect competition: each firm acts as if prices and market conditions are given, the entrepreneur has perfect information. Firms fail if they do not equate marginal revenue and marginal cost. This approach is most applicable to small, privately owned firms operating in a competitive setting.

In recent years the assumption that profit maximization governs the behavior of business firms has been challenged. Many sectors of the American economy are not characterized by perfect competition. Concentration is high. Firms do not perceive prices as a given. Managers of one firm realize that their decisions partially determine the actions of others. With the diversification of stockholding, owners are no longer managers. Two further approaches, satisficing and behavioral, that take account of these factors have been developed.

The satisficing model focusses on the problem of information. Firms rarely have perfect knowledge of the market. Classical assumptions place unreasonable demands on the choosing organism: payoffs must be associated with each outcome; unexpected results are not considered; outcomes must be ordered and probabilities determined. There is no evidence that these criteria are met in actual situations of any complexity. A more accurate picture emerges if it is assumed that the organism searches for some satisfactory level of payoff and will settle for any outcome that equals or exceeds this level. Business firms, like other complex decision-making organisms, can then be viewed as satisficers rather than maximizers. They attempt to secure one of many satisfactory outcomes based upon past experience and levels of expectation.[36]

Satisficing behavior is characteristic of large business firms. Information costs increase as the complexity of the organization increases. The complexity of the organization is, in part, a function of its size and diversity. A large firm with many divisions producing, marketing, and distributing different products may find it difficult to arrive at any decision concerning particular government policies.[37] Many corporations are both importers and exporters. Many have extensive foreign investments and at the same time produce import-competing goods domestically. In attempting to

[36] Simon, *Models of Man*, pp. 245-50.

[37] See Schelling, "Command and Control," for a discussion of decentralization in the firm, and Chandler, *Strategy and Structure*, for the general evolution of corporate organizational structure.

adapt themselves to the norms that exist in different countries, central corporate managers may be loath to specify general policy. During the debate over American tariff policies in the late 1950s, for instance, Du Pont and General Electric left their individual division managers to lobby as they saw fit.[38] In the mid-1960s Nestle's corporate headquarters in Switzerland supported an international cocoa agreement, while its American subsidiary, following the rest of the American industry, opposed it.

Another approach, the behavioral theory of the firm, focusses on the internal needs of the organization rather than on external economic objectives. It analyzes enterprises as coalitions that include managers, workers, suppliers, customers, and stockholders. Organizational survival requires that the firm have enough resources to meet the demands of members of its coalition. In an oligopolistic corporation little attention may be paid to considerations of cost as long as a decision does not affect existing arrangements with regard to the general level of profits, dividends, wages, and output—that is, as long as a decision does not dramatically affect the resources that are used to satisfy the demands of members of the coalition.[39]

Oligopolistic corporate managers have considerable discretion. They make decisions when the actual survival of the organization is not at stake. They coordinate the activity of other coalition members. Managers are likely to avoid risky behavior. If they perform badly, they may find themselves subject to a stockholders' revolt, dismissal by their board of directors, or takeover efforts by outside interests. If they perform well, the owners are not likely to provide them with equivalent rewards. Managers are faced with an asymmetry that induces them to avoid risky endeavors whose failure could threaten their position.[40] They aim at acceptable rather than optimal levels of profits, sales, and growth for their firms.

One kind of risky behavior that corporate managers are not likely to engage in is public conflict with the government. Busi-

[38] Bauer, Pool, and Dexter, *American Business and Public Policy*, p. 125.

[39] Cyert and March, *A Behavioral Theory of the Firm*, p. 53.

[40] Williamson, *The Economics of Discretionary Behavior*, and Monson and Downs, "A Theory of Large Managerial Firms," p. 349.

ness leaders are prone to keep a low profile. Direct confrontations with the state may focus attention on the firm that can lead to economic problems or increased government interference.[41] The enormous power possessed by private companies in America has never been fully legitimized by the dominant value system. There has been persistent strain between the economic aims of the company and general social goals.[42] Public exposure always presents the risk of catalyzing widespread public antipathy that political leaders can mobilize against the autonomy or profitability of the firm. The behavioral theory of the firm suggests that corporate managers are not likely to place themselves lightly in such an unpredictable and potentially threatening situation.

The behavioral theory also suggests that managers are motivated by nonpecuniary as well as pecuniary considerations. Robert A. Gordon has argued: "The most important spurs to action by the businessman, other than the desire for goods for the purpose of direct want satisfaction, are probably the following: the urge for power, the desire for prestige and the related impulse of emulation, the creative urge, the propensity to identify oneself with a group and the related feeling of group loyalty, the desire for security, the urge for adventure and for 'playing the game' for its own sake, and the desire to serve others."[43]

Chester I. Barnard, in his classic study *The Functions of the Executive*, maintains that nonmaterial rewards are the real cement holding organizations together. Prestige, personal power, and the attainment of dominating position are, he argues, much more important than material rewards, even in the development of commercial organizations.[44]

The behavioral theory implies that the government can expect neutrality if its policies do not threaten the level of resources necessary to satisfy all members of the coalition composing the firm. Even if official policies have a negative effect on economic performance, risk-avoiding managers may steer away from confrontations that could raise the saliency of an issue for stockholders, workers, or customers. Furthermore, large diversified firms

[41] Dahl, *Who Governs?* p. 78. [42] McKie, "Changing Views."
[43] *Business Leadership in the Large Corporation*, p. 305.
[44] *Functions*, p. 145.

have a great deal of flexibility. They can move from one product line to another. They can adjust their production methods. For such actors consistency of government policy may be more important than its actual substance.[45]

Nonpecuniary objectives open possibilities for the exercise of political leadership: political leaders can manipulate the preferences of private managers. Although the behavioral theory has dealt primarily with intrafirm transactions, there is no reason why managers cannot get some rewards from outside the firm. To secure nonpecuniary benefits managers may support official policies that are harmful to economic performance so long as resources are adequate to maintain the firm's internal coalition. If public leaders can cast their policy aims in terms of attitudes that are widely held within the society, uncooperative corporate executives will experience some cognitive dissonance. As managers come to regard themselves more as trustees of resources meant to serve the whole society, and less as profit maximizers concerned solely with the balance sheet of the firm, the probability of such psychological discomfort increases.[46] Provided that the policy advocated by public decision-makers does not threaten the corporation's ability to satisfy its immediate coalition members, managers can eliminate dissonance by accepting public initiatives.

A similar conclusion can be reached by viewing managers as citizens rather than private economic actors. David Truman, in a somewhat strained application of group theory, makes shared social values the central "balance wheel" of the American polity.[47] "How does a stable policy exist in a multiplicity of interest groups?" he asks, and answers that "in essence, however, it is that the fact that membership in organized and potential groups overlap *in the long run* imposes restraints and conformities upon interest groups on pain of dissolution or of failure."[48] The most important "potential interest group" is manifest in the "behavior

[45] The chairman of Exxon reportedly said: "We're flexible. We can play the game any way you [the U.S. government] want—if somebody will tell us what the rules are." Quoted in Mikdashi, *The International Politics of Natural Resources*, p. 52.

[46] Preston, "Corporation and Society," pp. 434-35.

[47] *The Governmental Process*, p. 514.

[48] *Ibid.*, p. 168.

and the habitual interactions of men" that reflect widely accepted "ideals and traditions."[49] Hans Morgenthau, who writes from a different orientation, comes to a similar conclusion. "Consensus and consent of the governed," he argues, "indispensable for an effective foreign policy in a democracy, flow from the allegiance of a citizen to his nation—its nature, institutions and objectives"—rather than from particular social or economic interests.[50] The existence of such sentiments has recently received some empirical corroboration from a study of the attitudes of American business leaders that concludes that their ideological beliefs are a more important determinant of their general foreign policy outlook than the specific economic interests of their firms.[51]

The problem for the state is to transform these latent loyalties into an active political force, or at least to use them to neutralize potential opposition to state initiatives. This may be done through appeals to individuals or groups. In *War and the Private Investor* Eugene Staley writes:

> Some governments are able to appeal to another powerful non-profit motive which strongly influences more men, and, one may suspect, acts with special effectiveness on those who have already reached the pinnacle of success in finance and business. This is the striving for distinction that is fostered and satisfied by the granting of patents of nobility, order of merit, knighthood. Instances are probably rare where a capitalist has received such recognition as the immediate result of compliance with his government's wishes in the placement of funds abroad, just as direct bribes are relatively unimportant in the influence of investors on governments. Rather, like good jobs with oil companies and banks for former state officials, these distinctions are legitimate prizes, endowed with social approval, which dangle before the eyes of aspirants and supply an incentive to act generally in a seemly and becoming manner.[52]

[49] *Ibid.*, p. 51.

[50] "Comments," p. 99.

[51] Russett and Hanson, *Interest and Ideology*, pp. 126-27.

[52] *War*, pp. 289-90.

Obviously, the granting of patents of nobility has not been very salient in the United States. But there are functional equivalents including awards, ambassadorships, and White House dinners.

More important than appeals to specific individuals is the ability of state actors to define issues in ways that touch upon the general concerns of citizens. Foreign policy is distant from the specific experience of most individuals. Even corporate managers engaged in disputes over foreign investment may find it difficult to determine what course of action they should follow. The information they must analyze is political as well as economic. Their long-term economic objectives may not be well defined. Political leaders, on the other hand, may be able to define their own goals more clearly. They may be able to place a specific dispute over a foreign raw material investment in a broader political context. They may be able to feed corporate officials additional information, such as assessments of the political stability of a host-country government, that will lead managers to change their estimates of what action would be best for their firm. The exercise of effective leadership, then, involves changing the perceptions of private actors by defining problems and by appealing to the notion that managers are trustees of social resources, or to their loyalties as citizens, or to their private drives for status and prestige.[53]

In sum, satisficing and behavioral theories of the firm suggest that interests cannot simply be taken as a given. Political leaders may be able to change the goals of private managers. Such leadership will be most difficult when dealing with privately owned economic units operating in a competitive market. Owners of relatively small firms are more likely than the executives of large diversified ones to be able to perceive the impact of government

[53] The concept of leadership as it is used here can be understood in terms of what Parsons has called influence and the activation of commitments. The former refers to the ability of one actor to change the opinions of another, the latter to cashing in on existing norms. These processes are distinct from two other forms of power, physical coercion and bargaining, in which actors exchange resources. The bargaining situation is much more prevalent in France or Japan where the state can offer loans or other material incentives to private firms. On these general distinctions see Barry, "The Economic Approach to the Analysis of Power and Conflict," pp. 192-95.

policy. They lack the status and prominence that would give them access to national decision-making arenas. Although some individuals may be capable of acting altruistically even if their sacrifices go unrecognized, they are surely a tiny minority. Purposive kinds of motivations are usually accompanied by solidary ones. Selfless behavior can only rarely be sustained without group recognition.[54] Large corporate managers who accede to the entreaties of public officials are likely to be recognized; the owners of small firms who act in the same way are not.

The probabilities of convergence between the preferences of public and private officials are, then, higher when private units are larger and more complex and issues are identified as being vital to widely held national goals. This convergence is not simply a function of objectively defined economic interests; it is also determined by the general value structure of the society and the ability of political leaders to attach these values to specific policy initiatives. It is, in sum, a function of political leadership as well as material rewards. The presence of large complex corporations presents political opportunities for increasing the coincidence of public and private preferences. The political resources of large corporations may not be mobilized against the state if managerial perceptions are altered by political leaders.

POLICY-MAKING ARENAS

While natural convergence or effective leadership can result in many areas of agreement between public officials and corporate managers, their preferences are obviously not entirely coincident. Political leaders may attempt to implement policies that are opposed by businessmen, and conversely, private managers may press the state to behave in ways that are antithetical to the general aims of stability, security, or greater competition in raw materials markets. The outcome of such struggles depends, in part, on the decision-making arena in which they take place. Private firms have often been frustrated in their efforts to secure public support, particularly for foreign investments, because the White House and State Department, where most investment policy is made, are rel-

[54] Wilson, *Political Organizations*, Ch. 3.

atively impervious to private pressure. On the other hand, public officials have had great difficulty accomplishing their objectives when such decisions have been taken in Congress or in bureaus that have been penetrated by societal groups.[55]

The degree to which either governmental functions are captured by societal groups or public purposes are frustrated by private interests varies from one issue area to another. Neither the pluralist contention that all interests are automatically represented, nor the power-elite argument that narrow socio-economic groups always prevail, is borne out. There are many examples of laws, such as health, environmental, and antitrust regulations, that impose palpable burdens on powerful and specific economic sectors. On the other hand, there are many attitudes widely held in the society that are never manifest in public law. Rather than treating public policy-making in the United States as a single uniform process, it is necessary to divide it into several separate ones. Different issues are treated in different ways. The inherent fragmentation and decentralization of power in the American political system can be mitigated if decisions are taken by state institutions—the White House, the State Department, and a few other central bureaus—that are insulated from specific societal pressures.

The relevance of issue areas to the policy-making process has its recent origins in the work of E. E. Schattschneider. Even in his first book, which dealt with the 1930 Smoot–Hawley Tariff and focussed primarily on interest groups, Schattschneider suggested this line of argument.[56] In *The Semisovereign People*, published twenty-five years later, he contended that the outcome of every political conflict is determined by its scope—that is, the number of people involved in its resolution. The scope determines the setting in which it is decided. Different kinds of actors have different resources that are effective in some settings but not in others. So long as the scope of conflict remains narrow, it is likely to be settled in Congress and particular interest groups are likely to prevail. When the scope of a conflict broadens, however, it is likely to be

[55] For a discussion of the impact of decision arenas on U.S. trade and monetary policy see Krasner, "U.S. Commercial and Monetary Policy."

[56] Schattschneider, *Politics*, p. 288.

settled by party rather than committee politics. Special interest groups do not play a major role in party politics, because they cannot decisively contribute to winning elections.[57]

The concept of scope has been further refined by Theodore Lowi and James Q. Wilson. Lowi's typology of policies—distributive, regulative, redistributive—is based upon their incidence. Distributive policies involve resources that are perceived to be unlimited. Decisions can be disaggregated so that all interested parties can get some payoff. The likelihood of government coercion is remote, and the applicability of coercion when it does take place is individual rather than collective. Distributive policies are generally dealt with in legislative committees and even subcommittees. Particular interest groups are powerful. The prime example of distributive politics is tariff setting until 1934, when the passage of the Reciprocal Trade Agreements Act transferred the locus of power over commercial policy from Congress to the President.

Lowi's second major issue area is regulative. Here policy cannot be disaggregated. Large sectors of the public are affected in the same way, and a direct choice must be made as "to who will be indulged and deprived."[58] Peak associations rather than individual firms are involved in bringing pressure on the government. Decisions are made by the whole Congress rather than by individual committees. Examples include laws against unfair competition and for the elimination of substandard goods.

The third major kind of issue is redistributive. Here broad groups of the population, approaching social classes, are affected in the same way. Decisions on such issues are generally taken within the executive rather than the legislative branch. Examples include progressive taxation and social security.[59]

James Q. Wilson has offered an alternative classification of issue areas. He suggests that the basic parameters should be the concentration and diffusion of costs and benefits. Typically, a pol-

[57] Schattschneider, *Semisovereign People*, Ch. 1.

[58] Lowi, "American Business," pp. 690-91.

[59] *Ibid.*; Lowi, "Decision Making vs Policy Making"; and Lowi, "Four Systems." Lowi also delineates a fourth category, "constituent politics," which is not relevant for this study.

icy that involves concentrated benefits and diffuse costs will lead the potential beneficiaries to organize; particular societal groups are likely to develop symbiotic relations with those government agencies that make decisions directly affecting them. Adversely affected groups are unlikely to be effective because the free-rider problem makes it difficult for them to organize. A similar situation develops when benefits are diffuse, but costs concentrated. Here specific groups are likely to organize to oppose government initiatives. Public actors can overcome this resistance, but only by effectively exercising political leadership in the form of mobilizing broadly held sentiments within the general population. Leadership is also necessary in a situation when benefits are diffuse, even if costs are also diffuse. There may be little organized resistance, but political figures must generate their own support. When both costs and benefits are concentrated, there is likely to be a high level of group conflict with shifting coalitions involving public and private actors.[60]

How can these schemata be applied to questions of international raw materials policy? At a first cut this issue area can be classified as narrow in Schattschneider's terminology, as distributive in Lowi's, and as involving either concentrated costs and diffuse benefits or concentrated benefits and diffuse costs in Wilson's typology. For instance, increasing the price of a particular raw material through the imposition of a tariff or the toleration of oligopolistic practices provides large benefits to particular firms, but diffuses cost throughout the society. Failing to protect a foreign concession may have substantial costs for a specific firm, but a very modest impact on the general economy. Under such conditions, all three formulations suggest that the government will confront well-organized and powerful political interest groups. Decisions are likely to be taken in arenas that maximize the power of these groups, most notably Congressional committees or executive departments like Agriculture and Interior that are responsive to a narrow range of societal groups.

Questions involving the pricing and ownership of raw materials are not, however, invariably decided in such narrow arenas. A

[60] Wilson, *Political Organizations*, Ch. 16.

second cut at classification is necessary because international politics presents options that are not available for purely domestic issues and because political leaders can themselves redefine a dispute and change both its scope and the arena in which it is decided. Although it has become very fashionable to claim that there is little difference between domestic and international politics, the fact remains that there is no domestic equivalent to war, and there are few analogs to the kinds of solidary appeals that political leaders can make when the state acts in the international system. Politics never really ends, but the claim that it should can only be staked out at the water's edge.

Decisions about the use of military force are taken in arenas, most notably the White House and State Department, that are heavily insulated from particular domestic pressure groups. Central decision-makers are not immune to the entreaties or even, as we have too clearly seen in recent years, the purses of major corporations, but they are subject to such pressures to much less a degree than, say, a Congressman from Texas voting on oil quotas. The points of access for interest groups "can be hundreds of times greater" for a decision involving tariffs than for one about diplomatic or military action.[61] Most of the resources that Presidents need to govern, and to be reelected, cannot be provided by private companies or particular economic sectors.

Of all the executive departments State is least subject to pressure-group tactics. State is charged with defending general interests rather than those of particular domestic groups such as labor (Labor Department), business (Commerce Department), or agriculture (Agriculture Department). It does not make the large expenditures that have so intertwined the Defense Department with particular industries and geographic areas. While this constrains its ability to mobilize societal support, it also limits the pressures that can be placed upon it. When a question involving international raw materials policy can lead to the use of force or diplomatic confrontation, private corporations are not likely to be able to compel the State Department to defend their interests at the expense of broader national goals.

[61] Milbrath, "Interest Groups and Foreign Policy," p. 236.

A second cut at classifying international raw materials policy is also necessary because the way in which an issue is decided may depend upon the way in which it is defined. The pre-1934 tariff is everyone's favorite example of a policy that was settled through log-rolling pressure-group politics. But in 1934 the way in which tariffs were set began to change. At least until the Trade Act of 1974, increasing power was given to the President. The influence of particular groups declined. Log-rolling became more difficult. The natural proclivity to protectionism was overcome.

The change in law was itself a reflection of the way in which tariffs were viewed. At least for political leaders, such as Secretary of State Hull, the Reciprocal Trade Agreements Act was the product of a vision: the world would be made more prosperous and peaceful through free trade. The Great Depression had given this idea new force. Tariffs were no longer seen simply as a device to provide material benefits for particular sectors of the American economy, but rather as a matter that affected the whole nature of the international system. This change in vision led to a change in policy-making processes, and this change in policy-making processes changed the relative influence of political groups. Political leaders thus can redefine issues and, by doing so, alter both the process and substance of policy.

In international raw materials policy the opportunity to redefine issues has been important. The general goals associated with the pricing and ownership of raw materials suggest that these matters involve something other than the economic well-being of particular firms. The nation's ability to make war, the general health of its economy, the stability of its political system, its influence over other states can all be affected by the international availability of unprocessed goods.

This relationship opens possibilities for political leaders. By playing upon these broader themes, they can increase competitiveness and visibility, the two primary means by which the scope of conflict is increased.[62] By increasing the scope of conflict they can change the arena in which the issue is decided. Madison was

[62] Schattschneider, *Semisovereign People*, p. 16, and Wilson, *Political Organizations*, p. 355.

wrong to suppose in *Federalist No. 10* that the extent of the republic would be an adequate defense against the tyranny of factions. Such tyranny can only be avoided if political leaders are adroit enough to generate effective political pressures that would otherwise remain latent and, in doing so, thrust an issue out of arenas dominated by private corporations and into ones where other groups, both public and private, exercise greater power.

A third reason why raw materials policies cannot always be viewed as determined by pressure-group politics is that there are often conflicts within the private sector. Small domestic firms do not always share the same objectives as large international producers. Companies that still have hopes of keeping direct investments in a particular country may not support the same policies as those that have been nationalized. Financial institutions that have portfolio investments are more likely to advocate conciliation in the hope of preventing debt repudiation by a foreign state than are direct investors who have already lost their property. Such private disagreements open space for public initiatives. Governmental officials can mobilize support for a course of action even when there is strong opposition from some private actors.

Hence, if there is conflict between the aims of public actors and corporate managers, the former can at times prevail by exercising effective leadership. Such leadership involves appealing to the nonpecuniary motives of the managers of large oligopolistic firms, changing the way in which issues are viewed, and taking advantage of splits among private groups. Because a democratic state must admit the legitimacy of intermediate economic bodies, its leaders must act shrewdly to secure public purposes. The fragmentation of power in the American polity is an endemic disease, but not one that is necessarily fatal to the public interest.

In sum, the United States has a weak political system. The state—that is, central decision-making institutions, most notably the White House and the State Department—cannot directly alter the structure of their domestic society: they cannot establish new kinds of economic units such as state-owned firms or adopt policies that directly benefit some industries or firms at the expense of others, although obviously many macro-economic policies will indirectly have such an impact.[63] Furthermore, central decision-makers may find it difficult to overcome the resistance of specific societal interest groups, because political power in the United States is fragmented and decentralized. There are many points of access to the political system, especially in the Congress and some executive bureaus. Once an issue falls into these decision-making arenas, state preferences can be blocked. The American polity resembles a black ball system. Any major actor, public or private, can often prevent the adoption of a policy. However, as Table III-1 suggests, even in a weak political system the state is not merely an epiphenomenon: central decision-makers can still resist pressures from private groups; they can still formulate preferences related to general societal goals.

The weakness of the American state in relation to its own society does not mean that efforts to implement the national interest (the preferences of central decision-makers that are related to enduring general goals) will always be frustrated. Often public and private policy aims converge. Moreover, central decision-makers may exercise leadership by altering the preferences of private actors. Satisficing and behavioral theories of the firm suggest that this is most likely when the state is dealing with large oligopolistic companies. The managers of such units have considerable flexibility to adjust the activities of their firm or to satisfy their individual desires for status and prestige. The ability of public leaders to accomplish their goals also depends on the decision-making arena in which an issue is decided. If policy questions are settled in the Congress or executive agencies open to societal pressures, then private actors are likely to be able to block state initiatives. But if they are decided in the White House, the State Department, and other central agencies, it is much more difficult for the private sector to act effectively. The arena in which an issue is decided is partly a function of its inherent nature and partly a function of the way in which it is defined. Rulers can also exercise leadership by changing the way in which societal groups perceive a particular problem, thereby changing the arena in which it is decided and the

[63] For instance, an expansionary monetary policy will benefit debtors and hurt creditors; an open trade policy will benefit export-oriented industries and hurt import-competing ones.

final policy outcome. In sum, American politics most frequently follows a "weak" pattern in which the state can resist pressure from societal groups but is unable to overcome societal resistance; but through effective leadership political processes can be amended so that the power of the state follows a "moderate" pattern in which central decision-makers can not only resist societal pressures but also change the behavior of societal groups.

PART TWO

CHAPTER IV

The Promotion of Investments

The foreign expansion of American raw materials investment has been relatively free of conflict. In most instances the American government played little if any direct role in establishing the ownership and control of American corporations. Although U.S. officials worked assiduously, particularly in the period after World War II, to create a favorable worldwide climate for direct investment, in specific cases the resources possessed by private capital were usually sufficient to secure territorial access without explicit public support. Foreign capitalists controlled managerial and technical skills beyond the reach of the host-country government. They could raise the capital necessary to develop extensive mineral and agricultural ventures. They also, at times, helped procure loans for host-country governments or extended funds themselves. For poor countries even modest returns from new concession agreements were a bonanza. Their meager resource base and low level of administrative development made it very difficult for their governments to extract substantial sums from the local population. Most government receipts came from trade taxes.[1] Foreign corporations were more reliable taxpayers than native citizens. For backward countries the choice was almost always between leaving their resources undiscovered or unexploited and utilizing foreign capital. Thus, they generally welcomed new foreign investment.[2]

Although U.S. central decision-makers rarely have had to intervene to secure geographical access for specific ventures, nevertheless the ability of corporations to establish foreign subsidiaries has not gone unaffected by political power. Indeed, they have been critically dependent on political actors to create a gen-

[1] Hinrichs, *General Theory of Tax Structure Change*.

[2] Vernon, *Sovereignty at Bay*, Ch. 2. A more detailed description of the overseas expansion of raw materials investments is given in the Appendix.

eral environment in which they could operate effectively. Before the First World War Britain played the most important role in defining and upholding norms that facilitated the international movement of capital, although the British were far more heavily involved in portfolio than direct investment. The United States began to play such a role in the Caribbean around 1900 and in Latin America after the First World War.[3] After 1945 American central decision-makers began to project American power to all areas outside the Communist Bloc. From the late 1940s into the early 1960s not only was the United States the world's largest military and economic power, but it was also widely regarded as the most progressive. American policy-makers moved decisively to create an international economic order in which goods and capital could move freely across international borders.[4] They also adopted general policies that facilitated foreign investment. At the very least the tax structure did not discriminate against overseas activity, and in some ways it actively encouraged it. Beginning with the Economic Cooperation Act of 1948, the United States developed a number of investment guarantee programs that insured U.S. companies against some of the risks of foreign investment, such as currency inconvertibility and nationalization. On rare occasions the U.S. government even gave direct financial assistance to American companies to establish foreign mining and processing facilities. Host-country governments welcomed new capital not only because of its economic attractiveness but also because they were loath to challenge the power and policies of the United States.[5]

The persistence of official efforts to create an environment that facilitated foreign investment does not shed much light on the analytic concerns of this study. Such a policy is consistent with

[3] For Latin America see Tulchin, *Aftermath of War*.

[4] Aron, *Imperial Republic*; Gilpin, *U.S. Power and the Multinational Corporation*; Calleo and Rowland, *America and the World Political Economy*; Schurmann, *Logic of World Power*; Krasner, "State Power and the Structure of International Trade."

[5] Girvan, *Foreign Capital and Economic Underdevelopment in Jamaica*, pp. 21-22; U.S. House, Committee on Foreign Affairs, *Expropriation of American-Owned Property*.

Marxist analysis: support for foreign investment furthered the interests of powerful capitalist institutions. From a liberal perspective, this policy could be interpreted as a response to pressures from an important societal group. From a statist orientation, support for overseas direct investment, particularly in raw materials, could be understood to promote security of supply and, occasionally, to enhance overall U.S. influence in a particular country. Thus, the fact that U.S. policy-makers usually ignored specific investments, but worked assiduously to create a comfortable climate for private firms, is consistent with all three theoretical paradigms discussed in this book.

Most instances of new investment also offer little opportunity to further the second goal of this study—elaborating a statist approach. For a variety of economic reasons corporations were attracted to foreign operations.[6] Usually, the policies of private and public decision-makers were complementary. Furthermore, the ability of U.S. firms to negotiate their own terms of access to new areas conformed with the usual pattern of business–state relations in the United States. Both central state institutions (such as the State Department) and large corporations were leery of intimate involvements. Corporate managers distrusted the state. Policy-makers were afraid that their independence would be compromised. With the state and private corporations both pursuing the same goal, it is impossible to make judgments about power within the domestic political system.

Analytically, the most interesting cases are those that diverge from the modal pattern of general public support for private investment but only modest involvement in specific ventures. In the global spread of foreign raw materials investments, three cases stand out because of the duration and intensity of official backing: the entry of American oil companies into the Dutch East Indies and, more important, the Middle East during the 1920s; the establishment of a large rubber plantation in Liberia by Firestone during the late 1920s; and the creation of the Iranian oil consortium in 1954, which brought American companies into that country for

[6] See Vernon, *Sovereignty at Bay*, Chs. 2 and 3, for some explanations for corporate expansion.

the first time. There are also a few cases of divergence between private and public actors, either because corporations were unable to make investments owing to a lack of official support or because public officials wanted to interest private firms in a new venture that the companies did not find attractive.

These cases of extensive support or of divergence between public and private actors suggest that state action cannot be understood as an extension of private preferences. Extensive support occurred only when central decision-makers felt that state interests were at stake. American officials were not willing to sanction specific new investments unless they thought such action would increase security of supply or further more general foreign policy objectives. Promoting more competition was a peripheral concern. In the absence of such considerations support has been half-hearted or nonexistent. When corporate expansion conflicted with broader public aims, the state opposed private companies.

Cases of divergence between public and private actors also illustrate the general pattern of power relationships between the state and corporations in America. Decisions about the promotion of new foreign raw materials ventures were taken primarily in the White House and the State Department, the two institutions most insulated from societal pressure. On those unusual occasions when private actors sought extensive public assistance to support a specific new project, they were unable to get it unless state actors felt that the project would contribute to security of supply or general foreign policy aims. On the other hand, when state actors pressed private firms to invest in a new area because they believed this would promote the national interest, they were sometimes unsuccessful or at least had to compromise other goals.

Where raw materials investments are concerned, the state and private firms can be envisioned walking in the same direction and holding the ends of a long rope that is usually slack. Neither party can influence the other very effectively by pulling on its end of the rope. State actors will be susceptible to private pressures or will themselves try to influence corporations only when state goals, in particular promoting security of supply and furthering general foreign policy aims, are at stake.

THREE CASES OF EXTENSIVE STATE INTERVENTION

In general, U.S. central decision-makers tried to avoid becoming involved in specific disputes arising out of corporate efforts to establish new foreign raw materials ventures. They were prepared to give diplomatic support, but this was often quite perfunctory. There were, however, three projects to which U.S. leaders contributed extensively over several years: rubber in Liberia, and oil in the Middle East and the Dutch East Indies, during the 1920s, and oil in Iran in the early 1950s. Each of these cases attracted the attention of leading state actors, including the President. They are the only instances that I have been able to discover in which U.S. officials actually sanctioned the specific arrangements that brought American firms into a new area. Even in other cases of extensive state support, state actors were usually content to let private corporations work out the detailed terms of their concessions once official action had created conditions that made the investment feasible. Thus, the stakes involved in these three ventures should give some indication of the ordering of preferences of American leaders. In both oil and rubber during the 1920s there was intense fear among American central decision-makers of serious supply shortages that could undermine the functioning of the American economy. The oil dispute in Iran touched upon the major fixation of American leaders in the period after the Second World War—the spread of communism. It was also the case that engendered the most extensive involvement of the President and his closest advisors, leading not only to economic and diplomatic pressure but also to the covert use of force.

For ordering the preferences of American leaders, these three instances of extensive state intervention suggest that general foreign policy aims and security of supply were more important goals than increasing competition. Although there was no conflict among state goals in the case of rubber, oil in the 1920s and in Iran did involve a tradeoff between security and greater competition. The Iranian case, the only one in which force was used, also points to the primacy of political objectives over economic ones: only when such goals were at stake have U.S. leaders gone beyond diplomatic and economic forms of pressure. Furthermore, the promotion both of rubber investments in Liberia and of oil in Iran indicates the difficulty that state actors may have in modifying the behavior of private corporations. Because of the weakness of the American political system, U.S. leaders were compelled to bargain with these domestic actors to achieve their international objectives; they did not have instruments of control that would have allowed them to force a change in private behavior.

Rubber in Liberia

In the late 1920s high American officials strongly supported the establishment of a large natural rubber plantation in Liberia by the Firestone Rubber Company. This investment furthered state goals. Liberian rubber was perceived as contributing to security and stability by developing a source of supply that was both owned by an American corporation and located in a country where American influence was substantial. It was also perceived as enhancing the potential for competitive behavior by increasing production outside the control of the British, who were engaged in restrictive arrangements to raise rubber prices. Despite the high priority that public officials placed on new rubber investments, the Liberian venture was launched only after considerable effort. Its economic riskiness, as well as the attitude of Liberian officials, made it necessary for the American government to play an active role in the negotiations between Firestone and Liberia. Furthermore, only two U.S. companies, Firestone and Ford, responded positively to government appeals for more rubber investments. The executives of both companies had economic and personal reasons for wanting to secure their own sources of raw materials. Only by taking advantage of divisions within the rubber industry (relating to Firestone's competitive position and the ethos of its president) were central decision-makers able to further state interests.

BACKGROUND

In the early 1920s the United States was the world's largest consumer of crude rubber: in 1922 it accounted for 74 percent of global imports and 75 percent of absorption. Some 20 percent of consumption was provided by reclamation. There were no substantial sources of synthetic rubber; the United States was virtually totally dependent on foreign production. About 67 percent of global exports in 1922 came from territory under British control, with Malaya alone accounting for more than half of all supplies.[7] The Dutch East Indies contributed 25 percent. None of the major producing areas were under direct American jurisdiction or within the sphere of influence exercised by the United States in the western hemisphere. For no other industrial commodity was the United States so completely dependent on areas outside of its political control.

The threat to security of supply inherent in this situation became manifest in 1922 with the imposition of rubber export controls in British territories. Confronted with falling prices at the end of the First World War, rubber planters had tried at first to establish a private arrangement for limiting exports. It failed because there were many planters and no mechanism for enforcement. The British government then stepped in and, acting on the basis of a report prepared by a committee chaired by Sir James Stevenson (who was personal financial advisor to Churchill and had investments in the rubber industry), adopted a system of compulsory production and export controls. Britain not only was concerned about the financial situation of her colonies, but also feared that American corporations would take over bankrupt plantations. Export restrictions, coupled with rising demand generated by the automobile industry in the United States, led to a rise in rubber prices from 20¢ per pound in 1922 to $1.24 per pound in 1925. Only at this point did the British act to increase production substantially. After 1925 prices fell, and by 1928 they had almost returned to their 1922 levels primarily because of increasing output in the Dutch East Indies, whose share of exports rose from 25 percent in 1922 to 35 percent in 1933. The Dutch had refused to participate in Britain's efforts at market control. Smuggling and greater use of reclaimed rubber also undermined British efforts.[8]

[7] Knorr, *World Rubber and Its Regulation*, pp. 248-49.

[8] *Ibid.*, pp. 93-101, 248; Brandes, *Herbert Hoover and Economic Diplomacy*, p. 85; Whittlesey, *Stevenson Plan*, p. 43.

PUBLIC REACTION

The initiation of the Stevenson Rubber Plan alarmed a number of American officials, in particular Herbert Hoover, who was then Secretary of Commerce. Hoover's policy prescriptions closely resembled those of the classical mercantilists. He opposed foreign direct investment in manufacturing on the grounds that it deprived American workers of jobs and limited export markets. He pressed for state regulation of foreign loans. He argued for high tariffs to promote self-sufficiency for important raw materials. He wanted an open market for American exports. He led the American drive against a number of foreign raw materials cartels that were established during the 1920s, claiming that they cost American consumers hundreds of millions of dollars and threatened American security.[9]

Interest was not limited to Hoover. Secretary of Agriculture Henry Wallace supported government efforts to develop new rubber supplies because of the danger that "war might interfere with shipments."[10] At least tangentially the White House was involved, and President Coolidge in 1926 publicly endorsed Firestone's plan to establish plantations outside of British control.[11] The Department of State carried on some desultory conversations with Britain, but was more active in arranging for Firestone's entrance into Liberia. Concern in Congress was high enough to get a $500,000 appropriation for a worldwide survey in 1923 to uncover new areas where rubber might be grown. Lengthy hearings on international cartels took place before the Interstate and Foreign Commerce Committee in 1926. Thus, foreign efforts to control markets, particularly the Stevenson Plan, prompted widespread, albeit with the exception of Hoover not very intense, interest within the American government.

A number of measures including reclamation, control of loans, and conservation were instituted to combat foreign cartels. Here our attention will be devoted to the state's efforts to promote foreign investment. This did not prove an easy task, despite the vigorous activity of the Commerce Department in particular. Agents of the Rubber Division of the Bureau of Foreign and

[9] Brandes, *passim*.

[10] Quoted in Lief, *Harvey Firestone*, p. 232.

[11] *Ibid*., p. 246.

Domestic Commerce had numerous discussions with rubber company executives. In October 1923 a special agent of the division spoke with about twenty manufacturers in Akron and reported that "some expressed their willingness to contribute their share toward the establishment of rubber plantations preferably in Tropical America, provided the findings of the final report [of the government-sponsored rubber survey] would justify such investments."[12] Bureau representatives suggested to the United Fruit Company that abandoned banana plantations might be converted to rubber production. Hoover himself travelled to Cleveland and New York in May 1924 to urge rubber companies to invest in non-British-controlled areas.[13]

PRIVATE RESPONSES

All of this activity, however, had relatively little effect. What was in the interest of the state was not necessarily in the interest of private industry, particularly those corporations that already owned rubber plantations in British areas. Higher prices contributed to their profits. Restrictions on output gave them a competitive advantage because they had preferred access to their own production. The only companies that acted vigorously to establish new production were the Firestone Rubber Company and the Ford Motor Company. The former proved more important; Ford's efforts in Brazil never produced significant quantities of crude rubber.

Firestone's action was not just the result of government prodding. Harvey Firestone, the president and founder of the company, opposed the Stevenson Plan immediately after it was initiated. The day after it became public he told some of his associates that no "government has the moral right to make a law restricting the output of a produce of the soil so universally used as rubber," and went on to call the restrictions a "vicious plan which will result in making Americans pay exorbitant prices."[14] Firestone from the outset advocated a government-sponsored survey, an

[12] Memorandum on Status of Work Planned Under the Raw Materials Survey, Oct. 22, 1923, Records of the Department of Commerce, Bureau of Foreign and Domestic Commerce, File 621.2, U.S. National Archives.

[13] *Ibid.*

[14] Quoted in Lief, pp. 288-89.

American buying pool, and the establishment of new plantations. Even before the final report of the government-sponsored raw materials survey, Firestone had dispatched his own team of experts to Latin America and Asia. His employees examined areas that the Commerce Department had ignored, including Liberia. Firestone eventually secured leases in Mexico and Panama as well as Liberia, although the South American options were never developed.[15]

Firestone's attitude was in marked contrast with that of the rest of the rubber industry. Whereas the company's 1923 annual report began with a vigorous attack on the Stevenson Plan, it was not even mentioned in the reports of any of the other large American companies.[16] In 1923 the industry trade association, the Rubber Association of America, entered into negotiations with the British Rubber Growers Association. The U.S. companies expressed formal opposition to the Stevenson Plan, but they accepted informal assurances that the scheme would be flexibly administered. The consuming companies were more concerned about price fluctuations that could bring large inventory losses than with absolute price levels. Harvey Firestone was so incensed by these dalliances that he quit the Rubber Association. It was not until 1925, when the British refused to check a precipitous price rise by releasing stocks, that the rest of the industry began to voice concern.[17]

There are several explanations for why Firestone's attitude was so at variance with those of his compatriots. His was the fourth largest of the leading American rubber companies. The industry structure is illustrated by the following table. Firestone might have felt he could improve his competitive position by developing a source of natural rubber in an area where American influence was high. Goodyear already had a plantation in Sumatra, and United States Rubber was tapping its own trees in Sumatra and Malaya. United States Rubber's operation in Sumatra was, in

[15] *Ibid.*, p. 230; Memorandum on Status of Work Planned Under the Raw Materials Survey, Dec. 11, 1923, Records of the Department of Commerce, Bureau of Foreign and Domestic Commerce, File 621.1, U.S. National Archives.

[16] *Annual Reports* for Firestone, Goodyear, U.S. Rubber, and B. F. Goodrich.

[17] Whittlesey, pp. 135-38.

TABLE IV-1

The U.S. Rubber Industry in 1923

Firm	*1923* *Gross Sales (in millions of dollars)*	*Profits (in millions of dollars)*
U.S. Rubber	186.2	12.2
Goodyear	127.9	6.5
Goodrich	107.1	7.1
Firestone	77.6	6.1
General Tire	n.a.	1.6

Sources: *Annual Reports* and *Poor's and Moody's Industrials*, 1924.

1920, one of the largest in the world, supplying about 25 percent of the company's needs.[18]

Personal factors also contributed to Firestone's behavior. Harvey Firestone was the only founding father still running a large rubber company and as such was more likely to pursue profit maximizing than satisficing behavior. Within the company, investment in Liberia was regarded as being so risky that Firestone was forced to buy out one of his close associates who opposed the operation. Firestone might also have been particularly sensitive to British restrictions because he had encountered such practices while serving as president of the Rubber Association during the First World War. Even at that time he had advocated rubber development in the Philippines. The significance of Firestone's personal experience in explaining his differences with other industry leaders is further reinforced by the fact that Henry Ford, the only other American entrepreneur to take up Hoover's call for new rubber investment, was a close personal friend. Ford, Firestone, and Thomas Edison went on long, highly publicized camping trips during the 1920s. The three men formed a private company to seek new rubber-producing plants, and Edison had developed a strain of goldenrod with a seven percent rubber content by the time of his death.[19] (Hay-fever sufferers must be glad that this development never came to fruition.)

[18] Goodyear Tire Co., *Annual Report*, 1923; U.S. Rubber, *Annual Report*, 1923; Lief, p. 235.

[19] Lief, p. 229.

The Firestone decision to go into Liberia reflected the weakness of the American state as much as its power. Despite the concern of at least one very prominent public official, the American industry was not responsive. Only because of divisions among firms was it possible to move toward establishing new sources of supply under American control. Most rubber companies were not very concerned about the impact of the Stevenson Plan, and the risks of starting new plantations in unfamiliar areas were great. The possibility of creating a government-owned enterprise was never considered, despite the lukewarm private response. When the government tried to get new rubber investment, it almost found itself pushing on a string. The Liberian venture came to fruition only because some private and public aims converged.

STATE SUPPORT

Still, the role of the state was decisive: without public support Firestone's Liberian plantation would probably never have been developed. The initial suggestion that Firestone examine possibilities in Liberia might have come from the American consul in Monrovia. The company wanted government support. The political and economic stiuation in Liberia was strained and uncertain. If the enterprise collapsed before the new rubber trees had reached maturity after five years, the entire investment would be lost.[20]

The Liberians were anxious to get foreign capital. Their financial situation was precarious. Nevertheless, they were extremely cautious about becoming entangled with large foreign enterprises, and Firestone was not so anxious that it would accept any terms that were given. Liberia's initial offer was rejected by the company in June 1924, and Liberia found Firestone's subsequent revisions unacceptable. The final arrangement was not concluded until October 1926 after several other sets of terms had been turned down by Firestone, the Liberian executive, or the Liberian legislature.[21]

The United States government used diplomatic and economic

[20] Letter from S. P. Hood to Harvey Firestone, Nov. 11, 1923, Bureau of Foreign and Domestic Commerce, File 254, U.S. National Archives; U.S. Dept. of State, *Foreign Relations of the United States*, 1925, Vol. 2, pp. 369ff.

[21] *Foreign Relations*, 1927, Vol. 3, pp. 148-49.

resources to bring the project to a successful conclusion. Many of the actual negotiations involving the concession and loan agreement were carried out by the American consul in Monrovia. The United States also engaged in one minor diplomatic foray on Liberia's behalf. While the Firestone concession was being negotiated, Liberia sought the good offices of the United States in settling a boundary dispute with France that had festered since 1885. Liberia had lost territory in 1892 and 1908, and feared further encroachments. Her leaders hoped that an indication of American displeasure would put an end to French expansion. The United States responded by urging the early completion of a boundary demarcation survey that had been provided for in earlier negotiations, and the issue was satisfactorily resolved.[22]

Far more important, however, was the prime instrument of policy during this episode—foreign loans. The Liberians were in desperate economic straits. After the war they had been unable to float a $25,000 issue. The State Department pointed out that it would be impossible for Liberia to get new financing unless the Firestone deal went through. Liberia could not, without new export receipts, generate revenue to amortize substantial foreign obligations. As a condition for letting the concession, the Liberians asked for a five million dollar loan. They were anxious to have the American government involved because they felt it would be safer than working directly with Firestone.[23]

Although the loan was finally made through a subsidiary Firestone organized for that purpose, The Finance Corporation of America, the American government played an active role. The consul in Monrovia helped negotiate the loan. It was approved by the State Department. Under the terms of the Loan Agreement signed in 1926, the President of the United States designated a financial advisor to be appointed by the President of Liberia. The United States also agreed to recommend two officers for the Liberia Frontier Force and to appoint an arbiter to settle disputes that could not be resolved directly by Firestone and Liberia. The first two provisions extended practices already in effect.[24] Given the laborious negotiations involved in establishing Firestone's

[22] *Ibid.*, 1925, Vol. 2, pp. 495-99; 1926, Vol. 2, p. 536.

[23] *Ibid.*, 1925, Vol. 2, p. 432.

[24] *Ibid.*, 1927, Vol. 3, p. 151.

rubber plantations, the risks of the venture, Liberia's reluctance, and dissension within the company, it is not likely that the enterprise would have been brought to fruition without the active support of the State and Commerce Departments.

CONCLUSION

The lessons of the rubber investment in Liberia are subtle but important. Here was a situation in which all major public economic aims were furthered. Firestone's investment meant weakening the potential for cartelization as well as enhancing security of supply. Rubber was an important industrial product. The Stevenson Plan had attracted wide attention in the United States. A powerful government official, Herbert Hoover, spearheaded state efforts. Despite all of these advantages, the state made only modest progress toward its objectives. Only two American companies responded to public appeals. Only one, Firestone, went ahead with extensive development plans, and the results even then were not impressive: Liberia accounted for less than five percent of world rubber output when the Second World War began. The American government did not have the power to compel other corporations to diversify their crude rubber holdings. Firestone entered Liberia only because public and private aims converged. The company could not act without the state, nor could the state without the company.

Oil in the Middle East and the Dutch East Indies

Fears of petroleum shortages have seized American central decision-makers at various times during the twentieth century. The first such episode occurred during the First World War and the early and mid-1920s. Before this period American investments in foreign oil production were modest; supplies came from within the country's territorial boundaries. In the middle and late 1920s domestic production increased substantially with the discovery of new fields in the Southwest. During and after the war, however, policy-makers feared that reserves within the United States would be exhausted and the most promising overseas fields would fall under the control of foreign powers, primarily Great Britain. They felt this posed a threat to the functioning of the economy in general and naval capabilities in particular. During the war the State Department indicated its general support for foreign oil investments, but would not endorse specific projects. The oil companies for their part refused to act without clearer official support, and during the early 1920s central decision-makers actively backed American firms in Central America, Colombia, Venezuela, Albania, and, most vigorously, the Middle East and the Dutch East Indies.[25] In the last two areas American companies encountered substantial opposition from European colonial powers. This endangered the interests of U.S. firms as well as those of the state. Through the use of diplomatic and economic pressure, central decision-makers gained access for U.S. companies. Yet, in obtaining greater security of supply, they contributed to the creation of private institutional structures that helped make the petroleum industry the most effective oligopoly that the world has ever known. This case suggests that in ordering preferences American leaders were willing to sacrifice goals associated with competitiveness and lower prices for those that enhanced security of supply.

AMERICAN CONCERNS

The earliest concerns about oil shortages were voiced by public officials before World War I had ended. In 1916 Mark L. Requa, who worked for the Fuel Administration, warned that foreign oil supplies would be vital in the postwar period. Van H. Manning, the Director of the Bureau of Mines, also drew attention to this problem, as did Franklin K. Lane, the Secretary of the Interior. In 1919 the State Department established an interagency coordinating committee on government oil activity and ordered American consuls to collect information.[26]

In the immediate postwar years many Americans thought that continental reserves would soon be depleted. The fear of major shortages reached hysterical levels among some public officials, Congressmen, journalists, and oil company executives. James D.

[25] For a discussion of activities in Latin America see Tulchin, Ch. 4; for Albania see *Foreign Relations*, 1922, Vol. 1, pp. 605-9; 1923, Vol. 1, p. 376; 1925, Vol. 1, pp. 493-511.

[26] DeNovo, "Aggressive American Oil Policy," pp. 862-70.

Phelan, a Senator from California, warned the Secretary of the Interior in 1919 that the British were attempting to control the world's richest oil fields, and that the nation that secured such control would have "an overwhelming advantage on land and sea."[27] Arthur C. Millspaugh, the Foreign Trade Advisor to the State Department, expressed similar sentiments, arguing shortly after the war that the United States should support foreign oil investment for strategic reasons "whether . . . monopolistic in tendency or not."[28] The Director of the United States Geological Survey wrote that the "position of the United States in regard to oil can best be characterized as precarious."[29] These fears were exacerbated by the possibility that two foreign companies, Royal Dutch Shell and the Anglo-Persian Oil Company (later Anglo-Iranian and still later the British Petroleum Company), would be able to secure control of all important foreign reserves.[30]

Oil company executives became aware of the need for foreign sources of crude at the end of the war. The only American foreign operations actually in production were in Mexico and Rumania. While U.S. companies accounted for 70-80 percent of world production in 1918, British ones controlled 50 percent of known reserves. In addition, the relative cost of developing U.S. crude was greater because legal practices made it necessary to negotiate leases with individual land owners, rather than working through concession grants of large tracts of territory.[31]

Officials of Standard Oil of New Jersey (later renamed Exxon) were particularly worried. Jersey was basically a refining and marketing company. In 1918 it had to buy more than 84 percent of its crude. The company's 2.3 percent share of world output was

[27] Telegram from Phelan to Secretary Lane, May 2, 1919, General Land Office, General Leasing Act, Alien Ownership, Records of the Department of the Interior, File 2-208, part 1, U.S. National Archives.

[28] Quoted in DeNovo, *American Interests*, p. 172.

[29] Quoted in U.S. Senate, Committee on Foreign Relations, Subcommittee on Multinational Corporations, *Multinational Oil Corporations*, Report, p. 33.

[30] Krueger, *International Oil*, p. 40; Nash, *United States Oil Policy*, p. 49; Feis, *Diplomacy of the Dollar*, pp. 49-50; U.S. Senate, *Multinational Oil Corporations*, Report, p. 33.

[31] DeNovo, "Aggressive American Oil Policy," pp. 855-65; U.S. Federal Trade Commission, *International Petroleum Cartel*, pp. 39-40.

surpassed by that of its great competitor, Royal Dutch Shell, which accounted for 6.1 percent. Even in the United States Shell produced more crude than Jersey. Jersey's position became increasingly vulnerable as its rivals began to integrate downstream, establishing their own transportation, refining, and marketing networks. The appointment as president in 1922 of W. C. Teagle, who had previously directed foreign operations, indicated the company's concern.[32]

Once the large American companies, particularly Jersey and Standard Oil of New York (Socony, later Socony-Vacuum and now Mobil), became committed to developing foreign sources of supply, industry organizations as well as particular firms pressed the American government for assistance. The American Petroleum Institute was established in 1919. It grew out of the Petroleum Committee for War, the industry group that had helped plan oil strategy for World War I. The Institute immediately urged official support for foreign oil investment. It was joined by the American Institute of Mining and Metallurgical Engineers, which represented technical personnel.[33] Thus, the expansion of foreign oil activities represented a clear convergence between corporate economic goals and state objectives associated with security of supply.

FOREIGN OBSTACLES

When American companies attempted to expand their foreign operations, they encountered resistance from the British in the Middle East and from the Dutch in the East Indies. The end of the First World War left the Middle East in disarray. Among the many uncertainties precipitated by the collapse of the Ottoman Empire was the legal status of concession agreements. Shortly before the outbreak of the war British, French, and German interests had concluded an arrangement with the Grand Vizier of Turkey for petroleum development in the Baghdad and Mosul *vilyats* (provinces), which became part of Iraq. It was confirmed in a letter from the Vizier, but was not ratified by the Ottoman parliament. On the basis of this arrangement, which established the

[32] Gibb and Knowlton, *History of Standard Oil*, pp. 106-109, 275-78.

[33] DeNovo, "Aggressive American Oil Policy," pp. 867-68.

Turkish Petroleum Company, the British and the French concluded the San Remo Agreement in 1920, which covered aspects of oil activity in Rumania and Russia as well as Mesopotamia (later Iraq): in Rumania enemy concessions were to be divided fifty-fifty; in Mesopotamia 75 percent of oil would go to the British, 25 percent to the French; both countries would jointly support the nationals of either seeking concessions in Russia; the French were to allow pipelines across their sphere of influence in Syria; finally, the agreement provided for exploration in each other's colonies by companies composed two-thirds of interests from the metropolitan power and one-third from the other state. The San Remo Agreement completed arrangements between the British and the French concerning spheres of influence and petroleum activity in the Middle East initially formulated in the secret Sykes–Picot Agreement of 1916.[34]

Had the claims of the Turkish Petroleum Company been accepted, and the provisions of the San Remo Agreement put into effect, American corporations would have been frozen out of the Middle East. In 1919 and 1920 the British prevented American companies from operating or exploring in Palestine or Mesopotamia on the grounds that no arrangements could be made until new governments were established. Meanwhile, representatives of British firms (Shell and Anglo-Iranian) were active in the area.[35]

The Dutch opposed the expansion of American holdings in their East Indian possessions. The Shell Oil Company, initially Dutch, which became the half-Dutch, half-English Royal Dutch Shell Company, was consistently favored. The 1918 Dutch Mining Law restricted petroleum concessions to nationals, inhabitants of Dutch territory, or companies domiciled on Dutch territory a majority of whose directors were Dutch nationals or residents.[36]

[34] *Foreign Relations*, 1920, Vol. 2, pp. 655-58; Memorandum from the Office of the Foreign Trade Advisor, Oct. 11, 1921, Records of the Department of State, Decimal File No. 890g 6363/49a, U.S. National Archives; Shwadran, *Middle East, Oil*, p. 199.

[35] DeNovo, *American Interests*, pp. 172-79.

[36] U.S. Senate, Special Committee Investigating Petroleum Resources, *Diplomatic Protection*, p. 33.

Production in the East Indies was the major source of Shell's strength. Shell and Anglo-Persian were the only international rivals of the major American companies. Efforts by both Sinclair and Jersey to secure promising territories in the East Indies were rejected in the early 1920s.

PUBLIC INITIATIVES

Central decision-makers felt, then, that foreign powers were threatening America's economic well-being. The oil companies could do little on their own. Unlike backward nations, the British and the Dutch were not desperate for the capital, technical skill, and market knowledge that the companies possessed. This predicament led American leaders to depart from their modal pattern of behavior, which eschewed extensive intervention on behalf of particular foreign investments. Before 1916 the American government had not paid much attention to the establishment of new foreign oil ventures.[37] When the fear of shortages receded in the middle and late 1920s, they again adopted a more circumspect attitude. The increase in state activity was related to a perceived threat to a national security goal—insuring security of supply.

U.S. officials began their pressure on Britain with ideological arguments. Negotiations after the war were couched in terms of the Open Door. Free access for investment was a principle that Britain endorsed. The unimpeded movement of goods and capital had been the touchstone of British foreign economic policy during much of the nineteenth century. Sterling continued to play a key role in the international monetary system. Great Britain was, in the 1920s, in the peculiar and ambiguous position that confronts all imperial powers during their decline. National interests might best have been served by adandoning the principles of free trade, but such action would be extremely difficult. It would imply that the nation's status had changed and would be opposed by powerful domestic interest groups.[38] Inconsistency could decrease Brit-

[37] They were, however, concerned with existing investments in Mexico. This case is discussed in Ch. VI.

[38] See Krasner, "State Power and the Structure of International Trade," for an elaboration.

ain's prestige with third parties by making her behavior appear self-serving and unprincipled.[39] In diplomatic exchanges with the United States, Britain persistently endorsed the principle of the Open Door.[40] The arguments presented by the American government were not without their effect, because statesmen in both countries were influenced by the same basic principles.

In addition, the British could not ignore the economic and political consequences that might flow from an acrimonious dispute with the United States. Britain was the primary regulator of the postwar world, but she lacked the power to carry out her task alone. American capital was needed to rebuild Europe. Explicit American rejection of the Middle East mandates could spark nationalist revolts, which Britain was ill-prepared to handle: only with difficulty had a 1920 uprising in Iraq been suppressed. At the Lausanne conference of 1923 Turkey implicitly threatened to settle its territorial claims to the south by force. It was not clear that the British had the military capability to deal with a Turkish invasion of Iraq. An American condemnation of British policy could have led to a Turkish attempt to annex territories including the Mosul oil fields. Thus, American diplomatic protests both appealed to common principle and carried an implied threat of political and economic sanctions.

By 1924 the British had acquiesced in American participation, although the actual negotiations between the companies continued for three more years. The final settlement gave the Americans a 23.75 percent interest in the Turkish Petroleum Company (later the Iraq Petroleum Company). The French got the same share as did the Anglo-Persian (British) and Royal Dutch Shell (British-Dutch) companies. The remaining five percent went to Calouste S. Gulbenkian, a British citizen of Armenian extraction whose prior claims to the concession were recognized in British courts. The American group was originally composed of Standard Oil of New Jersey, Standard Oil of New York, Gulf, Atlantic, and Pan-American, but by 1931 all but the first two had dropped out.[41]

[39] For a discussion of this argument see Franck and Weisband, *Word Politics*, pp. 6-7.

[40] Grew, *Turbulent Era*, pp. 495, 501; *Foreign Relations*, 1920, Vol. 2, pp. 663-67; Shwadran, p. 391.

[41] Wilson, *American Business*, p. 195; Shwadran, p. 238.

Diplomatic appeals were much less effective in dealing with the Netherlands. The Dutch were not wedded to equal access for all investors. When the American government first became aware through Jersey that the Netherlands intended to grant concessions for the promising Djambi field in the East Indies to a quasi-public Dutch enterprise without opening public bids, the United States brought economic pressure to bear through the 1920 Leasing Act, which provided that nationals of foreign countries that denied access to American corporations could be barred from public lands in the United States. In practice this law was directed against the Royal Dutch Shell Oil Company, which was a major producer in the United States. The American Minister read this Act to the Dutch Secretary for Foreign Affairs. In September 1920 the United States informed the Netherlands that the Secretary of the Interior had determined that Dutch practices were discriminatory under the provisions of the Act, and that no more leases would be granted to companies whose controlling stock interest was held by Dutch citizens. The Dutch were unmoved, and in 1921 the Djambi concession was let to Shell.[42]

Still, American officials persisted. In 1922 the Secretary of the Interior, Albert Fall, rejected Shell's request for a lease on public lands in Utah on the grounds that American firms were not granted similar access to Dutch territory. Shell withdrew its application. Several months later Fall rejected a Shell application for a grant on Indian lands, although this action was reversed by his successor, who ruled that the provisions of the Leasing Act did not apply to Indian territory.

The dispute was not resolved until the Dutch changed their policy. In 1927 they announced their intention to grant four tracts in the East Indies to a Jersey subsidiary, provided that Holland was declared a reciprocating country under the terms of the 1920 Leasing Act. After discussions lasting several months an agreement, reflected in an exchange of memoranda between the Dutch foreign affairs minister and the United States representative in the Netherlands, was reached. The Dutch averred that the East Indian mining law would no longer be used to discriminate against American

[42] U.S. Senate, Special Committee Investigating Petroleum Resources, *Diplomatic Protection*, pp. 34-35, 44.

citizens and granted promising territory to a Jersey subsidiary. The United States declared Holland a reciprocating country.[43]

THE OUTCOME

American international oil policy after the First World War was clearly successful in securing access for American corporations. To the extent that this prevented major sources of crude from falling entirely into non-American hands, it contributed to security of supply for the United States. Foreign companies are beyond the state's legal jurisdiction. The state can, however, appeal to the nationalistic and patriotic sentiments of its own nationals, who head multinational corporations. It can also exercise legal jurisdiction over the company's assets that are within its own borders. This is likely to make domestic companies more susceptible to state initiatives than foreign ones.

In furthering security, however, American political leaders undermined the possibility of creating a competitive world oil market. Ideologically, the principle of the Open Door had been pervasive in the position taken by U.S. central decision-makers. The State Department persistently argued that no single company should be granted monopoly control in a particular country. In the Turkish Petroleum Company (TPC) dispute this issue was manifest in a technical debate about subleasing within the territory covered by the TPC concession and oil development in the rest of what had been the Ottoman Empire. To be consistent with an Open Door policy, U.S. leaders should have argued that all companies be free to develop areas within the concession that were not exploited by the Turkish Petroleum Company within some reasonable period of time, and that other areas be open to all comers. However, the British and their companies were not interested in such a free-wheeling arrangement, one that could result in a large role for aggressive non-British firms, most of which were bound to be American. Confronted with the possibility that this issue would preclude U.S. participation in the development of Middle East oil, American officials essentially gave up their efforts to secure a more competitive market. In June 1922 Secretary of State

[43] *Ibid.*, pp. 38-47; Wilson, p.198; Nash, pp. 65-66.

Hughes told a representative of Standard Oil that it was necessary to distinguish between the Open Door "principle and its application." The Secretary indicated that "he did not want to be so impractical as to take a position which would prevent American interests from having that opportunity [to develop oil in Iraq] that our representations had been made to obtain for them."[44]

Arrangements for subleasing and the development of other areas within the Ottoman Empire were worked out in 1924 and embodied in what became known as the Red Line Agreement of 1928, which formally established the new Iraq Petroleum Company (IPC).[45] The Agreement, signed by Anglo-Persian, Royal Dutch Shell, Compagnie Française des Pétroles (CFP), Jersey, Standard Oil of New York, Gulf, Atlantic, and Pan-American (the companies involved in the Turkish Petroleum Company), was a clear violation of the spirit of the Open Door. Prior to World War II it was the basic instrument used by the oil firms to control crude production. The Agreement obligated the signatories "not to be interested directly or indirectly in the production or manufacture of crude oil in the Ottoman Empire in Europe or Asia, except in that part which is under the administration of the Egyptian Government or of the Sheik of Koweit, or in the transferred territories on the Turco-Persian frontier, otherwise than through the Turkish Petroleum Company."[46] That is, no signatory could independently develop new sources of petroleum anywhere in the Middle East except Kuwait. The Agreement gave lip service to the Open Door principle by ostensibly allowing American companies to bid independently for areas within Iraq. This provision had no real effect because any American company could easily be outbid by the other members of the TPC consor-

[44] Memorandum of Conversation Between Secretary of State and Representative of the Standard Oil Company, June 22, 1922, Records of the Department of State, Decimal File No. 890g 6363/147, U.S. National Archives.

[45] The delay in arriving at a final settlement was complicated by several issues, including the role to be played by Calouste Gulbenkian, a British entrepreneur with a prior claim to the concession area. See *Foreign Relations*, 1924, Vol. 2, pp. 222-41.

[46] *Foreign Relations*, 1927, Vol. 2, p. 822. This self-denying clause was originally formulated by the Dutch and British in 1914. See Blair, *Control of Oil*, p. 31.

tium: 76.25 percent of their purchase price would be returned since they owned 76.25 of the company.[47] There was never, in fact, any independent activity by TPC members within the Red Line until after the Second World War. When the associate general counsel of Standard asked if there would be any objection to American firms signing the Red Line Agreement, the Secretary of State wrote that he perceived "no objection on the grounds of policy to the American Group taking up the proffered share participation in the Iraq Petroleum Company. . . ."[48]

The restrictive aspects of the Iraq concession became even more apparent during the 1930s. In 1931 a new concession gave the Iraq Petroleum Company (the name was changed in 1929) control of most land east of the Tigris and eliminated any provision for subleasing. The area west of the Tigris was let to a new group, the British Oil Development Corporation, in 1931. In 1942 this area too passed to the Iraq Petroleum Company. In 1938 the Basrah Petroleum Company, a subsidiary of the Iraq Petroleum Company, secured a concession for the area of Iraq not covered by the other two grants.[49] Furthermore, three of the five American participants had dropped out of the IPC by 1931, leaving only Mobil and Jersey. Hence, by the early 1940s all of Iraq's oil was controlled by a consortium of five of the eight largest oil companies. The Red Line Agreement was explicitly sanctioned by the State Department, and later arrangements tacitly accepted. They contributed to oligopoly control of the oil market through the Second World War and beyond.

Aside from the self-denying ordinances of the Red Line Agreement with respect to production, the formation of the Turkish Petroleum Company initiated the concept of production companies owned by several U.S. firms, a critical factor in the industry's later ability to restrain competition. Ironically, the American government played an important role in establishing this new institutional form. The initiative for the formation of a joint American effort in Iraq came from public officials, particularly Secretary of Commerce Herbert Hoover. He called a meeting of large

[47] U.S. Federal Trade Commission, *International Petroleum Cartel*, p. 59; Blair, pp. 33-34.

[48] *Foreign Relations*, 1927, Vol. 2, p. 823.

[49] Shwadran, p. 239; DeNovo, *American Interests*, p. 201.

American oil companies in 1921 to try to interest them in the Middle East. Up to that time only Jersey and Socony had been involved in the area. Hoover urged the State Department to secure American participation through a joint operation with European companies, although he would have preferred that U.S. companies be independent of French and British interests. The Department did not support a separate American company, but it did endorse the concept of joint ownership. Jersey took the lead in forming an American consortium specifically because the State Department indicated the inappropriateness of its backing a single firm. Although this stance might be interpreted as a commitment to a more competitive policy, the Department's later acceptance of restrictive schemes suggests that the fear of becoming involved in disputes among domestic companies was the more salient concern.[50]

After 1928 joint ventures became the typical pattern for oil development. Ownership of the Kuwait Petroleum Company was divided fifty-fifty between Gulf and Anglo-Iranian. The Bahrein Petroleum Company, initially held by Socal, became a joint operation with the Texas Company (Texaco) in 1936. By 1948 the Saudi Arabian American Oil Company (Aramco) was owned by Jersey, Socal, Texas, and Socony. Except in Iran there were no individual production concessions in the Middle East until the late 1940s.

Many of these joint ventures initially included provisions not to upset the market shares of partners. Although these explicit restrictions were probably eliminated during the 1950s, the requirement that each partner in an operation announce in advance its production needs helped keep the major companies informed of each other's intentions. This reinforced collusive behavior by mitigating the possibility that the market would be upset by surreptitious increases in output.[51]

CONCLUSION

Oil investment in the Middle East and the Dutch East Indies in

[50] Shwadran, p. 205; Letter from Hoover to Hughes, April 17, 1922, Records of the Department of State, Decimal File No. 890g 6363/96, U.S. National Archives; Krueger, p. 41.

[51] Adelman, *World Petroleum Market*, pp. 82-89.

the 1920s followed a pattern similar to that of rubber. In both cases there was a convergence of interests between the state and private corporations. Public officials were not dragged, pressured, or bribed into the promotion of foreign investment. They believed that the expansion of American corporate activity would provide the U.S. economy with more secure sources of raw materials.

At the same time, however, these cases revealed the structural weakness of the American political system. The government had to work through private industry. The possiblity of government ownership was not seriously considered. That it was not was particularly striking in the case of oil, where foreign models suggested this as a reasonable policy. The British government had bought into Anglo-Persian in 1914, and the French government into the CFP in the 1920s. In the United States a suggestion made by Senator Phelan in 1919 that a quasi-public oil company be formed never gained support. Banbridge Colby, the Secretary of State, rejected it on the grounds that such a firm would have difficulty doing business in foreign countries.[52] There was some merit in this argument, for Venezuela did pass a law in 1922 prohibiting concessions to companies owned by foreign governments. Still, Anglo-Persian and CFP were working effectively in the Middle East, and there was nothing that logically prevented the United States from supporting different kinds of operations in the eastern and western hemispheres. The more fundamental difficulty in creating a public corporation was the resistance of the private sector. Any attempt to create a state-owned operation would have thrown the whole issue into decision-making arenas, particularly the Congress, where the power of the industry was greatest. It became increasingly clear that the state's need for security could only be furthered by working through the major oil companies.

In sum, the promotion of petroleum in the Middle East and the Dutch East Indies indicates that U.S. central decision-makers preferred security of supply over greater competition. They were willing to approve the restrictive clauses of the Red Line Agreement. Although there is no evidence that they understood that the formation of jointly owned enterprises would further market control, this was the inadvertent consequence of their policy. A state

[52] DeNovo, "Aggressive American Oil Policy," p. 872.

more concerned with promoting competition might have looked more carefully at such tactics, or at least tried to monitor the subsequent behavior of joint operations.

With respect to more general macro-theoretical issues, the promotion of oil investments in the Middle East during the 1920s does not provide much evidence for deciding among statist, liberal, or Marxist approaches. There were never any serious differences between private corporations and state actors. While U.S. policy could be explained from a liberal or Marxist perspective in terms of the preferences of powerful private (or capitalist) groups, it was likewise consistent with a statist interpretation, at least if maintaining security of supply is a more important goal than promoting competition and lower prices. The same is true for the promotion of rubber investment in Liberia, except here government action also contributed to conditions that made it marginally more difficult to control the market.

Oil in Iran, 1951-1955

Although the dispute that followed Iran's nationalization of the British-owned Anglo-Iranian Oil Company in 1951 is often cited by radicals as an example of the fundamental importance of economic considerations in foreign policy,[53] American behavior is better understood from a statist perspective. The United States was reluctant to become involved. Central decision-makers made proposals that led to the entrance of U.S. oil companies into Iran only after they became convinced that no Iranian government could accept an exclusively British-owned operation. U.S. leaders were moved not by economic considerations associated with either security of supply or the interest of private corporations, but rather by their unease about the domestic political structure of the Iranian government. American policy-makers were willing to use covert force as well as economic instruments to eliminate what they increasingly perceived as a regime that could increase communist influence.

BACKGROUND

Iran was the largest oil producer in the Middle East at the con-

[53] See, e.g., Joyce and Gabriel Kolko, *Limits of Power*, pp. 412-20.

clusion of World War II. It was also a country where the threat of Soviet influence was palpable. The Russians had occupied parts of northern Iran at the conclusion of the Second World War and procured an oil concession in the same area. Both of these initiatives were successfully blocked by the Western Powers. The Soviets, however, were not the only source of tension. Although Iran had never directly fallen under colonial rule, British influence had been dominant for half a century. All of Iran's oil production was controlled by the British-owned Anglo-Iranian Oil Company (AIOC). This situation encouraged nationalist disaffections that were focussed upon the 1933 oil concession, which based payments to the government on the company's dividend policy. Both parties found this arrangement unsatisfactory, and negotiations were opened in 1949. A Supplemental Agreement to the 1933 concession was concluded calling for an increase in royalty payments from four shillings per ton to six and for other modifications. These changes would probably still have left Iran in a worse position than the fifty-fifty profit-sharing formula that began in Venezuela during the 1940s. At any rate, the agreement was opposed by a coalition of left- and right-wing elements led by Mohammed Mossadegh, and the Iranian parliament failed to ratify it before elections were called. The new parliament passed consideration of the Supplemental Agreement to an ad hoc Parliamentary Oil Committee chaired by Mossadegh, which rejected it in December 1950. The parliament accepted this decision in January 1951.[54]

The Parliamentary Oil Committee then resolved in principle to nationalize the oil industry and asked the Premier, Ali Razmara, to report on the practicality of such a measure. Ali Razmara indicated that nationalization was not practical, but he refused to champion the Supplemental Agreement because he did not want to appear to be befriending the AIOC. The possibility of a moderate settlement ended with the assassination of the Premier by a member of a radical Moslem sect on March 7. Razmara's successor was unable to secure the support of parliament, and on April 27 the Shah named Mossadegh as the new Premier. On May 1

[54] Shwadran, pp. 89-98.

details for the nationalization, the first such action in the Middle East, were announced.[55]

The British then imposed economic sanctions on Iran. In April 1951 the AIOC halted payments to the Iranian treasury. Tanker shipments from the refinery at Abadan were stopped in June when government officials tried to secure receipts from the ships' captains indicating Iranian ownership of the oil. In October Iranian soldiers took over the refinery, locking out the British technicians. By the end of the month all British staff had left the country. The British broke commercial relations and forbade the export of scarce materials such as railroad ties. When Iran did manage to send off some small shipments of oil in 1952, the AIOC brought suits in Aden, Italy, and Japan claiming that it was the rightful owner. From 1951 to 1953 Iranian crude exports were negligible.[56]

The British also tried to use diplomatic maneuvers, and compromises, to resolve the dispute. Britain requested arbitration under the terms of the 1933 concession, but this was rejected by the Iranian government. Britain then submitted the issue to the World Court, also under the terms of the old concession, but the Court did not give a clear ruling. In June 1951 the British indicated willingness to form a company with a mixed board of directors, which would at least formally recognize Iranian ownership. This offer too was rejected by the Mossadegh government.[57] Tensions mounted, culminating with the breaking of diplomatic relations in October 1952.

THE AMERICAN RESPONSE

From the outset U.S. leaders were fundamentally concerned with the internal political situation in Iran and the danger of Russian influence. The United States did not act to get additional oil supplies for the western world: Iran's liftings had been replaced by increased production in other countries. It did not act to further the interests of specific American corporations. Policy-makers did

[55] Longrigg, *Oil in the Middle East*, 3rd edn., pp. 161, 162.

[56] Longrigg, 2nd edn., pp. 164, 170; Shwadran, pp. 116-20.

[57] Longrigg, 2nd edn., p. 166.

not devise the idea of an international consortium, including American and French as well as British companies, until they concluded that the Iranians would never reestablish an operation that was entirely owned by the British. U.S. officials persuaded the major American oil companies to join this enterprise, but at the cost of terminating a criminal antitrust suit designed to end collusive practices in the world oil market. While policy-makers were hesitant about introducing U.S. oil companies into Iran, they were decisive in their efforts to change a regime they considered to be tainted with communism. Covert U.S. assistance contributed to the success of the military coup that overthrew Mohammed Mossadegh in 1953.

American leaders were very disturbed by the stand taken by the British in Iran. Both Attlee and his successor, Morrison, as well as the Conservative government that followed, rigidly opposed compromise with Mossadegh, while American officials counselled moderation and caution. In late 1950 George McGhee, Assistant Secretary of State for Near East Affairs, asked the British to accept Iran's outstanding demands for changes in the pending agreement. The British refused. The United States also informed Britain that it would oppose the use of troops unless there were a Russian invasion, communist coup, invitation from the Iranian government, or need to evacuate British nationals.[58] In June of 1951 Truman sent letters to Mossadegh and the British urging new negotiations. Harriman visited Iran during the following month as a special envoy of the President. Other conversations were held with Mossadegh while he was at Walter Reed Army Hospital in the fall of 1951. All of these, plus other initiatives and forms of pressure, were ineffective. Through 1952 animosity increased.

American officials became increasingly concerned about a drift to the left in Iran. Mossadegh's position was weak. He was not always able to control his own supporters, including the left-wing Tudeh party. Street riots occurred frequently in 1951 and 1952. In the summer of 1952 Mossadegh concluded ten oil sale agreements with buyers in Eastern Europe.[59] In December 1952 the State De-

[58] Acheson, *Present at the Creation*, pp. 503, 506.

[59] Lenczowski, *The Middle East in World Affairs*, p. 234.

partment announced that American dealers were free to buy Persian oil at their own risk. This reversed an earlier policy of complete support for the oil companies' embargo, and it reflected fears of a takeover by left-wing groups.

In May 1953 Secretary of State Dulles made a three-week trip to the Middle East and concluded that the Arab world could slip out of the Western Bloc. In June Eisenhower personally rejected an appeal from Mossadegh for additional aid; the United States had granted substantial assistance in 1951 and 1952.[60] State Department officials saw a growing danger of communist influence in Iran. There were rumors that Mossadegh was about to get a large loan from the Russians. Because the oil companies had succeeded in virtually cutting off all Iranian exports, the country's financial situation was becoming more precarious.

The fear of a lurch to the left in Iran led American central decision-makers to abandon efforts at moderation. In August 1953 the Shah fled the country after an unsuccessful effort to unseat Mossadegh. Four days later the military seized power. The United States gave strong backing in the form of emergency materiel shipments. The Shah returned. The CIA was almost certainly involved in this episode.[61]

While these political and military developments were taking place, American leaders were trying to devise ways to bring Iranian oil back onto the world market. They were not motivated by immediate concerns about economic security: additional output from other countries in the Middle East had easily replaced losses from Iran. They were not pressured by U.S. oil companies: proposals made by U.S. officials in 1951 for a compromise settlement did not involve the entry of American companies into Iran. U.S. leaders wanted to get Iranian oil flowing again because they felt this was necessary to maintain a stable noncommunist regime. By the fall of 1952 they concluded that the restoration of the AIOC would be unacceptable to Iran: nationalist sentiments made it impossible for any regime to restore a wholly British-owned operation. The largest non-British institutions that could produce and

[60] Eisenhower, *Mandate for Change*, p. 162.

[61] LaFeber, *America, Russia and the Cold War*, p. 156; Engler, *Politics of Oil*, pp. 205-6.

ship oil were the major American oil companies. In November 1952 Truman instructed the Secretary of State to enter discussions with the Anglo-Iranian Oil Company and the American majors. The initial meetings were held with Gulf, Socony, Jersey, Socal, and Texas on December 4 and 9, 1952.[62]

Bringing the U.S. majors into Iran presented a double problem for the State Department. First, the companies themselves were not enthusiastic. Second, such a policy would conflict with the criminal antitrust suit that was about to be brought against the very same oil companies by the Justice Department.

At the initial meeting between corporate and government officials it was clear that the firms were not anxious to move Iranian oil. They had already increased production elsewhere. Reintegrating Iran into the market would present a threat to oligopoly control: outlets would have to be found for her oil; production would have to be cut back elsewhere if prices were to be held. Corporate reluctance was also associated with the pending antitrust case, for the courts were the one institution in the American polity that could deal the industry a decisive blow. They were the one arena in which the very core of the enterprise was at stake. The situation was highly uncertain and fluid. It was not surprising that corporate managers proceeded cautiously. Throughout most of 1953 they continued to express reluctance about being involved in Iran. Bringing Iranian oil back into the world market would require a high level of intercorporate coordination, but the antitrust suit made such coordination potentially very dangerous.[63]

Only in December 1953 did the companies accede to the government's request, and even then they continued to play the reluctant bride. In a letter to the Secretary of State dated December 4, Standard Oil of New York indicated that it preferred AIOC to work out its own arrangements with Iran, but understood that American officials thought this to be impossible. The letter went on to note that the company had no interest in joining a consortium from "a strictly commercial viewpoint," but was prepared to

[62] U.S. Senate, *Multinational Oil Corporations*, Report, p. 61; U.S. Senate, Committee on Foreign Relations, Subcommittee on Multinational Corporations, *Iranian Consortium*, p. 26.

[63] U.S. Senate, *Iranian Consortium*, pp. vii and 27.

make reasonable efforts being "very conscious of the large national security interests involved."[64] Several years later a representative of Gulf Oil claimed that it had been forced into the Iranian consortium by the State Department.[65]

By the time the American majors were brought to the altar, however, they had already gotten one concession from the government that they wanted very much—a downgrading of the antitrust suit from a criminal to a civil action. This seemed not so much the result of corporate pressure as a recognition by public officials that the foreign policy goals involved in restoring Iranian oil production inherently contradicted the desire to make the oil industry more competitive.[66] The State Department opposed the suit when a grand jury investigation was first announced in April 1952. Secretary of State Acheson argued that antitrust proceedings would "not help the achievement of the foreign policy aims of the United States in the Middle East. . . ."[67] This position was fully etched out in a report submitted to the National Security Council by the Departments of State, Defense, and the Interior in January 1953. It maintained that oil would be lost to the free world not only if countries went communist but also if foreign corporations were expelled. Only the major companies, it contended, had the ability to restore output in Iran rapidly. Furthermore, oil was a major source of income for producing states and was needed for economic growth and political stability. The report drew a relationship between the ideological struggle with the Soviet Union and the pending criminal antitrust suits: "In this struggle of ideas," the report stated, "on which our security depends, the oil companies of the United States play a significant role. . . . In many foreign countries they are the principal contact of the local inhabitants with American enterprise. What such people think of the oil companies, they think of American enterprise and the American system; we cannot afford to leave unchallenged the assertions that these companies are engaged in a crimi-

[64] *Ibid.*, p. 58.

[65] U.S. Senate, Subcommittee on Multinational Corporations, *Multinational Corporations*, Hearings, Part 8, p. 561.

[66] U.S. Senate, *Multinational Oil Corporations*, Report, p. 60.

[67] U.S. Senate, *Iranian Consortium*, p. 5.

nal conspiracy for the purpose of predatory exploitation."[68] The report concluded by recommending that the suit be changed from a criminal to a civil complaint. This recommendation was adopted, and on January 12, 1953, President Truman personally ordered the Justice Department official in charge of the case to change it to a civil proceeding.[69]

The consortium itself was put together in late 1953 and early 1954. Acting on the advice of Herbert Hoover, Jr., special American representative on oil, the chairman of Anglo-Iranian invited the five American majors to a meeting in December 1953. In January 1954 the Justice Department ruled that American participation in the consortium would not, in light of the security interests involved, constitute an unreasonable restraint of trade.[70] Given the choice between more competition in the industry and broader political goals, American political leaders opted for the latter.

I do not mean to argue that participation in the Iranian consortium meant any economic sacrifice for U.S. oil companies. It was clearly in their interest to maintain a stable market situation. Some companies, especially Socony-Vacuum, could not fill their needs from supplies they owned. Others, such as Exxon, were not crude short, but the creation of the consortium in Iran did extend the pattern of jointly owned companies to the one Middle East country where operations had been governed by a single major firm. Even though the final settlement left Iran with formal ownership of her oil, effective control was exercised by the international companies. This denouement could only suggest that nationalization was not to be taken lightly, a message the companies were anxious to get across.[71] However, it is clear that the impetus for participation came not from the private sector but from the state. Had U.S. political leaders not pushed, American oil companies would not have entered Iran.

Furthermore, the majors did not get everything they wanted.

[68] U.S. Senate, *Multinational Corporations*, Hearings, Part 8, p. 5.

[69] U.S. Senate, *Multinational Oil Corporations*, Report, pp. 63-64.

[70] U.S. Senate, *Iranian Consortium*, p. vii.

[71] For a discussion of company aims see Wilkins, *Maturing of Multinational Enterprise*, pp. 322-23.

The nature of the suit was changed, but it was not entirely abandoned. More important, the companies agreed to take a number of smaller firms into the consortium, as a result of pressure from the independents themselves and from the Justice Department. In 1955 seven American companies were formed into the Iricon group and given one-eighth of the 40 percent American share of the consortium. This was tokenism, but it was tokenism that had a cost, for the growth of independents through the consortium and otherwise eventually made market control far more difficult for the majors.[72]

CONCLUSION

American policy in the Iranian dispute cannot easily be explained in terms of corporate interests. First, only after U.S. leaders became convinced that nationalism would make it impossible for any Iranian government to accept a venture exclusively controlled by British interests did they push for the entry of American oil companies; a new role for U.S. firms was not an important part of their initial efforts to bring about a settlement between Iran and Britain. While the final consortium agreement provided for 40 percent American participation, it also included Shell and the French-owned CFP. Second, even though Mossadegh had nationalized a major international corporation, U.S. officials did not initially take an unambiguously negative attitude toward him. They extended considerable aid in 1951 and 1952. In 1951 Mossadegh was treated at Walter Reed Army Hospital. Only after American leaders became convinced that no compromise was possible, and that communist influence in Iran could dramatically increase, did they endorse the covert use of force.

This is not to say that the final outcome violated the preferences and interests of U.S. firms. On the contrary, they got most of what they wanted as far as thwarting government efforts to initiate a criminal antitrust suit was concerned. The compromise that central decision-makers were forced to make reflects the weakness of the American political system. U.S. leaders could not compel firms to go into Iran. They could only get corporate cooperation

[72] U.S. Senate, *Multinational Oil Corporations*, Report, p. 71. See Vernon, "An Interpretation," pp. 1-14, for a discussion of the impact of the independents.

by buying them off. Given the importance they attributed to the general foreign policy goal at stake—preventing a communist regime in Iran—American leaders were not terribly reluctant to abandon efforts to create a more competitive oil market.

Unsuccessful Efforts to Expand

Although American firms usually succeeded when they wanted to make new raw materials investments, they did experience some failures. In some cases, U.S. political leaders were not willing to give private actors the support that would have been necessary to overcome the resistance of host-country governments. There is also one example of a situation in which central decision-makers wanted to promote investment in a particular area (iron ore in Liberia in the late 1930s) but were unable to secure the cooperation of private firms. These cases suggest that the state has some independence from societal actors. When central decision-makers have not seen a clear relationship between an investment and general societal goals, they have rejected private efforts to get extensive government support. In at least two cases, political leaders opposed specific foreign investments that they felt would make it more difficult to accomplish general foreign policy aims. However, policy-makers have not always been able to get private corporations to accede to their policy preferences. Whenever there has been a clear divergence between public and private aims, neither party has been able to do very much.

Despite their economic resources, American corporations acting on their own have not always been able to establish new foreign raw materials operations. Attempts to launch oil ventures in Burma and the Dutch East Indies before the First World War were frustrated by the Indian and Dutch governments. The former had imposed restrictions on non-British investment in oil as early as 1883. When Jersey applied for a concession in Burma in 1902, the Viceroy's office informed the American legation that "it was not desired by the Government of India to introduce the American Oil Companies, or their subsidiaries, into Burma. . . ."[73] Simi-

[73] *Foreign Relations*, 1922, Vol. 2, p. 353.

larly, in the Dutch East Indies, Jersey's efforts to obtain a concession before World War I were not successful.

The American government did make some diplomatic protests on behalf of American companies.[74] But they were not very vigorous. The authors of the most extensive history of Jersey Standard, who had access to the company's files, claim that the government offered no support whatsoever between 1912 and 1917.[75] This was a period during which there was no concern about supply shortages in the United States. Even after the war in Europe had begun, no extensive planning efforts were undertaken within the American government. Absent a clear rationale for vigorous state intervention, U.S. central decision-makers refused to depart from their usual policy of maintaining considerable distance from the specific efforts of U.S. firms to establish new foreign ventures.

A second case in which a U.S. investor failed to get state support occurred during the interwar years and World War II. The American entrepreneur Percival Farquhar unsuccessfully attempted to develop the Itabira iron ore deposit in Minas Gerais, Brazil. He encountered opposition from both local and national political leaders. Other American interests that held land adjacent to Farquhar's also opposed his project. The concession was finally nationalized during the Second World War. Farquhar, who did receive some compensation, blamed the American government for Brazil's action. At the very least he got almost no official backing. His efforts, to secure a loan from the Export-Import Bank or Reconstruction Finance Corporation, for instance, were turned down in 1941, because the State Department would not approve when Brazil refused to provide a guarantee.

The American government was more interested in cementing good relations with Brazil than in finding new iron ore deposits. Farquhar's endeavor could only have aggravated relations between the two countries. His accusation that the United States had actually encouraged the nationalization of his concession is supported by the fact that the Export-Import Bank extended a $20 million loan to the newly formed Brazilian National Steel Com-

[74] Wilkins, *Emergence of Multinational Enterprise*, pp. 84-86.

[75] Gibb and Knowlton, p. 107.

pany in the early 1940s. This was the first major funding ever given by the American government for a publicly owned raw materials industry in a developing country. It was prompted in part by reports that Brazil had discussed the project with Nazi Germany. The state's concern with broader security issues outweighed the interests of an individual investor. Given the nexus of decision-making within the executive, Farquhar was unable to affect government policy.[76]

Finally, there are at least two cases where the American government actively opposed foreign investments, because they conflicted with broader political objectives. In the early 1920s the oil operator Harry Sinclair, in one of his more brazen endeavors, sought American diplomatic support for an oil concession that he had signed with the Far Eastern Republic for northern Sakhalin. This presented two problems. First, the United States did not recognize the Far Eastern Republic, which was incorporated into the Soviet Union in 1922. Second, the Japanese, not the Russians, military controlled northern Sakhalin. Nevertheless, Sinclair sent two expeditions across the ice from Siberia. Both were deported by the occupying authorities. The State Department consistently refused to make any interventions to the Japanese.[77]

A second instance occurred in Ethiopia in 1935. Stanvac, a subsidiary of Socony and the Vacuum Oil Company, had negotiated a large oil concession. The American legation was so ignorant of these proceedings that it originally thought that Jersey was the company involved. When the agreement was publicly announced, it was opposed by some groups within Ethiopia, and by the British, who felt that it could complicate Ethiopia's dispute with the Italians. The State Department, following the British lead, advised the company to renounce the concession. This advice was accepted.[78]

I do not want to make too much of any of these cases, but it is worth remembering that in all of them central decision-makers were either unattracted by, or opposed, the activities of private

[76] Gauld, *Percival Farquhar*, Chs. 16-18.

[77] *Foreign Relations*, 1923, Vol. 2, pp. 798-812; 1924, Vol. 2, pp. 697-701; 1925, Vol. 2, pp. 678-81.

[78] *Foreign Relations*, 1935, Vol. 1, pp. 778-84.

entrepreneurs. The actions of central decision-makers were consistent with the proposition that their primary concern was to further certain general state goals. In the case of petroleum investments before World War I, they were not willing to go beyond diplomatic intervention because they did not feel that the United States confronted any shortage of crude oil. In Farquhar's iron ore venture in Brazil, Sinclair's oil in Sakhalin, and Stanvac's concession in Ethiopia, they refused any support because the activities of these firms were thought to jeopardize general foreign policy goals. Furthermore, despite some strong appeals, private actors were not able to alter official behavior. Decisions on these issues were taken primarily in the State Department where the political resources of private firms could not be put to much use.

There is one final example of unsuccessful overseas expansion that illustrates in a particularly graphic way the weakness of the American state in relation to domestic societal actors. This is a case in which the initiative for making a new investment came not from the private sphere but from state actors.

During the late 1930s the State Department tried unsuccessfully to interest American steel firms in Liberian iron ore. This effort was prompted by political rather than economic concerns. Liberia had been within America's traditional sphere of influence, both politically and economically. In December 1936 the American legation in Monrovia reported that a firm called Neep, registered in Holland but possibly controlled by Germans, was negotiating for an iron ore concession. The Department immediately raised questions with the Liberian government about the possibility of foreign infiltration and the financial resources of Neep.[79]

The State Department tried to find an American firm that would bid for a concession. Samples of ore from Liberia were given to U.S. Steel, Bethlehem, and Republic. The Department also took care to include Liberia in a law that allowed the federal government to send U.S. civilian employees to foreign countries, so that Americans could do a minerals survey.

All of this activity came to naught. U.S. Steel did send its own geological team to Liberia in 1938, but the following year the

[79] *Foreign Relations*, 1937, Vol. 2, pp. 829-57.

company reported that it had not found any deposits that would warrant commercial development.[80] No investments were actually made until after the Second World War. During the Depression new foreign undertakings were not, in general, economically attractive, and Liberia did not offer any special promise. In the face of corporate indifference, there was nothing that State Department officials could do in spite of their concerns about the possibility of increased Nazi influence in Liberia.

Conclusion

In the expansion of foreign raw materials investments the American government and private industry were like two men on the ends of a long slack rope. Most of the time the corporations had enough leeway and power to act on their own. They did not need government assistance, because their own economic resources were sufficient to secure access to foreign areas. When private companies were frustrated, the state was often ready to help, but the commitment of public resources depended upon the extent to which policy-makers perceived new investments furthering public interests. When a clear national interest was thought to be at stake, as was the case for rubber and oil during the 1920s and oil in Iran in the 1950s, state actors were willing to become extensively involved in specific projects. They used diplomatic and economic pressure and, in Iran, covert force. This made it possible to create a new oil consortium, but the entry of U.S. firms was incidental to the broader political objective of eliminating a government that American policy-makers perceived as falling increasingly under communist influence.

When there were no clear state interests, policy-makers did not give much support. Some ventures, such as oil investment in Burma and the Dutch East Indies prior to the First World War and iron ore in Brazil in the interwar years, were never successfully consummated. When the State Department and White House were determining policy, companies could push, but not pull, on their end of the rope. This inability to move the government was par-

[80] *Foreign Relations*, 1938, Vol. 2, pp. 773-817; 1939, Vol. 4, pp. 623-30.

ticularly clear in those rare cases of official opposition—Sinclair's investment in Sakhalin and Stanvac's in Ethiopia—that violated what public officials perceived to be the national interest.

However, if corporations could not push the state, neither could the state push the corporations. The response to Hoover's appeal to increase American rubber investment during the 1920s was feeble. Efforts to get American companies to invest in Liberian iron ore during the late 1930s were unsuccessful. Only rarely did federal officials have some resource that allowed them to pull on their end of the rope rather than pushing it. In the early 1950s it was the antitrust suit, as well as the ambiguous economic position of the oil companies, that made it possible to create the Iranian consortium. But to further broader diplomatic objectives, the state had to sacrifice the economic principles embodied in the Sherman, Wilson, and Clayton Acts. It was not the first time, nor the last, that the possibilities for a more competitive market were placed at the bottom of the government's list of priorities.

In sum, pulling on the rope is rarely possible in the American political system. In promoting foreign investment there was almost always a happy convergence of interest between the state and private corporations that made this lack of power less costly as far as achieving public purposes was concerned. When divergences occurred, neither party was able to do very much. This conclusion should not comfort those who view the American polity as an efficiently functioning system, nor instrumental Marxists or liberals who see state policy as the result of societal pressures. However, no firm judgment can be drawn about the relative merits of statist and structural Marxist arguments from this situation.

PART THREE

CHAPTER V

An Overview of the Problem of Nationalization

Although the promotion of new raw materials investments has not usually involved much disagreement between private actors and the state—indeed, specific ventures rarely came to the attention of central decision-makers—the protection of projects once they have actually been established has been a much more vexing problem. For both political and economic reasons, direct investments have come under attack from host-country governments. Raw materials companies can no longer prevent the loss of formal ownership, and in recent years their real control has eroded. Managers have frequently appealed to the state. However, the expenditure of state power that would be needed to protect the position of private American firms may well be disproportionate to the general economic benefits, in terms of security of supply and lower prices, that would result from a successful defense. In particular, military as well as economic and diplomatic action might be necessary to defend the "rights" of U.S. concessionaires.

The case studies in Chapters VI-VIII suggest that central decision-makers have successfully resisted private pressures: instruments of public power have not been put in the service of U.S. companies because decisions about the use of force, and about diplomatic and economic coercion, have been taken in the White House and the State Department where private influence has not been great. American leaders were only willing to use covert or overt force when they felt that broader political goals were at stake. In particular, they used force to further ideological objectives associated with minimizing the prospects for communist regimes in host countries. This goal came to dominate American policy after the Second World War, although it was presaged by the attitude of Woodrow Wilson toward the Mexican Revolution between 1912 and 1920. The increase in prominence of ideological goals is intimately related to the growth of American power during the twentieth century. Only an imperial or hegemonic state, a country so powerful that it need not concern itself with protecting its territorial integrity or economic security, can enjoy the luxury of trying to remake the world. The importance of ideology's influence on American foreign policy is discussed more fully in Chapters VIII and IX.

The first part of this chapter reviews some of the general reasons why American raw materials investors have been attacked by host-country governments after new ventures have begun actual production. The second part discusses the general response of American central decision-makers to the problem of protecting foreign raw materials investments.

The Problem of Nationalization

Foreign investment holds the seeds of its own destruction. There is a dialectic that is particularly compelling for raw materials activities in less developed areas, one that leads from initial host-country enthusiasm, to moderate dissatisfaction, to a desire to eliminate completely foreign control. The apogee of international raw materials operations completely under the dominion of private companies is past. Beginning in the 1960s, disputes between multinational corporations and host-country governments became more frequent and involved more fundamental issues.

Changes in host-country policies have both political and economic roots. The economic causes of tension have been clearly described by several scholars.[1] Host countries, particularly less developed ones, usually welcome new foreign investors because they bring capital, technical skill, and market knowledge. Export earnings and revenues from hitherto undeveloped natural resources can be a bonanza, providing additional economic and political resources without imposing any costs on the domestic population. When corporations first enter a country, they have almost always gotten very favorable terms.

[1] Vernon, *Sovereignty at Bay*, esp. Ch. 2; Vernon, *Storm over the Multinationals*, p. 151; Wells, "The Evolution of Concession Agreements"; Moran, *Copper in Chile*.

Once a project becomes viable, however, the bargaining position of the host-country improves. Foreign corporations then have large fixed investments that can only be liquidated at substantial costs. New investors are waiting in the wings, willing to offer more lucrative payments for concessions of demonstrated profitability. Host-country nationals learn skills that had previously been monopolized by foreign personnel: they develop the technological capability necessary to operate a complex enterprise by working for foreign investors or attending foreign universities. After initial capital outlays, companies usually finance additional needs through earnings generated within the host-country; their ability to offer new capital becomes less important. The economic benefits offered by the foreign investor erode. Host-country governments can profit from the revision of concession terms, land tenure practices, tax provisions, and even from expropriation or nationalization.

The political causes of host-country dissatisfaction have been at least as important as the economic ones. Governments, particularly in the Third World, have taken actions against foreign investors that have been economically self-defeating or at best neutral. The desire to weaken or eliminate foreign control is generated by the enormous economic and political salience of such enterprises in many less developed states. Oil-exporting nations, such as Saudi Arabia, Libya, Abu Dhabi, and Kuwait, which have received more than 90 percent of their foreign exchange from the operations of a single industry, are but the most extreme examples of countries in this situation. As nationalism grew during the twentieth century, Third World regimes found that attacking foreign investors offered political rewards, at least in the short run.

At first the presence of large raw materials operations did nothing more than stimulate the avarice of the local elite. In Venezuela, for instance, two American asphalt companies were taken over in 1904 and 1905 by politically influential Venezuelans who wanted to increase their own wealth.[2] A decade and a half later the dictator Juan Vincente Gomez manipulated the sale of petroleum concessions to feather the nest of his entourage. Before the

[2] U.S. Senate, *Correspondence Relating to Wrongs Done to American Citizens by the Government of Venezuela*, pp. 95ff. and 124ff.

Second World War it was difficult to separate the personal income of local potentates from national treasuries in the Arabian peninsula: higher returns meant more wealth for the king as well as the country.

In recent years the desire for personal wealth has been far less important than the desire for political power and control. The looming presence of foreign corporations as employers, taxpayers, and exporters has made them a target of nationalist resentment and, conversely, opposition to such enterprises a source of political support for new regimes. This circumstance first became evident in Mexico. Every Mexican president since 1910 has publicly viewed foreign investment with suspicion. The nationalization of the petroleum industry in 1938 raised President Cardenas to the stature of a folk-hero.[3] In 1937 the Bolivian military regime, which had come to power through a coup in 1936, secured additional support from virtually all sectors of the society by nationalizing the local subsidiary of the Standard Oil Company of New Jersey.[4] When Jacobo Arbenz was elected President in 1951, Guatemala passed an agrarian reform law that led to the takeover of United Fruit, a symbol of Yankee imperialism.[5] When Paz Estenssoro, another leftist leader, came to power in 1952, Bolivia nationalized the tin mines; if the new regime had not taken this action, its support among the workers and middle class would have fallen.[6] When Colonel Kassem took control of Iraq in 1958, one of his first acts was to press publicly for renegotiation of the Iraq Petroleum Company concession, a move that enjoyed great popular approval.[7] One of the reasons Colonel Khadaffi of Libya demanded higher prices from the oil companies in 1969 was that he wanted to discredit existing arrangements negotiated by the

[3] Baklanoff, *Expropriation of U.S. Investments*, p. 43; Cline, *The United States and Mexico*, p. 239.

[4] Ingram, *Expropriation of U.S. Property in South America*, pp. 110-15; Klein, "American Oil Companies in Latin America," pp. 63-65.

[5] U.S. House, Committee on Foreign Affairs, *Expropriation of American-Owned Property*, p. 19.

[6] Ingram, p. 126.

[7] Penrose, *The Large International Firm*, pp. 70-73; Tanzer, *Political Economy of International Oil*, p. 60.

previous regime.[8] The first important act of the military regime that came to power in Peru in 1968 was to nationalize the International Petroleum Company, an Exxon subsidiary; it celebrated the occasion by declaring October 9 a Day of National Dignity.[9] Kenneth Kaunda nationalized the Zambia copper industry in 1969 at least in part to forestall attacks from the left.[10] Perhaps the clearest example of the attractiveness of nationalization for a regime seeking political support occurred in Bolivia in 1969, when General Ovando nationalized Gulf Oil to identify his new government with Peru's reformist military. However, Bolivia surreptitiously brought Gulf back through a Spanish subsidiary during the following year because Bolivia could not operate the concession alone. When this fact became known, it contributed to Ovando's fall from power.[11] The frequency with which attacks on foreign corporations have been associated with nonconstitutional changes of regime suggests that political leaders, particularly in less developed states, have seen such actions as a way to increase their domestic support. Taking over foreign companies enhances legitimacy based on nationalist sentiments.

Labor relations have also led to action against raw materials investments. The 1938 Mexican nationalization was precipitated by a labor dispute. Strikes and unrest among workers forced governments in Venezuela in 1936, Peru in 1930, 1941, and 1960, and Bolivia in the 1940s to an uncomfortable choice between appearing to back foreign companies by using the military to control workers and allowing the country's largest industry to remain idle. In the late 1950s the International Petroleum Company in Peru exacerbated labor unrest by cutting production and forcing the layoff of a thousand workers in retaliation against a government price freeze on oil products.[12]

Foreign policy concerns have also occasionally been a source

[8] U.S. Senate, Subcommittee on Multinational Corporations, *Multinational Oil Corporations*, Report, pp. 121-22.

[9] Ingram, p. 60.

[10] Sklar, *Corporate Power in an African State*, p. 34.

[11] Ingram, pp. 155-56; *New York Times*, Jan. 24, 1970, 9:1; May 17, 1970, 29:4; *Washington Post*, Nov. 24, 1969, 4:3.

[12] Martz, "Venezuela's 'Generation of 28'," p. 29; Ingram, pp. 31, 40-41.

of host-country dissatisfaction with foreign investors. Bolivia wanted to nationalize Jersey's holdings in 1937 in part because her leaders hoped to gain diplomatic support against Paraguay by reletting the operations to Argentina. After the Second World War Chilean leaders were irked when American bans on strategic sales to the Soviet Bloc were extended to Chilean copper produced by American companies.[13]

These political considerations, coupled with increasing economic bargaining power, enabled host countries first to get more income and later formal ownership and greater effective control. Concession renegotiations to give host countries higher returns began early in the century, usually by changing from royalties (fixed in terms of the quantity of output) to payments based on the value of exports. This shift took place in the oil industry in Venezuela, Iraq, and Iran before the Second World War. Tax payments were also increased in other sectors, such as copper, during the 1920s. More dramatic changes in the distribution of economic rent came after the Second World War, must notably the institution of fifty-fifty profit-sharing arrangements in the oil industry beginning with Venezuela in the mid-1940s. American companies were not happy with these developments. Higher payments could cut into corporate profits. More important, constant renegotiation of concession terms undermined the principle of sanctity of contract, which the companies wanted to preserve.

Disputes over ownership and managerial control, rather than the distribution of economic rent, led to more acrimonious quarrels. The first major takeovers occurred in Mexico, beginning with land holdings in the 1910s and culminating with the nationalization of the oil industry in 1938. From that date until 1959 only Guatemala challenged corporate control. In fact, during the 1950s several countries liberalized their mining and petroleum codes.[14] Castro brought this quiescent period to an end. During the late 1960s there were numerous takeovers, and the pace of nationalization rapidly accelerated after 1970. The value of property expropriated in Cuba, estimated at over one billion dollars, was the largest to that date. Between 1968 and 1972 some two billion

[13] Wood, *Making of the Good Neighbor Policy*, pp. 169-70; Moran, *Copper in Chile*, p. 76.

[14] Ingram, p. 29; Moran, *Copper in Chile*, Ch.4.

dollars' worth of American property was taken in Latin America alone, an amount that exceeded the value of all expropriated holdings (including those in Cuba) during the previous decade.[15] The total value of property disputes that were settled between 1971 and July 1973, or unsettled at the latter date, was as high as $3.5 billion. A good part of this amount was accounted for by raw materials investments: of the 143 nationalization disputes outstanding in 1973, 55 percent involved resource or resource-related industries.[16] If the value of the American oil holdings affected by "participation" agreements is judged to include crude reserves, this figure would be much higher. Takeovers of U.S. resource exploitation investments are given in the following table.

This list is not complete (no full record exists), but it does give an accurate general picture. Before 1965 only two countries adopted policies that threatened substantial U.S. raw materials investments: Mexico and Cuba. Since 1965 virtually every foreign holding has come under pressure or been taken over.

American corporations have not usually been able to prevent host-country takeovers, although they have sometimes been able to increase their level of compensation. The most effective weapon possessed by corporations has been their influence in world markets. At times this enabled them to limit the sales of a raw material that was vital to the political and economic well-being of a host-country. In the early 1950s British Petroleum was able to virtually stop Iranian output by withdrawing technicians and supplies and by bringing lawsuits in third countries. Bolivia was unable to market much oil after its 1969 nationalization because of Gulf's legal actions and control of the nearest refinery capable of processing Bolivian crude. In both of these instances, private companies did regain virtually complete effective control. In Iran, as in Indonesia in the mid-1960s and Guatemala in 1953, the restoration followed a change of regime that was partly the result of U.S. covert intervention. These few cases are the exception, not the rule. Despite their ability to influence output and exports, corporations have usually been unable to reverse nationalizations.

[15] Paarlberg, "United States Attention to the Third World," p. 206.

[16] U.S. Dept. of State, "Disputes Involving U.S. Foreign Direct Investment," pp. ii, 3.

Table V-1

Foreign Takeovers of U.S. Raw Materials Investments

Year	*Commodity*	*Country*	*U.S. Company*	*Settlement or Other Valuation Indicated When Available (in millions of dollars)*
c.1900-1907	Asphalt	Venezuela		
1906	Timber	Nicaragua	George D. Emory Co.	.60
1917-1930s	Land	Mexico	numerous	40
1928	Chicle	Guatemala	P. W. Shufeldt	.23
1937	Oil	Bolivia	Exxon	1.75
1938	Oil	Mexico	numerous	24
1952	Tin	Bolivia	Some American ownership but companies controlled by non-Americans	
1953	Land	Guatemala	United Fruit	Rescinded by government that came to power in 1953
1959	Land (mostly sugar)	Cuba	numerous	1,400 (1963 estimate of U.S. State Department for all American properties, sugar accounting for about 25 percent)
1961	Oil	Iraq	Mobil, Exxon	
1961	Bauxite	Guinea	Alcan (incorporated in Canada but with considerable U.S. stock ownership)	
1964-1965	Rubber	Indonesia	Goodyear, Uniroyal	Returned by new government
1966 (1967, 1969)	Copper	Chile	Kennecott, Anaconda	345 agreed to in 1974 for full nationalization
mid-1960s	Oil	Algeria	numerous	
mid-1960s	Nonferrous Metals	Mexico	Asarco	
1967	Sulphur	Mexico	Panamerica Sulphur, Texas Gulf Sulphur, Gulf Resource and Chemical	

1968	Oil	Peru	Exxon	Shared in 76 given by Peru to settle outstanding claims in February 1974
1968	Land	Peru	Cerro	
1969	Sugar	Peru	Grace	
1969	Oil	Bolivia	Gulf	94
1969	Oil	Libya	Chappaqua	
1970	Timber	Ecuador	Georgia Pacific	.1
1970	Oil	Libya	Gulf	.350 (valued by Gulf)
1971	Tin	Bolivia	Harvest Queen Mill and Elevator Co.	1.4
1971	Zinc	Bolivia	U.S. Steel and Phillips Bros.	13.4
1971	Copper	Chile	Cerro	42
1971	Iron Ore	Chile	Bethlehem	22.3
1971 and later	Oil	Venezuela	5 U.S. majors and numerous independents	1,000+
1971	Nitrates	Chile	Anglo-Lautaro	4
1971	Bauxite	Guyana	Alcan	53.5
1972	Bauxite	Ghana	Reynolds, Union Carbide	
1972	Bauxite	Guinea	Olin Matheson	
1972	Oil	Ecuador	7 U.S. independents	
1972	Phosphates	Togo	W. R. Grace	
1972-1974	Copper, Iron Ore	Peru	Marcona	
1972	Oil	Iraq	Exxon, Mobil	
1973	Oil	Ecuador	Amerada Hess and Aminoil	
1973	Oil	Iran	5 U.S. majors and 7 independents with 40% interest in Iranian consortium	

TABLE V-1 (*cont.*)

Foreign Takeovers of U.S. Raw Materials Investments

Year	*Commodity*	*Country*	*U.S. Company*	*Settlement or Other Valuation Indicated When Available (in millions of dollars)*
1973	Oil	Libya	numerous	
1973	Fishmeal	Peru	Cargill, General Mills, and others	Shared in 76 given by Peru to settle outstanding claims in February 1974
1974	Copper	Peru	Cerro	75-79
1974	Iron Ore	Gabon	Bethlehem	
1974	Iron Ore	Venezuela	Bethlehem and U.S. Steel	101.4
1974	Bauxite	Guyana	Reynolds	14.5
1974	Bauxite	Jamaica	Kaiser, Revere	15.0+
1974-1976	Oil	Saudi Arabia	Exxon, Mobil, Socal, Texaco	
1974-1976	Oil	Abu Dhabi	Exxon, Mobil	
1974-1976	Oil	Kuwait	Gulf	
1974-1976	Oil	Nigeria	Gulf, Mobil, Socal, Texaco	
1974-1976	Oil	Qatar	Exxon, Mobil	

Sources for Table V-1: Wilkins, *Maturing of Multinational Enterprise*; U.N. Economic and Social Council, *Permanent Sovereignty over Natural Resources*, A/9716; U.N. Economic and Social Council, *Permanent Sovereignty over Natural Resources*, E/C.7/53; U.S. Dept. of State, "Nationalization, Expropriation and Other Takings of United States and Certain Foreign Property Since 1960"; U.S. Dept. of State, "Disputes Involving U.S. Foreign Direct Investment"; First National City Bank v. Banco Nacional de Cuba, "Brief for Respondent"; U.S. Senate, Committee on Foreign Relations, *Major Instances of Expropriation*.

Corporations have been more successful in increasing their compensation. When the major oil companies were taken over in the 1970s, their market power made it possible for them to secure not only compensation (amounting in Venezuela, for example, to over one billion dollars) but, more important, preferred access to crude nominally owned by host countries. The Patino Company gained better terms from Bolivia in the mid-1950s partly because it had a large interest in the only British smelter that could process Bolivian tin ore, but its ownership was not restored. When Kennecott was nationalized by the Allende regime, the company brought pressure through lawsuits in the United States and elsewhere against Chilean property, including the jets of Lanchile. In addition, Kennecott got international support because its customers and creditors in Western Europe and Japan brought pressure on their own governments. These tactics, however, did not reestablish Kennecott's legal control of Chilean mines.[17]

How effectively corporate officials have used bribery and other questionable monetary payments to protect their holdings is not known. During 1975 and 1976 many major American firms admitted to illegal foreign payoffs. Most of these involved the sale of manufactured goods. (Lockheed's payoffs are the most highly publicized example.) In the raw materials sector, United Brands probably used bribes to get Honduras to lower her export tax on bananas from $1.00 to 25¢ per box, undermining the banana-producing states' attempt to create a cartel. It is impossible to say with certainty that corporate bribes did not prevent nationalizations, but given the frequency of takeovers after 1965, few payoffs could have been successful. It is not surprising that money could not guarantee property rights. The financial rewards that corporations could offer were politically less potent than the nationalist sentiments that could be tapped by attacking foreign companies.

State Policy for the Protection of Investments: A Preview

Because corporations have not been able to defend themselves

[17] Ingram, p. 132; Moran, *Copper in Chile*, pp. 147-50.

against host countries, they have been tempted to appeal to their own governments. Such appeals have been made by American firms in spite of a business ethos that generally dictates keeping public officials at arm's length. Private pressure has presented public decision-makers with two problems: one of policy preferences and one of policy implementation.

Policy Preferences

As far as policy preferences are concerned, the maintenance of control by American corporations can further security of supply, but the use of state power to accomplish this objective can violate more general foreign policy aims. In addition, the use of force always involves risks and uncertainties, yet it may be the only alternative if a host-country regime has committed itself to nationalization. In cases concerning the protection of foreign raw materials investments, American policy-makers have consistently placed general foreign policy aims above security of supply, and security of supply above more competitive markets.

Official pronouncements about nationalizations indicate a desire to distance public institutions from private interests. The United States has never denied that foreign states had the right to take over property, but has held that such action must be pursued in a nondiscriminatory way, undertaken for public purposes, and accompanied by prompt and adequate compensation. This position was enunciated as early as the first decade of the twentieth century when Venezuela took over several American-owned asphalt companies. It was reiterated when Mexico acted against American-owned property in the second and third decades of the twentieth century. It has remained unchanged. The 1971 National Security Council Decision Memorandum on expropriation dealt with compensation, not with the restoration of ownership.

There is an interesting contrast between American and British doctrine. In both Mexico in 1938 and Iran in 1951 the British denied the right of nationalization. About 70 percent of the Mexican oil industry was owned by British interests, primarily Royal Dutch Shell, and the Chamberlain government informed Mexico that it regarded the expropriation as unwarranted and unjust and demanded the return of British assets. The British claimed that

Iran's nationalization of the Anglo-Iranian Oil Company was a breach of contract.[18] In both cases the United States accepted a foreign state's right to take over property within its borders.

I am not trying to argue that Britain has been a vigorous defender of her companies, while the United States has let American firms fend for themselves. As early as 1860 American officials asserted the right to intervene on behalf of citizens when a foreign government broke a contract with them.[19] The United States has rejected the claim that acceptance of the Calvo clause (which states that disputes between host countries and foreign companies will be resolved entirely between the two parties) precludes American intervention on behalf of corporate citizens. However, I do want to argue that official doctrine does not identify the interests and power of the United States solely with the prerogatives of its foreign investors. And in practice decision-makers have always placed more general foreign policy aims above the interests of private corporations. American legal doctrine toward nationalization has always been ambiguous: the United States has never denied that foreign sovereigns have the right to nationalize property if owners are compensated, but it has asserted its own right to intervene even if a private corporation had eschewed appeal by assenting to the Calvo doctrine, and it has never made entirely clear what would constitute prompt and adequate compensation.

Policy Implementation

In actually carrying out policy, American officials have almost always been successful in placing public objectives above private ones, despite the political resources of U.S. multinationals. Nationalized companies have not been able to use state power for their own ends. Two factors have enabled central decision-makers to resist pressures: divisions within the business community, and the concentration of policy-making in arenas that are relatively insulated from societal interest groups.

[18] Ward, "The Mexican Oil Problem," p. 508. See Shwadran, *Middle East, Oil*, p. 109, for Britain's challenge in Iran.

[19] U.S. Senate, *Correspondence Relating to Wrongs Done by Venezuela*, pp. 111-13, 118.

Divisions within the private sector have arisen from several sources. While companies that have been nationalized have often pressed for vigorous U.S. government support, financial institutions holding portfolio investments have generally favored moderation, fearing that hostility would precipitate debt renunciation. Other direct investors may also refuse to support a company that has been nationalized because they are afraid of retaliation against their own holdings. Finally, even the nationalized firm may be divided, since a hard line could jeopardize its investments in other countries or the prospects for liberal compensations.

Policy-makers have also been able to maintain the priority of public goals over private interests because most decisions concerning the response to nationalizations have been made in the White House and the State Department. These institutions are relatively impervious to private pressures. Actions initiated in Congress have more closely reflected corporate preferences. The Hickenlooper and Gonzalez amendments, which mandated economic retaliation against host-country governments that failed to provide prompt and adequate compensation, originated in Congress. But even their effects have been muted by executive discretion.

Individual nationalizations of American raw materials investments now number in the hundreds. It is impossible to analyze all of them. Chapter VI deals with the three major cases involving raw materials supplies that arose before the conclusion of the Second World War: land and oil in Mexico, oil in Bolivia, and oil in the Arabian peninsula. The American reaction to the Mexican Revolution between 1910 and the mid-1920s illuminates many of the patterns that recurred in later years as nationalizations became more frequent. American central decision-makers were willing to use diplomatic and economic instruments to protect what they understood to be the legitimate rights of American investors. However, while such measures could insure some compensation, they could not restore ownership and control. At least some elements in the private sector pressed the state to engage in armed intervention. These entreaties were rejected by central decision-makers. President Wilson did use American troops twice in Mexico, but these actions can be seen to be more consistent with an interpretation of American policy that focusses on political goals—

establishing a democratic regime or insuring Mexican support during World War I—than with one that emphasizes objectives related to the desires of American investors. Similarly, in American reactions to Bolivian and Mexican nationalizations of their oil industries in 1937 and 1938, U.S. policy was guided by broader political concerns associated with the fear of Nazi penetration of Latin America rather than by specific corporate interests.

The protection of American oil investments in the Arabian peninsula during and immediately after the Second World War is one of the most analytically significant cases discussed in this book. In the midst of the Second World War the highest American officials, including the President, the Joint Chiefs, and several cabinet officers, concluded that the public interest would be served by the government purchase of the Saudi concession then owned by Standard Oil of California and Texaco. However, central state actors were unable to carry out this policy, because the private sector was successful in moving the locus of policy-making from executive agencies to the Congress. Later proposals for the government construction of a pipeline across the Arabian peninsula and for an oil agreement with Britain also came to naught. Confronted with strong industry opposition to initiatives requiring legislative approval, the state was unable to implement its preferences.

Chapter VII deals with nationalizations that have taken place since the Second World War in countries where there is no indication that the American government used overt or covert force. This is the modal category for cases involving the protection of foreign investment. The four cases discussed in this chapter—copper in Zambia, copper in Chile from 1960 to 1970, oil and other products in Peru from 1967 to 1975, and the oil crisis of the 1970s—illustrate the caution that U.S. leaders exercised when confronting what they perceived as purely economic issues. American policy-makers were unwilling to use more than diplomatic or economic instruments when only security of supply or protection of corporate prerogatives were at stake. Furthermore, the Peruvian case illustrates the learning process that took place among U.S. political leaders as they came to realize that in the face of strong nationalist sentiments any kind of pressure could be counterproductive. Having reached this conclusion, they not only resisted pressure from the private sector but also succeeded in educating corporate managers about the political realities they confronted in doing business in the Third World.

Finally, Chapter VIII deals with four cases of nationalization of raw materials investments in which the United States did use covert or overt force: Guatemala in 1954, Cuba in the early 1960s, the Dominican Republic in 1965, and Chile under Allende. In each of these cases American economic interests were jeopardized, and radical analysts have frequently pointed to these instances to demonstrate the primacy of economic considerations in U.S. foreign policy. However, in each of these countries U.S. leaders also saw the prospect or existence of a communist-dominated regime. In general, the United States has used force only under such circumstances. The response to economic nationalism, which has been a much more frequent cause of attack on foreign investors, has prompted only diplomatic or economic pressure. For delineating the underlying preferences of American central decision-makers, this pattern suggests that general foreign policy goals have been more important than economic ones.

All of the cases discussed in Chapters VI through VIII can be understood from a statist approach. Many of them clearly strain either interest-group or instrumental Marxist interpretations. Neither of these two approaches can explain the existence of state goals that are not related to pressures from any particular societal group, or even from public opinion in general. Neither can deal adequately with the ability of central decision-makers to resist pressures from private groups.

Establishing the superiority of a statist interpretation over a structural Marxist one, however, is far more difficult. Both of these paradigms recognize the autonomy of the state: both see the state acting to protect the general structure of the society; neither tries to relate specific state actions to the desires of private corporations. Where they differ is in their definition of societal goals and the kinds of objectives that the state will seek to maximize. In the end, even a structural Marxist argument must understand state actions to be preserving the coherence of capitalist society. The goals sought by the state must ultimately be conceived in materialist terms. A statist perspective, on the other hand, can countenance nonmaterial objectives. While a state whose territorial and political integrity are threatened can be expected to act to protect these core objectives, as even a structural Marxist argument would predict, a state that is so powerful that it need not concern itself with these basic aims might well pursue other ends. And these other goals need not be related to material concerns.

Establishing the merits of a statist interpretation against those of structural Marxism hinges critically on several cases. One of these is the effort by the American government to take over the Saudi concession during the Second World War. This violation of the norms of capitalism (through the assertion of state ownership) cannot be clearly connected with any aim of maintaining the coherence of capitalism in America. Unlike unionization, or social security, or unemployment compensation, it cannot be equated with mollifying societal groups that could disrupt the system as a whole. More important, the six cases discussed in this book in which the United States used overt or covert force—Mexico in 1914 and 1916, Iran in 1953, Guatemala in 1954, Cuba in 1961, the Dominican Republic in 1965, and Chile in the early 1970s—cannot be adequately explained as involvements preserving the coherence of American capitalism. In many of these cases, the relationship between U.S. intervention and societal coherence was extremely tenuous. Few of them attracted wide public attention. While all involved economic interests, they also impinged on more general policy objectives usually associated with minimizing the presence of communist regimes in less developed countries. One can think of other cases of forceful intervention besides, including Korea, Lebanon, and Vietnam, where there were no direct economic interests but where the same general political goal was threatened. The American fixation on stopping communism was a product of a set of ideological precepts (Lockean liberalism) and America's extraordinarily powerful position in the international system, particularly after World War II. The precepts provided the goals of policy, and America's power made it possible to pursue these ends with little regard for economic or strategic interests. Moreover, as Vietnam revealed most clearly, American behavior has often been nonlogical in the sense that

U.S. leaders either misperceived the external situation (by exaggerating the communist threat) or failed to make prudent calculations about the costs and benefits of a particular policy. Such behavior is more easily understood from a statist perspective than from a Marxist orientation that emphasizes economic objectives and logical action.

CHAPTER VI

The Protection of Investments before 1950

During the first half of the twentieth century there were few attacks on American investments in general, or raw materials activities in particular. Although nationalist sentiments were already apparent, particularly in Latin America, the economic bargaining power of host countries remained weak; they did not have the market knowledge, capital resources, or technical skills to challenge the multinationals. The regimes of most host countries were conservative: the institution of private property was not under attack.

However, there were several major exceptions to this tranquil situation. The most obvious was the Soviet Union. There were a number of American manufacturing enterprises in Russia before the revolution. All were lost. Investors received little compensation. At the time of the revolution there was virtually no American activity in the area of raw materials exploitation, although Standard Oil of New Jersey did pay several million dollars for a share of Nobel's Russian oil concession after the revolution had taken place.[1] (Confidence in the inevitable triumph of capitalism was stronger then.)

The country that did present a major threat to American operations was Mexico. When the revolution began in 1910, Mexico was the largest single recipient of U.S. raw materials investments. Although serious questions have been raised in recent years about how revolutionary the revolution actually was, the rhetoric of Mexican leaders was egalitarian and nationalistic. And American investors were clearly a target.

For twenty-five years American policy-makers struggled with both Mexico and American investors in an ultimately successful

[1] Gibb and Knowlton, *History of Standard Oil Company*, p. 337.

effort to maintain the primacy of state objectives over private interests. The United States was willing to use diplomatic and economic pressure to secure adequate compensation, but it was not willing to use force. When American officials saw the possibility of a German-Mexican liaison during World War I and Nazi infiltration in Latin America before the Second World War, they opted decisively for security interests, despite the strenuous opposition of the American oil industry. In dealing with Mexico, central decision-makers were successful in preserving the primacy of public aims, because decisions were taken primarily in the White House and the State Department. The levers of power on Pennsylvania Avenue were not easily reached.

The other major case examined in this chapter involves oil investment in the Arabian peninsula during the Second World War. Here American policy-makers were fundamentally interested in security of supply. To achieve this they felt it was necessary to introduce state participation into the international oil industry through the public ownership of oil fields or pipelines. The industry adamantly opposed such action. The executive could not secure the financial resources needed to implement this project without going to Congress. The levers of power in the Congress were within the industry's grasp. Private preferences prevailed.

In these instances, the conception of national interest held by American officials was not vague and amorphous, or simply the product of an agglomeration of private aims. They first sought general foreign policy aims, then security of supply, then greater competition. What was confusing was the implementation of policy. Central decision-makers did not always get what they wanted, not because they did not know what they wanted, but because when they could not hold decisions within executive agencies, the fragmentation of the American political system prevented them from implementing their priorities.

Mexico, 1910-1928

In Mexico during the second and third decades of the twentieth century American investors first encountered the kind of intense nationalist reaction against foreign investment that was to dog them in later years. The management of this situation illustrates both the relative importance of different state policy goals and the political interaction between central decision-makers and private corporations. American leaders consistently gave broader foreign policy objectives concerned with the nature of the regime in Mexico and with prevention of German incursions a higher priority than economic aims associated with either insuring supplies or protecting private corporations. In dealing with Mexico, U.S. leaders were able to implement their preferences fairly well because decisions about the use of force, economic coercion, and diplomacy were kept away from institutions like Congress where investors might have more effectively brought their power to bear.

Mexican Policy

The Mexican Revolution produced the first major thrust against American foreign investments. There had been earlier attacks on property in Venezuela and Nicaragua, but the value of the losses was not great and, in any case, the attacks were motivated by personal cupidity rather than national ideology. In Russia also American raw materials investments were modest. But Mexico was a different story. Porfirio Diaz, who ruled from 1876 to 1911, had actively encouraged foreign investment. American holdings in mining, petroleum, and agriculture grew rapidly, particularly after 1900. A 1912 consular report made the following estimates for the Mexican mining industry:

TABLE VI-1

Value of Foreign Mining Investments in Mexico
(in thousands of dollars)

	American	*British*	*French*	*Mexican*	*Other*
Mines	223,000	43,600	5,000	7,500	7,830
Smelters	26,500	—	—	7,500	3,000

Source: Bernstein, *The Mexican Mining Industry 1890-1950*, p. 75.

By far the largest mining interests in Mexico were those of the Guggenheims, who operated through the American Smelting and Refining Company (Asarco) as well as other companies. But there were many other American mining investors whose holdings included mines, processing plants, and railways. Mexican petroleum production began during the first decade of the century. The first substantial commercial operation was the Mexican Petroleum Company controlled by Edward Doheny. After 1906 Doheny was challenged by the British Mexican Eagle or El Aguila Petroleum Company. There were also extensive American agricultural holdings. These included not only large plantations but also a number of small- and medium-sized farms. By 1910 two-thirds of Mexico's total accumulated investment outside of handicraft and agriculture was foreign controlled. One-seventh of the land surface of the country was owned by foreigners. U.S. holdings were greater than all other foreign holdings combined.[2] This situation prompted a nationalist reaction, which made limiting the activities of non-Mexican, particularly American, companies one of the cardinal principles of Mexican political life.

The reaction against foreign control had begun even before 1910. Diaz and members of his entourage became increasingly concerned about the huge American presence. Given past experience (the Mexican–American War), the possibility of American annexations of Mexican territory could not be ignored. Beginning around 1905, Diaz adopted policies that favored British oil interests. In 1906 he granted a concession to a British firm, S. Pearsons and Sons, which later became the Mexican Eagle Oil Company. Pearsons received terms that were more favorable than those given to American oil men. The new company's board of directors included Diaz's son and his finance minister. In 1910 the Mexican government, or more precisely the Mexican National Railway, imposed a 50 centavo per ton tax on oil shipped from Tampico. This affected the American companies, but not Mexican Eagle, which sent its oil through a pipeline to tankers waiting offshore at Tuxpan. This tax was several times greater than the royalties that the companies were paying. The president of the

[2] Bernstein, *The Mexican Mining Industry*, pp. 50-60; Mexican Petroleum Company Ltd. of Delaware, *Consolidated Balance Sheet and Profit and Loss Account*, 1914, p. 9; Rippy, *Oil and the Mexican Revolution*, p. 153; Baklanoff, *Expropriation of U.S. Investments*, p. 34; Bemis, *Latin American Policy*, pp. 43, 170.

Mexican National Railway in 1910 was also the head of the Mexican Eagle Oil Company. Aside from petroleum, Diaz also took modest steps in other areas. In 1910, after several years of discussion, a new mining law was passed. Although it hardly represented a fundamental attack on foreign investment, it was somewhat less favorable than previous legislation.[3]

In the decades after the Mexican Revolution there were many differences among the men who ruled Mexico. For both political and economic reasons, however, they all adopted policies more antagonistic to foreign investment than those of Diaz. Nationalist sentiments made attacks on foreign investors a potent source of popular support. Mining and petroleum exploitation represented a major potential source of revenue for governments that were constantly strapped for funds; after the revolution even the most conservative of Mexico's leaders imposed new taxes on large mineral and agricultural operations. Some public encroachment on private capital was inevitable.

Perhaps even more important for foreign investors was the civil strife that lasted for a decade. The oil zone was the scene of serious fighting only in 1914, but until 1920 peace and order were provided by a local caudillo. The operations of many other foreign enterprises, particularly in the mining sector, were more seriously curtailed. Only 14 out of 110 mining companies were able to work steadily from 1914 to 1919. Many small American farmers were driven from their homes, particularly after the landing of American troops at Vera Cruz in 1914. The losses incurred by U.S. investors between 1910 and 1920 have been estimated as high as $500 million, although the actual awards granted by the Special Mexican Claims Commission in 1938 came to only $5.2 million. Petroleum was the only area of foreign activity where investments actually increased during the first decade of the revolution.[4] It was also the one that produced the greatest political tensions.

[3] Rippy, 135-36; Bernstein, pp. 78-83; U.S. National Archives, Records of the Department of State Relating to Internal Affairs of Mexico, 1910-1929, M274, Microfilm Reel 214, Decimal File No. 812.6363/124 (henceforth cited as Records Relating to Internal Affairs of Mexico).

[4] Bernstein, 105; Wilkins, *Maturing of Multinational Enterprise*, p. 39.

Diaz fell from power in 1911, driven out by forces supporting Francisco Madero. Madero was a political reformer and an economic conservative. He came from one of Mexico's leading industrial families. But he did take some modest measures to curb the prerogatives of foreign enterprises and to make Mexico more independent. In 1912 he imposed a special 20¢ per ton tax on petroleum. The state of Vera Cruz also levied a tax. Madero tried, moreover, to increase the number of Mexicans working in the railway system, which was largely foreign owned. Members of Madero's family had mining and petroleum interests that brought them into conflict with outside investors, particularly the Guggenheims. More important for foreign investment, Madero was not able to establish control over the country. While his forces held Mexico City, fighting continued in other areas. There was also an increase in labor unrest.[5] The lack of civil order represented a greater problem for foreign companies than Madero's modest reforms.

In 1913 Madero was overthrown and probably murdered by one of his own generals, Victoriano Huerta. Huerta was identified with those elements of the Diaz regime that had continued to support foreign investment. He was certainly the most conservative political leader in Mexico during the first decade of the revolution. However, even he felt compelled to take some measures that infringed upon the prerogatives of alien capitalists. By 1913 he was in deep financial difficulties (in part because of economic sanctions imposed by the United States). He raised the special oil tax from 20¢ to 75¢ per ton. He imposed irregular levies on foreign corporations, which some of them categorized as blackmail.[6] Huerta also was unable to establish suzerainty over the countryside, and as we shall see, his position was undermined by American opposition and the occupation of the port of Vera Cruz. In 1914 he was defeated by a coalition of dissident leaders that included Pancho Villa, Venustiano Carranza, and Emiliano Zapata.

[5] Records Relating to Internal Affairs of Mexico, Reel 214, Decimal File No. 812.6363/124; Meyer, *El Conflicto Petrolero*, p. 47; Bernstein, pp. 98-101.

[6] Records Relating to Internal Affairs of Mexico, Reel 214, Decimal File No. 812.6363/90; Bernstein, p. 97; U.S. Senate, Committee on Foreign Relations, *Investigation of Mexican Affairs*, pp. 284-87.

This coalition quickly disintegrated, however. In 1915 Carranza took control of the capital. He treated foreign investment less favorably than Diaz, Madero, or Huerta. Carranza was particularly concerned with the petroleum sector. It was the most attractive area for reform from the standpoint of internal politics. Its legal status was peculiar because Diaz had given foreign companies ownership of subsoil rights; under Roman law these were generally reserved to the state. Oil was dominated by foreigners. Attacks on the industry tapped powerful anti-American sentiments. Petroleum taxes could become a major source of revenue for the new government. Even before he had consolidated his power, Carranza had taken modest measures against the industry, such as requiring state approval for the transfer of ownership in the oil zone. In 1915 he began imposing new taxes. He also ordered additional exploration and development stopped until new legislation had been promulgated. The attitude of the Carranza regime was formalized in Article 27 of the 1917 Constitution, which vested subsoil rights in the state and thus left uncertain the status of concessions granted by the previous government. A new petroleum law passed in 1918 imposed higher taxes and required the oil companies to reregister their holdings with the government.[7]

In 1920 Alvaro Obregon became President. Tensions began to ease. In 1923 the United States and Mexico signed the Bucareli Agreement, which provided that confiscated land would be compensated for with Mexican bonds, and that Mexico would honor oil concessions if some positive development had taken place prior to the promulgation of the 1917 Constitution. However, the 1925 oil law, which included the Calvo clause and required companies to apply for confirmatory concession, led to new problems. In June of 1927 the Mexican army prevented oil companies that had not complied with the law from drilling. This phase of the dispute was resolved by the Morrow–Calles Accord of 1928 between the United States and Mexico, in which Mexico confirmed the ownership of petroleum concessions held prior to 1917, while the companies implicitly recognized Mexico's ownership of sub-

[7] Meyer, pp. 79-88; Cumberland, *Mexican Revolution*, pp. 247-51; Smith, *Revolutionary Nationalism in Mexico*, p. 117.

soil rights.[8] The situation remained relatively quiescent until 1938 when Mexico nationalized her petroleum industry.

In sum, the Mexican Revolution led to nationalist attacks on U.S. investments. It would have been virtually impossible for any Mexican regime to restore the prerogatives enjoyed by foreign investors in 1900. However, there were substantial variations in the attitudes of different Mexican leaders. During the first decade of the revolution Huerta appeared to offer the most favorable prospects for American private economic interests.

The American Response

The Mexican Revolution began at a time when the United States was actively expanding its control in the western hemisphere. Although the Monroe Doctrine had been enunciated almost a century before, it had had little practical effect. During the nineteenth century Britain had regularly stationed gunboats off Mexico and Peru to protect investments. At various times Britain had blockaded Nicaragua, Argentina, and El Salvador. In 1897 German gunboats had threatened Port-au-Prince, Haiti; in 1900 the French had moved against Santo Domingo in the Dominican Republic; in 1901 Britain, France, Germany, Belguim, and Italy prepared to occupy Guatemalan ports; and in 1902-1903 Germany and Britain blockaded Venezuela. The pretense for most of these actions was economic, particularly the failure of Caribbean countries to meet loan payments to European financiers.[9]

The United States began to translate her economic and military strength into political control in the Caribbean around 1900. The Spanish–American War established U.S. dominance in Cuba and Puerto Rico. Support for the Panamanian revolt in 1903 insured American control of the canal across the isthmus. In 1905 Theodore Roosevelt announced that the United States would take a more direct interest in the financial affairs of the Caribbean republics, because this was the only way in which the pretense for

[8] Kane, "American Business and Foreign Policy," p. 310, n. 52; Smith, *Revolutionary Nationalism in Mexico*, p. 254; Cline, *The United States and Mexico*, p. 230.

[9] Preston and Major, *Send a Gunboat!*, p. 85; Munro, *Dollar Diplomacy*, pp. 14, 65, 87, 143.

European intervention could be eliminated. The United States took over customs collection, the largest source of government revenue, for several Caribbean countries. Naval interventions to protect American lives and property occurred in the Dominican Republic and Central America. In 1911 American troops were sent into Honduras, in 1912 into Nicaragua, in 1915 into Haiti, and in 1916 into the Dominican Republic.[10]

The growing American military presence corresponded with an increase in economic activity. American direct investments and foreign loans grew rapidly after 1900. Under Taft the State Department consciously moved to become the major source of credit for the Caribbean. Loans were an instrument of foreign policy. Debtor countries changed their political and military policies to gain access to the financial markets of more powerful countries. However, prior to the First World War, European investments in the Caribbean were still larger than American.[11]

There can be no empirical resolution of the question whether American policy after 1900 should be explained in terms of strategic objectives (excluding European influence from the Caribbean) or economic ones (protecting American investors), because American expansion coincided with both growing military and economic power. Although military intervention is the most costly instrument of policy, it was still cheap when used against the small and weak republics of the Caribbean. The presence of a hundred marines was sufficient to maintain civil order in Nicaragua.

Mexico presented American policy-makers with far more difficult problems. The country was large and intervention would require substantial forces: there was no easy military resolution to the Mexican problem. For this reason Mexico offers a much more interesting case for answering two of the major questions of this study, about the aims of American policy-makers and about the relationship between the private sector and the state. The Mexican Revolution presented a threat to several goals of American leaders. The clearest were economic interests. Next to Canada,

[10] Munro, pp. 107-11, 130-33, 148-49, 228, 307; Van Alstyne, *Rising American Empire*, p. 168.

[11] Munro, pp. 16, 163ff.; Feis, *Europe*, for the relationship of capital and international politics.

Mexico had the largest amount of American foreign investment in 1914, and the book value of petroleum and mining holdings was greater than in any other country.[12] Mexican oil was perceived as being important to meet the needs of the United States and, during the war, of her allies. Once war with Germany became imminent, Mexico presented a strategic problem: the Germans tried to entice Mexico into a neutral position and entangle the United States in a way that would have precluded an active military role in Europe. Finally, the Mexican Revolution impinged upon the visionary objectives of American foreign policy, the desire to fashion a world system composed of states created in the American image. Events in Mexico between 1910 and 1920 involved private interests, security of supply, and more general foreign policy aims.

To arrive at a judgment about which of these objectives was paramount, it is necessary to ask how far American officials were willing to go in protecting each of them. In terms of costs to the domestic polity, the cheapest instrument is diplomatic protest, next economic sanctions, and finally military intervention. The United States twice intervened in Mexico: once in 1913 and 1914 when American troops occupied the port of Vera Cruz, and once in 1916 when some 12,000 men were sent across the Mexican border in pursuit of Pancho Villa. Neither of these episodes can be explained by economic interests. Vera Cruz is only comprehensible in terms of Woodrow Wilson's world vision. The Pershing expedition of 1916 was prompted by a raid on American territory and was terminated to insure Mexican neutrality during the First World War.

The protection of the private sector was limited to diplomatic and economic pressure in spite of growing demands by some groups for direct intervention. Economic nationalism in Mexico was a potent force. At least in the minerals sector, American investors were not willing to compromise, even with the conservative regimes of Madero and Huerta. Foreign companies resisted higher taxes and changes in legal regulations. The antagonism of direct investors increased during Carranza's rule. Although the American government was assiduous in its diplomatic protection of American firms, it refused to use force despite private en-

[12] Wilkins, *Emergence of Multinational Enterprise*, p. 110.

treaties. Public decision-makers were able to resist pressure because the use of force was the prerogative of the White House, and because there were divisions within the private sector, particularly after 1920.

DIAZ AND MADERO

In the struggle that led to the overthrow of Diaz in 1911, the United States took no firm stand. At least in Washington, there was a strong consensus against intervention. The Secretary of State, Philander Knox, argued that it would be impossible to protect American lives and property in a country as large as Mexico. On balance decisions taken by the United States were probably mildly supportive of Madero. The rebellion was partly organized in the United States, where many of Madero's supporters were living. U.S. neutrality in 1910-1911 hurt Diaz.[13]

However, once Madero had taken power in Mexico City, but was unable to impose order in the countryside, the weight of American policy swung against him. Henry Lane Wilson, the American Ambassador to Mexico, had persistently urged more vigorous intervention. He openly supported Huerta in 1913 and was probably involved in the coup itself. In August 1912 the United States posted naval vessels off Mexican ports, and in September a strong note about threats to American lives and property was sent. Taft also ordered 20,000 troops to the Mexican border. The State Department protested Madero's increase in petroleum taxes.[14]

There was no sharp distinction between the policy implemented by the United States toward Diaz and Madero and the preferences

[13] Haley, *Diplomacy with Mexico*, pp. 25, 30-31; Bemis, p. 171.

[14] Haley, pp. 25-44; Bemis, pp. 171-74; Meyer, pp. 49-50; Blasier, "The United States and the Revolution," pp. 34-35. Blasier argues strongly that Ambassador Wilson was heavily involved in Madero's overthrow and that, in supporting those who opposed Madero, Wilson exceeded his authority. Blasier attributes Wilson's behavior primarily to his personality. Wilson's independence can be seen as a manifestation of a weak political system. In America the problem of controlling ambassadors may have been exacerbated because until recently most were appointed for political reasons and their political loyalties were not necessarily to the President. In Henry Lane Wilson's case, his brother, who died in 1912, had been a powerful Republican Senator.

of the private sector. Diaz's efforts to offset American influence by encouraging European investment had disaffected oil and mining interests. In 1911 Edward Doheny of the Mexican Petroleum Company had opposed American intervention on behalf of Diaz on the grounds that it would only benefit the British. Some American oil companies may have given financial assistance to Madero.[15]

Once Madero came to power, however, he proved no more favorable to U.S. investors. He did not change the differential tax structure for British and American petroleum that had been established by Diaz. The Guggenheims became involved in a dispute with members of Madero's family who were engaged in mining. Most important, Madero's inability to bring peace to all of Mexico presented a threat to American companies. There was no strong support for Madero within the private sector.[16] For analyzing American foreign policy, the early years of the Mexican Revolution are not very revealing, for both public and private decision-makers were confused. Neither group had ever had to deal with a full-scale revolution. The reaction of both to Diaz and Madero was negative, but still hesitant and indecisive.

HUERTA

The American response to the regime of Victoriano Huerta is analytically far more interesting: Huerta's rule was as close as Mexico came to a restoration of pre-1910 policies, although even he was constrained by nationalism and financial stringency. Despite his political and economic conservatism, Huerta was strongly opposed by Woodrow Wilson. This opposition took the form not only of diplomatic pressure but also of the occupation of the port of Vera Cruz in 1914. Wilson made his first diplomatic proposal to Huerta in June of 1913, four months after Huerta had secured control of Mexico City. Wilson offered to try to end hostilities between Huerta and the Constitutionalists, whose main

[15] Meyer, p. 41; Rippy, pp. 138-39; Wilkins, *Emergence of Multinational Enterprise*, p. 130.

[16] Meyer, p. 45. See Records Relating to Internal Affairs of Mexico, Reel 214, Decimal File No 812.6363/115 for a report that Jersey Standard and Asarco had opposed both Diaz and Madero.

leaders were Carranza, Villa, and Zapata, if Huerta would hold a free election in which he himself would not be a candidate. Huerta rejected what was in effect a demand to abdicate. President Wilson dismissed Henry Lane Wilson in August 1913 because the Ambassador supported Huerta. To circumvent the State Department, he sent a number of his own specially appointed representatives to Mexico. In January 1914 Wilson sanctioned the sale of arms to the Constitutionalists (who were opposing Huerta), despite the formal embargo that was still in effect. In February he lifted the embargo altogether, an act that benefitted the Constitutionalists, who controlled the northern part of the country. Wilson condemned European powers, particularly Britain, for extending diplomatic recognition to Huerta. He attributed their action to a desire to protect oil holdings, and ultimately forced the British to withdraw recognition because of their need for American support in the First World War.[17]

American pressure against Huerta was not limited to these more or less conventional means. In April 1914 Wilson seized upon a petty incident to land some 20,000 American troops at the port of Vera Cruz. His basic objective was to overthrow Huerta, although he was not willing to launch a full-scale American invasion of Mexico.[18] U.S. forces did not actually fight against Huerta, but they did weaken his position by denying control of Mexico's major port. In August 1914 the Constitutionalists defeated Huerta. U.S. troops left Vera Cruz in November.

It is not possible to explain American behavior in terms of economic interests or economic pressure. The initial reaction of American investors to Huerta was very favorable. Banking, railway, and minerals investors all urged recognition. The positive attitude of American private interests continued through the summer of 1913. In 1920 Senator Albert Fall held a series of hearings on the Mexican situation in which American investors made it clear that they felt Huerta was their last best hope. Many witnesses, including small farmers as well as large investors, testified

[17] Link, *Woodrow Wilson*, pp. 113-14, 119-20; Baker, *Life and Letters*, p. 262; Bemis, pp. 176-78; Haley, pp. 123ff.; Meyer, p. 56.

[18] Smith, *Revolutionary Nationalism in Mexico*, p. 34; Link, p. 123; Haley, pp. 131ff.

that their troubles in Mexico began with the American occupation of Vera Cruz and the fall of Huerta. They saw Huerta as the one man who could have brought order to Mexico.[19]

The private sector did begin to turn from Huerta during the latter part of 1913, but this shift occurred only after Wilson's refusal to extend recognition and U.S. financial sanctions had placed Huerta in a difficult position. Huerta raised petroleum taxes from 20 centavos to 75 centavos per ton in October of 1913. He did not change the differential tax benefit enjoyed by British firms. This behavior was hardly surprising given the diplomatic support he got from London in the fall of 1913. American companies protested the increase in taxes and asked the State Department for assistance. In addition, Doheny claimed in 1920 that he stopped paying taxes to Huerta (who never had physical control of the oil fields) when the American government refused to recognize his regime, although this public testimony might only have been an effort to ingratiate the Mexican Petroleum Company with the Carranza regime.[20]

As Huerta's government disintegrated, American investors were confronted with the same problems of disorder that had plagued them since 1910. In September the president of one small oil company complained that both Huerta and the Constitutionalists were demanding rental for land on which the company held a lease from the Mexican National Railway. Americans could not avoid the widespread armed clashes. The transportation system was in chaos. Sales of the Mexican Petroleum Company, the largest American producer, fell from 12.3 million barrels in 1913 to 8.2 million in 1914.[21]

When fighting actively took place in the petroleum zone in the spring of 1914, a number of petroleum companies urged the United States to take immediate steps to protect the oil fields. However, Wilson refused to extend the occupation of American

[19] Link, pp. 108-9; Daniels, *The Wilson Era*, p. 181; Meyer, pp. 50-51; Baker, *Life and Letters*, pp. 245-47; U.S. Senate, *Mexican Affairs*, pp. 773-77, 1427, 1430, 2174, 2177-78, 2243-44, 2422, 2615.

[20] U.S. Senate, *Mexican Affairs*, pp. 277-79; Meyer, p. 56.

[21] Records Relating to Internal Affairs of Mexico, Reel 214, Decimal File No. 812.6363/133; Mexican Petroleum Company, *Balance Sheet*, p. 17.

troops beyond the port of Vera Cruz. The State Department did try to get Carranza and Huerta to declare the oil-producing area a neutral zone, but Carranza refused because this would have given his opponent a military advantage. The State Department did not press the point, but accepted assurances from both sides that American lives and property would not be molested.[22]

The economic difficulties that led private investors to drop their support for Huerta were the result of the actions of the American government as well as internal developments within Mexico. It was Woodrow Wilson's opposition that, at least in part, prevented Huerta from consolidating his regime. This opposition can only be explained by reference to Wilson's general foreign policy objectives. Wilson wanted to create an international system composed of democratic states. Huerta had murdered his predecessor and dismissed the Mexican legislature. This behavior Wilson found intolerable, even though Huerta had indicated that he would treat American business interests favorably. In Mexico the pattern Wilson was later to follow in Europe was already apparent. He eschewed selfish motivations. He rejected the pleas of American private interests. He saw British recognition as a selfish effort to protect their oil investments. In his biography Ray Stannard Baker suggests that Wilson identified Huerta as an enemy in the same way that he had earlier identified Dean West at Princeton in the dispute over the location of the new graduate school, and was later to focus on Lodge in the struggle over ratification of the League. This is a telling analogy given the psychological difficulty Wilson had in reaching compromises with strong-willed opponents.[23] Huerta had to go, even though (or for Wilson, perhaps, because) he would have served identifiable American economic and political interests better than any other Mexican head of state after 1910. For Wilson, backing Huerta would have been selfish and unprincipled. American policy was Wilson's, and American investors tried to accommodate themselves to it as best they could.

[22] Records Relating to Internal Affairs of Mexico, Reel 213, Decimal File Nos. 812.6363/29/33/34/38/67.

[23] Baker, *Life and Letters*, p. 311. See the Georges, *Wilson and House*, for a brilliant analysis of Wilson's personality.

CARRANZA

Wilson's domestic political problems in dealing with Carranza were the opposite of those he had confronted with Huerta: he wanted to be less aggressive than private investors, rather than more. Wilson had initially looked with favor on the Constitutionalists, for he saw them as a legitimate alternative to Huerta. He had first offered help to Carranza, but when the Mexican leader made it clear that he would consider any American direction undue interference, Wilson turned to Pancho Villa, who appeared to be more pliable.[24] However, Wilson was never able to find a Mexican protégé, and the attention of the United States was forced to more mundane objectives: the protection of American investors and the prevention of a Mexican alliance with Germany. The problem was to design a policy that would secure these goals. Wilson ultimately settled on a formula of protecting private citizens through diplomatic intervention and economic sanctions, but not military intervention. A full-scale invasion would have violated broader foreign policy objectives, particularly commitment to the war in Europe, and might also have pricked Wilson's conscience.

The United States made frequent diplomatic protests against many Mexican efforts to change the rules governing foreign investment. In 1914, even before Carranza had consolidated his rule, the State Department supported the oil companies when they refused to pay higher taxes. In 1915 the companies, with official support, objected to signing a decree that would have obligated them to obey all new petroleum legislation. The State Department disputed another decree in January 1915 that, at least at first, appeared to halt all petroleum activity until new legislation could be promulgated. The United States ominously threatened "serious complications and consequences."[25] Carranza later explained that his action was meant to apply only to new operations. When Carranza tried to get higher taxes from mining activities, most of which were under Villa's rule in the north, the State Department indicated that it did not recognize his edicts as having force out-

[24] Link, pp. 121-31.

[25] U.S. Senate, Special Committee Investigating Petroleum Resources, *Diplomatic Protection of American Petroleum Interests*, p. 52.

side the territory he controlled. At the same time, the United States vigorously protested regulations by Villa providing for the forfeiture of unworked mining concessions.[26]

Diplomatic activity increased with the promulgation of the new Mexican Constitution in 1917. Both the companies and the American government complained about the petroleum legislation passed in 1918 that required the companies to apply for new drilling leases. Such applications would have tacitly implied that the government owned subsoil rights, that the companies were concessionaires rather than owners.[27]

Pressure was not limited to diplomacy: the United States also used economic instruments to protect private investors. By 1917 American export restrictions made it difficult for Mexico to secure certain commodities. The Secretary of State informed Carranza's government that the United States would not sign a trade agreement until Mexico recognized the rights of American property owners. More important, the federal government limited loans to Mexico. In 1916 and 1917 several American bankers turned down Mexican applications because the State Department would not approve them. Such approval was made conditional on respect for the claims of American investors.[28]

There was also during the Carranza period a second episode of armed intervention by the United States. In March 1916 Pancho Villa raided Columbus, New Mexico, and murdered sixteen Americans. This action came after Wilson had recognized Carranza rather than Villa. It led to an immediate military response by the United States. A military expedition under General Pershing was sent after Villa. By June Pershing had some 12,000 men under his command and was 300 miles into Mexico. This action was originally undertaken with Carranza's approval. The Mexican border had been turbulent for many years, and hot pur-

[26] Dunn, *Diplomatic Protection of Americans*, p. 328; Records Relating to Internal Affairs of Mexico, Reel 214, Decimal File Nos. 812.6363/146-149/152; Meyer, pp. 68-71.

[27] Smith, *Revolutionary Nationalism in Mexico*, p. 106; Cumberland, p. 395; Meyer, p. 99.

[28] Smith, "The Formation and Development of the International Bankers Committee on Mexico," p. 576; Smith, *Revolutionary Nationalism in Mexico*, p. 114; Kane, p. 298; Meyer, p. 98.

suit of bandits across the boundary line was not uncommon. However, Carranza had not expected such a large-scale American intervention. Pershing was able to disperse Villa's men, but he was not able to catch Villa. By June there had been armed confrontations between Carranza's forces and U.S. troops. In September negotiations began on American withdrawal. The United States tried to link Pershing's recall with the protection of American lives and property, but Carranza rejected this effort. With the imminent entry of America into the First World War, the troops returned without conditions.[29]

Without doubt the Pershing expedition was more than an effort to capture Villa. Large numbers of American troops in Mexico did have political implications. Yet it was not simply an effort to force Carranza to change his policies. It did have at least the initial approval of the Mexican government. Villa did present a real threat to the security of border areas. Furthermore, the troops were unconditionally withdrawn. As Wilson had shown at Vera Cruz, he was willing to use force to advance American objectives in Mexico, but it is difficult to understand these objectives simply in terms of the prerogatives of American private investors.

This conclusion is further supported by the fact that American policy toward Carranza was not entirely negative despite the diplomatic, economic, and military pressure that was brought against him. The war in Europe presented the danger of German encroachment in the western hemisphere through an alliance with Mexico. This possibility led to *de facto* American recognition of Carranza in 1915; *de jure* recognition was extended after the United States received ambiguous assurance that any action implementing the 1917 Constitution would be "nonconfiscatory."[30]

These conciliatory steps were designed to make sure that Mexico did not establish a liaison with Germany. As bizarre as this possibility appears in retrospect, it was actively pursued by the Germans. German agents made contact with Huerta after he had been driven from power and tried to fund a counterrevolution

[29] Smith, *Revolutionary Nationalism in Mexico*, Ch. 3; Meyer, p. 84; Link, pp. 136-44; Haley, pp. 188ff.

[30] Smith, *Revolutionary Nationalism in Mexico*, p. 109; Bemis, p. 183; Meyer, pp. 84-85.

that they hoped would so embroil the United States that it would be impossible for substantial numbers of American troops to go to Europe. Later the German Foreign Minister Zimmermann sent a telegram to Carranza suggesting the possibility of regaining territory that Mexico had lost to the United States seventy years before. This was intercepted by British intelligence and passed to U.S. officials.[31] Despite the unhappiness of private investors, the American government tempered its diplomatic opposition to Carranza in order to lessen the possibility that he would establish ties with Germany.

Throughout the Carranza period many American investors advocated stronger American action, including outright military intervention. The larger oil companies were especially insistent. They consistently resisted changes in Mexican legislation providing for, among other things, higher taxes, claims to ownership of subsoil rights, and requirements for new drilling permits.[32]

To some extent, American investors were able to protect themselves. The oil companies operated in the Tampico area, where the central government was not able to establish its authority. *De facto* control was exercised by a local leader, Manuel Palaez. Palaez's position was strengthened by payments from the investors, who argued that otherwise the wells might be destroyed. The State Department strongly defended this practice on the grounds that the companies had no choice.[33]

Buying a local caudillo, though, was not enough. Palaez did not claim national power. The port of Tampico, through which most of the oil was exported, was under the control of the central government. The companies' own resources were not sufficient to protect their interests. They appealed to the American government.

Private entreaties were addressed to the White House and the Fuel Administration as well as the State Department. At the diplomatic level, the State Department did protest every major effort

[31] Munro, p. 270; Link, pp. 133-35, 200; Blasier, *Hovering Giant*, pp. 106-16; Rausch, "The Exile and Death of Victoriano Huerta," *passim*.

[32] Meyer, pp. 94-97.

[33] Smith, *Revolutionary Nationalism in Mexico*, pp. 102-3; Meyer, pp. 72-73; U.S. Senate, *Mexican Affairs*, pp. 280-82, 839, 944-45.

by the Mexican regime to change the economic and legal framework that had been established by Diaz. But in 1915 and 1917 investors failed to persuade Washington to withhold recognition until Carranza pledged that he would respect their claims. In both cases the American government acted as if avoiding a clear break, which could have sent Mexico into closer relations with Germany, was more important than protecting the immediate interests of U.S. corporations.[34]

The sharpest failures of private direct investors to secure government support came not in the diplomatic arena, but in the military one. From 1913 to 1919 there was a well-organized campaign, spearheaded by Senator Albert Fall and William Buckley (legal representative for a number of oil investors), to use military pressure to turn Mexico into an American protectorate. After the promulgation of the 1917 Constitution, this position gained new supporters. In 1918 the head of Jersey Standard's Mexican operations wrote his superiors that only U.S. intervention could save the Mexican situation. He himself had been severely beaten and robbed. In the same year Jersey's counsel advocated the withdrawal of recognition and the dispatch of American warships. In August of 1918 Wilson explicitly rejected an oil company proposal that included military intervention.[35]

Pressure continued to build through 1919. By the end of the year those advocating intervention included not only many members of the private sector but also the Secretary of the Interior, Franklin K. Lane (who accepted a lucrative offer from Doheny in 1920), Wilson's son-in-law William Gibbs McAdoo, and Thomas Gregory, who had been Secretary of the Treasury and Attorney General respectively earlier in Wilson's administration. But in December 1919, in one of the first official meetings after his stroke, Wilson propped himself up in his sickbed and said no to a delegation that was led by Senator Fall.[36]

[34] Wilkins, *Maturing of Multinational Enterprise*, p. 34; Smith, *ibid.*, pp. 95-96.

[35] Gibb and Knowlton, pp. 88, 361; Trow, "Mexican Interventionist Movement," pp. 46-72; Smith, *ibid.*, p. 24.

[36] Smith, *ibid.*, pp. 168-175; Trow, "Mexican Interventionist Movement," pp. 48, 63. For additional members of the private sector supporting intervention see U.S. Senate, *Mexican Affairs*, pp. 1438, 2190, 2245-46.

In sum, American policy during the first decade of the Mexican Revolution sheds light on both of the analytic problems associated with elaborating a statist paradigm: policy goals and policy implementation. For defining the objectives of American central decision-makers, it indicates that the general foreign policy goals of influencing the nature of the regime in Mexico and preserving solidarity in the western hemisphere were more important than the specific economic goals of enhancing security of supply and backing U.S. investors. Relations with Mexico also illustrate how the American political system structures business–state relations. Private companies wanted the United States to take a strong stand, including the use of force against Mexican regimes that threatened the prerogatives of American investors. However, this issue was decided in the White House, where the political resources of economic groups were not particularly potent. Wilson was willing to use diplomacy and economic pressure so long as they did not violate other objectives, but he was not willing to use American troops to further public or private economic aims.

After Carranza's death in 1920 there was movement toward reconciliation. The United States returned to diplomatic pressure to secure greater protection for American investors. Recognition of Carranza's successor, Obregon, was withheld until 1923. The State Department also discouraged J. P. Morgan from providing credits to the new regime. This pressure was largely successful. In late 1922 and 1923 the two governments reached a number of agreements dealing with debt repayments, compensation, and oil taxes. In addition, the Mexican Supreme Court ruled that provisions of the 1917 Constitution were not applicable to oil properties that had been developed prior to 1917. There was further controversy over a new oil law passed in 1925, but this dispute was dampened by a 1927 ruling of the Mexican Supreme Court that some provisions of the new law were not constitutional. Controversy sputtered to a close in 1927 with the signing of the Morrow–Calles Agreement, which included the stipulation that future oil disputes would be settled through local means.[37] This agreement ushered in a period of quiescence in Mexico's raw ma-

[37] Kane, p. 309; Smith, *ibid.*, pp. 176-88, 234; U.S. House, Committee on Foreign Affairs, *Expropriation of American-Owned Property*, p. 11.

terials industry that lasted until the nationalization of the petroleum industry in 1938.

Within the private sector there were serious disagreements about American policy after 1920. The large oil companies continued to take a hard line, and there were still occasional calls for armed intervention. Many oil companies and landowners opposed the recognition of Obregon in 1923. However, there was growing support for a more conciliatory policy, particularly from American bankers. They had large amounts invested in Mexico, and they needed a stable political situation if they were to be repaid. In the early 1920s many American manufacturers and exporters saw Mexico as an attractive market; they needed foreign outlets for wartime capacity. Finally, some of the smaller oil companies also favored a more conciliatory position. They feared their larger competitors more than they feared Mexico. Small producers in the United States were not unhappy about higher Mexican taxes, which improved the competitive position of stripper wells in the Southwest.[38]

Conclusion

The outcome of American pressure on the fate of U.S. investors in Mexico was mixed. Landowners suffered the sharpest losses. After 1914 many small- and medium-sized American farmers were driven out of Mexico. The value of U.S. direct investment in Mexican agriculture fell from $70 million in 1914 to $58 million in 1929, while global agricultural investment increased 256 percent (see Appendix, Table 1). During the same period the value of mining investments fell from $302 million to $248 million, while global values increased by 70 percent (see Appendix, Table 2). The petroleum industry fared better than others. The book value of U.S. holdings did increase. Profits of Doheny's Mexican Petroleum Company fell in 1914 and 1915, but they began to pick up in 1917 and continued to rise until the mid-1920s.[39] The physical plant of the oil companies escaped with minimal damage, largely because the Mexican central government was reluctant to carry out military operations in the oil

[38] Smith, *ibid.*, pp. 197-99, 224, 241; Kane, pp. 303-6.

[39] Mexican Petroleum Company, *Annual Reports*, various years.

zone lest the destruction of property lead to American intervention. The United States also succeeded in securing its main legal objective, preventing the retroactive application of the 1917 Constitution.

Even in oil, however, American policy was not a total success for private investors. Mexico was able to make some changes, particularly in the area of taxation. In retrospect, it is not clear that Mexico could have accomplished much more than it did during the first two decades of the revolution. In agriculture, where local skills were available, there was a dramatic increase in the degree of Mexican control. In the oil industry, where Mexico was much more deficient in capital, technical skills, and knowledge of the market, full-scale nationalization in the 1910s or 1920s would probably have been economically disastrous. As indigenous capabilities increased during the 1930s, Mexico was able to move in the petroleum sector as well.

It is difficult to understand American policy in Mexico from an analytic viewpoint that does not regard the state as an autonomous actor; statist or structural Marxist perspectives are more appropriate than interest-group or instrumental Marxist ones. The costs of the Mexican Revolution fell upon a well-defined group of American investors. Even so, Woodrow Wilson intervened against Huerta when the private sector would have preferred conciliation, and refused to intervene in 1919 when American investors wanted armed action. Once the decision against military action was firmly taken, consensus within the private sector began to disintegrate. By eliminating the most extreme option, the state had changed the parameters within which decisions about Mexico would be made. Wilson's actions turned certain possibilities into nondecisions, options that could no longer be seriously considered by any parties involved in the policy debate. This situation is exactly the reverse of that usually associated with the concept of nondecision, which is generally applied to circumstances where certain policies are never contemplated because of the underlying structure of the economic system.[40] A statist or structural Marxist approach is more sensitive to this possibility than liberal or instrumental

[40] See Bachrach and Baratz, "Two Faces of Power," for a discussion of the nondecision concept.

Marxist arguments. Investors had to search for a second-best policy, and they were unable to arrive at any clear consensus about whether recalcitrance or accommodation would be preferable. Disagreements among private groups, themselves partly a function of the state's unwillingness to use force, gave official policy-makers more leeway.

The Bolivian and Mexican Oil Nationalizations of 1937 and 1938

In 1937 Bolivia nationalized the local subsidiary of the Standard Oil Company. This operation had always been very modest, with production peaking at 450 barrels a day in the 1930s, but it was the only field in Bolivia.[41] In 1938 Mexico nationalized almost all of her oil industry. U.S. firms accounted for 30 percent of production with Jersey holding the largest share, followed by Sinclair (9 percent), Cities Service (5-6 percent), and Gulf (4-5 percent). Royal Dutch Shell pumped about 60 percent of Mexico's crude.[42] The disputes arising from the Mexican and Bolivian takeovers were settled in the early 1940s with agreements for relatively modest compensation—$1.5 million to be paid by Bolivia, and $24 million by Mexico. Despite the clear threat that these nationalizations posed to American corporations, the official policy and behavior of the United States can only be explained by broader foreign policy concerns—the deteriorating situation in Europe and the danger of German infiltration in Latin America.

The Background

Both the Bolivian and Mexican nationalizations were precipitated more by political than economic circumstances: the legitimacy of the regimes in both countries became intimately tied to the assertion of national sovereignty over their petroleum resources. In early 1936 left-wing military officers seized power in Bolivia following the country's defeat in the Chaco War with Paraguay. After a short period of what appeared to be a conciliatory attitude toward Standard Oil, the new leadership became

[41] Larson, Knowlton, and Popple, *History of Standard Oil Company*, p. 122.
[42] Wilkins, *Maturing of Multinational Enterprise*, pp. 225-26.

more negative: in June all concessions not being actively worked were cancelled, and in December a state oil company was established. On March 13, 1937, the largest operation in the country, Bolivian Standard, was taken over. Criminal charges were lodged against the company for failing to pay taxes and for illegally exporting oil to Argentina in 1926 and 1927.[43]

In an endemically unstable political system made worse by the Chaco War, Standard became a focus of discontent, and dramatic actions against it a source of legitimacy for the government. The takeover was ordered partly to bolster the faltering regime of Colonel David Toro. When Toro was replaced by Germán Busch in 1937, suspicions that the coup was backed by the company were so strong that the new government issued a denial the day after it took office. The hopes of the American legation in La Paz for a settlement in September were dashed when Busch publicly confirmed the criminal charges brought against the company. In November Jersey's Bolivian lawyer was deported, although a company representative sent from New York was allowed to stay. The military leaders regarded a Bolivian's involvement with Standard as unpatriotic. In 1939 Bolivia rejected a settlement proposed by the United States, because it implied that Bolivia had an "obligation" to pay Jersey. When the nationalization was debated in the Bolivian Congress in the spring of 1941, sentiment ran so high that it was necessary for several cabinet members to be present to defend the government's efforts to arrive at a settlement.[44] The final judgment was promulgated by Bolivia without public discussion.

Bolivian antipathy toward Standard was aggravated by the nation's international situation. Bolivia had been defeated by Paraguay in the Chaco War. During the course of hostilities the company had been accused of shipping equipment out of the country and refusing to produce aviation fuel at its refinery, which was seized by the government in 1933. Bolivia was searching for

[43] Klein, "The Bolivian Experience," p. 64. The decree is reprinted in *Foreign Relations of the United States*, 1937, Vol. 5, p. 277. The company knew there was some question about these exports, but thought it had settled the matter in 1935. See Larson et al., pp. 123-25.

[44] Klein, p. 66; *Foreign Relations*, 1937, Vol. 5, pp. 297-305, 307, 309; 1939, Vol. 5, pp. 331-34; 1941, Vol. 5, pp. 467-77; Larson et al., p. 127.

effective diplomatic support, which it felt could only come from Argentina or Brazil. Reletting Standard's holdings to these countries was seen by Busch and Toro as a way to bolster Bolivia's shaky international position. The American legation reported in early 1937 that if Argentina was allowed to purchase the fields claimed by Standard, Argentina would guarantee that Paraguay would not again go to war.[45] In May 1937 the Bolivian Foreign Minister told the U.S. representative in La Paz, "We had to drive the Standard Oil Company out of Bolivia for political reasons."[46] Although Bolivian leaders were willing to pay compensation, the domestic political situation precluded any compromise of the March 1937 decree, which enshrined the state's right to abrogate Standard's concession unilaterally.

In Mexico as in Bolivia the nationalization of the petroleum industry was intimately associated with the domestic political situation. The general antipathy of the Mexican government to foreign investment following the revolution has already been noted. Lazero Cardenas, who became President in 1934, took a more militant stance than his immediate predecessors. In 1936 Cardenas brought 13,000 of 19,000 oil workers into a single union. He nationalized most railroads in 1937.[47]

The new union of oil workers pressed their employers for higher wages and greater worker autonomy. The two parties were unable to reach a settlement and the matter was submitted to an arbitration panel, which ruled that the workers were receiving inadequate salaries, and that the companies were trying to evade taxes and were unfairly exploiting Mexico's natural resources. The companies were alarmed, not so much by the proposed wage settlement as by the judgment that foreign technical personnel be replaced in three years and that management's ability to dismiss workers be limited. They appealed the Labor Board's decision to the Mexican Supreme Court, which rejected their suit on March 1, 1938. The companies still refused to implement the ruling and

[45] Klein, p. 57; *Foreign Relations*, 1937, Vol. 5, pp. 284, 286-87; Wood, *The Making of the Good Neighbor Policy*, pp. 169-77.

[46] *Foreign Relations*, 1937, Vol. 5, p. 284.

[47] Cline, p. 227; Padgett, *The Mexican Political System*, p. 36; Green, *Containment of Latin America*, pp. 28-29.

entered into negotiations with Cardenas himself. A wage settlement was reached. But the insistence of the foreign investors that the President commit himself in writing, and their refusal to accept limits on their control of workers, precipitated the nationalization of the industry on March 18, 1938. This action, which was widely applauded in Mexico, strengthened the domestic political position of the regime.[48]

Official U.S. Policy

The nationalizations in Bolivia and Mexico were the first major takeovers of nonagricultural foreign raw materials investments. The threat to American corporations was immediate and obvious; they could no longer assume that deeds or concession arrangements were equivalent to contracts between private parties. The effect on American state goals was not so clear. Even if both Mexico and Bolivia stopped sending their oil to the United States, the impact would be modest. American supplies had been swelled by new discoveries in the Southwest during the 1920s and 1930s; the Depression had limited demand. Bolivian output was never very large, and Jersey would not have reopened its Bolivian operation even if the company had regained possession. Mexican production, which had reached 42 percent of U.S. output in 1921, had been falling during the 1930s.[49] Security of short-term supply was not a salient consideration for the United States. Still, the loss of foreign concessions could weaken the security of America's crude resources in the long term. Indeed, the concerns of the early 1920s about the exhaustion of domestic supplies were to be rekindled during the mid-1940s.

However, the most serious dilemma confronting American policy-makers involved more general foreign policy goals—specifically, developing a firm alliance system in the western hemisphere to prevent German encroachment. As the Axis threat became more apparent, modest diplomatic and economic pressures

[48] Herzog, "Mexico's Case," pp. 515-17; Powell, *The Mexican Petroleum Industry*, p. 22; Ward, "The Mexican Oil Problem," pp. 505, 507; Larson et al., p. 131; Cline, p. 236; Padgett, pp. 37-39.

[49] *Foreign Relations*, 1937, Vol. 5, p. 290; U.S. Senate, Special Committee Investigating Petroleum Resources, *American Petroleum Interests*, p. 331.

intended to protect oil interests were abandoned, and the final compensation settlements not only went against the interests of American corporations but were largely funded by the American rather than the Mexican or Bolivian Treasury. For U.S. policy-makers, salient general foreign policy goals outweighed more tenuous considerations of maintaining the security of supplies in the long term. The ability of the large oil companies to subvert this set of preferences was limited by divisions within their own ranks, and by the fact that decisions were taken largely in the White House and the State Department: despite the weakness of the American political system, U.S. leaders were able to implement their preferences by taking advantage of the arena in which policy was decided, and by adroitly exploiting differing interests within the private sector.

American officials used, albeit in a half-hearted way, both diplomatic and economic instruments against Bolivia and Mexico. The initial diplomatic communication with Bolivia expressed regret over the conflict without taking any stand on the substance of the issue. This was followed by a personal message from Secretary of State Hull to the Bolivian Foreign Minister. In 1938 and 1939 the American government acted as an informal intermediary, offering several proposals for settling the dispute. The United States never, however, challenged the validity of the nationalization decree, or the Bolivian Supreme Court decision denying the company's right to bring suit against the state.[50]

In Mexico, where the economic stakes were larger, diplomatic maneuvering was more convoluted. While publicly stating that it would not intervene until the companies had exhausted local remedies, the State Department took immediate action. On March 21, 1938, the Undersecretary, Sumner Welles, told the Mexican Ambassador that Cardenas's policy was "suicidal."[51] Hull instructed the U.S. Ambassador in Mexico, Josephus Daniels, to see Cardenas and protest the expropriation in the strongest terms. However, this forceful initiative ran into opposition within the American government. Daniels undermined the policy of Hull and

[50] *Foreign Relations*, 1937, Vol. 5, pp. 282, 284-85; Wood, pp. 185-86; Green, p. 26.

[51] Quoted in Cronon, *Josephus Daniels in Mexico*, p. 187.

Welles by persuading the Secretary of State to have his note presented informally rather than officially, and by asking Roosevelt to overrule Hull's instructions that he return to the United States. Daniels had close personal and political ties with Roosevelt. He had been Secretary of the Navy during Wilson's administration when Roosevelt was the Assistant Secretary. At an impromptu press conference Roosevelt took a conciliatory attitude, stating that the United States did not have much sympathy for American investors trying to collect "excessive sums."[52]

Economic pressure paralleled diplomatic efforts; both were indecisive and, at times, contradictory. Until 1940 the United States did refuse to give economic assistance to Bolivia, and this sanction became an important element in Bolivia's desire to settle the dispute with Standard. As late as September 1939 Hull rejected proposals for extending assistance because public opinion, "which would be taken up by Congress," would oppose such action until the nationalization question was resolved.[53] This attitude changed as the international political situation became more threatening.

In Mexico the oil companies and the State Department initially pressed for extensive economic sanctions. Daniels and Treasury Secretary Henry Morgenthau, generally supported by Roosevelt, wanted a more moderate policy. This internal dispute first centered on Mexican silver. Under pressure from the State Department, which had the support of Key Pittman, the chairman of the Senate Foreign Relations Committee, Morgenthau agreed to halt the purchase of Mexican silver on March 27, 1938, and to lower the price of silver from 45¢ to 43¢ per ounce. This action contributed to depreciation of the Mexican peso. Yet the Treasury never firmly implemented this policy, continuing to buy spot silver without inquiring into its origins and then, in April, announcing that it would buy 200,000 ounces from Mexico. In the summer of 1938 Morgenthau refused Hull's request to lower silver prices further.[54]

On the question of purchasing oil from Mexico, American pol-

[52] *Ibid.*, pp. 195-201, quote from p. 200; Green, p. 32.

[53] *Foreign Relations*, 1939, Vol. 5, p. 320.

[54] Cronon, pp. 191ff., 216; Wood, p. 225.

icy was also uncertain. The State Department took a number of actions that supported the private boycott imposed by the large American oil companies. In 1939 Hull succeeded in preventing U.S. naval ships from purchasing Mexican oil. In the fall of the same year Mexico was omitted from an executive agreement providing for the import of oil from certain countries at reduced tariffs. In December 1939 Sumner Welles told the Mexican Ambassador that his country should not attempt to send any oil to the United States. Still, the State Department never took an absolute stand against private citizens buying oil, and Mexico did sell to a U.S. firm, Eastern States Refineries, as well as to Germany, Europe, and Latin America. She was able to procure the use of some seventeen tankers owned by an American, after the large companies had withdrawn their fleets. The value of foreign Mexican petroleum sales fell from 162 million pesos in 1937 to 78 million in 1938,[55] but Mexican shipments were never entirely cut off as Iranian exports were to be a decade later.

By 1940 the United States was trying to work out a settlement with both Mexico and Bolivia. With Bolivia the Reconstruction Finance Corporation began negotiating for a long-term tin purchase agreement because it wanted assured sources of ore for the smelting industry it was planning to finance in the United States. During 1941 the United States and Bolivia concluded agreements covering a military aviation mission, lend-lease aid of $8 million, and the purchase of tin, lead, and zinc. German airline interests and an Italian military mission were forced out of Bolivia. On January 12, 1942, Bolivia and Standard signed an agreement that provided for payment of $1.5 million in compensation. It was two paragraphs long. No mention was made of the legitimacy of the March 1937 decree. This denouement came about largely because of the State Department's pressure on the company; given the clear American government commitment to cement political and economic ties with Bolivia, the company had little recourse but to accept.[56]

[55] Green, p. 52; Cronon, p. 208; Wood, pp. 229-32; Powell, p. 118.

[56] *Foreign Relations*, 1940, Vol. 5, p. 524; 1941, Vol. 5, pp. 403-64, 466, 472; 1942, Vol. 5, pp. 587-88. Green, p. 51; Ingram, *Expropriation of U.S. Property*, p. 118; Klein, p. 69. Gardner, *Economic Aspects of New Deal Diplomacy*, p. 112.

Toward Mexico the State Department adopted an increasingly conciliatory stance as the international situation became more treacherous. In the fall of 1940 Department officials began, for the first time, to consider the possibility of a general settlement. They became increasingly impatient with the recalcitrant position of the companies, and with what they regarded as inflated demands for compensation. In the spring of 1941 agreement was reached on airfield transit rights and the purchase of strategic raw materials. Two American companies, Sinclair and Cities Service, concluded their own settlements with Mexico in 1940 and 1942 respectively, involving compensation of some $8.5 million to Sinclair plus preferential access to Mexican oil for four years, and of $1-2 million to Cities Service. The U.S. government had to negotiate the rest of the claims directly with Mexico, because the largest American oil company in Mexico, Standard of New Jersey, had refused to enter direct talks. By August 1941 Mexico and the United States had agreed to an initial $9 million payment for oil claims. In the following year a total sum of $24 million was set by a mixed Mexican-American claims commission that had been created at the suggestion of Mexico. The last payment was made in 1968. The United States, in effect, underwrote the payments to Standard by agreeing to spend up to $40 million a year to stabilize the peso, to purchase $25 million worth of silver a year, and to loan Mexico $30 million.[57]

Corporate Pressure

In acceding to and even facilitating a settlement, policy-makers had to resist the determined opposition of major corporations, particularly Standard Oil of New Jersey. Company officials feared that the actions taken by Bolivia and Mexico would set a precedent and threaten operations in many parts of the world. The economic stakes in Bolivia, in particular, were unimportant: Jersey had stopped drilling in 1932 and opened negotiations for the sale of its assets in 1936. The company took a firm stand because it did not want to give the impression that it could be forcibly expelled. Money was not the issue. Jersey rejected a settlement offer in

[57] Cronon, pp. 251, 262, 258-60, 268-69; Wood, pp. 250-58; Green, pp. 53-54; Blasier, *Hovering Giant*, pp. 121-28.

1939 because it would have left the validity of the March 1937 nationalization decree unchallenged.[58]

Oil industry leaders publicly stated that they would resist nationalization in Mexico. The chairman of the board of Jersey Standard urged the American government to support the company because Mexico's action could "set a precedent" for other nations. Corporate officials first hoped that their property would be restored as a result of U.S. pressure or a conservative victory in the 1940 Mexican elections. When these expectations proved futile, they switched to a demand for prompt compensation, including payment for subsoil rights, with the hope that Mexico would have to back off because the financial burdens of such an arrangement would be beyond the government's means.[59]

The corporations tried to use their own resources to reverse the nationalizations. They boycotted Mexican oil and denied use of their tanker fleets. Travel agencies owned by corporate interests discouraged tourism to Mexico. U.S. firms refused to export tetraethyl lead (needed for gasoline production) to Pemex, the Mexican state oil company. Some Jersey officials thought about underwriting revolution in Mexico, but they seem to have been dissuaded by the attitude of the Roosevelt administration. During the abortive 1938 revolt led by Cedillo, Roosevelt warned that any U.S. pilots participating in the insurrection would lose their licenses. The President bluntly informed Jersey's counsel that there would be no revolution in Mexico.[60]

Although company officials had many contacts with government policy-makers, their efforts to get U.S. support were not successful. In Bolivia one Jersey official convinced the American minister in La Paz that the company should try to stall and delay, but this proposal was rejected in Washington. State Department officials refused to back the company's efforts to avoid placing its case before the Bolivian Supreme Court. In March 1938 the Department even refused to allow a member of the U.S. delegation in La Paz to accompany Jersey's lawyer when he delivered a letter to the Foreign Minister indicating that the case was being submit-

[58] Wood, p. 168; Klein, p. 66; *Foreign Relations*, 1939, Vol. 5, p. 329.

[59] Cronon, pp. 186-87, 204, 207, 231, quote from p. 169.

[60] Engler, *Politics of Oil*, p. 195; Cronon, p. 212.

ted to Bolivia's judiciary under protest. The State Department went ahead with the 1941 preliminary settlement with Mexico even though it was condemned by the companies. The Department also rejected Jersey's plea that the United States press for international arbitration of the dispute rather than for a direct settlement between the company and Bolivia. When Jersey flatly refused to talk with Mexico, the Department itself negotiated the formal arrangements for compensation.[61]

The companies remained bitter about the State Department's policies even after the Second World War. Testifying before the Special Petroleum Committee established by the Senate, Jersey's general counsel stated that the company had invested $17 million in Bolivia and gotten back less than two. He also argued that Mexico's Labor Arbitration Board made "unconscionable awards to labor."[62] He described developments in Mexico as "unfortunate," and maintained that if taken as a precedent, they could "be far-reaching and harmful to the national interests of the United States."[63] A special report prepared by the industry for the Committee complained that the American government had neglected foreign oil investments after the mid-1930s. Diplomatic intervention was described as being *ex post facto*, coming too late to deal effectively with a crisis.[64]

Conclusion

American officials were able to resist corporate pressure because decisions were taken in the executive branch, where private influence was minimized. Reversing Bolivian and Mexican actions would have required concerted pressure by the American government, probably including the use of force. This public officials refused to consider. The consequences of covert or overt intervention were dangerous and uncertain, given the international situation and the political salience of nationalization disputes. Corporate managers did not have political resources that could compel government policy-makers to follow such a policy. How-

[61] *Foreign Relations*, 1937, Vol. 5, p. 291; 1938, Vol. 5, p. 324; Cronon, p. 269; Wood, pp. 193, 248.

[62] U.S. Senate, *American Petroleum Interests*, p. 87.

[63] *Ibid.*, p. 88.

[64] *Ibid.*, pp. 311-14.

ever, private firms could to some extent impede positive efforts to reach a settlement. Some refused to negotiate with Mexico. The danger that companies would lobby in Congress discouraged the State Department from negotiating a large loan agreement with Bolivia before the oil dispute was settled.

The moderate course pursued by the State Department was facilitated, particularly in Mexico, by divisions among private interests. Sinclair, the second largest American producer in Mexico, reached its own agreement in 1940. Sinclair got better terms by breaking the solid corporate front. The holdings of the Gulf Oil Company, although small, were not taken over in 1938. Seventy percent of Mexico's silver production was controlled by U.S. interests, and they did not want economic pressure to take the form of suspending silver purchases. The American Chamber of Commerce in Mexico urged the State Department to separate itself from the oil companies, because German manufactures were replacing American goods.[65]

Thus, in the oil nationalization disputes in Bolivia and Mexico, the pattern followed in earlier disagreements about Mexico's treatment of U.S. investors repeated itself, even though some important economic interests were threatened in a more direct way. General foreign policy goals prevailed against the interests and pressures brought by private corporations. State officials succeeded in implementing their preferences because decisions were taken in arenas where private influence had minimal force. This advantage was reinforced by divisions among economic groups. This pattern of developments is consistent with statist and structural Marxist perspectives, but cannot be easily understood from interest-group or instrumental Marxist ones. Examination of our next case, however, reveals that when the decision-making arena shifts, public purposes can be frustrated by private interests.

Oil Policy in the Middle East, 1940-1950

The Second World War brought new demands for oil, and new demands raised old fears about the exhaustion of supply. Ameri-

[65] Cline, p. 241; Gardner, p. 120.

can production during the 1940s accounted for about fifty percent of world output, while America's share of world reserves was declining because of new discoveries in the Middle East. The attention of senior officials was first drawn east of Suez by Texaco and Standard of California, the joint owners of the California Arabian Oil Company (the name was changed to the Arabian American Oil Company or Aramco in 1944), which were concerned about the security of their concession. When policy-makers became aware that Saudi reserves were at least as large as those in the United States, they began to search for measures that would insure that this new source of wealth and power would be firmly under American control. In 1943 a new government entity, the Petroleum Reserve Corporation, was established to purchase California Arabian. This attempt failed, as did efforts to construct a government-owned pipeline from the Persian Gulf to the Mediterranean and conclude an international oil agreement with Great Britain. Finally, in 1950 American officials found a policy they could implement—permitting taxes paid by the companies to host-country governments to be written off against U.S. tax liabilities. The United States could only protect its foreign investments by, in effect, transferring revenues from the U.S. Treasury to the purse of Ibn Saud. Other policies were frustrated by the opposition of one segment or another of the oil industry.

The American effort to increase the security of oil supplies from the Middle East during the 1940s is one of the most fascinating and revealing cases of American policy that I have encountered. Looked at in isolation, it gives strong support to either liberal or instrumental Marxist arguments. For here, as opposed to Bolivia and Mexico, central decision-makers were consistently frustrated by the private sector: they were not able to implement their policy preferences. This looks like an example of a nonexistent state rather than a weak one. However, the critical distinction between this case and the others discussed in this chapter is that Congress became an important arena for decision-making. None of the initiatives taken by the state could be put into effect without legislative approval. In Congress the oil industry's political resources were very potent. They could effectively frustrate the undertakings of central decision-makers.

The Effort to Purchase the California Arabian Oil Company

The Standard Oil Company of California (Socal), which secured the Saudi Arabian concession in 1933, and the Texas Company (Texaco), which bought a half share in 1936, were from the outset concerned about the security of their holding. It was the first production venture for both companies in the eastern hemisphere. Saudi Arabia was an unstable area, more a collection of tribes held together by the military prowess, prestige, and subventions of King Ibn Saud than a unified state. Great Britain was the dominant foreign power. During the 1930s the United States did not have a diplomatic representative accredited to any of the countries on the Arabian peninsula. The companies wanted the political support of the American government without sacrificing their economic autonomy.

Socal and Texaco, through their subsidiary the California Arabian Oil Company, first turned their attention to securing American diplomatic representation to Saudi Arabia. This was discussed within the company in 1937 and broached to the State Department before 1939.[66] In 1940 the American representative in Cairo finally presented himself to Ibn Saud.

But this initiative was hardly enough to protect American investors. In October 1940 the Italians bombed California Arabian's headquarters in Dhahran. This attack, coupled with wartime shipping difficulties, led the company to virtually close down its operations. Production did not begin to increase until 1943. In the meantime, King Ibn Saud demanded more money. The war threatened the stability of his regime. His main source of revenue, fees from pilgrims visiting Mecca and import duties, fell sharply. At the same time, he had to increase payments to tribal chiefs because revolts in Iraq made their loyalty more uncertain.[67]

The companies offered a loan of $6 million, but immediately tried to pass the burden to the American government. In 1941 James Moffett, chairman of the board of Caltex (the Social and

[66] U.S. Senate, Special Committee Investigating the National Defense Program, *Petroleum Arrangements with Saudi Arabia*, p. 25380.

[67] Wilkins, *Maturing of Multinational Enterprise*, pp. 249, 278; Feis, *Three Episodes*, pp. 107-9; U.S. Senate, *Petroleum Arrangements*, pp. 25380-81; Shwadran, *Middle East, Oil*, p. 315.

Texaco marketing subsidiary in the eastern hemisphere) and a personal friend of Roosevelt, saw the President and urged him to extend lend-lease to Saudi Arabia. Roosevelt opted instead for assistance through Great Britain, largely because he feared that direct American involvement would stir domestic isolationist sentiment.[68] This tactic was made necessary by the weakness of the American state. Roosevelt himself was acutely aware of the dangers confronting the United States in the international system. Yet he had to deal with strong isolationist beliefs among the general public that were well represented in Congress. He had to act with stealth to implement his policy preferences. In the case of subventions for Saudi Arabia, Roosevelt shifted the decision to an arena completely removed from domestic opinion, namely, Great Britain.

Rather than comforting corporate managers, this move only made them more anxious. They feared rising British influence as much as political unrest within Saudia Arabia. They had gotten the Saudi concession only because other companies were not really interested. Neither Socal nor Texaco had ties with the major British companies, while Mobil and Jersey shared joint ownership of the Iraq Petroleum Company with Anglo-Iranian and Shell, and Gulf shared the Kuwait Petroleum Company with Anglo-Iranian. Even before Roosevelt's lend-lease decision, Britain was giving the King financial assistance. Socal and Texaco claimed that a 1942 British expedition, ostensibly to control locusts, also included many geologists. Britain made plans to establish Barclay's as a bank of issue in Jiddah, which would have placed Saudi Arabia firmly in the sterling area and presented financial problems for American enterprises. Texaco and Socal officials feared that these developments would ultimately lead to the entry of British oil interests.[69]

In February 1943 they renewed their efforts to get direct American aid for Ibn Saud. The presidents of Socal and Texaco

[68] Wilkins, *Maturing of Multinational Enterprise*, p. 249; U.S. Senate, Committee on Foreign Relations, Subcommittee on Multinational Corporations, *Multinational Oil Corporations*, Report, pp. 37-38; Shwadran, p. 317.

[69] Shwadran, pp. 318-19; U.S. Senate, *Petroleum Arrangements*, pp. 24859-60.

visited Harold Ickes, the Secretary of Commerce and Petroleum Administrator for War, as well as the Secretaries of the Army, Navy, and State Departments. They offered to set aside a large in-ground reserve in Saudi Arabia from which the American government would be supplied at preferential prices. On February 18 Roosevelt authorized lend-lease.[70] The companies' proposal for preferential access and pricing was not heard of again, but corporate appeals had planted in Ickes's fertile mind a far bolder strategy to preserve the security of oil supplies.

Having been persuaded by the companies of the strategic importance of Saudi Arabian oil, Ickes concluded that private American firms could not compete with British corporations (partly government-owned) in Britain's sphere of influence. He proposed to Roosevelt that the United States establish a Petroleum Reserve Corporation, under the authority of the Reconstruction Finance Corporation Act, with the primary purpose of purchasing the Saudi and Bahrein concessions from Socal and Texaco. He was supported by the Joint Chiefs, James Byrnes the Director of War Mobilization, Secretary of War Stimson, Secretary of the Navy Knox, and other high officials. State Department representatives, particularly the Department's Foreign Economic Advisor, Herbert Feis, were not enthusiastic, preferring the companies' offer of a special government reserve, but they went along. On June 30, 1943, Roosevelt authorized the creation of the Petroleum Reserve Corporation (PRC). In August negotiations with Standard Oil of California and the Texas Company began.[71]

These steps marked the first decisive effort by the American government to participate directly in the ownership of petroleum reserves. It was not peculiar in the context of wartime policy, for public agencies had become intimately involved in many areas of

[70] U.S. Senate, *Petroleum Arrangements*, p. 24861; Shwadran, p. 319; U.S. Senate, *Multinational Oil Corporations*, Report, p. 38.

[71] For documentary and primary accounts see U.S. Senate, Committee on Foreign Relations, Subcommittee on Multinational Corporations, *A Documentary History of the Petroleum Reserve Corporation 1943-1944*; U.S. Senate, *Petroleum Arrangements*, pp. 25237-41; and Feis, *Three Episodes*, pp. 117-22. For secondary accounts see Wilkins, *Maturing of Multinational Enterprise*, p. 277, and Shwadran, pp. 320-25.

the economy, although the only foreign public oil project was the construction of a pipeline and refinery in Canada.[72] Socal and Texaco executives were nonetheless flabbergasted, and probably confused. They flatly refused to sell 100 percent of their interest. Ickes then briefly turned his attention to purchasing Gulf's share of the Kuwait Petroleum Company, but found the selling price prohibitively high (several hundred million dollars, while forty million was being offered for California Arabian). Discussions with Socal and Texaco proceeded, with the government reducing its proposed share to one-half and eventually one-third. At the meeting of the Board of Directors of the PRC, on September 28, 1943, the government's chief negotiator reported a tentative agreement that called for one-third public ownership, the right to preemptive government purchase of all production during wartime and 51 percent purchase in peacetime, and the power to control production if reserves became depleted "to the point of resulting in an insufficient supply for anticipated Government requirements."[73]

Two weeks later negotiations collapsed. Testifying in 1948 before a Senate committee, the president of Texaco recalled that it was Ickes who had broken off discussions. This interpretation seems disingenuous. Ickes felt that Socal and Texaco had worked out a policy of purposeful obstructionism. He stated at the same Senate hearings that once Rommel was stopped in Egypt the companies felt "more secure in their concession and more disposed to thumb their nose at us."[74] Herbert Feis, who was actually engaged in the negotiations, felt that it was the corporations that had turned the government down, as did James Byrnes.[75] On November 3, 1943, the effort to buy the concession was terminated. The official minutes of the PRC meeting read:

> The Board was unanimously of the opinion that the interests of the people of the United States and its foreign oil industry re-

[72] Wilkins, *ibid.*, pp. 273-75.

[73] U.S. Senate, *Petroleum Reserve Corporation*, pp. 30-32; Feis, *Three Episodes*, p. 131.

[74] U.S. Senate, *Petroleum Arrangements*, p. 25241.

[75] *Ibid.*, pp. 24868 and 25387; Feis, *Three Episodes*, p. 133.

quired the participation of the United States Government . . . in the protection of American oil resources. . . . The Directors expressed deep regret that the [California Arabian] representatives had been unable or unwilling to appreciate the urgency of and need for the assistance of the Government.[76]

How did this failure come about? Here was a resource deemed essential to the national security of the United States at a time when the country was fighting its most extensive foreign war. With the exception of the Secretary of State, all high officials from the President on down had strongly endorsed a policy of purchasing the Arabian, Bahrein, and possibly part of the Kuwait concessions. Such a policy would not have been out of line with practices in other industries.

That the companies resisted this initiative is not surprising. They feared government control and thought that public participation might make it more difficult for them to do business in other countries. (Venezuela had passed a law in 1922 prohibiting concessions for publicly owned firms.) The purchase of California Arabian would have changed the structure of the oil industry. What was at stake was not a marginal goal that could be accommodated by corporate slack. The nature of the corporation itself was the basic issue. It is difficult to conceive of any way in which public leaders might have cajoled or threatened Socal and Texaco into selling their Arabian concessions. Corporate executives probably realized that the United States would have to extend what protection it could to American concessionaires holding such valuable assets, whether or not the state itself held a proprietary interest.[77]

But how did the industry prevail? The answer lies in the location of the arena in which the decision to purchase the Arabian concessions would actually have taken place—the Congress. Ickes realized that any major or novel expenditures would have to be submitted to Congress. The PRC had not been directly authorized by the legislature. There was some question about its legal-

[76] U.S. Senate, *Multinational Oil Corporations*, Report, p. 40.

[77] U.S. Senate, *Petroleum Reserve Corporation*, p. 27; Feis, *Three Episodes*, p. 133.

ity. This need to go through Congress colored all of the government's deliberations. Congressional resistance was clearly manifested in early 1944 when Senators Moore of Oklahoma and Brewster of Maine introduced a resolution calling for the dissolution of the PRC in response to the more modest proposal to build a government-owned pipeline in Saudi Arabia. In 1943 the Congress had rejected a joint Navy–Socal project to exploit domestic Navy reserves. Although the PRC resolution was never acted on, the Senate did authorize the formation of a Special Petroleum Committee in the spring of 1944 with five out of eleven members from oil-producing states as well as Senator Brewster of Maine, who was ideologically opposed to government ownership.[78] Ickes testified in relation to the purchase that the oil industry "came up here to the Hill and built a fire under us. . . ."[79] The purchase of California Arabian could not be carried out solely by the executive branch, and it probably would not have passed the Congress. The combination of industry pressure and ideological distaste was strong enough to lead the Senate to create a new decision-making arena—the Special Petroleum Committee—where the influence of the private sector was even greater than in the full chamber.

The outcome of this episode can be understood from a liberal or instrumental Marxist position. As I will try to demonstrate in the conclusion of this chapter, it is also consistent with the statist interpretation offered in this book. However, the effort to buy the American concessions on the Arabian peninsula does not conform very well with a structural Marxist approach. Structural Marxism views the state as an autonomous actor. The state may sometimes act against the expressed preferences of the capitalist class. It may recognize unions and the right to strike, implement social security, approve unemployment insurance, and even nationalize certain industries, if these measures further long-term social stability. Such policies, which violate some of the fundamental tenets of capitalism, are most likely when there is some immediate danger to the system, such as unrest within the working class.

In the case of Arabian oil there was neither overriding need nor

[78] Feis, *ibid.*, pp. 118 and 127; U.S. Senate, *Congressional Record*, 78th Cong., 2nd sess., pp. 497, 1468.

[79] U.S. Senate, *Petroleum Arrangements*, p. 25240.

compelling social pressure. Production in the Arabian peninsula had hardly begun. State ownership might have contributed to future security of supply, but this was not an ineluctable outcome. What was certain was that buying Aramco would have undermined the basic precept of capitalism, the private ownership of the means of production. To explicate this case from a structural Marxist perspective it would be necessary to view the state as standing at a very great distance from its own society: central decision-makers attempted to act against the preferences of leading corporations and were willing to violate the principle of private ownership for a tenuous contribution to long-term social coherence. This is not a compelling position, because it explains too much. It is hard to conceive of any public policy that could not be justified in a similar fashion. From a structural, and even instrumental, Marxist viewpoint it is difficult to explain why the state tried to buy Aramco in the first place.

Furthermore, it would not be an adequate defense from a structural Marxist position to note simply that the policy never came off. This argument would imply that powerful capitalist groups are capable of blocking state initiatives. But such a close tie between the expressed preferences of private groups and government policy would undermine the fundamental premise of a structural Marxist position—namely, that the state is able to carry out an autonomous policy.

What a structural Marxist would have to maintain is that the system is geared to give the state enough autonomy to act when it is necessary, but not when policies reflect the caprice of individual decision-makers. This formulation is not illogical, but it is more convoluted. It introduces another variable into the analysis: determining whether the state itself is laboring under false consciousness—that is, misperceiving its true role and interests.

The durability of social theories is in large part a function of how well apparently anomalous data can be interpreted without fundamentally altering their basic frames of reference. Structural Marxism is a powerful and malleable paradigm, and the search for a definitive empirical refutation is bound to be futile. Nevertheless, the effort of U.S. central decision-makers to buy a major potential source of oil from private companies that were willing to develop it on their own, in the absence of any compelling pressure from the society, requires that a Marxist argument incorporate variables that delineate the inherent wisdom of state policy. This is not an easy task, and the results are likely, at the very least, to be inelegant.

Trying to distinguish a statist interpretation from a structural Marxist one is the most difficult analytic task in this book. The effort to buy the Arabian oil concessions during the Second World War is one of the few cases that supports the former paradigm better than the latter. The other critical cases involve the use of force and the protection of foreign raw materials investments. These are discussed in Chapter VIII.

The Saudi Arabian Pipeline

When the effort to purchase the concessions failed, high officials, particularly Ickes and Knox, looked for other ways to insure the security and control of Arabian oil. They settled upon building a government-owned pipeline from the Persian Gulf to the Mediterranean. In February 1944 the PRC and California Arabian signed a preliminary contract that provided for preferential government purchases and a State Department veto over sales, in exchange for the government's expenditure of $165 million to build the pipeline. Ickes felt that this was "practically as good as interest in the oil concession."[80] This policy was supported by the Joint Chiefs, the Secretaries of War and the Navy, and the Director of the Office of War Mobilization, who thought it would increase security and reduce the drain on domestic reserves while avoiding the pitfalls of direct government ownership. Roosevelt gave the plan at least oblique support.[81]

Texaco, Socal, and Gulf—the three companies that would benefit from the pipeline—supported the project.[82] Precisely how much hesitation there was over the government's veto power is not known. Anyway, the economic advantages were great, for the Arabian peninsula had produced very little oil before the war.

[80] *Ibid.*, p. 25244.

[81] *Ibid.*, pp. 25387-88; *New York Times*, March 4, 1944, 9:7, and March 22, 1944, 8:1; U.S. Senate, *Petroleum Reserve Corporation*, pp. 48-49.

[82] *New York Times*, April 26, 1944, 29:1, and May 5, 1944, 25:7.

Easy access to the Mediterranean could offer the decisive advantage necessary to penetrate the European market.

The rest of the American industry vigorously opposed Ickes's new initiative. Jersey and Mobil, which had been denied materials to build a pipeline from the Iraqi concession, did not want additional competition. The domestic industry saw their markets threatened by cheap Arabian oil, even then being pumped at a fraction of the American cost. The Independent Petroleum Association called the pipeline proposal a "fascistic approach."[83] The president of the Houston Oil Company called the PRC "un-American" and a threat to the very existence of the private oil industry.[84] A resolution against the pipeline was supported by fifty-two out of the fifty-five members of the Petroleum Industry War Council; Texaco, Socal, and Gulf cast the only negative votes.[85]

Opposition also came from other sources. The British were unhappy with the project, because it would weaken their influence in the Middle East and compete with oil produced by Anglo-Iranian and Shell. In March 1944 the *New York Times* printed two editorials against the pipeline. In April Herbert Feis, who had resigned as the State Department's Foreign Economic Advisor, publicly attacked the PRC.[86]

The power of the industry was directly felt in Congress. Although the administration had tried to slip the purchase of the Arabian concessions through, the pipeline proposal became public knowledge when the preliminary contract was signed in February. The response of the Senate was to approve the establishment of the Special Petroleum Committee. Senator Moore of Oklahoma, the co-sponsor of the resolution to create the committee, condemned the pipeline as "needless, useless, and impractical," and went on to state that it had "chilled the American oil industry with fear for its very existence." He also argued that Congress could stop the project by not appropriating funds, or by dissolving the PRC.[87] The interim report of the Special Petroleum Committee is-

[83] U.S. Senate, *Multinational Oil Corporations*, Report, p. 41.

[84] *New York Times*, March 10, 1944, 12:4.

[85] Feis, *Three Episodes*, p. 153; *New York Times*, March 3, 1944, 1:2.

[86] See *New York Times*, March 23, 1944, 10:1, for negative British reaction and March 3, 1944, 12:2, March 10, 1944, 14:3, and April 6, 1944, 9:1. For other opposition see Shwadran, p. 342.

[87] *New York Times*, March 17, 1944, 8:1.

sued in 1945 noted that it had asked the President for thirty days' notice before any final contract was signed. The report expressed doubt that the Reconstruction Finance Corporation Act authorized the establishment of the PRC in the first place.[88] The committee's final report, issued in 1947, stated that the advice given by its chairman to President Roosevelt "resulted in the abandonment of the [pipeline] project."[89]

Ickes backed off when the extent of Congressional opposition became clear. By the spring of 1944 the PRC and its pipeline were moribund. Aramco finally committed its own funds in February 1945.[90] Ickes and his compatriots found themselves unable to circumvent the industry's Congressional power. In the midst of America's most trying national crisis, private interests prevailed over the perception of the public good held by central decision-makers in the executive branch. Central decision-makers could not turn division within industry to their advantage. In the Congress, or at least the Special Petroleum Committee, what counted was the wealth and, probably more important, the number of people involved in the domestic oil industry. The weight of these political resources became more apparent when American policy-makers turned their attention to an oil agreement with Great Britain.

The Anglo-American Oil Agreement

During the same period when American officials tried to buy the Arabian concessions and build the pipeline, they also thought of a third device to insure the security and control of Middle East oil—an agreement with Great Britain. This scheme too was never brought to fruition, because of the opposition of the oil industry or, more specifically, domestic producers. Here the peculiarities and fragmentation of the American political system were even more apparent: it was the position of one Senator, Tom Connally of Texas, the chairman of the Senate Foreign Relations Committee in the 78th Congress (1944-1946), that prevented the treaty

[88] U.S. Senate, Special Committee Investigating Petroleum Resources, *Investigations of Petroleum Resources*, Report No. 179, p. 2.

[89] U.S. Senate, Special Committee Investigating Petroleum Resources, *Investigation of Petroleum Resources*, Report No. 9, p. 3.

[90] Feis, *Three Episodes*, p. 154; U.S. Senate, *Multinational Oil Corporations*, Report, p. 41; *New York Times*, June 21, 1944, 4:4; Shwadran, p. 337.

from being considered at a time when it would probably have been approved. When the committee actually did hold hearings (in the spring of 1947), both government officials and industry supporters had lost interest because economic and political circumstances had changed. Although the Anglo-American Oil Agreement was favorably reported by the Foreign Relations Committee (only Connally dissented) it was never presented for ratification to the full Senate.

The idea of concluding an oil agreement with Great Britain originated in the State Department in the spring of 1943. Herbert Feis, the Department's Foreign Economic Advisor, and others saw it as an alternative to the purchase plan that was then being advocated by Ickes. The possibility of a treaty was not widely broached within the government until the fall of 1944. A preliminary trip by Feis to London was scheduled for October, but then abruptly cancelled. Feis left the Department shortly thereafter.[91] The idea was then taken up by Ickes and others as a supplement to the projected pipeline. Indeed, Ickes testified that he saw the pipeline proposal as a way to show Britain that the United States really meant business in the Middle East, and he took credit for getting Roosevelt to initiate international negotiations.[92] When the pipeline scheme collapsed in the spring of 1944, those policy-makers most concerned with Middle East oil turned their full attention to an international pact. They basically saw it as a device for giving American companies protection against British pressure and easier access to areas within Britain's sphere of influence. There was also some concern with integrating new supplies into the world market once the war ended. A vaguely worded document providing for equal access to supply, respect for existing concessions, and the establishment of an International Petroleum Commission to analyze short-term problems of production, processing, and transportation was concluded by Britain and the United States in April 1944.[93]

[91] Feis, *ibid.*, p. 137. Although there is no direct evidence, Feis might have left because he lost this bureaucratic battle.

[92] U.S. Senate, *Petroleum Arrangements*, p. 25343.

[93] *Ibid.*, p. 25247; U.S. Senate, *Multinational Oil Corporations*, Report, pp. 42-43; Feis, *Three Episodes*, pp. 159-61.

The proponents of the arrangement wanted it to be treated as an executive agreement, which would have kept it out of Congress and minimized the influence of the industry. They were not successful. The Special Petroleum Committee argued in a letter to Roosevelt on May 24, 1944, that the agreement could not be binding on the United States until it was approved as a treaty. Senator Connally of Texas, the chairman of the Foreign Relations Committee, took the same position.[94] In August 1944 the executive acquiesced and the pact was transmitted to the Senate.

It immediately ran into opposition. Connally announced that it would not be accepted even before it was presented. The industry's dissatisfaction was apparent. Both the majors and the independents expressed their opposition: the former because they feared competition, the latter because they saw it as another government effort to limit their autonomy. Ickes, having already lost on the procedural issue, did not want another outright confrontation with the industry. Secretary of State Hull did not want a fight with the chairman of the Foreign Relations Committee. Because of industry objections, Roosevelt asked the Senate to return the treaty for revisions in the fall of 1944.[95]

There then ensued a period of very effective political leadership by U.S. policy-makers. They opened extensive negotiations with American producers before approaching Great Britain. The U.S. draft was revised to meet industry objections—specifically, by stating that regulation of domestic petroleum would not be affected. The American team that went to London had six industry advisors: the president of the American Petroleum Institute, the presidents of four independent oil companies including the head of the Independent Petroleum Association of America, and the vice-president of Chase National Bank in charge of oil matters (a surrogate for the majors).[96] A second Anglo-American Oil Agreement was quickly concluded. It was endorsed by all of the major industry trade organizations including the Independent Pe-

[94] Feis, *ibid.*, p. 168; U.S. Senate, *Investigation of Petroleum Resources*, Report No. 9, p. 3.

[95] U.S. Senate, *Petroleum Arrangements*, p. 25246; Feis, *ibid.*, p. 164; U.S. Senate, Committee on Foreign Relations, *Petroleum Agreement*, p. 25.

[96] U.S. Senate, *Petroleum Agreement*, pp. 92-93.

troleum Association of America (the main representative of solely domestic producers) and resubmitted to the Senate.[97] Had the pact been considered by the Senate in 1946, it would probably have been approved.

However, it was not considered during the 79th Congress. Tom Connally was chairman of Foreign Relations, and Texans were not happy with the Agreement, even if the rest of the industry was. Hearings were initially scheduled for January 1946. They did not actually begin until June 1947, after the election had given the Republicans a majority and Senator Vandenburg of Michigan had become committee chairman. By that time the delicate domestic coalition put together by State Department and other officials had begun to unravel, and the international situation had changed.

After the Second World War perceptions of the world were rapidly transformed. When William T. R. Fox introduced the term "superpowers" in his 1944 study, Great Britain was included along with the United States and the Soviet Union. By the winter of 1946 the English people were cold and hungry, their country bankrupt. The prospect of Britain thwarting the onward march of American oil enterprise was no longer taken seriously by U.S. policy-makers. Undersecretary of State Dean Acheson was the highest administration representative to testify at the 1947 Senate hearings on the treaty, and the transcript leaves the impression that he wanted nothing more than to turn the matter over as quickly as possible to Charles Raynor, the State Department's Petroleum Advisor, who accompanied him. Acheson was clearly unfamiliar with some of the treaty's provisions. The Undersecretary of the Interior also made a brief appearance. The War and Navy Departments sent a colonel (the executive officer of the Army–Navy Petroleum Board) to inform the Senate that they still favored the treaty. No cabinet-rank official testified.[98]

The Anglo-American Oil Agreement still had some support from the oil industry. It was clear by 1947 that there would be no glut, but the treaty did appear to institutionalize the principle of

[97] *Ibid.*, p. 99.

[98] See *ibid.*, pp. 23-30, for Acheson's testimony; see also pp. 187ff. and 246-47.

equal access to supplies, which concerned the international oil companies. The president of Jersey Standard, for instance, argued that the pact might help his company in Indonesia. Joseph E. Pogue, Chase's vice-president in charge of oil, also defended the treaty. The American Petroleum Institute, whose membership is composed of individuals in the oil industry rather than companies, endorsed the agreement with reservations (which were accepted by the State Department) stating that the treaty would not affect the domestic industry and would not be a first step toward international regulation. Even some independent oil men were favorable. A past president of the Independent Petroleum Association of America wrote the committee that international regulation would help the domestic industry by preventing the United States from being flooded with cheap foreign oil. At least thirty-eight other independent oil men informed the Senate of their support.[99]

But there was also vigorous and substantial private opposition, which came primarily from domestic producers. The Independent Petroleum Association of America reversed its earlier endorsement after two State Department officials said on a national NBC radio news program that they saw the treaty as a step toward a general international agreement. Opposition was particularly strong from Texas, where the Governor, the State Senate, several educational associations, the Agriculture Commissioner, and the Democratic State Convention all either testified or wrote against the treaty. The Oil Workers International Union of the CIO also urged the committee to reject the pact.[100]

What the independents fundamentally feared was that the treaty would change the arena of decision-making for the domestic oil industry. Production controls within the United States were set primarily by state regulatory agencies such as the Texas Railroad Commission and the Oil Conservation Board of Montana. In these agencies the industry had enormous power. If decisions were transferred to the federal level, where many other actors and interests could gain access, the industry's power would be diluted. Since legally treaty commitments take precedence over domestic law, even the vaguely worded Anglo-American Oil Agreement

[99] *Ibid.*, pp. 19, 36, 80-81, 171ff., 292-93, 393-96.

[100] *Ibid.*, pp. 68, 155, 176ff., 279, 280.

might, the independents felt, become an instrument for transferring the locus of decision-making from the state to the federal levels. And even worse, this result might be brought about through the judiciary in a way that circumvented the Congress altogether. A letter from the Governor of Texas to the Foreign Relations Committee stated the case bluntly: "The State of Texas will unalterably oppose any treaty or agreement that would ever permit any agency other than the Texas Railroad Commission . . . to regulate and determine the production, sale, and use of its oil and gas, except in time of war and of actual national emergency."[101] Sinclair Oil Company, the largest independent to testify at the hearings, employed the prestigious law firm of Root, Ballantine, Harlan, Bushby, and Palmer to write a brief making the argument that the treaty could change oil decision-making within the United States, despite explicit disclaimers to the contrary. A specific corollary of this concern was the possibility that the pact might open the American market to cheap foreign petroleum.[102]

Through adroit leadership public officials had been able to assuage these fears in 1945 and 1946. But the consensus they constructed was delicate, capable of being shattered by the statements of two middle-level State Department officials in a radio broadcast.[103] The executive was, after 1946, no longer willing to make the large commitment that would have been necessary to maintain wider industry backing for the agreement. Furthermore, the American majors, the private group most supportive of the pact, also lost interest in the late 1940s. Their initial concern was related to the expectation that the treaty would help prevent an oil glut at the end of the war. In fact, by 1947 there was a shortage of oil. Although the agreement might still have facilitated access to certain foreign areas, it is unlikely that the majors were very worried given the increasing weakness of Great Britain. The Foreign Relations Committee recommended the treaty, but it was never taken up by the full Senate. Thus, the Anglo-American Oil

[101] *Ibid.*, p. 79.

[102] *Ibid.*, pp. 372ff.; see p. 109 for the statement of Senator Robertson of Wyoming, who attended some of the hearings although he was not a member of the Committee.

[103] *Ibid.*, p. 68.

Agreement went the way of other postwar schemes such as the International Trade Organization. The fragmentation of the American political system led to delay. As time passed, circumstances changed. As circumstances changed, support withered.

Fifty-fifty Profit Sharing and American Taxes

American central decision-makers were unable to protect foreign oil investments through direct government ownership, by building a pipeline, or by signing a treaty with Britain, but even after the war the threat to American control did not disappear. The British no longer were much of a problem, but nationalism and host-country economic demands were.

In the 1940s and 1950s the governments of most oil-exporting states were more interested in increasing their revenue than in securing formal ownership. The State Department was sympathetic, and urged American oil companies to renegotiate their concessions. The companies were initially reluctant, both because they did not want to undermine the sanctity of their contracts, and because they were not anxious to increase their payments. American policy-makers nevertheless prevailed, but only by finding a device that, in effect, transferred the cost of higher taxes from the oil companies to the U.S. Treasury. First in Venezuela and then in the Middle East, American corporations concluded agreements that called for something like a fifty-fifty division of profits. (In fact, the actual distribution of profits under these contracts, which lasted through the 1960s, was initially below fifty percent for governments, but changed in their favor over time.) The United States allowed most of these higher payments to be written off against American tax liabilities under the provisions of the foreign tax credit. This statute, enacted in 1918, permitted firms to reduce their American taxes dollar for dollar against foreign direct (income) tax payments. The purpose was to avoid double taxation, which could place U.S. corporations at a competitive disadvantage.

Given the peculiar nature of profit calculations in the oil industry, it would have been reasonable to regard Saudi imposts as an indirect tax (based on output) rather than a direct one based on profits. Had this been done, the corporations would have been able to credit higher payments against their taxable income, but not directly against their tax liabilities.[104] The decision to treat higher payments to Saudi Arabia as direct rather than indirect taxes was determined by political considerations. It was made by the National Security Council, not the Internal Revenue Service. Its purpose was to minimize corporate resistance to host-country demands and to bolster the Saudi regime. Hence, the only policy to protect oil investments that American policy-makers were able to implement amounted to using the U.S. Treasury to increase the revenues of host-country governments.

VENEZUELA

Venezuelan pressure to increase oil revenues began with the death of the dictator Juan Gomez in 1935. New petroleum laws were passed in 1936 and in 1938, but they were largely ignored by the companies. The regime of Isias Medina became increasingly desperate in the early 1940s, as the wartime shortage of tankers cut deeply into Venezuelan exports. In the spring of 1942 Venezuelan officials told the State Department that concessions would be revised regardless of the company's attitude.[105]

The State Department did not want a rerun of Bolivia and Mexico. Undersecretary Sumner Welles, in particular, felt that the large profits generated by the development of oil fields in Lake Maracaibo warranted renegotiation of existing arrangements.[106] Once the Mexican nationalizations had taken place, and the war had broken out, the Department was very anxious to avoid another takeover that could jeopardize not only American business interests but also the strategic position of America's major ally, Great Britain.

Government officials wanted the corporations to adopt conciliatory policies. Policy-makers feared that if the question of oil pay-

[104] An example may make this point clearer. Assume a company has revenues of $1,000 and business costs of $900. Let us say that it pays $30 in taxes to a foreign country, and that the American corporate tax rate is 40 percent. If the foreign taxes are direct, then the U.S. liability of the company is $10 (.40 [1,000 − 900] − 30 = 10). If the foreign taxes are indirect, then the U.S. tax obligation of the company is $28 (.40 [1,000 − 900 − 30] = 28).

[105] Larson et al., pp. 479-81; Lieuwen, *Petroleum in Venezuela*, pp. 72-80, 95.

[106] Wood, p. 274.

ments was taken to the Venezuelan judicial system, it would become a salient domestic political issue and the Venezuelan government would be forced to adopt more radical policies. The oil companies were at first resistant, but at least in part because of effective state leadership changed their position. In 1941 the State Department urged Jersey to accept higher payments to Venezuela. The American Ambassador told the corporations that their position was tenable in the long run only if they adopted a conciliatory attitude. Secretary of State Hull met with representatives of the major firms in 1940. The State Department told Gulf a year later that the company would be wise to settle a tax issue with the Venezuelan government before it became a matter of public debate. In the same year the Department urged Jersey to accept higher payments. In September 1942 the State Department arranged for representatives of Jersey and Venezuela to meet in Washington. During these negotiations Venezuela was advised by Herbert Hoover, Jr., who had been hired on the recommendation of the State Department.[107] Buying off foreign talent was later to become a common practice, but for the American government to, in effect, send an advisor to negotiate with American corporations is rather striking.

These official interventions were probably decisive in determining Jersey's position. The company, facing a difficult and perplexing situation, was split. Jersey had just been nationalized in Bolivia and Mexico. Economically, both of these were far less important than Venezuela. The settlements with these two states had not been concluded when Venezuela escalated its pressure in the early 1940s. What strategy was likely to preserve the company's position?

Some corporate officials in New York urged a tough line. They feared that accepting Venezuelan demands would weaken the sanctity of their contracts all over the world. From the corporation's perspective, the ideal situation was one in which concessions with host-country governments would have the same force as contracts between private parties within states. Jersey's managers in Venezuela itself were particularly recalcitrant. However, others within the firm took a different tack. They argued that the

[107] *Ibid.*, pp. 268-71; Larson et al., pp. 481, 483-84.

company had done better in Venezuela than expected and, more important, that foreign operations could only survive if the interests of both the host-country government and the firm were satisfied. Concessions were not contracts. Sovereign states were not private parties. Besides, Venezuela was holding out the bait of extending some concessions that would soon expire, and confirming others whose legal validity had been challenged.[108] The conciliators triumphed: on November 27, 1942, Jersey's executive committee decided to enter into negotiations with Venezuela; two high officials in Venezuela later resigned.[109]

Certainly this decision was in part the result of a bold change by some Jersey officials. They had come to see that the American government was unwilling to support them with force. Without this ultimate sanction, the corporation's ability to stand against the demands of sovereigns was limited. The intervention of the State Department was also important, however. Public officials were much firmer and clearer in their views than their private counterparts. The Department nurtured those company executives who favored a placable position.[110] It was this combination of private flexibility and government leadership that defused a potentially serious disagreement with Venezuela.

Although it is often assumed that the government is muddled while private firms are decisive, this is not always so. Influence can move from the state to the private sector. When the state is dealing with large oligopolistic corporations, the private sector may be quite flexible. Jersey's existence was not on the line in Venezuela, regardless of the position the company finally took. By ruling out the use of force, taking advantage of differing positions within Jersey, and offering the incentive of having the U.S. government absorb the cost of higher taxes, state officials were able to implement their policy preferences in Venezuela. They were able to protect the firms' interests, which were congruent with increasing security of supply, more effectively than corporate officials themselves. This is a situation that conforms well with a statist or structural Marxist approach, but not with an ar-

[108] Larson et al., p. 482.

[109] *Ibid.*, pp. 483-85.

[110] *Ibid.*, p. 483.

gument that explains government policy in terms of private preferences.

Negotiations between Jersey and Venezuela resulted in the passage of a new petroleum law on March 13, 1943, which ultimately raised royalties and taxes to levels that approximated a fifty-fifty division of net earnings. The companies in turn got some old concessions confirmed and renewed for forty years.[111]

SAUDI ARABIA

In the Middle East the situation of American oil companies, temporarily salvaged by lend-lease payments during the war, again came under attack in the late 1940s when Saudi demands for increased payments became more strident. After the war, corporate profits increased and host-country governments wanted their share. Furthermore, Middle East producers were aware of new arrangements in Latin America, because of a mission sent to them by Venezuela in the late 1940s. The corporations were circumvented in this exchange. In fact, a Gulf executive was surprised to learn in 1950 that the Saudis knew what had happened in South America. Late in 1950 one Arabian-American Oil Company (Aramco) official told the State Department that King Ibn Saud might shut down operations if higher cash payments were not made.[112]

In September 1950 State Department officials invited executives of the major American oil companies to Washington, and gave them a policy paper expressing concern about "the threat of Communist aggression" and a "rupture of the flow of Middle East oil."[113] At a later meeting Assistant Secretary of State McGhee stated that "the [State] Department had been thoroughly convinced of the need for Aramco's making substantial increased payments at this time and impressed with the uselessness of trying to divert Saudi Arabian demands into different channels."[114]

[111] *Ibid.*, pp. 484-85.

[112] U.S. Senate, *Multinational Oil Corporations*, Report, p. 81, and *Multinational Corporations*, Hearings, Part 8, pp. 342, 349, 350.

[113] U.S. Senate, *Multinational Oil Corporations*, Report, p. 81.

[114] U.S. Senate, *Multinational Corporations*, Hearings, Part 8, p. 346.

American policy-makers had decided in Saudi Arabia, as they had earlier in Venezuela, that the best way to protect American investments was to satisfy demands for more revenue. Furthermore, the failure of the Petroleum Reserve Corporation and the Anglo-American Oil Agreement indicated that bolder options were not feasible.

At least by 1950, most of the American companies in the Middle East were willing to see their concessions rewritten. Yet this position did not come easily. Aramco had been rejecting Saudi demands for tax payments as opposed to royalties for several years. In 1967 John J. McCloy, then representing Mobil and Socal, sent a letter to Secretary of State Rusk indicating that the companies had only accepted a fifty-fifty arrangement in Saudi Arabia at the behest of the State and Treasury Departments. Prior to government entreaties, McCloy wrote, Aramco had "resisted for nearly four years intense pressures by the Saudi Arabian Government" for new concession terms.[115] This interpretation may have been a little disingenuous, since the minutes of the meetings between State Department officials and representatives of Aramco in 1950 suggest that there was a consensus on making higher payments. Even at that time, however, Gulf was urging the State Department to back a firm stand by the companies against host-country demands.[116]

It is likely that, as in Venezuela, the intervention of the State Department was important in defining the utility function of private executives. Faced with a complicated and confused situation, they could not see clearly how their firms' aims could best be achieved. Under such circumstances public officials could play a major role in establishing private preferences. In part, effective leadership means doing exactly this. The interests of private actors are not, as pluralist models assume, always clear. Rather they can, at least at times, be manipulated and formed by public officials.

All the same, no agency in the American government can escape the fragmentation of the American political system. The companies made some sacrifice in changing from a royalty to an

[115] *Ibid.*, Part 9, p. 116.

[116] *Ibid.*, Part 8, pp. 346-50.

income-tax-based system. They got something in exchange: a transfer of the cost of higher payments to the U.S. Treasury.

The Revenue Act of 1918 allowed corporations to write off foreign direct (income) taxes against their American tax liabilities. The question was: did payments to Saudi Arabia fall under the law? Aramco executives discussed this with the Treasury Department in late 1950. They got a preliminary judgment in their favor, but not a firm commitment. At the State Department, Assistant Secretary McGhee said that he could not take a stand because a legal issue was involved.[117]

The issue was finally decided on political, not legal, grounds. The Saudi Arabian income tax was an odd direct tax indeed. Aramco was not only the largest enterprise in Saudi Arabia, it was virtually the only one. The corporation was wholly owned by Socal, Texaco, Jersey (30 percent each), and Mobil (10 percent). The posted price on which tax payments were made was a transfer price established by the companies to preserve their oligopolistic position. Despite the very low cost of extracting oil in Saudi Arabia (about 10¢ per barrel), this price was set at levels that prevailed in the Gulf of Mexico. The majors preferred to take their profits at the exploitation, rather than the processing or marketing, stages because if they had set crude prices at levels approximating marginal costs, their downstream operations would have been more profitable. Higher profitability in processing and marketing would have attracted even more new firms into these activities, where the barriers to entry presented by capital costs and technical skills were not as high as those presented by the majors' control over crude supplies based on long-term concessions. As it was, the market share of the majors declined almost constantly after 1950. Treating taxes to Saudi Arabia as direct imposts meant accepting an artificial rather than a market price as the base for calculating profits: the tax decision implied tacit official support for collusive practices.

The decision to treat Saudi payments as a direct levy was taken not by the Internal Revenue Service of the Treasury Department, but by the National Security Council. The question whether

[117] *Ibid.*, p. 349.

posted prices were acceptable in establishing profits was never really addressed. Rather, central decision-makers acted to further foreign policy goals. For political and economic reasons they wanted to get more money to Saudi Arabia. They needed the cooperation of the oil companies. They offered a compelling incentive: the cost of the new arrangement would be borne by the American government. For the years 1962 to 1971 the percentage of taxes paid to the United States by the five largest oil companies ranged from 7.3 for Exxon to 2.6 for Texaco. Even as late as 1967, when there could be no doubt that posted prices were established by negotiation between the corporations and host-country governments, that is, were related to doing business, not to profits, a Treasury effort to reconsider the 1950 decision was overruled.[118]

Conclusion

Fifty-fifty profit sharing and the tax decision were the end of a long story that had begun with the Petroleum Reserve Corporation in 1943. It was not an unhappy tale from the point of view of American decision-makers: the oil industry was secure for nearly twenty years; dramatic increases in world demand were met at extraordinarily stable prices; institutional arrangements were not challenged. During the same period the United States achieved most of its broader political objectives. Although the Soviets did increase their influence in the Middle East, the conservative regimes bordering the Persian Gulf (Saudi Arabia, Kuwait, Abu Dhabi, and Iran) were preserved. This accomplishment the United States managed even while continuing its support for Israel.

In performing this political balancing act, public officials used the corporations as an instrument of American foreign policy, in part because private firms were outside of the formal political system.[119] It is not likely that the American Congress would have authorized direct subventions to Saudi Arabia. Ibn Saud and his successors were not exemplars of democracy, and the domestic

[118] *Ibid.*, Part 9, p. 133. U.S. Senate, *Multinational Oil Corporations*, Report, pp. 82-85, 92.

[119] I am indebted to Robert Paarlberg for suggesting this line of argument. See also Church, "The Impotence of the Oil Companies."

petroleum industry became increasingly apprehensive about foreign imports. This concern led to voluntary import controls in 1956 and mandatory ones in 1959. The oil companies were an institutional mechanism that central decision-makers could use to implement a policy of simultaneous support for Israel and some Arab states. In a stronger political system this policy might have been carried out more coherently, and without cost to the public treasury. In the United States such a first-best solution was not possible. Private corporations had to be paid off, but these payoffs were not without their more general political purpose.[120]

Conclusion

The three cases examined in this chapter offer some striking contrasts. In Bolivia and Mexico before World War II, American policy was virtually a complete success. This case conforms well with a structural Marxist or conventional state-centric unified actor interpretation of foreign policy: to maintain alliances, the United States forced a settlement upon resistant oil companies. The effort to further security of Middle East oil supplies during the war was almost a complete failure. This case closely conforms with instrumental Marxist or liberal interpretations: actual policy outcomes coincided with the expressed interests of at least some powerful parts of the petroleum industry. Efforts to cope with the Mexican Revolution were mixed: there were elements of clear state success, for instance, in resisting armed intervention to protect American investors; but government policy was hardly entirely liberated from the preferences of private groups.

Taken individually, each of these cases can be understood from either a liberal or a Marxist perspective. But it is a statist paradigm that offers the most powerful approach for dealing together with all three of these examples. American central decision-

[120] One might argue in retrospect that this whole policy was a mistake since it gave the oil-exporting states sufficient monetary reserves to establish effective market control in 1973. However, such foresight is really asking too much of policy-makers, and anyone else for that matter. Prior to the oil embargo in the fall of 1973, few experts predicted prices above $7 per barrel, which was generally viewed as the opportunity cost for developing new sources of supply.

makers did try to implement a consistent set of preferences. Achieving broad foreign policy goals was their most important objective. These goals were of two types. The first involved changing the nature of the regime in a foreign country, as illustrated by Wilson's opposition to Huerta. This, along with Pershing's expedition, is the only case discussed in this chapter in which American troops were actually used. The use of force is one indication of the importance attributed by state leaders to a particular foreign policy objective. The second broad foreign policy goal was to preserve relations in the western hemisphere when the United States confronted a European war. In Mexico after 1915, and in Mexico and Bolivia during the late 1930s, American central decision-makers were concerned about growing German influence, and this worry limited the support they would give to foreign investors.

The second most important objective for U.S. central decision-makers was increasing security of supply. If general foreign policy goals were not at stake, this was the aim that attracted their attention. The effort to purchase American concessions on the Arabian peninsula, build a pipeline, and sign an oil agreement with Great Britain were all associated with concerns designed to minimize the probability of crude oil scarcities. To try to further this goal, American central decision-makers were willing to oppose the American oil industry (or various of its parts) and, in trying to assume ownership of the Arabian concessions, violate one of the fundamental precepts of capitalist society. A public effort to take over a major capitalist enterprise without any public pressure or clear relationship to general social coherence is not a form of state behavior that can be easily explained by a structural Marxist argument.

Finally, promoting greater competition came at the bottom of the state's set of preferences. This is brought out by the tax arrangements concluded in Venezuela and especially Saudi Arabia. These tacitly recognized the oligopoly structure of crude petroleum pricing, because U.S. leaders felt that higher payments were necessary to promote security of supply and to maintain close political relations with host-country governments.

Although a statist interpretation requires demonstrating that there was consistency in the preferences of central decision-makers, it does not imply that actual government policy will be coherent. The ability of the state to implement its preferences depends upon the domestic political structure in which it must operate. In the United States political leaders have been able to carry out their programs, or at least resist private pressures, if policy was set in the White House or other central executive institutions. Decisions about the use of force are almost always taken in these arenas. This allocation of power made it possible for President Wilson to resist pressure for an armed American intervention in Mexico in 1918 and 1919. It also gave Wilson the ability to weaken Huerta by sending U.S. troops to Vera Cruz, even though this move was opposed by the private sector. However, pressure brought by investors through Congress (one example being the extensive hearings held by Senator Albert Fall) did mean that Wilson could not, even if he had wanted to, entirely ignore the pleas of U.S. ranchers, farmers, miners, and oil companies. Around 1940 the ability of central state organs to manipulate certain instruments of state policy (such as the level of diplomatic support and the purchase of silver) and adroit political leadership that took advantage of differing interests among U.S. oil companies were important factors in the success of American policy toward Bolivia and Mexico. Central decision-makers were able to maintain the primacy of foreign policy goals (cementing alliance ties with Latin America) despite the objections of some major oil companies.

When decision-making moves from central executive agencies to the Congress, however, U.S. political leaders confront a far more difficult situation. They are unlikely to be able to implement state preferences over the objections of the private sector. This is what happened in the case of Middle East oil during the 1940s. The oil industry, with its wealth and votes, was able to stifle one government initiative after another. Even when there were splits in the industry over the construction of the pipeline and the Anglo-American Oil Agreement, the state was still not able to prevail. The opposition of one powerful segment of the industry was enough to frustrate state initiatives when policy implementation required legislative approval.

In sum, all of the cases discussed in this chapter help demonstrate empirically the existence of a transitively ordered set of state objectives; but success in translating such preferences into government policy depended upon the state's ability to deal with groups in its own domestic society.

CHAPTER VII

The Protection of Investments after 1950: Diplomatic and Economic Pressure

After the Second World War the American imperium brought a period of tranquility for American raw materials investors. The foreign activity of firms increased dramatically. The Iranian crisis of the early 1950s was weathered with no negative repercussions for U.S. companies. Indeed, they emerged stronger not only in Iran but around the world; for Mossadegh's failure seemed to demonstrate that less developed states could not stand against the power of the multinationals, particularly if they were supported by the United States. The only major attack on American raw materials investments during the early 1950s was Guatemala's takeover of United Fruit's holdings in 1953. This effort suffered the same fate as Mossadegh's. Not only was the operation returned to private foreign control, but the regime that had chosen the policy was overthrown. In both cases covert American intervention was important.

Yet it was not simply American power that smoothed the way for private foreign investors. The outcome of the Second World War seemed to confirm the wisdom of America's economic and political system. Many Latin American regimes, which had toyed with fascism during the 1930s, now saw liberalism and free enterprise opening the broadest path to development.[1] During the 1950s a number of Latin American countries passed laws liberalizing the conditions under which foreign investors could operate. The Peruvian Mining Code of 1950 and Petroleum Law of 1952, promulgated by the conservative regime of General Manuel Odria, encouraged foreign investment. Bolivia passed a law to promote petroleum investment in 1955. Chile's 1955 min-

[1] Schurmann, *Logic of World Power*.

ing law was very favorable to foreign companies.[2] Canada and Australia also welcomed American capital. Most of Africa remained under European control.

Ultimately, this untroubled atmosphere was a manifestation of the tight bipolar structure of the postwar international system, of the pax-Americana imposed upon the noncommunist world. For host-country governments there were no alternatives to participating in the international economy through the activity of multinational corporations: the ideological, economic, and military might of the United States foreclosed other options.

This comfortable environment was shattered by events in Cuba in 1959 and 1960. Vice-President Nixon's experience during his Latin American tour two years earlier indicated that the American dream had already worn thin. There followed during the late 1960s and 1970s a mounting attack on American foreign raw materials investments. Because of their economic and political saliency, and the changing balance of economic bargaining power between the multinational corporations and host countries, holdings of this type drew more attention than those in manufactures.

The number of nationalizations increased dramatically after 1965. This was a worldwide phenomenon: it was no longer only in Latin America that U.S. investors found themselves in difficulty. The industries affected extended beyond petroleum, which had been the focus of most earlier disputes. The increased frequency of takeovers is brought out by the following table.

The apogee of global corporate control of raw materials has

TABLE VII-1

Frequency of Takeovers
of American-owned Raw Materials Firms

Period	*Latin America*	*Africa*	*Asia*
1900-1950	6	0	0
1951-1965	3	0	0
1965-1974	24	10	0

Source: Derived from information in Table V-1.

[2] Goodsell, *American Corporations and Peruvian Politics*, pp. 41-42; Furnish, "Days of Revindication"; Moran, "The Alliance for Progress," p. 7.

been passed. Multinational corporations in raw materials industries will not disappear from the international scene, but their autonomy and power will be eroded. The pattern of formal ownership has already changed dramatically. For instance, the proportion of copper-producing capacity in the noncommunist world at least partially owned by governments increased from 2.5 percent in 1960 to 43 percent in 1970.[3] In the world petroleum industry there was virtually a complete shift from private to public control in the 1970s. This formal change has also meant a change in actual control: albeit more slowly, decisions about pricing, production, and sales are passing to host-country governments. The discretion the central management has to direct the movement of capital, goods, and personnel is being increasingly circumscribed by national regulations. In some cases multinational corporations have given up formal ownership completely and are simply selling their services to host-country governments. The institutional structure that has governed the international movement of unprocessed commodities is crumbling.

In the final analysis, the takeover of foreign holdings is a reflection of a general waning of American power at the global level. Economic exchange does not take place in a political vacuum. While the United States is still extremely powerful (for even now its resources are greater in relative terms than those of Britain during the latter part of the nineteenth century), there are an increasing number of specific issue areas where it cannot prevail. More important, the United States no longer can set the structure—the basic rules of the game and institutional arrangements for the international movement of goods, capital, and technology. In particular, the United States is no longer able to defend and maintain a structure in which the exploitation, transportation, and marketing of raw materials is controlled by vertically integrated corporations based in the advanced industrial countries. Multinational corporations are flexible and resourceful institutions. They will not disappear, but their role will be more circumscribed in the future than it has been in the past.[4]

[3] Prain, *Copper*, p. 222.

[4] I have elaborated this argument more fully in "Raw Materials Markets." For a general treatment of the problem of protecting foreign investors, which should be contrasted with the interpretation offered here, see Lipson, *Standing Guard*.

This shift in the control of raw materials enterprises impinged upon both the economic and political objectives of the United States. There were unambiguous losses for the American firms involved. Few were put out of business, but the discretionary power of their managers was curtailed. Foreign takeovers also meant that supplies were less secure. The 1973 oil embargo made this predicament clear in the most vivid fashion. While the United States is still relatively self-sufficient in most natural resources, its major allies, the Western European states and Japan, are very dependent on foreign mineral sources.

The nationalizations of raw materials industries in the 1960s and 1970s presented American officials with hard choices. The way in which they made these choices illuminates both their underlying preferences and the pattern of decision-making in the American polity.

The main conclusions that emerge from an examination of the postwar protection of raw materials investments are:

1. American central decision-makers were unwilling to use state power when nationalizations threatened corporate prerogatives (ownership of managerial control), but compensation was paid, and broader foreign policy aims and security of supply were unaffected. In fact, under these circumstances corporate managers do not appear to have appealed for much public assistance. There was a large area of nondecision in postwar policy toward nationalization, of options not seriously considered by either public or private actors. All parties had come to realize that there were high costs involved in protecting foreign investors, and that these costs would not be incurred by state officials if purely private interests were at stake.

2. Corporations could successfully appeal for public support if they could demonstrate that their legal rights involving the payment of prompt and adequate compensation had been violated. But in such cases public officials were willing to use only economic pressure, and even this policy instrument was tempered as it became increasingly clear that such action was counterproductive. The attack on multinational raw material corporations came very swiftly. It was virtually encompassed within the span of three administrations—those of Johnson, Nixon, and Ford. Like

all rapid changes, it was not expected. At the very moment that the autonomy of multinationals was beginning to decrease, scholars were writing about "cosmocorp" and "sovereignty at bay." But a learning process did take place, and over time American policy became more accommodationist. The response to Peru's nationalization of the International Petroleum Company, an issue that poisoned relations between the two countries for nearly a decade, is particularly revealing of this shift in official strategy. The United States moved from economic coercion in the 1960s to conciliation in 1973 and 1974.

3. Only when nationalizations were associated with regimes that were perceived as being communist were American decision-makers willing to use covert force and proxy intervention. These cases—Guatemala in 1954, Cuba and the Dominican Republic in the early 1960s, and Chile in the early 1970s—are often cited to demonstrate that American policy was dictated by economic interests. However, when examined in the context of the whole range of American responses to foreign takeovers, as well as military interventions in areas where American economic stakes were very low (Korea, the Congo, Lebanon, and Vietnam), Guatemala, Cuba, the Dominican Republic, and Chile suggest instead that deeply held beliefs reflecting America's Lockean traditions were the fundamental determinants of American policy.

This chapter deals with the responses to takeovers of U.S. raw materials holdings in which covert or overt force was not an instrument of American policy. The following chapter deals with those cases in which force was used. This distinction has been made because the use of force is the best indication of what is most valued by policy-makers. Its costs to the domestic polity are more substantial than the burdens resulting from economic coercion or diplomacy. Analytically, the cases in which force has been used are the critical ones.

Before moving to the specific cases examined in this chapter, it will be useful to review some of the general American responses to the problem of nationalization. They suggest both the legalistic way in which U.S. officials tried to deal with the problem and the propensity of Congress to defend more decisively the narrow interests of foreign investors.

Laws and Doctrines in the Postwar Period

Although the response to the attacks on foreign investment that began in Cuba in 1959 was swift, it was not sure. It was not until 1971 that the National Security Council systematically addressed itself to the issue. There were several Congressional initiatives earlier, however. Beginning with the Johnson–Bridges Amendment to the Mutual Security Act of 1959 and ending with the Gonzalez Amendments of 1972, Congress passed a number of laws that mandated economic sanctions against countries that failed to compensate U.S. investors for nationalized property. Yet the provisions of these laws were rarely imposed.

The Johnson–Bridges Amendment called for the suspension of aid to any country that did not compensate U.S. investors within six months, but the final version gave the President discretion to waive its provisions if he felt this would be in the national interest. The Hickenlooper Amendment of 1962 mandated the automatic suspension of aid disbursements unless foreign governments took appropriate steps promptly to compensate U.S. investors for nationalized property. This amendment was expanded in 1963 and 1964 to include disputes arising over the nullification of contracts by foreign governments. In 1965 the Sugar Act was amended to provide for the suspension of sugar quotas for countries that did not, within six months, take appropriate steps to compensate Americans whose holdings had been nationalized. The Pelly Amendment passed in 1968 required the suspension of military sales and credit to any nation seizing U.S. fishing vessels more than twelve miles off their coasts. The Gonzalez Amendments of 1972 prohibited American approval of loans from international financial institutions to countries that had failed to take steps to satisfy U.S. investors.[5]

Despite their obligatory language, the executive found ways around these laws. The Hickenlooper Amendment was only officially invoked once—against Ceylon in 1962. The Pelly Amendment led to the suspension of military aid to Peru in February of 1969.[6] But these were the exceptions, not the rule, during the

[5] Lipson, "Corporate Preferences and Public Policies," pp. 397-98; Goodsell, *American Corporations*, p. 130; Einhorn, *Expropriation Politics*, p. 49.

[6] Einhorn, p. 39.

1960s. On January 10, 1972, however, President Nixon released a statement on expropriation that appeared to herald a tougher line on extending aid to countries that had not taken reasonable steps to provide adequate compensation.

Nixon's 1972 speech was as close as the American government came to explicit formulation of a coherent policy response to the takeover of American companies. In 1973 the mandatory provisions of the Hickenlooper Amendment were repealed; the President was again given discretion. American law had come full circle back to the Johnson–Bridges Amendment of 1959.[7]

There are two things analytically interesting about the provisions of American law dealing with nationalizations. First, policy continued to be formulated in the same narrow legalistic terms in which it had first been expressed during the early years of the twentieth century. Although the United States expected prompt and adequate compensation if the holdings of its citizens were taken, the right of foreign governments to nationalize property was never denied. Second, the initiative for automatic economic sanctions came from the Congress. Congressmen who took the lead in such actions were motivated by a variety of factors. For conservatives like Bridges and Hickenlooper, the major concern was a commitment to the sanctity of private property and the free enterprise system. From a "liberal" perspective, as manifest in the Alliance for Progress, foreign investment was considered necessary for economic development. For Pelly, it was the protection of American tuna fishermen. The State Department opposed the mandatory implementation of sanctions. In fact, since the executive was in a position to decide if "meaningful" negotiations were taking place, it was able to circumvent even those laws that dictated an automatic cut in aid. Central decision-makers were primarily concerned with broad foreign policy aims, emanating from a Lockean liberal ideology, not compensation for private firms. A case-by-case examination of the American response to nationalization suggests that policy must be understood in terms of general national goals rather than narrow legal principles, reflected in Congressionally initiated amendments, or the desires of private corporations. These goals prevailed in the actual im-

[7] For a detailed discussion see Einhorn.

plementation of policy because private actors could not get public ones to use the kinds of instruments that would have been necessary to maintain the prerogatives of U.S. firms. Decisions about the use of such instruments, particularly force, were made in the White House where corporate influence was not great.

This chapter examines in detail four cases of the nationalization of raw materials investments that did not involve the overt or covert use of force by the American government. These cases are: copper in Zambia, copper in Chile before 1970, oil and other commodities in Peru, and oil in the Middle East and Latin America during the 1970s (the oil crisis). Takeovers in which force was used are discussed in Chapter VIII. The four cases discussed here are not a random sample of the nationalization of raw materials ventures that have taken place in the last decade. To some extent, the selection has been based on the availability of information. (In the case of oil the problem is to avoid drowning.) At any rate, each does highlight some important facet of American policy preferences and the relationship between the state and large corporations.

The nationalization of the copper industry in Zambia illustrates a situation in which private corporations were able to reach their own accommodation with a host-country government. By the time that President Kaunda moved against the companies, they had already realized that they would be unable to maintain full ownership and control. They did not seek the assistance of the American government. The major American company operating in Zambia, American Metal Climax, was not very reliant on its Zambian operations. The corporate slack possessed by this enterprise made it relatively easy to give up direct ownership and, eventually, considerable control. By the 1970s this pattern of private settlement with little, if any, state involvement was probably the modal one. Although there are no strong analytic conclusions that can be drawn from this case, it does at least illustrate that the private and public American reaction to nationalization was not one of Pavlovian antipathy.

The second case discussed in this chapter involves copper in Chile from 1960 to 1970. It is of substantial analytic interest. It strongly suggests the dominance of general foreign policy objectives in the preferences of American central decision-makers. To bolster the regime of Eduardo Frei, U.S. leaders actively supported a Chilean effort to assume control of the copper industry, which was then virtually entirely owned by a few large American firms. The companies were compelled to adjust to a situation in which their own government was clearly not going to give much support. Kennecott and Cerro maneuvered far more effectively than Anaconda, the firm that had the highest stake in Chile.

The third case involves oil and other commodities in Peru from 1963 to 1975. This case attracted a high level of government attention, and it shows the learning process that American leaders went through over time. As they came to realize the potency of economic nationalism, they became increasingly circumspect in their defense of private investors. The United States moved from economic coercion to low-key diplomacy. American corporations were forced to accommodate themselves to the state's position.

This chapter concludes with a discussion of the oil crisis of the 1970s. The most important analytic conclusion that emerges from this investigation is the importance that American central decision-makers placed on maintaining conservative regimes in oil-exporting states; at least before 1973, this was their central objective.

In sum, all of these cases indicate a consistent ordering of preferences for American policy-makers. General foreign policy goals were more important than economic objectives associated with security of supply or corporate prerogatives. Decision-makers were able to implement their preferences because virtually all of the effective instruments of state policy for dealing with nationalizations were controlled by the White House or the State Department.

INACTION: COPPER IN ZAMBIA

Zambia is a one commodity country. During its first six years of independence (1964-1970) copper accounted for 45 percent of net domestic product, 60 percent of government revenue, and 95 percent of export earnings. The copper industry was controlled by two corporations. The Anglo-American Corporation, which was neither Anglo nor American but South African, produced about 52 percent of Zambia's copper. Roan Selection Trust (RST) accounted for almost all of the rest. Roan Selection Trust was owned by American interests with American Metal Climax (AMAX), with 42 percent of the shares, the largest stockholder.[8]

In August 1969 the President of Zambia, Kenneth Kaunda, "invited" the copper companies to sell 51 percent of their interests to the government. Agreement was quickly reached. Compensation was based on the book value of the companies' holdings and took the form of eight- and twelve-year government bonds bearing an interest rate of 6 percent. The companies were given the right to appoint the managing directors of the new jointly owned firms. They were also given a veto over certain financial and capital programs. Irreconcilable disputes were to be submitted to the Center for the Settlement of Investment Disputes of the World Bank. Limitations on foreign dividend remittances were removed, and Zambia agreed to pay management and marketing fees to RST and Anglo-American; as a result, the actual division of profits between the companies and the state (approximately 35 to 65 percent) did not change very much.[9] Zambia's 1969 action meant only a change in formal ownership.

In 1973, however, Zambia abrogated the 1969 agreement. The outstanding bonds were paid off in full. The foreign exchange privileges of the companies, and their management and marketing contracts, were terminated. The government also announced that it would appoint its own managing directors. Some effective control as well as formal ownership passed into the hands of the state.[10]

The companies did not raise serious objections to any of these developments. Indeed, they appear to have accepted them as a matter of course. The most careful study of the behavior of the copper companies in Zambia concludes that they assiduously adhered to public directives. Even Anglo-American, a South African corporation, obeyed Zambian embargo regulations against

[8] Sklar, *Corporate Power in an African State*, pp. 24, 30, 49.

[9] *Ibid.*, pp. 53-61, 189-90.

[10] *Ibid.*, pp. 189-90; AMAX, *Annual Report*, 1973, p. 23; AMAX, *Annual Report to the Securities and Exchange Commission*, Form 10-K, 1974, p. 17.

white-ruled Rhodesia. The annual reports of AMAX during the early 1970s reveal no indication of efforts to thwart Zambia's actions. No serious objections were raised by the companies when nationalization was first announced.[11]

Given their limited economic stake, the response of the American companies was not surprising. The market value of the companies' shares, particularly RST's, did fall. However, only about 14 percent of AMAX's total earnings in 1969 came from its Zambian operations. Furthermore, its foreign operations were relatively modest: in 1974 about 18 percent of its consolidated sales revenues came from outside the United States.[12] Zambia's actions did mean a real loss of corporate prerogatives—that is, the control managers exercised over economic resources—but nationalization did not threaten the company's survival.

Kaunda's "invitation" of August 1969 and subsequent events raised not a ripple of public response from the American government. Secretary of State Rogers visited Lusaka in February 1970 as part of a ten-nation tour of Africa. The statements released during his one-day visit were entirely amiable. No mention was made of foreign investment in general, or the copper nationalization in particular.[13] Nor was there any direct or indirect economic pressure. U.S. foreign aid grants, which had been running at about one million dollars a year from 1966 through 1968, did fall to under half a million in the early 1970s, but loans from the Export-Import Bank increased substantially to $4.3 million in 1971, $23.2 million in 1972, and $9.1 million in 1973. During the 1970s loans from the International Bank for Reconstruction and Development (IBRD) to Zambia also increased, reaching $74.5 million in 1973.[14]

From the perspective of narrow American economic interest, the lack of government response was unsurprising. America is

[11] Sklar, *passim*, esp. Ch. 5; *Wall St. Journal*, Aug. 15, 1969, 9; *New York Times*, Aug. 17, 1969, III, 1:1.

[12] Sklar, pp. 46, 49; AMAX, Form 10-K, 1974.

[13] U.S. Dept. of State, *Department of State Bulletin* 62 (March 23, 1970), pp. 373-75.

[14] U.S. Agency for International Development, *Overseas Loans and Grants*, May 1974, pp. 125, 193.

relatively self-sufficient in copper; in 1973 imports from Zambia equalled less than one percent of total American consumption.[15]

From a global perspective, however, Zambian copper is important. In 1969 it accounted for a little more than 10 percent of world production and a much higher percentage of world trade. It is a major source of supply for America's closest allies, and does have an indirect effect on the United States through the impact of Zambian sales on world, and thus American, copper prices. The loss of corporate control does make supplies at least potentially less secure: it is illusory to assume that the government of a less developed state will act in the same way as a large multinational corporation. Zambia's leaders do have political objectives, particularly with respect to white-ruled areas, which are not those of the American Metal Climax Company. Zambia is likely to be more interested (at least at times) in maximizing its short-run copper earnings rather than maintaining long-term price stability. Since 1967 Zambia, along with Chile, Peru, and Zaire, have tried (albeit unsuccessfully) to turn the Intergovernmental Council of Copper Exporting States (CIPEC) into an international cartel. Although it is improbable that any of these factors will lead to a denial of Western access to Zambian copper in the future, it is not impossible. It would be safer for the West if copper were still in the hands of the companies.

The absence of American response to the copper nationalizations in Zambia must be understood not only by appreciating the negligible direct threat they posed to American interests, but also by referring to a more general rational calculus. Economic pressure against Zambia would have threatened the broader foreign policy aim of maintaining noncommunist governments in the Third World. Covert political pressure was also risky. The southern part of Africa is particularly sensitive, because white minority governments are a constant source of tension. As events in Angola in 1975 and 1976 demonstrated, this situation did present an opportunity for the Soviets and their allies.

Not much can be concluded from the private and public American response to Zambia's copper nationalizations. AMAX, and

[15] U.S. Dept. of the Interior, Bureau of Mines, *Mineral Industry Surveys*, "Copper in 1973," March 6, 1974.

the other American owners of RST, did not see any alternative to accepting Zambian assumption of formal ownership and greater managerial control: their own resources could not halt this development, and their home-country government was unwilling to help. Zambia's care to pay mutually satisfactory levels of compensation eliminated the most obvious formal grounds on which American officials might have felt compelled to intervene. American central decision-makers did not have an automatically negative reaction to nationalization. The takeover of American companies was not in itself enough to generate even a diplomatic response.

ACTIVE ACCOMMODATION: COPPER IN CHILE, 1960-1970

After 1964 the American government strongly supported a reformist government in Chile that was determined to exercise greater control over the American-owned copper industry. The economic stakes for American firms in Chile were much higher than they were in Zambia. Even so, American central decision-makers fastened their attention on regime developments rather than on the specific needs of U.S. investors. In fact, some aspects of American policy, in particular support for land reform under the Alliance for Progress, positively weakened the position of the copper companies. This case, when taken in conjunction with the change in American policy toward Chile that took place after Allende was elected, strongly supports the proposition that American policy was guided by general foreign policy considerations rather than the needs or preferences of specific investors. Whether this is best explained by a statist interpretation or a structural Marxist one is a question I shall try to answer in Chapters VIII and IX. But such behavior does weigh against interest-group and instrumental Marxist approaches.

Chile, like Zambia, is a country highly dependent on one commodity. In the mid-1960s copper accounted for about 75 percent of Chile's export earnings. In 1964 copper-mining activities were almost entirely in the hands of three American companies—Anaconda, Kennecott, and Cerro. The country's economic dependence on minerals and growing nationalist sentiments made the ownership of the mines a major issue in the 1964 presidential campaign, which pitted the socialist Salvador Allende against the Christian Democrat Eduardo Frei. (The conservative candidate had withdrawn and thrown his support to Frei.) While Allende favored outright nationalization, Frei advocated a program of Chileanization, in which the state would assume partial ownership. Frei, who won the election, made this the linchpin of his presidential platform. Chileanization would meet nationalist aspirations and provide financial resources to finance other aspects of the Christian Democrat's plan for Chile.[16]

The first step in Chile's takeover of the copper industry was completed in 1967. It provided for a 75-25 split between Cerro and Codelco (the state copper company); 75-25 between Anaconda and Codelco for the company's two largest mines (Anaconda retained ownership of the new La Exotica mine); and 51-49 between Codelco and Kennecott's Braden Copper Company, which owned the El Teniente mine. The companies, particularly Kennecott, were generously compensated through tax reductions, new financing from the state, and liberal provisions for the expatriation of foreign exchange earnings. The next step in Chile's assumption of control came in 1969, when an agreement was signed raising Chile's share in Anaconda's two largest mines to 51 percent. In the same year Chile imposed a surtax designed to capture some of the profits accruing to the companies because of the Chilean government's 1966 decision to base prices on the London Metals Exchange rather than long-term contracts.[17] Thus, even before the 1970 elections, which brought Allende to power, Chile had moved a long way towards effective ownership and control of the copper industry.

Official Response

The reaction of the United States to these developments is striking and analytically revealing. There is no indication that American officials sought to prevent the takeover of the copper industry.

[16] Moran, *Copper in Chile*, p. 127.

[17] Moran, "Transnational Strategies," pp. 273-87; U.S. Dept. of the Interior, Bureau of Mines, *Minerals Yearbook 1967*, Vol. 4, p. 182. Levinson and de Onis, *The Alliance that Lost Its Way*, p. 157; *Wall St. Journal*, July 25, 1974, 8:3; Moran, *Copper in Chile*, pp. 145-46.

On the contrary, they lent strong support to the Frei regime; American backing of social reforms even undermined the position of the companies. Furthermore, American actions before 1970 stand in sharp contrast to those after the election of Allende. During the later period the United States intervened not simply through economic sanctions but also through covert political activity (including indirect involvement in the assassination of the chief of Chile's armed forces) to bring down the Allende regime. The post-1970 period will be examined in greater detail in the following chapter, but the contrast in official behavior does suggest that American policy-makers were not motivated simply by a desire to protect the prerogatives of private investors.

From the early 1960s the United States was heavily involved in internal Chilean affairs. Allende had lost the 1958 election to the conservative Jorge Alessandri by only 33,500 votes.[18] The fundamental objective of American policy in 1964 was to make sure that the Chilean left did not triumph at the polls. The United States threw its support to the Christian Democrats, even though the Chileanization of the copper industry was a major part of their program. More than 50 percent of Frei's campaign funds in 1964 ($2.6 million) came from the CIA. Resources were also provided during the 1965 and 1969 congressional elections. Moreover, the American government funded a propaganda campaign involving payoffs to individual writers and support for noncommunist papers including *El Mercurio*, the country's largest daily. These activities were directed by a high-level interagency task force.[19]

The Frei regime received large amounts of overt foreign aid. Between 1962 and 1969 Chile got more than one billion dollars in direct assistance, a higher per capita level than any other Latin American country. In 1968 public and private food donations from the United States were supplementing the diet of 25 percent of Chile's population. In 1966 Averell Harriman, acting as a special emissary for President Johnson, negotiated an arrangement for the sale of 100,000 tons of Chilean copper to American fabricators. In return for agreeing to a low sales price Chile received

[18] Levinson and de Onis, p. 91.

[19] U.S. Senate, Select Committee to Study Governmental Operations with Respect to Intelligence Activities, *Covert Action in Chile, 1963-1973*, pp. 7-9, 17.

a $10 million loan on very liberal terms and Anaconda agreed to pay additional taxes of $3.5 million.[20]

American officials also facilitated Chileanization of the copper industry. A $200 million Export-Import Bank loan to expand production was conditioned on corporate agreement to state participation. The U.S. Treasury sweetened Kennecott's 1966 deal with Chile by allowing the company to use losses from gold-mining operations in South Africa during the 1950s to lessen the capital gains tax liabilities from the sale of Braden. In 1969 the American Ambassador, Edward Korry, played an important role in the negotiations that gave Chile a 51 percent interest in Anaconda's two largest mines and a minority interest in the new La Exotica mine.[21]

American policy toward Frei was not simply a holding action against the left. The United States actively supported the land-reform program of the Christian Democrats. The Alliance for Progress called for social reform and land redistribution. Although the United States did not always act in accord with these principles, U.S. officials were far from hypocritical in Chile. Ralph Dungan, the American Ambassador during the first half of Frei's term, spoke out strongly in favor of agrarian reform.[22] Frei's program did not meet its target, but considerable land redistribution did take place.

Ironically, support for social reform undermined the position of the copper companies. Until the 1960s Anaconda and Kennecott had been able to count on the backing of conservative business and land-owning groups in Chile. These strata identified their interests with the United States and private property. U.S. support for social reform undercut their position. In retaliation they turned against foreign mining interests. This dissatisfaction was manifest even under the conservative Alessandri regime. After Frei came to power, Chilean conservatives tried unsuccessfully to tie guarantees to the copper companies with the ending of land reform. In 1969 the right-wing National Party indicated that it would not

[20] *Ibid.*, p. 4; Levinson and de Onis, p. 239; Moran, *Copper in Chile*, p. 142.

[21] Levinson and de Onis, pp. 157-58; Moran, "The Alliance for Progress," p. 15.

[22] Levinson and de Onis, p. 238.

support Anaconda against the government's desire to take majority control. The full bitterness of conservative sentiment against the United States is suggested by the fact that the 1970 constitutional amendment proposed by Allende, which provided for the complete nationalization of the copper industry, was unanimously passed by the Chilean legislature even though conservatives and Christian Democrats held a majority of the seats.[23]

American officials had not intended to weaken domestic support for the companies. But they had failed to understand that their desire for social reform in Latin America was incompatible with preserving the position of foreign corporations. The image of the Alliance for Progress, of internal change and continued foreign capitalist activity, was not politically feasible. This misperception favored the left, just as another misperception in Peru during the same period contributed to undermining the strength of the center. While inaccurate images led to inconsistencies in the results of policy, the central objectives of American decisionmakers remained the same: the promotion of Latin American regimes that would not move their countries ideologically and economically towards communism took precedence over the protection of specific private American business interests.

Private Responses

The reaction of American corporations to Frei's Chileanization plan reflected a recognition of the limited support that could be expected from the American government. However, the two largest American companies, Kennecott and Anaconda, had different stakes and adopted different strategies. Kennecott had invested very little in Chile after 1945. It had large reserves of copper ore in the United States. Operations of El Teniente accounted for 30 percent of production, but only 13 percent of the company's total earnings in the mid-1960s. Anaconda, on the other hand, was very heavily involved in Chile. It had made large new expenditures in the 1950s, and its operations there accounted for 51 percent of its total production and 67 percent of earnings by the time Frei came to power.[24]

[23] Moran, "The Alliance for Progress," *passim*.

[24] Moran, "Transnational Strategies," p. 275.

By the late 1950s Kennecott officials had come to the conclusion that their position in Chile was tenuous at best. They sought an accommodation with the government that would minimize their risks and still provide financial remuneration. In 1964, even before Frei's election, Kennecott indicated that it wanted to sell a majority share of El Teniente. Corporate officials had decided that a privately owned company could not get the guarantees they felt were necessary to justify undertaking a major expansion in Chile. The arrangement Kennecott negotiated in 1966 provided for new capital, not from the company's coffers, but from the Export-Import Bank and Chile itself. In addition, Kennecott arranged for financing from banks in Europe and Japan. This spreading of risks ultimately provided Kennecott with a generous settlement after the Allende regime had fully taken over its operations in 1971, because of the international legal and economic pressures that were brought against Chile. Cerro followed a similar policy. Anaconda, on the other hand, was more reluctant to divest itself of its Chilean operations, if only because these were such a major part of its total activities. When nationalization finally came, Anaconda received relatively less compensation, and the company's top management was fired in the early 1970s.[25]

Conclusion

Developments in Chile during the 1960s illustrate the limited leverage that private corporations could exercise over American policy. Decisions about diplomatic initiatives and Alliance for Progress programs were taken in the executive branch. The United States was not willing to use overt or covert force to protect corporate prerogatives. Furthermore, divisions within the industry made it easier for policy-makers to implement their preferences. Cerro and Kennecott, with less to lose in Chile, decided at an early date that they would try to protect their financial position even if they could not maintain their ownership and control. Once they had adopted this course, it became far more difficult for Anaconda, which was less happy with developments, to generate support for a more vigorous American defense of the company's position.

[25] Moran, *Copper in Chile*, pp. 128ff.; Moran, "Transnational Strategies," *passim*.

Still, private accommodation does not warrant the conclusion that firms were happy about what was going on. Even though none of them went out of business, there were real losses. Corporations would prefer a climate in which their ownership rights are not subject to challenge. The course that was voluntarily adopted by Kennecott and Cerro, and forced upon Anaconda, was a second-best solution. American policy in Chile is compatible with an interpretation of American foreign policy that emphasizes the importance of long-term political and economic goals (including security of supply and greater market competition), but not with one that sees the decisions of American policy-makers reflecting the needs of particular U.S. investors.

Economic Coercion and Accommodation: Peru, 1963-1975

From the early 1960s through the mid-1970s the American government was involved in an extended dispute with Peru over the treatment of nationalized American firms. This case illustrates the motivations of Third World regimes (particularly the relationship between domestic political legitimacy and policy toward international corporations), the evolution of policy within the American government (particularly the change to a more accommodating position), and the gradual adjustment of private corporations to the growing power of host-country governments.

Concern about foreign investments in Peru initially focussed on one company—the International Petroleum Company (IPC), a subsidiary of Exxon.[26] It was a dispute that went back to 1914, a year after Jersey assumed control of the La Brea y Parinas concession from British interests. For many years the core of the problem was that the La Brea concession, as opposed to all others in Peru, apparently vested the ownership of subsoil rights with the concessionaire rather than the state. Peru tried to increase taxes in 1914, but was forced to accept international arbitration in 1918 after Canada (possibly at IPC's request) had requisitioned the two tankers that were used to ship oil from the field to Lima. The arbitration was not concluded, however, before the conservative regime of Augusto Bernardino Leguia came to power in 1918. In

[26] More precisely, IPC was a subsidiary of Exxon's wholly owned Canadian subsidiary.

1922 an agreement was reached that was very favorable to the company. The issue was taken up in the 1930s and 1940s, but no fundamental changes were made in the company's relationship with the state.[27]

The La Brea controversy became prominent again in the late 1950s. To put pressure on the government to raise gasoline prices, which were fixed by the state, IPC laid off a thousand workers in 1958. The company was in fact running at a loss. The price increase was granted in 1959, but it engendered a storm of negative publicity that reopened the whole issue of taxation rates and subsoil rights.[28]

By the 1960s the La Brea controversy had become a central political concern in Peru. The success of any regime depended in part on its ability to demonstrate that it was not subservient to Standard Oil of New Jersey. Once the petroleum issue became this salient, the company could no longer protect its interests: it could not give Peruvian political leaders any substitute for the popular legitimacy they needed to preserve their tenure in office.

In 1963 the IPC dispute fell into the lap of the newly elected president, Fernando Belaúnde Terry.[29] Belaúnde promised a settlement within ninety days. However, the internal political struggle between Belaúnde and the APRA party, which controlled the national legislature, made it impossible for the Peruvian government to formulate a coherent policy. The issue dragged on. Belaúnde had some sixty meetings with IPC officials. Finally, in 1967 Peru took nominal control of the subsoil rights of the La Brea field, which by that date accounted for about 30 percent of IPC's output. In November the Peruvian Tax Commissioner ruled that the company owed $144 million in back taxes. In August of the following year a settlement was apparently reached: IPC ceded its subsoil rights in exchange for Peru's cancellation of the tax bill.[30]

[27] Goodsell, *American Corporations*, pp. 52, 121; Ingram, *Expropriation of U.S. Property*, pp. 35-37; Gibb and Knowlton, *History of the Standard Oil Company*, pp. 102-5.

[28] Goodsell, *American Corporations*, pp. 143-44.

[29] These elections were held under the watchful eye of the military, which had taken over in 1962 to prevent the APRA party from winning control of the government.

[30] Levinson and de Onis, p. 154; Ingram, p. 58; Furnish, p. 63.

This agreement (the Act of Talara) was never implemented. In early September 1968 the head of the state oil company accused the IPC of suppressing the last page of an ancillary contract governing crude oil sales. IPC denied the existence of the page. Meanwhile, the original accord lost political support. On October 3 the military escorted Belaúnde at gunpoint to a plane bound for Argentina and political exile. The new leaders stated that the August accord was the "final criminal act" that had prompted their intervention. Six days later the military seized the La Brea concession and IPC's Talara refinery, and declared October 9 a "Day of National Dignity."[31]

In February 1969 Peru announced that the IPC owed $690 million in back taxes and seized the rest of the company's holdings (its distribution network and the Lima oil field). The company appealed this decision through the Peruvian courts, but to no avail. The government did not deny its obligation to pay compensation for property that had been seized, but claimed that back taxes far outweighed the value of IPC's holdings. The company had valued the nationalized property at $120 million.[32]

In the course of the next five years Peru moved against the holdings of the two largest remaining foreign raw materials companies, Cerro and Grace, as well as other U.S. operations. In 1968 Peru took Cerro's landholdings. These had been acquired initially because Cerro's smelter had polluted the surrounding land; they were substantial, but ancillary to the company's primary interest, which was in mining. In August 1969 the government took over almost all large sugar estates; Grace was a major landholder. The following year Cerro opened negotiations to sell the rest of its property to the state, but talks collapsed after two years. Cerro was nationalized in January 1974.[33] In July 1975 another large American company, Marcona, which mined and shipped iron ore, was expropriated. This takeover was striking not only because it was one of the few large foreign operations left in the country, but also because Marcona had appeared to maintain

[31] Goodsell, *American Corporations*, p. 54; *New York Times*, Dec. 8, 1968, 25:1; U.S. Senate, Committee on Foreign Relations, Subcommittee on Western Hemisphere Affairs, *United States Relations with Peru*, pp. 100-102.

[32] Furnish, pp. 63-84; *New York Times*, March 26, 1970, 8:2.

[33] Goodsell, *American Corporations*, p. 124; Ingram, pp. 21, 95.

good relations with the government and had voluntarily renegotiated its concession four times between its entry into the country in 1952 and 1970.[34] Furthermore, the U.S. Undersecretary of State for Economic Affairs, Charles Robinson, had been an executive of one of Marcona's parent companies before he took office. During the early 1970s a number of other U.S. operations ranging from construction to fish meal were also nationalized. Thus, by 1975 almost all large American raw materials companies had been taken over by Peru.[35]

Official U.S. Response

Peru's claims on the IPC were one of the earliest challenges to raw materials investors from a regime that U.S. officials did not perceive as communist. The way in which public officials grappled with this issue illustrates both their ability to learn and their unwillingness to use force to protect U.S. investors when more general foreign policy aims were not at stake. U.S. policy moved from economic pressure in the mid-1960s to accommodation in the 1970s as policy-makers came to realize that strong nationalist sentiments made it impossible for any Peruvian regime to accept a dominant role for foreign investors. Furthermore, the evidence that is available indicates that the impetus for accommodation came from the state, not the corporations. Exxon in particular was uncertain about how best to protect its interests, and was therefore susceptible to a redefinition of the problem by state officials. Divisions within the American business community also made it easier for decision-makers to take an active role in negotiating final settlements between Peru and a number of U.S. investors. Given the unhappiness of some private investors, and the legal obligation of

[34] Goodsell, *American Corporations*, p. 51.

[35] The most important exception was the development of the $600+ million Caujone copper mine by a consortium of mining companies led by Asarco. Also, Marcona retained control over the marketing and shipping of Peruvian iron ore, and Belco continued to develop petroleum resources. In August 1975 Juan Velasco Alvarado was replaced by a more conservative group of officers. By this time the Peruvian economy was in bad shape. Foreign debt had risen sharply. Although the new regime adopted a more conciliatory attitude toward foreign investment, U.S. firms were not anxious to commit new resources to Peru. See *Wall St. Journal*, Jan 31, 1977, 6:1.

the Hickenlooper Amendment to impose economic sanctions on countries that nationalized without compensation, U.S. leaders were able to implement their preferences only because they exercised adroit leadership toward private firms and could take advantage of divisions within the business community.

When Belaúnde took office, the U.S. government put economic pressure on Peru to force a satisfactory settlement with IPC. After a visit to Lima in 1963, Teodoro Moscoso, the Administrator of the Alliance for Progress, recommended a freeze on U.S. aid authorizations. Moscoso regarded this as a temporary measure, one that would give the Peruvians an incentive to reach an accord. However, when Thomas Mann took over Moscoso's responsibilities as Assistant Secretary of State for American Republic Affairs in 1964, he made the freeze permanent, although he did not explicitly tell the Peruvians why aid had been cut off. This policy was not reversed until 1966, when Lincoln Gordon became Assistant Secretary. In 1968 aid was again frozen, after Peru purchased a number of supersonic jet fighters from France. This measure was taken under provisions of the Foreign Assistance Act providing for aid reductions to countries that made unnecessary military expenditures.[36]

When Nixon took office several months after the Talara refinery and La Brea field had been nationalized, he continued the earlier policy of economic pressure. The IPC case was placed on the National Security Council's agenda. Undersecretary of State Elliot Richardson took responsibility for supervising the issue. In February 1969 the United States threatened to cut $25 million in aid and $65 million in sugar quotas. At a March news conference Nixon stated that the United States would have to impose economic sanctions if the IPC dispute were not settled. The aid cutoff that the Belaúnde regime had suffered during its last years in office continued through most of 1970 and included not only a reduction in American assistance but also a dramatic fall in loans from the Inter-American Development Bank and the World Bank. In both of these institutions a large share of votes gave the United States considerable influence. Although the Export-Import Bank did

[36] Levinson and de Onis, pp. 150-51; Ingram, pp. 51, 57; Goodsell, "Diplomatic Protection of U.S. Business in Peru," p. 248.

grant some loans in fiscal year 1969, aid to Peru from all sources fell to $9 million in 1969.[37]

In April 1969, however, came a hint that the United States might be reconsidering. Secretary of State Rogers and Henry Kissinger decided that the provisions of the Hickenlooper Amendment would not be formally invoked against Peru, although the six-month deadline for its implementation was approaching. While aid reductions continued, the American government took a new tack by sending John Irwin, a New York lawyer, on a special mission to Peru. It also announced that a $12 million credit was being released by the Inter-American Development Bank, and that Peru's sugar quota was being increased. Irwin had three rounds of meetings in Peru between April and August. He made another visit in September, but no final settlement was reached.[38]

In July 1973, after a number of other American companies had been taken over, Nixon appointed James Greene, executive vice-president of Manufacturers Hanover Trust, as his special representative to Peru. In February 1974 Greene concluded an agreement. It called for Peru to pay $150 million in compensation of which $76 million was to go to the U.S. government, which would then distribute it to Grace, Cerro, International Proteins, Star-Kist, Goldkist, Cargill, General Mills, Socal, H. B. Zachry, Brown and Root, and Morrison–Knudsen. The remaining $74 million went directly to Cerro ($58 million), Grace, Star-Kist, Goldkist, and Cargill. Nixon called the settlement a "successful outcome" to a dispute that had "clouded relations between our two governments for the past five years." The IPC was not explicitly mentioned, but did share in the funds.[39]

The American government was also instrumental in bringing about a settlement between Marcona and Peru in 1975. The July nationalization halted all foreign iron ore shipments, because Japanese purchasers were glad to use the threat of a Marcona lawsuit

[37] Einhorn, p. 27; Ingram, p. 64; Goodsell, *American Corporations*, pp. 130-31; Powelson, "International Lending Agencies," pp. 137-50; Chadwin, "Nixon Administration Debates New Position Paper on Latin America," p. 106.

[38] Einhorn, p. 27; Goodsell, *American Corporations*, p. 131; Ingram, pp. 65ff.; *New York Times*, March 26, 1970, 8:2, and Aug. 24, 1969, 22:3.

[39] *Wall St. Journal*, Feb. 20, 1974, 4:1; Ingram, p. 95.

to refuse to take deliveries during the economic recession. In December 1975 an interim settlement was reached through negotiations in which the State Department took an active role. Peru agreed to pay some compensation and to allow Marcona to continue to manage foreign sales; Marcona dropped its threat of legal action.[40] Thus, from 1969 to 1975 the United States moved from a policy of fairly staunch resistance to Peruvian takeovers, most clearly manifested in the reduction of foreign aid, to one of accommodation, reflected in the Irwin and Greene missions and the settlement of the Marcona dispute.

Private Responses

Corporate preferences followed a pattern similar, but not exactly identical, to the public one. U.S. companies initially favored a tough line. During the mid-1960s Exxon was the only U.S. company being threatened. Peru's pressure confronted Exxon with a difficult choice. Corporate officials were primarily concerned with the demonstration effect of Peruvian initiatives. The company wanted to prevent changes in the terms on which it operated, not because IPC was economically important—Peru accounted for only a small fraction of Exxon's total crude production and profits—but because changing concession terms and limiting managerial autonomy might lead to similar challenges in other countries. Jersey supported a strong stand by the American government, and urged that economic sanctions be used to force a settlement acceptable to the corporation. There were extensive contacts between company officials and State Department personnel in Washington and Lima. No American company protested against economic sanctions before 1969.[41]

A hard line had its own dangers, however. It could threaten the company's position in other countries by making Exxon a more salient target for nationalist attacks. During the mid-1960s the advocates of firm resistance prevailed, but by 1967 or 1968 there was a change. The corporation's decision-makers came to believe that stubborn resistance would only make the company appear

[40] *New York Times*, Dec. 13, 1975, 43:1.

[41] Levinson and de Onis, pp. 149-50; Goodsell, *American Corporations*, p. 131; Einhorn, p. 42.

more reactionary. This more conciliatory attitude led to the conclusion of the August 1968 agreement with Peru. The absence of strong sentiments about the utility of economic sanctions by the late 1960s was revealed in the response of an Exxon official to a query from Senator Church about the Hickenlooper Amendment, during hearings before the Foreign Relations Committee in 1969.

> I really do not have any particular view on it. It is the law of the land. I would rather not express an opinion from a legal standpoint, because I am not qualified to speak in that fashion. I think its greatest use must be as a deterrent, and I guess you have to say in this case it has not worked yet.[42]

Exxon did not formally lobby for the application of the Hickenlooper Amendment in 1969, although there was still some sentiment within the company for tough American action.[43]

Once the IPC was actually nationalized, a number of other American investors expressed their opposition to economic sanctions. They regarded IPC as a separate case because of its long and controversial history, and feared that formal sanctions would jeopardize their own position.[44] The president of Marcona led the fight against the automatic suspension of aid. In a private memorandum written in April 1969 he argued:

> In summary, there is at least a remote possibility that IPC could obtain compensation through direct negotiations with the Peruvian Government without State Department pressure. However, it is very clear that there is no hope for IPC so long as our government insists on invoking the Hickenlooper amendment. Furthermore, U.S. relations in all of Latin America are in jeopardy, if we continue to follow this course. Certainly other U.S. investors in Peru are now suffering and will continue to suffer from a continuation of this completely unsound policy which ignores the basic facts of life in Latin America.[45]

During the months following the expropriation of IPC, Belco Petroleum, Marcona, and the Southern Peru Copper Company announced plans to expand their operations. Cerro, Xerox, and ITT

[42] U.S. Senate, *Peru*, p. 112.

[43] Goodsell, *American Corporations*, p. 131; Einhorn, p. 50.

[44] Ingram, pp. 93-94.

[45] Einhorn, p. 49.

declared that they were not in danger of being nationalized.[46] At a meeting with business executives in October 1969 President Juan Velasco Alvarado stated, "We are not going to establish a communist society."[47] In November Peru took out a full-page ad in the *New York Times* encouraging new foreign investment.[48]

The honeymoon did not last. As the general antibusiness attitude of the Velasco regime (most clearly manifest in new nationalizations) became apparent, American investors grew more hostile. After Peru offered only $10.1 million in nonnegotiable bonds as compensation for Grace's two sugar plantations, the company lobbied for an amendment to the Sugar Act that would have provided additional payments to the company from Peruvian sugar sold in the United States under the American sugar import program. Pressed by Representative Pelly (a spokesman for U.S. fishing interests threatened by Peru's claim of a 200-mile coastal zone), the House Agriculture Committee made the provision even more stringent, and the Senate Finance Committee recommended reducing Peru's quota. However, the final version of the bill left the invocation of sanctions to Presidential discretion.[49]

American business interests split over the "Grace Amendment." It was supported by Cerro, the largest U.S. company still operating in Peru, but the chief of Goodyear's Peruvian subsidiary, which made large truck tires, asked its corporate headquarters in Akron to lobby against the measure. The American Chamber of Commerce in Peru wrote letters to both the Senate and House committees opposing Grace's initiative and reductions in Peru's sugar quota.[50]

By February 1974, when the Greene mission was concluded, American investors had accommodated themselves to Peruvian nationalism. Even Exxon, which was not formally included in the settlement, was no longer pressing its case.

Conclusion

It is not easy to draw clear conclusions about the relationship between the American government and private corporations from

[46] Ingram, pp. 70, 80; Einhorn, pp. 34-35.

[47] *New York Times*, Oct. 30, 1969, 4:3.. [48] *Ibid.*, Nov. 16, 1969, 14.

[49] Goodsell, *American Corporations*, pp. 83-84, 135-36.

[50] *Ibid.*, p. 136.

the Peruvian case. Over the course of a decade both groups changed their attitude toward the way in which nationalizations should be confronted. Thomas Mann's freeze on funds in 1964, and even Moscoso's earlier recommendation of a temporary cutoff, can be explained either by corporate pressure or the desire to maximize global security of supply by preserving U.S. corporate control. Although it is clear in retrospect that this policy weakened the kind of regime that the Alliance for Progress was supposed to promote, American officials almost certainly failed to recognize at the time what a salient issue oil was in Peruvian domestic politics. Peru's challenge to IPC was one of the earliest attacks on a U.S. raw materials corporation by a regime that was not perceived as being communist. But economic coercion did not work because Belaúnde could not appear to be knuckling under to imperialist pressures without undermining his internal legitimacy; he also could not ignore the Peruvian Air Force's desire for supersonic jets in 1968 even though this too led to a reduction in American aid. The seizure of American tuna boats (with the consequent imposition of the provisions of the Pelly Amendment) was also not simply an economic issue, but one involving the assertion of national sovereignty and independence. The change in American policy from the early 1960s to the early 1970s can be seen as a learning process. Each new failure of sanctions made U.S. decision-makers more aware of the strength of economic nationalism within the Peruvian polity. Since force was not seriously considered, and economic sanctions did not work, accommodation proved the best alternative.

There is at least some evidence that new initiatives came first from government officials. The original freeze on aid to Peru was ended in 1966 by a new Assistant Secretary of State, Lincoln Gordon, a change that infuriated Exxon officials, who pressed for a tough line through most of 1967.[51] Deputy Assistant Secretary of State Julius Katz testified against the "Grace Amendment" in 1971. He did not inform Grace officials of the position he would take even though he had seen them two days earlier.[52] In 1974 and

[51] Treverton, "United States Policy-making in the IPC Case," p. 22.

[52] Goodsell, *American Corporations*, p. 137.

again in 1975 the State Department helped work out an accommodation between Peru and nationalized U.S. companies. At the very least the Peruvian case does not support the argument that the state was simply the handmaiden of private interests. Once it became apparent that economic sanctions were counterproductive, public officials were unwilling to escalate their pressure against a regime that showed no indication of changing its basic ideological or economic allegiance. Peru was not seen as another Cuba.[53]

The decade from the early 1960s to the early 1970s was one in which the position of American raw materials investors dramatically changed. The Peruvian case, which was a critical focus of debate within the American government for an extended period, suggests that the American response was one of gradual accommodation rather than stubborn resistance. American officials were unwilling to risk aggravating relations with Peru purely to protect corporate prerogatives.

The Oil Crisis

In the history of international raw materials markets no set of events has been as stunning as those that took place in the oil industry during the 1970s. Formal ownership was transferred from multinational firms to host-country governments. In the fall and winter of 1973-1974 some exporting states imposed a successful production cutback. From 1970 to 1974 prices rose nearly 600 percent.

These developments had a dramatic impact. They strained the cohesion of the Western alliance. They increased the dangers inherent in the political situation of the Middle East. They made the international monetary system more unstable by creating a new source of potentially volatile international liquidity, petrodollars (excess reserves held by oil-exporting states in the form of short-term funds). They helped plunge the industrial West into its most severe economic crisis since the 1930s. They imposed a huge additional economic burden on some less developed states. Although there were some positive effects, such as higher prices for

[53] For a counterargument see Lipson, "Corporate Preferences."

American crude oil producers, the overall impact of the oil crisis on the objectives of American policy-makers was negative.[54]

An assessment of American policy can best be made if it is divided into two time periods. Until the winter of 1973-1974 U.S. officials were primarily concerned with protecting conservative regimes in oil-producing states; they accepted changes in ownership and prices, despite objections from the multinational oil companies. After early 1974 American decision-makers confronted the more difficult task of limiting further price increases and preventing another production cutback without undermining the governments of those oil-producing states that were still anticommunist.

The pre-1974 period does yield some interesting analytic conclusions. First, it again shows that American policy-makers were more concerned with broader foreign policy objectives, specifically regime types in host-country governments, than they were with the prerogatives of corporations or the price of oil. In the triangular relationship involving the corporations, the American government, and conservative regimes in the Middle East, American central decision-makers allied themselves more often with the hereditary rulers of Iran and Saudi Arabia than with their own corporate executives. Second, the two efforts that American leaders did make during this period to try to control prices, both of which were directed at Libya, failed because of the weakness of the American political system: U.S. leaders were not able to get the oil companies to support each other against a Libyan strategy of picking them off one by one, and they were not able to stop a

[54] A number of commentators have argued that the oil crisis really served American interests, especially by improving the competitive position of U.S. industry, which was far less dependent on foreign oil than manufacturing operations in Western Europe and Japan. For an example see V. H. Oppenheim, "The Past: We Pushed Them." I find this contention implausible. First, it ignores a wide range of U.S. policies in the postwar period that did not serve narrow U.S. economic interests: in particular, support for the EEC despite the Common Agricultural Policy, and acceptance of Japanese restrictions on trade and investment. Second, the American government has allowed domestic oil prices to increase very substantially, thus vitiating the competitive advantage enjoyed by U.S. manufacturers. Finally, it is difficult to believe that any government would willfully open itself to the kind of grief and uncertainty resulting from the energy crisis.

major East Coast supplier, the New England Petroleum Company, from purchasing Libyan oil after Khadaffi had nationalized a number of American firms.

The period after 1973 must be approached with great hesitancy; it is still too much with us. The most prominent issues in the mid-1970s are not directly related to the immediate concerns of this book—foreign raw materials investments. Still, a study of raw materials cannot completely sidestep the broader issues associated with the oil crisis. Price hikes by the Organization of Petroleum Exporting Countries (OPEC) to more than $11 per barrel had a severe impact on state objectives. While U.S. central decision-makers had some success in working out arrangements with other industrial countries to mitigate the impact of higher oil prices, state programs encountered great difficulties within the United States. Some of these were technical and geological, not political. But others intimately reflected the weakness of the American political system. It has been difficult for the executive to implement a coherent and decisive plan because so many specific interest groups are affected by energy and the dispersion of power in the United States has made it possible for them to block policy at a large number of decision-making nodules. I do not want to argue that it is impossible for the United States to have an effective energy program. President Carter introduced his energy program in the spring of 1977 with a speech to the American public, an address to Congress, and a news conference. The Congress, however, was not very cooperative. Leadership, manifest in the President's ability to change the perceptions of private groups and their influence in Congress, through his hold on the general electorate, may prevail, but this is not usually the case: the fragmentation of power in the American polity is a major impediment to any effective program.

For convenience of exposition, the discussion in this section will be divided into two issue areas: nationalization and pricing.

The Background

NATIONALIZATION

The takeover of foreign oil companies followed several different patterns, although the final result (the loss of formal majority ownership) was the same. The most abrupt changes occurred in Iraq, Libya, and Algeria. These countries unilaterally nationalized all or part of their oil industry. Iraq's actions against the Iraq Petroleum Company (IPC) owned by CFP, British Petroleum, Exxon, and Mobil began in 1958, when the left-wing regime of Abdul Kassem came to power. Under its concession the IPC had petroleum rights in all of Iraq. In 1961, after three years of fruitless negotiations, Iraq took all of the land that was not actively producing. This amounted to 99.5 percent of the nation's territory, including some areas where commercial quantities of crude had been located but not developed. The companies had offered to relinquish 75 percent of the territory immediately and another 15 percent after seven years. Iraq refused to submit the dispute to arbitration or to pay compensation. This issue did not, however, come to a head until the early 1970s when Iraq tried to sell oil from the nationalized area, which had been developed with technical and financial assistance from the Soviet Union. Corporate efforts to put pressure on Iraq by limiting production led to the takeover of the rest of IPC's operations in June 1972. A settlement was reached in early 1973.

Algeria took 51 percent control of her oil industry in February of 1971, but this involved the two largest French companies, CFP and ERAP, not American operations. Virtually no compensation was paid.[55]

In December 1971 Libya nationalized British Petroleum's assets, which consisted of 50 percent of the Sarir field; the other half was owned by an American firm, Bunker Hunt Oil Company. This action was justified as retaliation against Great Britain for allowing Iran to occupy two small islands in the Persian Gulf. In June 1973 Hunt's assets were taken, and in September Libya issued a decree calling for state control of 51 percent of all oil operations. When Texaco, Standard of California, Atlantic Richfield, and Royal Dutch Shell balked, they were completely nationalized in February 1974. In April Exxon and Mobil concluded an agreement giving the government a 51 percent share in their operations.[56]

[55] *Petroleum Press Service* 39 (Sept. 1971), p. 323.

[56] *Wall St. Journal*, April 17, 1974, 14; *Petroleum Press Service* 39 (Jan.

For American companies, however, experiences in Iraq and Libya were the exception, not the rule. The more typical pattern of movement from corporate to state ownership was not the abrupt and arbitrary exercise of power that is associated with the term "nationalization," but rather a negotiated settlement described as "participation." Although in its initial formulation participation was supposed to lead to shared ownership and responsibility between corporations and host countries, the final outcome was not very different from nationalization. Nevertheless, the two procedures did engender somewhat different responses from American corporate managers and public decision-makers.

The concept of participation was the invention of Sheik Zaki Yamani, Saudi Arabia's petroleum minister. He had floated the idea as early as 1965. For Yamani, participation resolved serious political and economic dilemmas. Saudi Arabia was governed by a feudal regime that, on the one hand, did not want to alienate the United States but, on the other, was not immune to the nationalist pressures of the Arab world that were directed in part against foreign corporations. Participation was a way of demonstrating independence without offending American policy-makers. Furthermore, Yamani recognized that the corporations played an important role in maintaining the oligopolistic structure of the international oil industry. Were they to be suddenly expelled, prices, which were around $2 per barrel in 1970, could move downward toward marginal costs of 15¢ per barrel or less.[57]

The Organization of Petroleum Exporting Countries first passed a resolution calling for participation in 1968. A serious commitment was made in October 1971, and in January 1972 Yamani was delegated to negotiate for the producers of the Arabian peninsula (Saudi Arabia, Qatar, Kuwait, Iraq, and Abu Dhabi) with some twenty-three oil companies.[58] These discussions dragged on for almost a year. They involved not only the share of ownership to be taken by the state, but also the compensation that would be

1972), p. 4; U.S. Senate, Committee on Foreign Relations, Subcommittee on Multinational Corporations, *Multinational Oil Corporations*, Report, p. 137; *Washington Post*, Oct. 26, 1973, A17:1.

[57] *New York Times*, Jan. 4, 1976, III, 4, and Feb. 19, 1972, 43:6.

[58] *Petroleum Press Service* 39 (Sept. 1971), p. 322; *New York Times*, Nov. 3, 1971, 14:1, and Feb. 19, 1972, 41:5.

paid to the companies and, most important, the price that the corporations would pay for the share of production that would now be owned by the government. This so-called buy-back oil was a critical part of the package, for so long as the corporations had privileged access to production, the structure of the market would not be disturbed. The more oil the exporting states marketed on their own, the more tenuous the hold of the majors would become.

An initial agreement reached in October 1972 called for the government to assume 25 percent ownership immediately, rising to 51 percent in 1983. In December Saudi Arabia and Abu Dhabi approved this settlement, although the date when the state would take majority control was moved up by one year. But Kuwait's rulers did not accept this arrangement because they encountered difficulties in the relatively radical and nationalist Kuwaiti legislature. With more than half of the population drawn from other areas of the Moslem world, including many Palestinians, the aristocratic Kuwaiti regime had to be responsive to nationalist sentiments. At any rate, the late 1971 settlement did not last. The Saudis asked for 51 percent in November 1973. (By this time the 1973 Arab-Israeli War had transformed the political situation in the Middle East.) In January 1974 Kuwait signed a participation agreement giving the state an immediate 60 percent share. A month later Qatar made a similar arrangement. In May Saudi Arabia raised its stake to the same figure. In December 1975 Kuwait moved to 100 percent control. Most other Middle East producers followed suit.[59]

In other major exporting states the form varied, but the substance was more or less the same. Venezuela took full ownership of her oil industry on January 1, 1976. Her president raised the flag over the first oil well in Zulia state to the accompaniment of the national anthem and the sound of a squadron of jets roaring overhead. In Iran, where the 1951 nationalization had never been

[59] *New York Times*, Aug. 30, 1972, 47; Oct. 18, 1972, 61; Oct. 15, 1972, III, 1:4; Jan. 4, 1976, III, 1:3; *Petroleum Press Service* 39 (Dec. 1972), p. 459; *Washington Post*, Sept. 26, 1973, A17:1; Dec. 11, 1973, A18:5; Feb. 21, 1974, A6:1; *Wall St. Journal*, Feb. 1, 1974, 4; May 10, 1974, 7; Texaco, *Annual Report*, 1975, p. 6.

formally reversed (although the consortium of oil companies formed in 1954 did have effective control), the state renegotiated new arrangements in the summer of 1973.[60] Other producers in Africa, Latin America, and Asia assumed at the very least formal majority ownership by the end of 1975.

These arrangements meant a change in substance and not just in form for the international oil companies. They usually did receive compensation. Kuwait paid a little over $50 million for a 60 percent share of the Kuwait Oil Company; Saudi Arabia about $500 million for 25 percent of Aramco; Venezuela $1.1 billion for its entire industry. These were far short of the sums that the companies had originally sought, taking into account not only book value but also future profits. In Saudi Arabia such a sum would have amounted to ten times what the companies actually received.[61] The companies lost their sole control over the level of production. They also lost the power to set prices. In addition, the creation of national oil companies in all of the major states further undermined the ability of the majors to control the international petroleum market.[62] The takeovers of the early 1970s involved matters of vital interest to both American corporations and, after 1973, to the American state.

PRICING

Coincident with changes in ownership was a sharp increase in international petroleum prices. From 1950 to 1970 the price of crude oil was steadier than that of any other commodity because of the effective market control of the international oil companies.[63] But between 1970 and 1974 the price of oil rose sharply.

Increases began in Libya. When Khadaffi seized power in 1969, he demanded higher payments from the companies, at least in part to demonstrate the corruption and ineffectuality of the previous regime. In Libya, unlike most other countries, there were many oil companies operating, not just one or two. Some of

[60] *New York Times*, Jan. 2, 1976, 35:7; May 25, 1973, 45:2.

[61] *Oil and Gas Journal* 70 (March 27, 1971), p. 48.

[62] *New York Times*, Feb. 4, 1976, 43:1; Jan. 4, 1976, III, 1:3; Jan. 2, 1976, 35:7; Dec. 2, 1975, 69:5.

[63] Krasner, "Raw Materials Markets."

these, in particular the Occidental Petroleum Company, were very dependent on their Libyan supplies. The Libyan regime initially concentrated its pressure on Occidental, and in September 1970 the company capitulated, accepting a higher posted price and an increase in the tax rate from 50 to 58 percent. This change destroyed the stability that fifty-fifty agreements had given to the oil industry for two decades. Other Libyan producers also bowed to pressure. In December 1970 Venezuela imposed a flat 60 percent tax and assumed the right to unilaterally fix reference (posted) prices on which tax payments were based.[64]

Other major producing states in the Mediterranean area and the Middle East made claims on the basis of what Libya had gotten. Higher prices for the Persian Gulf producers were codified in the Teheran Agreement of January 1971, which provided for a 30¢ per barrel increase in payments, rising to 50¢ by 1975. Libya then made new demands, and got a 65¢ per barrel increase in March 1971. Further price hike agreements were concluded at Geneva in January 1972 even though the Teheran Agreement was supposed to have lasted for five years. New increased prices were set in 1973. Between 1970 and October 1973 prices rose from about $2 per barrel to about $3.25 per barrel.

Then the October War precipitated a dramatic rise in oil prices. The members of OPEC unilaterally raised posted prices on October 16, 1973, and on January 1, 1974. The fiction of negotiating with the oil companies was ended.[65] Prices went to nearly $12 per barrel. Since 1974 OPEC has dictated further increases. These developments are summarized in the following diagram.

Corporate Responses

Nationalization and price increases have not put the major oil companies out of business. The sharp rise in prices after January 1974 even gave them large temporary boosts in profits. Nevertheless, developments associated with the oil crisis did present some

[64] U.S. Senate, Committee on Foreign Relations, Subcommittee on Multinational Corporations, *Multinational Corporations*, Hearings, Part 5, pp. 111-12; *Petroleum Press Service* 39 (Sept. 1971), p. 327.

[65] U.S. Senate, *Multinational Oil Corporations*, Report, p. 143; *Oil and Gas Journal* 70 (Jan. 17, 1972), p. 65; *Oil and Gas Journal* 70 (May 18, 1972), p. 29; Gulf Oil Company, *Annual Report*, 1974, p. 48.

Figure VII-1

Changes in Posted Price of Saudi Arabian Crude Oil*

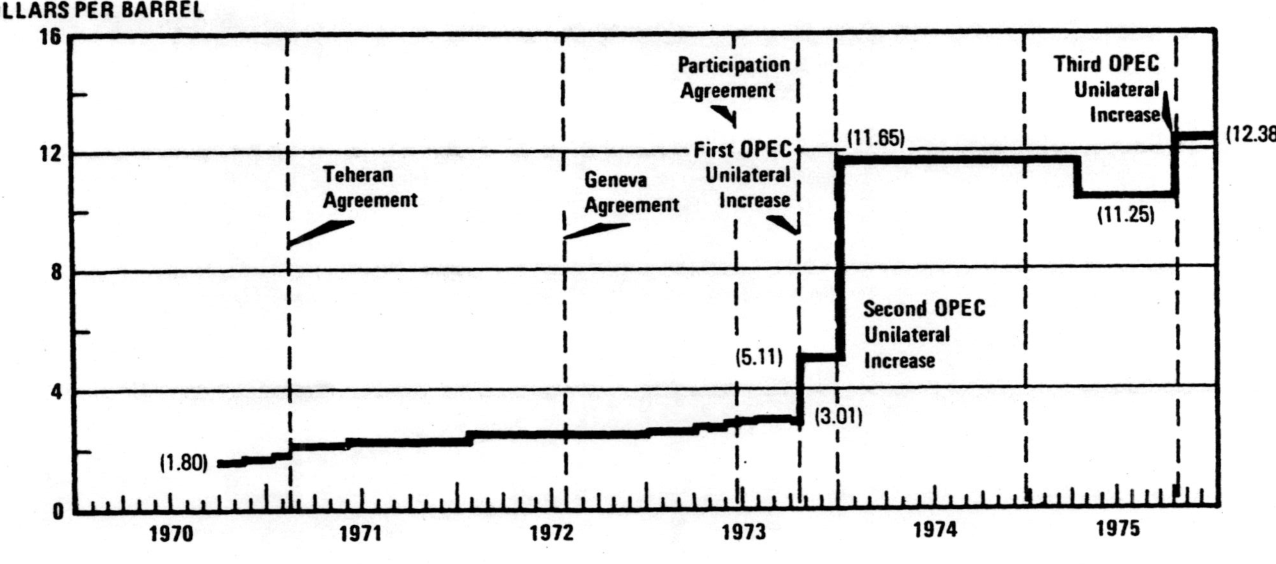

* Arabian Light 34°.

Source: From John M. Blair, *The Control of Oil* (copyright © 1976 by Pantheon Books), Chart 11-1, p. 263. Reprinted by permission of Pantheon Books, a Division of Random House, Inc.

serious problems for the private sector. The oil companies did make some attempt to prevent price increases and nationalization. They received no serious support from the American government, however. In fact, U.S. policy-makers undermined corporate efforts to check price increases in 1971. Without state support they could not resist pressures from even weak states. By the mid-1970s the oil industry had moved to accommodate itself to OPEC.

NATIONALIZATION

The dispute that followed Iraq's 1961 takeover of nonproducing territory was the most extended in the oil industry after the Second World War, and the one in which the companies put up the most resistance. In part, this was a matter of timing: during the 1960s American companies continued to challenge changes in concession agreements. In part, it was a response to the arbitrariness of Iraq's action and the refusal to pay any compensation. In an environment that was constantly being turned topsy-turvy, corporate officials looked for simple rules, and one of these was to resist unilateral uncompensated changes in concession arrangements.[66] The dispute over the 1961 decree came to a head only in late 1971 when Iraq began to market oil from the North Rumelia field, which was part of the territory that the IPC had been forced to relinquish. Some of IPC's parent companies threatened to bring legal action against this oil. This did present Iraq with some marketing difficulties in the spring of 1972. More decisively, the IPC cut back production from the fields it still controlled in Iraq, which accounted for almost all of the country's output. The government retaliated by nationalizing all of IPC's assets. Private attempts to block sales were undermined by the willingness of Russia, East Germany, and Bulgaria to take oil from Iraq and, more important, by a French decision not only to buy oil but also to operate some of the nationalized fields. Kuwait and Abu Dhabi provided Iraq with funds.[67]

In Libya the companies were even less successful. British Pe-

[66] For the importance of simple rules in complex situations see Steinbrunner, "Beyond Rational Deterrence."

[67] *New York Times*, April 7, 1972, 45:3; *Oil and Gas Journal* 70 (Jan. 10, 1972), p. 42; U.S. Senate, *Multinational Corporations*, Hearings, Part 8, p. 505; *Petroleum Press Service* 39 (Aug. 1972), p. 301.

troleum, Texaco, and Socal did bring legal actions against a number of parties that purchased oil from their concessions. Libya nevertheless was able to sell to the Soviet Union, Bulgaria, Rumania, Brazil, Italy, and even the United States. Furthermore, the companies did not meet their obligations to provide support for the most vulnerable producers, the independents such as Bunker Hunt and Occidental, which got a large proportion of their crude from Libya. In 1971 the corporations active in Libya had signed an agreement known as the Libyan Safety Net, under which they would supply any member cut off in a dispute with the government. But when Bunker Hunt was taken over in the summer of 1973, most independents and the crude-short majors such as Mobil did not fulfill the terms of the agreement, and Hunt was forced to capitulate.[68]

Host-country demands for participation, as opposed to nationalization, were more cordially received by the major corporations. Here too, however, they initially put up some resistance, Aramco particularly. Owned by Exxon, Socal, Texaco, and Mobil, it was the focus of discussions between Yamani and the oil companies in 1972. Exxon officials spoke out most forcefully in public. In November 1971 the company's vice-president in charge of the negotiations called the new participation demands "contrary to the word and spirit" of the Teheran Agreement concluded in early 1971.[69] Exxon's chairman echoed this sentiment, stating that participation would be "contrary to the 1971 agreements." He said that the companies were "sympathetic" to the countries' desire for a share of ownership, but that "it would be extremely difficult to implement in existing conditions."[70] However, the American majors were not united. Gulf took a more conciliatory position: one of the company's executive vice-presidents told a meeting of security analysts that "participation is not a nasty word."[71] At the initial meetings with Yamani in the winter of

[68] *Oil and Gas Journal* 70 (Jan. 10, 1972), p. 42; U.S. Senate, *Multinational Corporations*, Hearings, Part 5, pp. 45ff.; *New York Times*, April 17, 1974, 63; June 13, 1974, 65:1; Nov. 8, 1975, 35:1; Dec. 5, 1975, 57:2; *Wall St. Journal*, Feb. 19, 1976, 10:1.

[69] *Oil and Gas Journal* 69 (Nov. 8, 1971), p. 41.

[70] *Ibid*. 46 (Nov. 15, 1971), p. 106.

[71] *New York Times*, Nov. 3, 1971, 14:4.

1972, Aramco's negotiators took a tough stand. At least publicly they refused to accept participation, even in principle. They asked for compensation based not only on book values but also on future profits. They offered a very modest premium over their existing tax-paid costs for any crude they would buy from the government. Very little progress was made during the winter of 1972.

The owners of Aramco finally capitulated in the middle of March, one day before a meeting of OPEC was scheduled to begin in Beirut. They agreed in principle to 20 percent participation. Other companies followed suit, but, the negotiations continued to drag on. The companies were still hoping for large compensation and guaranteed access at reasonable prices to the government's share of crude. Then, in April, Iraq nationalized IPC. In June the Secretary General of OPEC warned that if the companies did not agree to participation, other producing states would follow Iraq's lead.[72] In July King Faisal of Saudi Arabia officially announced that his government was "determined to take all necessary measures" to secure participation. The companies were accused of "procrastination and evasiveness."[73]

At this point corporate resistance broke. Faisal, despite the conservative nature of his regime, had put himself publicly on the line. He could not back down, because it would undermine his domestic political position. As we shall see, it was already apparent that the companies could expect only limited support from the American government. U.S. policy-makers were more concerned with keeping a lid on the political situation, and maintaining the authority of conservative governments, than they were with the prerogatives of the oil companies. At Exxon's 1972 annual meeting the company's chairman argued that there were advantages to having the producing countries as partners.[74] By 1974 the corporations had clearly resigned themselves to their new status. Exxon's chief executives stated in their annual letter to the stockholders:

We see no indication that any major producing country is about

[72] *Oil and Gas Journal* 70 (March 20, 1972), p. 32, and 70 (March 27, 1972), p. 48; *New York Times*, June 6, 1972.

[73] *New York Times*, July 11, 1972, 45:1.

[74] *Oil and Gas Journal* 70 (1972), p. 39.

> to eliminate private companies from the scene all together. Quite the contrary. Companies like Exxon have the extensive and complex logistical systems needed to move petroleum into world markets and to distribute it to consumers. We have the technical and managerial skills backed by research and development capabilities which these countries will need to develop their resources further. So we believe that there is a sound basis for continued relationships between producing countries and the industry, though the relationship will be different from those which existed when the companies were discovering and developing the oil and gas reserves from which those countries now derive their economic power.[75]

This from the company that a decade before had urged the American government to use all of its economic power to pressure Peru in a conflict involving a trivial percentage of the company's operations!

PRICING

Responses on demands for higher prices followed a pattern similar to the one established in dealing with questions of formal ownership. The corporations did put up some initial resistance. But by the time the OPEC nations unilaterally arrogated the right to set prices in the fall of 1973, corporate managers had become passive. In the absence of strong political support from the governments of consuming states, their bargaining power depended upon market conditions. Although they were able to secure some marginal adjustments in 1975 when supplies became more abundant, they made no fundamental challenge to the quadrupling of oil prices.

Libya played a critical role in the price increases that occurred between 1969 and the fall of 1973. Had prices been checked there, the world might have been spared $12 per barrel oil. The companies failed badly in their initial encounter with Colonel Muhammed Khadaffi, who assumed control in Libya in 1969 and was determined to demonstrate the ineptitude and corruption of the previous monarchical regime by getting a better deal from the oil companies. Libya first put the squeeze on Occidental, a com-

[75] Exxon, *Annual Report*, 1974, p. 2.

pany that was very dependent on its Libyan supplies. Occidental did try to resist. The company's president, Armand Hammer, asked Exxon to provide supplies if Libya closed down her production. Without such support Occidental was very vulnerable because it had no alternative sources of crude. But the request was rejected by the chairman of Exxon's board of directors.[76] Occidental capitulated, touching off a long series of price increases.

If the oil companies had been able to put up a common front at this early date, both they and the consuming nations might have fared much better. But their shortsightedness is not surprising. From an economic perspective, Occidental was an upstart disrupting the market control of the majors. A general increase in Libyan prices alone would benefit the majors, which had other sources of supply, and hurt the competitive position of the independent companies dependent on Libya.

The oil corporations learned quickly, however. When Libyan demands were followed by cries from the Persian Gulf countries, the companies moved to form a solid front. In late 1970 they indicated to OPEC that they wanted joint negotiations on prices that would include all of the producers and all of the companies. They secured an antitrust waiver from the Justice Department to carry out such discussions. The companies felt that a general agreement was the only way to prevent price leapfrogging, as producers in one area sought to catch up with or surpass increases granted to those in other areas.

But this play failed: the Gulf producing states rejected joint negotiations. King Faisal and the Shah argued that if conversations were carried on with all of OPEC, the most radical demands would prevail. Faced with this resistance, the companies proposed a clever modification. They agreed to carry on discussions only with Persian Gulf producers. But at the same time they asked that these talks cover not only crude shipped from tankers through the Gulf but also that sent by pipeline to the Mediterranean. This approach would create a "hinge" between Gulf and Mediterranean prices that could prevent price ratcheting. Saudi Arabia, however, and Iran, rejected this proposal. When the American government, in effect, backed the position of the exporting states,

[76] U.S. Senate, *Multinational Corporations*, Hearings, Part 5, p. 109.

the companies gave in: the Teheran Agreement of January 1971 covered only oil shipped from the Persian Gulf. As corporate managers had foreseen, this did lead to price increases over the following years.[77]

Evidently, once the companies had lost this initial battle, they made no attempt to put up stiff resistance to subsequent demands. Despite some temporarily higher profits, the oil companies were hurt by price changes. Although none of them was put out of business, they were compelled to make adjustments in their operations. A number of companies began to search for more investment opportunities outside of the oil area. More important, the precipitous increase in prices as well as shortages made the companies a salient political target. Political decisions could no longer be made in narrow arenas where the corporations exercised considerable power. The oil industry became a focus of public attention. A focus of public attention is not likely to be ignored by the Congress or the White House. The 1975 Tax Act ended the depletion allowance for large companies. A bill to split up the vertically integrated petroleum companies successfully cleared the Senate Judiciary Committee in 1976. In voting for the measure Senator Scott of Pennsylvania, not one of the Senate's most progressive members, indicated that he thought a measure of such import should be decided before the whole chamber. The quadrupling of prices tore the veil of complacency that had shielded corporate operations from public view. For managers, this was not a welcome development. Even without new legislation, increased public scrutiny meant some loss of autonomy.

Official Reaction

The inability of the multinationals to resist host-country demands, and the rapidity with which they reconciled themselves to changing circumstances, reflected decisions taken implicitly or explicitly by the American government. Before the October 1973 war U.S. decision-makers were primarily concerned with protecting the prerogatives of the conservative governments of the Mid-

[77] For a discussion of this episode see U.S. Senate, *Multinational Corporations*, Hearings, Part 5, pp. 138-40, and *Multinational Oil Corporations*, Report, pp. 129-30.

dle East. They made no concerted effort to prevent host-country takeovers and did not challenge price increases. They frequently ignored the preferences of the oil companies. Since policy was determined in the White House or the State Department, the private sector was unable to block government initiatives.

But the embargo, production cutbacks, and quadrupling of prices in 1973-1974 presented U.S. officials with a much more complicated situation. Purely economic considerations—prices and access to supplies—became a vital concern. Policy-makers were faced with the difficult task of guaranteeing supplies at reasonable costs without undermining the position of political elites in countries like Iran and Saudi Arabia. The ability to accomplish these objectives was complicated because energy policy became a salient public issue, attracting the attention of the Congress as well as the White House and State Department. While central decision-makers were reasonably successful in implementing their aims at the international level, where they still had some discretion, they had great difficulty establishing their priorities domestically, where energy policy had become enmeshed in the morass of a fragmented political structure.

NATIONALIZATION

As far as the public record now shows, the American government never protested against participation. So long as the legal formalities of a negotiated settlement were observed, even if the threat of unilateral action by host countries was made explicit, American decision-makers did not intervene. In 1971 the U.S. oil companies received an antitrust waiver from the Justice Department that allowed them, among other things, to carry out joint negotiations on the question of participation. No explicit provisions were made for including government officials in this process. The Deputy Assistant Secretary of State for Economic Affairs testified that the Department was informed of the discussions between Aramco and Saudi Arabia that led to 60 percent state control in 1974, but expressed no judgment.[78] When the Saudi Arabian oil minister came to the United States in early 1976 to speak

[78] U.S. Senate, *Multinational Corporations*, Hearings, Part 5, p. 22, and Part 9, p. 164. For a general discussion of the ignorance of the American government see Church, "The Impotence of the Oil Companies," p. 46.

with Aramco's parent companies about a full Saudi takeover, he met with corporate representatives in Florida before flying to Washington.

Even in cases of nationalization (Iraq and Libya), where the form of negotiated settlement was not adhered to, American officials used only diplomacy to defend American corporations. In both of these countries, with their more radical regimes, American leverage was not what it might have been in Saudi Arabia. There was little in the way of economic assistance that could be cut off. During the 1960s the State Department did support the Iraq Petroleum Company by dissuading other American companies from investing. It also made diplomatic representations to Japan and Italy in 1967, after receiving information that companies from these states were interested in Iraq.[79] When Iraq moved against the remaining company holdings in 1972, the United States expressed "regret."[80]

The Libyan case is more complicated: it illustrates both the fragmentation of the political system and the preferences of policy-makers. Libya was an important source of low sulphur crude for the East Coast of the United States. In particular, the New England Petroleum Company (NEPCO) purchased large amounts from Standard of California and Texaco for major utilities in the New York metropolitan area. After the Libyan nationalizations of February 1974, both Socal and Texaco threatened NEPCO with legal action if it continued to buy from Libya. State Department officials also told New England Petroleum that it might be legally prevented from using any oil bought from Libya. NEPCO officials, who claimed that they had no other sources of supply that could meet environmental requirements, were unmoved by this pressure, and arranged to have their purchases from the Libyan state oil company refined in Italy.

They explained their position in a letter to Kissinger, but received no reply. The State Department did not ask American courts to consider the legality of Libya's action. Without such a request legal practices dictate that the courts assume the acts of a foreign sovereign to be legal.[81] The State Department did not have

[79] *Ibid.*, Part 8, pp. 532-33, 545, 551.

[80] *New York Times*, June 2, 1972, 37:3.

[81] U.S. Senate, *Multinational Corporations*, Hearings, Part 5, pp. 45-56.

the power to secure alternative supplies for NEPCO, and without alternative supplies, action against Libyan oil could have meant brownouts or additional pollution in the most heavily populated area of the country. For NEPCO, Libyan oil was vital to the company's survival. Against such unambiguous corporate interests, potentially backed by powerful domestic groups and a large Congressional delegation, the State Department had no leverage. And given such potentially strong resistance, there was no way that Texaco and Socal could compel the State Department to support their claims against Libya more decisively.

A second manifestation of the limited power of the Department was its inability to secure adherence to the Libyan Safety Net Agreement. This arrangement was strongly backed by the State Department, because it appeared to give the major independents in Libya some ability to resist being picked off one by one. However, when Bunker Hunt was taken in 1973, other producers did not fulfill their obligations. Some did not have supplies they could easily redistribute. Furthermore, they were not very anxious to maintain the position of a company with which they competed. While it was in the interest of the United States and the industry as a whole to thwart Libyan pressures, individual companies were inevitably torn. This tension could have been relieved if the American government itself had had the power to coordinate additional supplies for Bunker Hunt. The amounts involved were not very great. But such power did not exist in the American political system. Indeed, the very fact that the Libyan Safety Net Agreement was a private arrangement from the outset is indicative of the limited ability of the American state to play a decisive role in the private sphere.

Given the shifting balance of power between the corporations and host-country governments, there is probably little that the United States could have done to preserve the prerogatives of formal ownership. Before 1973, in any event, American central decision-makers were not much interested in making any efforts.

PRICING

The preferences of American policy-makers are brought out more clearly by an examination of official reaction to price increases. Little interest was taken in the rise in crude prices from about $2 to $3.25 per barrel from 1970 to October 1973, despite the concerns of the private sector. Official attention was focussed on preserving good relations with conservative governments in producing states. Only after the price of crude had quadrupled to $12 per barrel did economic matters come to the fore. But even then the United States was unable to implement domestic policies that would have enhanced the possibility of undermining the oil cartel.

Before 1974 there was even sympathy within the American government for higher oil prices. In 1969 Libyan demands for higher prices struck a responsive chord, at least in some quarters. James Akins, Director of the State Department's Energy Office (later Ambassador to Saudi Arabia), privately told the companies that the Libyan demands were reasonable because of differences in transporation costs between Libya and the Gulf. He never questioned the artificial basis on which prices were determined. Akins told the Senate Subcommittee on Multinational Corporations that "if the Libyans concluded they were being cheated, this I thought guaranteed a breakdown in relations with the companies and all sorts of subsequent problems."[82] Akins also spoke with the British Embassy in Washington, although not directly with British Petroleum, which had a substantial stake in Libya.[83] As we have seen, the companies were not quite so convinced of the justice of Khadaffi's demands.

In the negotiations that took place in Teheran in January 1971, the American government helped secure the settlement that was desired by Faisal and the Shah by undermining the bargaining tactic adopted by the oil companies. The companies wanted to confront OPEC as a united bloc. This plan was extensively discussed with high American officials at the beginning of January 1971. The Justice Department issued a business review letter exempting the coordinated activities of the companies from antitrust action. Corporate managers feared that if they did not get a unified agreement, their payments to host-country governments would be persistently ratcheted upward by price differentials between the

[82] *Ibid.*, p. 6. [83] *Ibid.*, pp. 3-7.

Mediterranean and the Gulf.[84] The companies went to Teheran in January 1971 with the aim of a united negotiation, but resistance from the Gulf states forced them to fall back to their "hinge" proposal, which linked the two geographic areas by setting prices for crude transported by pipelines as well as tankers. Both Saudi Arabia and Iran rejected this proposal.

In the midst of these negotiations, the American Undersecretary of State for Economic Affairs, John Irwin, was dispatched to the Middle East on one day's notice. On January 18, after talking with Arab and Iranian leaders for only two days, Irwin recommended that negotiations only deal with tanker sales in the Gulf. He said that he was convinced that an attempt to sign an agreement with all of OPEC would lead to an impasse, and that an agreement with the Gulf producers really would provide stability. By the end of January, after further pressure from the American Ambassador to Iran, the companies accepted this position.[85] The vice-president of Exxon in charge of the negotiations told the Senate Subcommittee on Multinational Corporations:

> I was disappointed because I thought it was going to make my life harder. I don't think it was catastrophic in your words, because there is always more than one way to solve a problem, but I thought it was going to be harder, much harder.[86]

He indicated his disappointment to the American Ambassador in Iran, stating that he doubted the stability of any agreement in the Gulf if Libya succeeded in getting better terms.[87] Hence, private resolve to resist demands for higher prices, or at least to establish a more stable situation, was weakened by the support of the American government for the position taken by the oil-exporting states.

How can American policy be explained? It can partly be attributed to ignorance. If Irwin believed what he said, then he could not have understood the "hinge" proposal of the companies, which excluded Libya and other radical states from the negotia-

[84] U.S. Senate, *Multinational Oil Corporations*, Report, pp. 127-28.

[85] U.S. Senate, *Multinational Corporations*, Hearings, Part 5, pp. 149, 169, 172; Weisberg, *Crude Oil Pricing*, pp. 56-60.

[86] U.S. Senate, *Multinational Corporations*, Hearings, Part 5, p. 221.

[87] *Ibid.*, pp. 221-23.

tions. Given the haste with which Irwin departed on his mission, and the symbolic distance that had separated the American government from the companies (itself a reflection of the fragmentation of the American political system), ignorance is not an entirely unsatisfactory explanation. However, it is not entirely convincing either. The fact is that American policy did satisfy the objective of keeping the Shah and Faisal happy, even if it did not keep prices down. American policy-makers acted to preserve the stability of noncommunist regimes even though this strategy meant accepting higher prices and opposing the preferences of the oil companies.

It was only after 1973 that prices themselves became a matter of concern. The increases unilaterally declared by OPEC in the fall and winter of 1973-1974 helped precipitate the most severe economic downturn experienced by industrial market economies since the 1930s. At least some high American officials brooded about the political and social effects of a recession, particularly the possibility of communist governments in Western Europe.[88] In addition, the accumulation of large amounts of liquid capital, petrodollars, strained the international monetary system. Under the modified floating rate regime that was emerging at the same time, the transfer of petrodollars from one currency to another could lead to precipitous exchange-rate changes. The decline of the British pound during the first half of 1976 was due in large part to the flight of Arab capital from sterling.[89]

To deal with higher prices after 1973, the United States used diplomatic and economic instruments, both with limited success. They first made positive appeals. Almost immediately after prices were raised, American officials began to elaborate on the theme of interdependence, arguing that both producers and consumers could be harmed if the world economy was destroyed. In January 1974 President Nixon stated that "severe disruptions of economic activity and the world monetary system, whether caused by insufficiency of supply or abrupt price movements, could prove disastrous for both consumers and producers alike."[90] At the Sep-

[88] *New York Times*, Oct. 6, 1974, 5:1.

[89] *New York Times*, Jan. 18, 1977, 50:5.

[90] *Washington Post*, Jan. 11, 1974, A4:7, and Jan. 4, 1974, A1:2 for a statement by Kissinger.

tember 1974 meeting of the United Nations, President Ford linked world trade in food and oil as manifestations of interdependence. Later in September both Ford and Kissinger warned that continued high oil prices could lead to a breakdown of the international economy.[91]

There were also intimations of economic retaliation against OPEC states, particularly with reference to food.[92] It quickly became apparent, however, that the imports of the oil exporters were too small, and their wealth too great, to implement a counterboycott. One concrete action was taken against OPEC: the Trade Act of 1974 excluded its membership from most favored nation status. In May 1976 the United States warned Mexico, which was showing signs of becoming a substantial oil exporter, that it would lose its most favored nation status if it joined OPEC. Seventy percent of Mexico's exports go to the United States.[93]

American policy did not succeed in rolling back prices. It is doubtful that diplomacy or economic threats could have had any effect after October 1973. By that time the oil-exporting states were primed for increases, and the reaction to the oil embargo and production cutbacks demonstrated how high prices could actually go. The opportunities for changing outcomes existed only before the October War. If Occidental had been provided with crude, it would not have had to capitulate to Libya. If the American government had indicated strong dissatisfaction with price increases to Iran and Saudi Arabia in 1971 or 1972, they might have relented. These conservative regimes could not have lightly contemplated alienating the United States. Had prices been held in check before 1973, expectations would have been different, and the oil-exporting states might have settled on lower prices even after production cutbacks revealed how tight market conditions were. Opposing higher returns to OPEC states, however, would have placed the United States in conflict with Faisal and the Shah. American policy-makers did not want such confrontations, be-

[91] *New York Times*, June 20, 1974, 5:1; Sept. 19, 1974, 18:5; Sept. 27, 1974, 1:6; Oct. 6, 1974, 5:1.

[92] *Washington Post*, Jan. 9, 1974, A3:5.

[93] *Wall St. Journal*, May 21, 1976, 10:3.

cause their fundamental aim was to preserve the political power of these regimes.

This is not the place to review all of American energy policies, but some of its aspects do illustrate one of the major arguments of this book: the fragmentation of power in the American political system. Every American President since October 1973 has said that the United States must reduce its dependency on Middle East oil. In the end, this goal can only be achieved by increasing energy supplies from politically safe sources (including new technologies within the United States itself) and reducing consumption. Yet once the implementation of policy preferences becomes dependent on institutions other than the White House and central bureaucracies such as the State and Treasury Departments, it becomes very difficult to carry out a coherent policy. Energy policy now involves a large number of groups and institutions including labor, environmentalists, state governments, and various elements of the oil industry. Most programs require Congressional action. The result has been stasis or at best modest progress. It took more than two years after the oil embargo to pass a new energy bill. This act was a hodgepodge of compromises. It was 250 pages long, with 18 pages alone devoted to the pricing of crude oil. Price controls on oil were extended through the 1976 elections. Some modest mandatory efficiency levels were imposed on automobiles. Voluntary, not mandatory, conservation targets were suggested for industry. The 1975 Energy Act also provided for the creation of a stockpile equal to 6-12 months' worth of imports from Arab countries.[94] President Carter's energy program was emasculated in Congress where one man, Russell Long, chairman of the Senate Finance Committee, was able to play a critical role.

American policy has not proceeded just through the Congress. Many other institutional actors have been involved. The following is merely a sample of developments in 1976 and 1977. The California Coastal Commission blocked a $110 million Exxon plan to develop its oil reserves in the Santa Barbara Channel. A Miami

[94] *Ibid.*, Jan. 28, 1976, 28:1; March 18, 1976; 4:1; April 15, 1976, 2:3; *New York Times*, Nov. 13, 1975, 1:5; Dec. 10, 1975, 17:1.

lawyer, interested in building up his environmental law practice, was able to force a $71 million delay in the construction of a nuclear power plant in Florida by arguing that the licensing board of the Nuclear Regulatory Agency, which had approved the project, had not done an adequate alternative site search. A delay occurred in a nuclear power project in New Hampshire because of confusion between the utility building the plant and a regional official of the Environmental Protection Agency. A federal judge in Brooklyn voided 93 offshore leases in the Mid-Atlantic region on the grounds that the Interior Department had not conformed with environmental laws; the suit in this case was brought by two Long Island counties, five townships, and a citizens group. His decision was reversed six months later. The Secretary of the Interior cancelled oil and gas lease sales on 60 million federally controlled acres along the Pacific Coast from Southern California to Washington, as well as a number of leases in Alaska; state and local officials had protested the accelerated leasing program.[95]

While these are simply anecdotes (the number could easily be multiplied), aggregate behavior tells a similar story. During 1976 petroleum imports increased by 21.6 percent over the previous year. Imports accounted for 40.6 percent of total consumption; purchases from the Middle East approximately doubled. During the first half of 1977 daily oil consumption in the United States was 8.8 percent higher than it had been in the first half of 1973. For the same period, consumption had *fallen* by 0.7 percent in Japan, 5.0 percent in Italy, 8.6 percent in France, 10.8 percent in Germany, and 19.5 percent in the United Kingdom.[96] The chairman of a Twentieth Century Fund Study on Energy summarized the situation well in January 1977 when he said that the "tendency of our energy policy of the last several years has been to temporize and delay."[97]

Implicitly, the United States has opted for the Saudi solution to energy needs. Without significant conservation and the develop-

[95] *Los Angeles Times*, Feb. 19, 1977, II, 1:6; *Wall St. Journal*, Feb. 18, 1977, 3:1; Jan. 11, 1977, 36:1; Jan. 7, 1977, 8:1; March 4, 1976, 6:4.

[96] *Wall St. Journal*, Aug. 17, 1976, 43:8; Jan. 14, 1977, 11:4; Oct. 31, 1977, 1:6.

[97] Quoted in *New York Times*, Jan. 12, 1977, D5:5.

ment of new sources it is unlikely that prices can be lowered, or exposure to political pressure from exporting states diminished. It is possible that the OPEC cartel will collapse because of cheating.[98] It is possible that central state actors will be able to implement an effective energy program. Given the fragmentation of power in the American political system, however, this will be a very difficult task. It will require leadership, manifest in the President's ability not only to convince the public of the efficacy and fairness of his program but also to make the program so salient that particularistic pressures can be ignored in Congress. And even then, the possibilities for impediments in the courts and in various state and local agencies remain high.

Conclusion

For the analytic concerns of this study, the period after 1973 offers little guidance about the ranking of preferences of American central decision-makers. The actions of OPEC states had a negative impact on general foreign policy goals, security of supply, and price levels. A policy that furthered one of the aims would also have some positive effect on the others. The post-1973 period does, however, reveal much about the pattern of policy-making in the American political system. For other cases discussed in this chapter—Zambia, Chile during the 1960s, and Peru—there is little evidence of the weakness of the state. The reason is that decisions were taken in the White House and the State Department. These central state agencies were able to implement their preferences because they could ignore pressure from the private sector. In the oil crisis after 1973 the situation was different. For the state to accomplish its aims required the cooperation of many other institutions including state and local governments, the judiciary, the Congress, environmental groups, several federal agencies, and the oil companies. Here the fragmentation of power in the American political system became apparent. Central decision-makers have had great difficulty increasing supplies and reducing consumption because they have not been able to overcome resistance from various private actors and nonstate

[98] For this possibility see Moran, "The Future: OPEC Wants Them."

governmental institutions (agencies other than the White House and central federal bureaucracies).

The period before 1974 is analytically somewhat more revealing, although here too, because of the coalescence of objectives, caution is necessary. U.S. leaders did appear to be primarily concerned with general foreign policy objectives, namely, preserving conservative regimes, rather than the prerogatives of private companies, or lower prices. Obviously, maintaining the power of the Shah and the Saudi monarch is consistent with an interpretation that focusses on economic aims: feudal regimes looked like reliable allies. But as recent events have demonstrated, the choice was not all that obvious. During the postwar period American central decision-makers have consistently tended to ignore the dangers presented by economic nationalism so long as regimes were not perceived as being influenced or dominated by communists. Yet the conservative oil sheikdoms have imposed stunning costs on the United States and its allies. Despite what American bankers like to think, the interests of these countries are not identical with those of the industrialized West. It is true that it is probably better to have a Faisal than a Khadaffi, but the difference may be marginal.

The period before 1974 also illustrates how the decision-making arena affects the ability of policy-makers to implement their preferences. During 1970 and 1971 U.S. oil companies did want greater support from the state against the pressures that were being placed on them by Saudi Arabia and Iran. However, decisions on this issue were taken in the White House and the State Department, institutions that could ignore corporate desires in favor of minimizing conflict with conservative regimes. In the case of pricing pressures and nationalization in Libya (a government U.S. leaders were less enamoured of), resistance would have required active cooperation from the private sector in the form of adherence to provisions of the Libyan Safety Net Agreement and the ability to provide domestic purchasers, in particular the New England Petroleum Company, with a substitute for Libyan supplies. U.S. leaders, however, did not have the capability to alter the behavior of actors in the private sector. In sum, when implementation is in the hands of the White House and the State

Department, central decision-makers can secure their preferences, but when it requires actions by other institutions, such as private oil companies, state goals will be satisfied only if central decision-makers exercise vigorous leadership.

Conclusion

The cases reviewed in this chapter—copper in Zambia and Chile, oil and other commodities in Peru, and oil in the Middle East—all concerned situations in which American firms were nationalized and the U.S. government did not respond at all, or used diplomatic and economic pressure but not covert or overt force. There are many other cases that follow the same pattern. Indeed, this was the modal American reaction to the general loss of formal ownership, and at least some managerial control, that took place in the late 1960s and the 1970s.

The relatively modest defense that American central decision-makers were willing to offer to protect the prerogatives of U.S. firms is more easily understood from a statist or structural Marxist perspective than it is from an interest-group or instrumental Marxist one. During the 1960s and into the early 1970s major American raw materials investors did want their government to defend them against the demands of host-country governments. Exxon supported economic sanctions against Peru. At Teheran in January 1971 the major oil companies did try to put up a common front against demands for higher prices. In Iraq, Libya, and even Saudi Arabia until mid-1972 they tried to resist nationalization and participation programs. Anaconda did not want to relinquish a large share of its ownership of its Chilean copper mines. However, American central decision-makers were not willing to give extensive support to U.S. firms, particularly after they became sensitive to the strength of nationalist sentiments in host countries. When firms did accommodate themselves to nationalist pressure, such as AMAX in Zambia, and Kennecott and Cerro in Chile, one reason may have been that they did not anticipate much backing from the American government.

Of the cases discussed in this chapter, Peru is the one in which the United States took the strongest stand. Extensive economic sanctions were imposed during the 1960s. Chronologically, Peru is also the earliest case. As American leaders came to realize that diplomatic and economic pressure was likely to be counterproductive, they became more circumspect. In Chile U.S. pressure for land reform helped undermine what support there was for foreign ownership of the copper mines.

In those cases where firms did resist nationalization, the initiative for a more conciliatory policy often came from the state. In 1966, when Assistant Secretary of State Lincoln Gordon reduced economic sanctions against Peru, Exxon still wanted strong pressure. The State Department also pushed Anaconda to accept Chileanization of the copper industry. In Middle East oil negotiations before 1974, U.S. policy-makers sided with host-country governments rather than American corporations.

Now it is true that most private investors accommodated themselves to these changes fairly comfortably. Given the flexibility and resources of large multinational raw materials firms, especially the oil companies, they could adjust their behavior. These corporations have been able to maintain a profitable and intimate relationship with oil-exporting countries. Many of them have also expanded into other business activities often remote from petroleum, of which the most notable example is Mobil's purchase of Montgomery-Ward. In American industry, control of financial resources has become as important as expertise in a particular kind of economic activity. When difficulties are encountered in one area, many firms can enter new lines of business. Thus, most raw materials companies did not put up strong resistance when they found that central decision-makers were not willing to support their claims.

I do not want to claim that the evidence in this chapter gives decisive support for the statist propositions of this study as opposed to versions of the Marxist position that grant the state some autonomy. American actions can be interpreted as being perfectly consistent with the long-term needs of an advanced capitalist society. The Third World has not been closed to investment. While activity in raw materials sectors has been subject to restraints, activity in manufacturing has continued to grow in many countries. Furthermore, during the mid-1970s loans to less developed countries have become an increasingly important source of income for international banks. A more vigorous defense of private raw materials investors could have radicalized regimes in the Third World and created a climate much less hospitable to major capitalist enterprises.

In sum, although divergences between the preferences of some specific firms and the American government cannot be readily explained by interest-group or instrumental Marxist arguments (especially in countries where nationalized raw materials companies were the only large American investors), the overall pattern of American behavior is consistent with either a statist interpretation that focusses on general political aims or a structural Marxist one that emphasizes the long-term needs of capitalist societies. The problem of distinguishing between statist and structural Marxist formulations is directly addressed in the following chapter. The willingness of American policy-makers to use force only when certain ideological goals were threatened, even when such action undermined the coherence of American society, offers strong evidence in support of a statist perspective.

CHAPTER VIII

The Protection of Investments after 1950: The Use of Force

Private accommodation, diplomatic protest, and economic pressure have been the most common American responses to the takeover of raw materials companies, but not the only ones. The cases that have attracted the most attention, and are analytically the most interesting, involve the use of covert or overt force. Since the Second World War the United States has engaged in four overt interventions: Korea, Lebanon, Indochina, and the Dominican Republic. It has supported at least two proxy interventions (the use of non-American troops to overthrow a regime): Guatemala in 1954 and Cuba in 1961. It has been involved in several assassination attempts: Lumumba in 1961, Trujillo in 1962, Diem in 1963, Castro during the early 1960s, and General Schneider in Chile in 1971. The United States also supported the Iranian military when it overthrew Mossadegh in Iran in 1953. We cannot say with certainty that the list of covert activities is exhaustive. However, it is likely that these nine countries include a large sample, if not the whole universe of instances, where the United States has used force to try to change a foreign regime.[1]

These are critical cases for two of the central problems of this study. First, for illuminating a statist paradigm by inductively defining the national interest, they help show which objectives American central decision-makers found to be paramount. Second, these cases suggest that a statist paradigm offers a better explanation of American foreign policy than not only instrumental Marxist or pluralist arguments (which we have already seen are often inadequate) but also structural Marxist ones.

[1] For a discussion of overt interventions see Tillema, *Appeal to Force*; for covert interventions see U.S. Senate, Select Committee to Study Governmental Operations with Respect to Intelligence Activities, *Alleged Assassination Plots* and *Covert Action in Chile*.

Turning first to the question of objectives, we can see that in cases in which force was used the paramount aim of American policy was to oppose communist governments. The costs that a state is willing to incur to achieve different goals is an indication of their relative importance. Lodging a diplomatic protest is not a decisive act. The application of this instrument of policy shows that rulers attribute some positive value to a goal, but does not reveal how much. Economic pressures usually involve higher costs, since they frequently entail some material losses for the country imposing sanctions. The use of economic instruments of policy indicates that a state places a higher value on a particular objective than if only diplomatic maneuvers are employed.

Force, particularly overt force, is the most solemn, and potentially the most costly, instrument of power that a state has at its disposal. Its use is a sign that central decision-makers place a very high value on the objective they are pursuing. Since the beginning of the twentieth century overt intervention has not been cheap. The era of gunboat diplomacy, in which a single vessel might compel a change in the behavior of another state or a few hundred occupying troops guarantee acceptable policies, is over. Even the least developed countries in the present international system have some ability to resist incursions. Greater social mobilization has made populations accessible to political leaders. Nationalism is a potent source of unity, at least in the face of a foreign threat. Better training and greater availability of new weapons have increased the firepower less developed countries can muster; the proliferation of nuclear weapons is but the most extreme manifestation of this trend. Even the most powerful states cannot undertake overt military interventions without incurring significant costs in money, material, and life. When combat continues for several years, as it did in Korea and Vietnam, there have been serious domestic political repercussions: in both cases, the longer the war continued, the more the public turned against it.

Covert interventions do not have the same costs, but they too are particularly revealing of basic preferences. They are risky. If they are discovered, the regime they are directed against can rally domestic support. The revelation of covert intervention can undermine a nation's prestige (and thus its power) because such behavior violates extant norms in the international system—that is, the sense of what is right and proper held by most political elites. Covert interventions also impose psychic costs on central decision-makers: they force them to lie. It is not just a matter of prudence that leads to secrecy in cases of intervention in the domestic affairs of other states. Such actions are not revealed because they are not legitimate.

Thus both overt and covert force are costly policy instruments. Central decision-makers are not likely to employ such tactics unless they perceive vital national interests to be threatened. Finding the thread, the common element that is shared by all of the cases of American covert and overt intervention, can suggest the underlying motivations of American policy-makers.

Let us turn first to direct economic interests, and particularly raw materials investments. The extent of American economic involvement in countries where intervention has taken place has ranged from negligible to extensive. This is indicated in the following table.

TABLE VIII-1

Value of U.S. Direct Investment in Countries Where the United States Has Intervened (in millions of dollars)

Country	*Year*	*Value*
Cuba	1959	1,956
Chile	1970	748
Dominican Republic	1960	105
Guatemala	1954	101
Vietnam	1960	less than 25
Korea	1950	less than 10
Lebanon	1958	less than 40
Iran	1953	less than 1
Congo	1960	less than 20

Sources: U.S. Dept. of Commerce, *U.S. Balance of Payments, Statistical Supplement*, 1963, pp. 208-9; U.S. Dept. of Commerce, *Survey of Current Business*, Vol. 51, No. 10 (Oct. 1971), p. 32; U.S. Dept. of Commerce, Bureau of Economic Analysis.

These cases fall into three categories: Chile and Cuba, where the value of U.S. holdings was very high; Guatemala and the Dominican Republic, where they were moderate; and Vietnam,

Korea, Lebanon, Iran, and the Congo, where they were low. In all of the states where American economic interests were high or medium, raw materials investments were significant. Sugar was important in Cuba and the Dominican Republic, copper in Chile, and bananas in Guatemala. In addition, both Iran and the Congo were important sources of raw materials for American allies, even though there was no significant American investment at the time intervention took place.

This table shows no clear positive relationship between economic interests and the use of force. Indeed, three out of America's four overt interventions took place in areas where American investments were low. In two of the others, the Dominican Republic and Guatemala, the value of U.S. holdings was modest, far less than in many other countries where American policy-makers did not use force. Furthermore, as the following pages indicate, in neither Cuba nor Chile was American action touched off by nationalizations. Castro had begun to move against American holdings some nine months before the Eisenhower administration tried to forcibly remove him; American copper companies in Chile had already been largely nationalized before Allende came to power, and it was evident by 1970 that no Chilean government, regardless of its position in the political spectrum, would continue to accept foreign ownership of the mines.

What these cases do have in common is not a direct economic stake, but a political one. The United States intervened when central decision-makers perceived the imminent danger of a communist takeover. This was the necessary, if not the sufficient, condition for the use of force to change a foreign regime.

Let us now turn to the macro-theoretic issue: the relative merits of a statist as opposed to a structural Marxist argument. We should first pause to review the lessons of the empirical cases that have been presented so far. Again and again there are serious disparities between the aims of central decision-makers and those of private corporations. Despite the weakness of the American political system, the state has generally prevailed because issues have been decided in the White House and the State Department, although where Congress has been intimately involved, as in the protection of Middle East oil during the 1940s, the industry has been able to prevent the implementation of state preferences. The divergence between public- and private-sector goals weighs against both instrumental Marxist and interest-group arguments. Neither of these is able to give an adequate explanation for state preferences that are sharply different from those of private actors that are directly affected by a specific policy issue, particularly when there is a diffuse impact on the rest of the society.

Evaluating structural Marxist and statist approaches, however, has been much more difficult. Both expect differences between state and corporate preferences. What kind of empirical data can be used to distinguish between these two arguments? The most compelling evidence bears upon the basic nature of the objective that is pursued and the way it is pursued. Structural Marxist arguments must ultimately relate state behavior to the economic interests of the ruling class, even though that class might not perceive where its own best interests lie. In addition, for structural Marxists, the state will strive to act rationally; there will be a clear relationship between means and ends, even though inherent contradictions may prevent policy-makers from ultimately accomplishing their goal. The cases in which the United States has used overt or covert force do not conform with structural Marxist expectations. They are better explained by ideological considerations than by materialist ones: American goals are more closely linked with a Lockean vision of how societies should be ordered than with any economic aims. Furthermore, this ideological objective was pursued in a nonlogical way in two senses: the subjective perceptions of American policy-makers often did not correspond to objective reality (they saw communists under every bed rather than nationalist army officers trying to dodge American bullets); and there was often no clear calculation of a relationship between means and ends.

The nonlogical behavior of American central decision-makers is critical in defending a statist approach against a structural Marxist one: it contradicts the underlying epistemology of a materialist paradigm to see the behavior of political leaders in other than logical or rational terms. The obvious structural Marxist retort to an ideological interpretation is that ideology was merely a blind, a rationalization, for underlying economic motives. A Marxist argument would still expect to find a logical relationship between means and ends. But a critical characteristic of the cases involving the use of force is that there is little evidence of such a relationship. Instead, there was frequent misperception. There was often no sense of costs or limits. At times, there was no clear specification of objectives. There was, in short, behavior much more compatible with the proposition that opposing communist regimes was an end in itself rather than a means to further the coherence of capitalist society. Indeed, one case, Vietnam, dealt a serious blow to that coherence. A structural Marxist position cannot credit the state with supreme prudence and calculation in some cases and misperception and miscalculation in others. However, a foreign policy characterized by ideological goals pursued in a nonlogical way is compatible with a statist approach, particularly in the case of an imperial or hegemonic state. In the conclusion of this study I shall try to show why very powerful countries are likely to pursue ideological goals.

This chapter examines in detail four cases of overt or covert intervention in the period since the Second World War that occurred in countries that had American raw materials investments: Guatemala, Cuba, the Dominican Republic, and Chile. At the end of this chapter we shall return to a discussion of the relationship between statist and structural Marxist arguments.

Guatemala

In 1954 the government of Jacobo Arbenz was overthrown by a group of Guatemalan rebels invading from Honduras led by an army officer, Carlos Castillo Armas. American officials had tacitly, and possibly explicitly, approved Castillo Armas as the leader of this rebellion. The rebels had been trained and armed by the CIA. When Castillo Armas's forces lost two of their three planes during their invasion, Eisenhower personally approved indirect American resupply. U.S. ambassadors in several Central American countries assisted Castillo Armas. The United States spent several million dollars to overthrow Arbenz.[2] Why had this intervention taken place?

[2] Schneider, "Guatemala," pp. 573-74; Blasier, *Hovering Giant*, pp. 161-62.

One obvious answer is that Arbenz threatened American economic interests. His land reform program included the nationalization of 234,000 acres owned by United Fruit. He also supported labor legislation introduced by the previous government that infringed upon managerial prerogatives. United Fruit was a salient target. It was the largest economic operation in Guatemala: the company's products accounted for a major share of Guatemala's foreign exchange; it owned a number of critical facilities including railroads and port facilities; it was the nation's largest employer. Its reputation was, to say the least, unsavory.

United Fruit strongly opposed Arbenz. The company protested against developments in Guatemala within the State Department and the Congress, where it found considerable support from the Massachusetts delegation (United Fruit is based in Boston) and conservative Republicans. At one point a corporate official introduced a potential leader of the anti-Arbenz movement to two CIA representatives. The company rejected the compensation offered by Guatemala, which was in the form of long-term bonds and was well below the company's own estimate of the value of its nationalized property. The State Department vigorously backed United Fruit, acting almost as legal representative for the company. As we have seen, this aggressiveness was quite unusual: the Department's standard operating procedure was to take a more distant stance, usually providing good offices rather than direct advocacy.[3]

But American decision-makers did not perceive Arbenz's policies being limited to narrow economic matters: they felt that his actions would lead to communist domination in Guatemala. In October 1953 the Assistant Secretary of State for American Republic Affairs charged that Guatemala's independence was being prejudiced by "the international Communist conspiracy."[4] A week after Arbenz was overthrown, Secretary of State Dulles said on a national television and radio broadcast that events in Guatemala exposed "the evil purpose of the Kremlin to destroy

[3] U.S. House, Committee on Foreign Affairs, *Expropriation of American-Owned Property*; Schneider, pp. 566-67; Wise and Ross, *Invisible Government*, p. 170; Blasier, *Hovering Giant*, pp. 89-90, 163.

[4] Quoted in Blasier, *Hovering Giant*, p. 160.

the inter-American system. . . ."[5] In his memoirs Eisenhower wrote that Arbenz "soon created the strong suspicion that he was merely a puppet manipulated by Communists."[6] He went on to note that Guatemala was playing the communist game when it accepted the contention that the United States had used bacteriological warfare in Korea.[7]

There was some basis for these views. The Communist Party had grown rapidly in Guatemala after the Second World War. By 1953 it had 4,000 members. Arbenz fully legalized the party in 1952, and named several of its members to run on the government party's election ticket in 1953. Communists were influential in the Congress. They also dominated the labor and peasant unions, the real base of their support. Arbenz became increasingly dependent on the left for electoral support. In 1954 Guatemala bought arms from Czechoslovakia.[8]

Considering the full spectrum of political power in Guatemala, however, American leaders almost certainly exaggerated the strength of the communists. Communists did not control the armed forces. There is no evidence that Arbenz had any extended contacts with Eastern European countries. The Soviet Union and Guatemala had established diplomatic relations in 1945, but neither country had sent resident diplomatic missions. There were no communists in Arbenz's cabinet. Furthermore, Arbenz's increasing dependence on the left was partly a result of American pressure. He turned to Eastern Europe for weapons because the American government had blocked exports from the United States and Europe for six years. The staunch support that the State Department gave to United Fruit placed him in a very difficult position: no nationalist regime could have compromised with the company without losing its domestic support. In sum, there was a certain blindness to the American position.[9]

Superficially, the Guatemalan episode offers strong support for an interest-group or instrumental Marxist position. American pol-

[5] Quoted in Blasier, *Hovering Giant*, p. 171.

[6] Eisenhower, *Mandate for Change*, p. 421.

[7] *Ibid.*, p. 422.

[8] Schneider, *passim*; Blasier, *Hovering Giant*, p. 155.

[9] In assessing the influence of communist elements in Guatemala I have drawn heavily on Blasier, *Hovering Giant*, pp. 154-58.

icy followed the preferences of the most directly affected economic interests. United Fruit was able to press its case in Congress; it also had previous business ties with a number of State Department officials.

This interpretation is questionable for three reasons. First, as most of the cases discussed to this point indicate, this was not the usual pattern of American behavior. U.S. officials were willing to use diplomacy and economic pressure to protect corporate interest, but not force. Furthermore, the issue of compensation has rarely been a decisive one because the U.S. government has often indirectly provided the funds necessary to repay American companies. This was true in Bolivia and Mexico before the Second World War, in Chile during the 1960s, and in Bolivia when the tin mines were seized in 1952.

Second, there is a development specifically related to the Guatemalan case that weighs against the argument that U.S. policy was guided by the interests of United Fruit. One week after Arbenz was overthrown, the Justice Department brought an antitrust suit against the company. The timing of this action suggests that U.S. leaders were trying to counter assertions that the state was merely a fop for the corporation.[10] Unlike many antitrust cases, this one did have a significant impact. In the consent agreement that ended the case in 1958, United Fruit agreed to divest its banana selling operation, end certain restrictive practices, divest itself of its Central American railway, and, most important, create out of its own resources a competitor capable of importing nine million stems of bananas into the United States, an amount equal to about one-third of United Fruit's annual sales.[11]

Third, another episode that occurred at about the same time provides an interesting contrast with U.S. behavior in Guatemala. In 1952 the Movimiento Nacionalista Revolucionario (MNR), led by Victor Paz Estenssoro, came to power in Bolivia. It had the support of the armed forces and of the powerful mine workers union. One of its first acts was to nationalize the tin mines, which in 1950 accounted for almost half of the government's income and a major share of the country's export receipts. The mines were

[10] This is suggested in Blasier, *Hovering Giant*, p. 166.

[11] Kronstein and Miller, *Modern American Antitrust Law*.

owned by three firms. Only the largest, Patino, had any American connections: it had American stockholders and was incorporated in the United States. Like United Fruit in Guatemala, the tin companies were a focus of nationalist discontent, and the MNR, which was dependent on the mine workers union, had no choice but to nationalize. The MNR also launched a number of other reforms involving land ownership and government regulation of large sectors of the economy. At its outset this looked like a genuine social revolution.[12] The MNR's programs became more conservative over time. In the late 1950s Bolivia accepted a number of measures that were hardly revolutionary, such as a new petroleum code favoring foreign investment and a restrictive monetary policy presented by the IMF. But in 1952 it could not have been completely clear that the Bolivian revolution would be so easily tamed.

The American response to events in Bolivia was strikingly different from its stance in Guatemala two years later. The United States recognized the new regime after seven weeks. When a provisional settlement was reached on compensation for the nationalized mines in 1953, the United States immediately agreed to accept new tin shipments at the government-owned smelter in Texas. Even more startling, the United States committed itself to an extensive foreign aid program. From 1953 to 1960 American subventions accounted for a third of Bolivia's budget. On a per capita basis Bolivia received more American aid than any other Latin American country during the 1950s.[13]

What can account for the contrast between Bolivia and Guatemala? Both occurred during Eisenhower's first term, so the difference was not produced by a change of government in the United States. There was also not very much difference in the way in which the issue of compensation was handled, although Bolivia did stick more closely to the legal niceties of prompt and adequate payment. The mine owners originally asked for $60 million; Bolivia countered with a back tax bill of over $500 million. The

[12] Alexander, *The Bolivian National Revolution*, p. 99; Patch, "Bolivia," p. 109; Blasier, "United States and Revolution," pp. 53-54.

[13] Ingram, *Expropriation of U.S. Property*, p. 144; Blasier, "United States and Revolution," pp. 65, 88; Alexander, p. 112.

parties finally settled on $20 million. This was paid out over a decade, and although an interim agreement was reached in 1953, final terms were not concluded until the early 1960s. While Bolivia's payments were probably adequate, they were not very prompt.[14] Guatemala's offer to United Fruit was less attractive, but the Arbenz regime did not challenge the right to compensation.

Another possible explanation of the difference in American response in the two countries is that the corporate interests at stake were not identical. United Fruit was a large enterprise that was unambiguously American. Patino was the only tin company that had U.S. ties, but its majority ownership was foreign (Patino was Bolivian). Still, corporate distinctions do not adequately account for the variation in U.S. behavior. The United States did not simply ignore the Bolivian dispute on the grounds that extensive American interests were not involved. The State Department did make representations on behalf of American stockholders.[15] The United States has even become involved in disputes where no American capital was at stake, as in Iran in the early 1950s, the Congo in the early 1960s, and Guyana in 1971 (after the nationalization of Alcan). These cases involved the use of covert force or economic sanctions, not just diplomatic protests.

Differences in corporate political power in the United States also fail to account for official policy. No doubt United Fruit's political influence in the United States was greater than Patino's. Although this variation might explain strong sanctions in Guatemala and weaker ones or neutrality in Bolivia, it cannot account for the positive support that the United States gave to Paz Estenssoro. It was not simply that American officials ignored the tin nationalizations; it was that they financially underwrote the government that had carried them out even though the issue of compensation was not settled for a decade. American policy-makers were interested in something other than protecting the sanctity of property rights.

A more convincing explanation is that Paz Estenssoro and Ar-

[14] Ingram, p. 132; U.S. House, *Expropriation*, p. 18; First National City Bank vs. Banco Nacional de Cuba, p. 70; Alexander, p. 106.

[15] U.S. House, *Expropriation*, p. 18.

benz were perceived as having very different impacts on broader American political objectives. Central decision-makers saw Arbenz as the opening wedge for communist infiltration in the western hemisphere; they saw Paz as a viable alternative to communism. In part, this was the result of the explicit policies of the Bolivian government. When the MNR took power, it tried to calm American fears. The new regime said that it would protect private property. It formally requested recognition from the United States. Bolivia's president claimed that the MNR was the last bulwark against communism.[16]

At any rate, the United States was convinced thoroughly and quickly. Milton Eisenhower, who was a special advisor to his brother on Latin American affairs, offered a positive assessment after his visit to the country in 1953. In a book published a decade later he stated that the MNR and its leader, Paz Estenssoro, were not communists, although "his Minister of Labor was an extremist of Marxist leanings, and many believed he belonged to the local Communist Party."[17] In November 1953 a Congressional delegation, which included two conservative members (Senators Bricker and Capehart), visited Bolivia and issued a basically favorable report.[18] In 1955 a State Department official justified the extensive aid being given to Paz as a way "to counteract Communist pressure."[19] "Rapid peaceful social change," Milton Eisenhower wrote, "is the only way to avert violent revolution in Bolivia; physical strife would be the surest way of giving the Communists control."[20]

Despite the close relationship between corporate preferences and state action in Guatemala, the contrast with Bolivia and the prosecution of a meaningful antitrust suit against United Fruit suggest that a statist interpretation is more satisfactory than an instrumental Marxist or a pluralist one. However, the more interesting macro-analytic issue involves distinguishing between statist and structural Marxist approaches. The Guatemalan episode of-

[16] Blasier, "United States and Revolution," p. 64.

[17] Eisenhower, *Wine is Bitter*, p. 67.

[18] Blasier, "United States and Revolution," p. 76.

[19] Quoted in Blasier, "United States and Revolution," p. 78.

[20] Eisenhower, *Wine is Bitter*, p. 68.

fers an example of one kind of nonlogical behavior that was frequently manifest in American foreign policy after the Second World War: a persistent tendency to overestimate the importance of communist influences in foreign regimes. This same tendency can be seen in one other case discussed later in this chapter, the Dominican Republic. It is also apparent in Lebanon in 1958. The perception of communist influence, whether accurate or exaggerated, touched off a reaction in which prudent calculation was not evident. Although the overthrow of Arbenz did not have any significant negative consequences, imprudent behavior in other situations, particularly Vietnam, severely damaged social coherence in the United States itself. This is not an outcome that can be easily understood from a structural Marxist perspective. But if U.S. policy is understood to be oriented toward ideological rather than material goals, it can be explained by a statist paradigm.

Cuba

The American success in Guatemala issued in a short period of quiescence in American relations in the western hemisphere. By the time of Vice-President Nixon's trip to Latin America in 1958, however, it was apparent that anti-American sentiment was substantial.[21] The next direct challenge to American interests, both political and economic, came in Cuba. By 1959 the corrupt dictatorship of Fulgencio Batista was entering its last months. Initially, American central decision-makers were not certain what a new regime under Fidel Castro would bring. Ultimately, the American efforts to topple Castro's regime involved both covert force and economic sanctions.

About 25 percent of the extensive American investments in Cuba were in agriculture, primarily sugar. Because of the strategic importance of Cuba and Castro's eventual unambiguous identification with the Soviet Union, it is difficult to impute a clear hierarchy of values to American decision-makers from this case: Castro threatened economic, ideological, and strategic interests. Still, a close examination of the chronology of American actions

[21] Nixon encountered hostile demonstrations in several countries and was physically threatened in Venezuela. See his *Six Crises*, Ch. 4.

does suggest, albeit modestly, that the decision to use violent means to try to remove Castro was taken only after it became clear that he would move Cuba towards the Communist Bloc, not in response to attacks on American property. The conclusion that general political objectives, rather than specific economic ones, guided American policy is reinforced by the antipathy shown to Batista during his last year in office.

Cuban Initiatives

Before Castro came to power, Cuba was economically very closely tied to the United States. American investments were worth about $1.5 billion, the largest nonoil stake in any country. American interests controlled 40 percent of Cuban sugar production, 90 percent of public utilities, and 25 percent of bank deposits. The United States was Cuba's largest trading partner. This trade moved within an institutional structure that made Cuba very dependent on its northern neighbor: the United States purchased more than half of Cuba's sugar under a preferential quota arrangement that usually maintained prices considerably above those on the world market; American manufactures were given reduced tariffs by Cuba.[22] In the period after the Second World War, sugar accounted for 25-33 percent of Cuba's national income and 75-85 percent of foreign exchange earnings.

Castro ended this dependence, but he did not do it immediately. Before he came to power, and during his early months in office, it was not clear what his ultimate political objectives were, although Cuban policies did indicate that the period of complete American economic domination was at an end. In March 1959 Cuba took control of (but did not formally nationalize) the telephone company, an ITT subsidiary. Seizures of American land began after the passage of an agrarian reform law in May 1959.[23] Nevertheless, much American investment remained.

Castro began to act against American political as well as economic interests only in the fall of 1959. Cuba abstained on the question of admitting Communist China to the United Nations.

[22] U.S. House, *Expropriation*, p. 17; Baklanoff, "International Economic Relations," pp. 252-54; Johnson, "U.S. Business Interests in Cuba," p. 443.

[23] Blasier, "United States Influence," p. 61.

Castro accused the United States of complicity in a bombing attack on Havana by a Cuban exile pilot. He more openly identified himself with the Cuban Communist Party. He attacked the United States Ambassador, Philip Bonsal, during a TV broadcast.[24]

On February 4, 1960, Anastas Mikoyan, First Deputy Chairman of the USSR Council of Ministers, arrived in Cuba. On February 13 the two countries concluded a trade agreement: Russia agreed to buy large amounts of Cuban sugar, provide a loan of $100 million, and send petroleum and technical advisors. Cuba established diplomatic relations with Russia and Communist China. Trade agreements were also signed with East Germany and Poland. On March 28 Castro abrogated the Rio Treaty of 1947, the basis for collective defense of the western hemisphere.[25]

After March 1960 Cuba drew closer to the Soviet Bloc. Ties with the World Bank (one of the pillars of the western postwar economic order) were broken. Russia became Cuba's largest trading partner. Two American diplomats were expelled during the summer. Arms were bought from the Eastern Bloc. In July 1960, as tensions with the United States increased, Khrushchev hinted that Russian troops would be used to support Cuba.[26]

The nationalization of American property moved in step with Cuba's growing political alienation from the United States. By the summer of 1960, however, less than half of these holdings had been taken. Then, in August, Castro formally nationalized the telephone company and several oil refineries that had refused to process Soviet crude. After the 1960 harvest some 275,000 acres of land were confiscated. At the end of October Castro seized all remaining U.S. property.[27]

The American Response

Because economic actions against American concerns and

[24] Gonzalez, "Partners in Deadlock," pp. 18-19; Thomas, *Cuba*, p. 1262; Bonsal, *Cuba, Castro*, p. 97.

[25] Blasier, "United States Influence," p. 60; Thomas, pp. 1265-67; Johnson, "U.S. Business Interests in Cuba," p. 445.

[26] Bonsal, p. 157; Blasier, "United States Influence," pp. 69, 71; Baklanoff, "Economic Relations," p. 259; Thomas, p. 157.

[27] Blasier, "United States Influence," p. 67; Thomas, pp. 1297, 1284; Bonsal, p. 160.

threats to more general American objectives occurred at almost the same time, only modest conclusions can be reached about the underlying values of American central decision-makers from their reaction to Cuban developments. Still, the timing of the decisive turning point in American policy—the decision to topple Castro by force, if necessary—as well as earlier policies toward Batista do suggest that broader political considerations were more important than specific economic ones.

The United States began to withdraw support from Batista nearly a year before he was defeated. On March 14, 1958, the State Department suspended arms shipments. When Castro kidnapped 43 Americans in July, there was no strong protest. They were later released. Late in 1958 the United States did try to establish a third force in Cuba by getting Batista to resign in favor of a military junta with civilian participation. This never materialized.[28]

These actions were the result, not of direct threats to American business, but rather of a developing American view of the relationship between dictatorial regimes and the rise of communism. During the 1950s American officials came to believe that oppressive regimes bred radical revolution. While visiting Latin America in 1958 Vice-President Nixon said in Paraguay that the best way to fight communism was "by establishing a government based on political and economic freedom," not by setting up another totalitarian system.[29] Support for Batista was withdrawn because he could not provide stability.

Once it became apparent that Castro could control Cuba, the United States quickly recognized his government. The American Ambassador, whose antipathy toward the revolutionary leader was well known, was replaced by Philip Bonsal, a career diplomat with a measured attitude toward the new regime. There was no sharp American response to the first round of nationalizations that began in March 1959. Bonsal claims that he received no explicit instructions from Washington on how to react to the "intervention" (assumption of managerial control) of the Cuban Telephone Company. When the first land reform program was promulgated in May 1959, the United States sent a diplomatic

[28] Blasier, "United States Influence," pp. 47-48.

[29] Nixon, p. 191.

note expressing sympathy for its objectives and recognizing the right of expropriation, but insisting on prompt and adequate compensation. During 1959 the sugar quota, the major economic link between Cuba and the United States, was slightly increased by the Agriculture Department.[30]

This is not to say that all was sweetness and light. Eisenhower refused to see Castro when he visited the United States in April 1959. Nixon did, and concluded that Castro was either "incredibly naive about Communism or under Communist discipline."[31] The administration did not disassociate itself from mounting press and Congressional attack, or firmly control anti-Castro activities in the United States, which included some sabotage missions.[32] Thus, into the fall of 1959 American policy toward Cuba was indecisive, despite the nationalization of some large American properties. As in Iran, an attack on foreign investment per se did not trigger an unambiguously negative American response.

As Castro moved closer to communism both internally and externally, however, American attitudes hardened. A last effort at conciliation was made in January 1960. But the estrangement between the two countries had already gone too far. A month earlier the CIA had begun to recruit Cuban exiles for an invasion force. Eisenhower gave the go-ahead for what was to become the Bay of Pigs fiasco a month after Mikoyan's visit. In December 1959 the administration had also begun considering a cut in the Cuban sugar quota, and in January 1960 it asked Congress for the authorization to take such action.[33]

After March 1960 U.S. pressure on Castro grew. It included virtual suspension of the Cuban sugar quota in July, a trade embargo in October, and the formal breaking of diplomatic relations in January 1961. In October 1960 the plane that Castro had used to fly to the United Nations was impounded for nonpayment of debts, and he had to borrow an aircraft from the Russians to get

[30] Blasier, "United States Influence," p. 49; Bonsal, pp. 47, 71; Thomas, p. 1240.

[31] Quoted in Gonzalez, p. 18.

[32] *Ibid.*, pp. 16-18.

[33] Blasier, "United States Influence," pp. 56-57, 59, 64; Baklanoff, "Economic Relations," pp. 258-59; Gonzalez, p. 19; Thomas, pp. 1254, 1263; Bonsal, p. 128.

back to Havana. American pressure culminated in the ill-fated Bay of Pigs invasion in April 1961. Later the CIA tried to assassinate Castro and supported sabotage raids on Cuba.[34]

American business interests did not object to these tough measures, although there is no evidence that they spurred on government decision-makers. By the spring of 1960 it was becoming clear that the position of all American investments on the island was untenable. At the request of Treasury Secretary Robert Anderson, Texaco and Standard Oil of New Jersey refused to process Soviet oil at their Cuban refineries. Shell also went along with American policy. This action precipitated nationalization of the refineries. This was not the course that the oil companies would have followed on their own. Before Anderson's intervention they had agreed under protest to process the Russian oil. Yet it was so unclear how corporate executives could protect their investments that they readily acceded to public initiatives.[35]

In sum, American policy moved in step with Cuba's growing communist identification. Perhaps the two countries were enmeshed in a vicious circle forged by American anticommunism and Cuban nationalism.[36] Still, the critical breaking point for American policy appears to have been Mikoyan's visit. Only after February 1960 did Eisenhower give approval for the use of covert military pressure against Cuba. The attack on a wide range of American properties had begun almost a year earlier. The American decision to forcibly overthrow Castro coincided with his clear identification with the Eastern Bloc, symbolized by Mikoyan's reception and the trade agreement with the Soviet Union, not with the expropriation of American property.

The Dominican Republic

Between 1960 and 1965 the United States brought the full range of its foreign policy instruments to bear against the Dominican Republic. American actions included diplomatic protests, economic pressure, covert assassination attempts, and overt mili-

[34] Thomas, p. 1295; U.S. Senate, *Alleged Assassination Plots*, pp. 71ff., 177.

[35] Bonsal, p. 149; Blasier, "United States Influence," pp. 64-65.

[36] Gonzalez, *passim*.

tary intervention. In the Dominican Republic there were substantial American investments including ownership of much of the sugar industry. However, the Dominican case illustrates far more clearly than the Cuban the primacy of general political objectives in American foreign policy. It also illustrates, as did American actions in Guatemala, the potential for misperception that afflicted American policy-makers. One indication of their pursuit of an ideological foreign policy was a tendency to exaggerate the danger of communist penetration.

Dealing with Trujillo

In the late 1950s American concern about the Dominican Republic grew. Rafael Trujillo, who had come to power some thirty years earlier with the blessings of the United States, was becoming increasingly autocratic and corrupt. U.S. policy-makers feared that this situation could lead to a communist takeover, as had happened in Cuba. Trujillo was seen as another Batista, even though there was no figure in the Dominican Republic who could be identified as another Castro. By the beginning of 1960 the United States wanted a new government in Santo Domingo.[37]

American misgivings were reinforced when Trujillo tried to assassinate Romulo Betancourt, the President of Venezuela, a man American policy-makers viewed as an exemplar of democracy in Latin America. (This was the same man who had pressed for revision of the oil concessions in the 1940s.) In August 1960 the United States joined all other members of the Organization of American States in breaking diplomatic relations with the Dominican Republic.[38]

American officials were not prepared to limit their pressure to conventional diplomatic measures. In April 1960 Eisenhower approved a plan calling for the removal of Trujillo through "political action." The United States indicated to Dominican dissidents that it would provide political, economic, and military support to a new government. When diplomatic relations were broken in Au-

[37] U.S. Senate, *Alleged Assassination Plots*, pp. 191-92; Atkins and Wilson, *Trujillo Regime*, p. 102; Lowenthal, *Dominican Intervention*, pp. 24ff.

[38] U.S. House, Agriculture Committee, *Extension of the Sugar Act of 1948*, p. 28.

gust, the Consul General, the highest U.S. official remaining in Santo Domingo, became the chief conduit for contacts between the CIA and anti-Trujillo groups. In December 1960 or January 1961 the "Special Group" (a committee of high officials from State, Defense, the White House, and the CIA that passed on covert operations) approved a plan giving monetary support for dissident forces in the Dominican Republic to be used for the arming of a yacht and the purchase of weapons.[39]

Trujillo was killed in May 1961. Although no American official or material was actually involved, the CIA did know who the plotters were, and the United States had let it be known that it would support a new government. The day before the assassination Kennedy personally authorized a telegram to the Consul General in Santo Domingo stating that the United States could not condone assassination; but the same message ordered continued support for those groups opposing Trujillo.[40] The United States probably could have stifled any effort to kill Trujillo simply by indicating that the perpetrators of such an attack could not expect American support. While Kennedy was anxious to avoid the possible opprobrium of actually ordering the death of a head of state, he was not unwilling to see the blood spilled by other hands. An imperial power cannot avoid involvement, even if it does nothing.

These efforts to remove Trujillo can be more easily explained by ideological considerations than by economic or strategic ones. It was a view of a global world order that moved American policy-makers, not any concern for the needs of specific industries. They were safe enough under Trujillo. It was only a rather complicated and probably incorrect political calculus relating authoritarian regimes with the rise of communist ones that led the United States to try to remove Trujillo through the use of force.

The absence of official concern for specific U.S. investments is further revealed by the economic pressure brought against Trujillo. The administration sought to limit the benefits that the Dominican Republic would derive from the American sugar import program, despite the rewards accruing to U.S. firms with Dominican sugar holdings. The sugar program, begun in 1934,

[39] U.S. Senate, *Alleged Assassination Plots*, pp. 192, 194, 196.

[40] *Ibid.*, p. 213.

separated the American market from the rest of the world through domestic and foreign quotas. Since it generally kept American prices above those that could be obtained on the world market, a share of the U.S. market was an economic plum. Until 1960 the primary beneficiary of this program was Cuba, which along with the Philippines had accounted for almost all of the foreign quota. When Eisenhower suspended Cuba's allocation in 1960, a great deal of money was up for grabs.

American policy-makers did not want Trujillo to benefit from new sugar arrangements. After the unsuccessful attempt to assassinate Betancourt, and the subsequent OAS condemnation, the administration asked Congress for authorization to prevent the Dominican Republic from receiving a share of the Cuban quota. Testifying before the House Agriculture Committee in August 1960, Undersecretary of State for Economic Affairs Douglas Dillon argued: "To reduce the sugar quota of a country with a leftist dictator only to grant a substantial portion of that quota to a dictator whose activities have been formally condemned by all American States would seriously handicap the conduct of our foreign relations throughout the hemisphere."[41]

It is, however, important to note that the administration was not asking to cut off the Dominican Republic altogether. It did not request a change in the Dominican Republic's basic quota, which amounted to 155,000 tons and had been raised because of a higher general authorization for sugar imports. What it did ask for was that some 322,000 tons, freed by the suspension of shipments from Cuba, not be given to the Dominican Republic.[42]

The administration proposal touched off a sharp dispute between the White House and the Congress (or more precisely the chairman of the House Agriculture Committee), which perfectly illustrates how the outcome of policy in the United States can be determined by the arena in which it is made. After securing Congressional approval to suspend the Cuban quota in July 1960, the President asked for discretion in allocating these supplies. This request went first to the House Agriculture Committee, the critical forum for sugar legislation. Such bills had to originate in the House because they involved raising revenue (through import duties). Chairman Cooley was not entranced with the prospect of

[41] U.S. House, *Sugar Act*, p. 28. [42] *Ibid.*, p. 49.

giving the administration any power over foreign sugar sales in the United States. Indeed, he had even been reluctant to give the executive power to cut the Cuban quota. Cooley had said during that battle that he had "no intention of surrendering the responsibility and authority of Congress, nor do I intend to create a sugar king or sugar czar in any Executive department."[43] After being accused of being soft on communism, Cooley was forced to relent on Cuba, but he wanted to keep control over the Dominican Republic's share of the U.S. market. On August 30 the House approved a bill that allowed the President to adjust quotas only if the Organization of American States voted and implemented economic sanctions against the Dominican Republic by October 15. There was little possibility that the OAS would act by that date. After some rangling with the Senate, the House version was finally accepted.[44] The policy adopted by central decision-makers was, at this point, thwarted by their inability to control the Congress.

What were Cooley's motives? He might have genuinely believed that Trujillo was a bulwark against communism.[45] He might have liked dealing with the well-paid lobbyists hired by various foreign governments.[46] Regardless of his specific motivation, what was critical for Cooley was that decisions about foreign quotas remain with his committee. For even though Cooley was a weak chairman, willing to relinquish power, sugar was one issue that he controlled. There was no sugar subcommittee; sugar bills went to the full committee. And at least on this issue Cooley held sway.[47] Congressional action on the 1960 Sugar Bill left the administration in a difficult position. Trujillo was perceived as a threat to the broad political objectives of the United States. But Congress had apparently quadrupled the amount of Dominican sugar that would enjoy preferential access to the American market.

The White House was not to be frustrated. On September 23, 1960, the Agriculture Department authorized the purchase of 322,000 additional tons from the Dominican Republic, but at the

[43] Quoted in *Congressional Quarterly Almanac*, 1960, p. 211.

[44] *Ibid*., pp. 214-15.

[45] Price, "Politics of Sugar," p. 214.

[46] Berman and Heineman, "Lobbying by Foreign Governments," p. 422.

[47] Jones, "Representation in Congress," pp. 358-67.

same time imposed an additional import levy of 2¢ per pound, which offset the benefits of higher American prices.[48] By changing the decision-making arena—in this case, by changing the nature of the decision (from a quota allocation to a tariff level)—the White House was able to change the policy outcome.

The following year the President did get authorization to cut the Dominican quota. Here the executive was helped by divisions within the domestic sugar industry, which included domestic beet and cane growers and processors, as well as importers and foreign suppliers. American sugar beet growers were happy to see foreign allocations cut, since they wanted to supply a larger share of the American market. Companies with interests in the Dominican Republic were not so enthralled. About one-third of Dominican production was controlled by an American-owned firm, the South Puerto Rican Sugar Company. The company attacked efforts to limit imports from the Dominican Republic and, when this attempt failed, sought unsuccessfully to recover the $7 million it had paid in special import duties through special Congressional legislation and court action.[49] Thus, the administration, with the backing of domestic economic interests, was ultimately able to secure a policy that was perceived as serving the general foreign policy objectives of the state. By that time Trujillo's death had presented the United States with new problems.

Overt Intervention

After Trujillo's assassination in 1961, the Dominican Republic entered a period of political instability that deeply involved the United States. Trujillo was succeeded by a Council of State that was strongly supported by the United States, most dramatically in the form of a naval armada that patrolled the Dominican coast for several months after the dictator had been killed. Early in 1963 Juan Bosch was elected President with American backing. Bosch was overthrown by a military coup seven months after he had taken office. After some misgivings the United States recognized the new regime. By 1965, however, this government was in serious economic and political difficulties. On April 24, 1965, pro-

[48] South Puerto Rican Sugar Co., *Annual Report*, 1960.

[49] *Congressional Quarterly Almanac*, 1961, p. 129; U.S. House, *Sugar Act*, pp. 71-76; South Puerto Rican Sugar Co., *Annual Report*, 1962 and 1964.

Bosch supporters precipitously launched a coup. On April 28 President Johnson authorized the landing of American marines. Within ten days there were almost 23,000 troops in the Dominican Republic. It was the first time since Roosevelt had enunciated the Good Neighbor policy that U.S. forces had actually been landed in the Caribbean. This was one of four explicit U.S. interventions in the period after World War II. What had prompted such a severe American response.? [50]

The overriding concern of American policy-makers was that the Dominican Republic would become another Cuba. This fear was reinforced by a fixation on the activities of known communists in the rebel movement. From the outset U.S. intelligence officers filed a stream of reports on the activities of communists. Well over half of the dispatches sent during the week beginning on April 24 dealt with this topic. Three days after antigovernment activity had begun the American Ambassador was reporting that rebel radio broadcasts had a "definite Castro flavor."[51] By this time he had concluded that the struggle in Santo Domingo was between communists and anticommunists, and Washington soon accepted this interpretation. In his memoirs Lyndon Johnson states: "A number of people, then and later, thought the Communist threat in the Dominican Republic was overestimated. I did not and do not think it was."[52] The decision to use troops was taken with hardly a dissent within the administration. U.S. central decision-makers felt that they had no choice.

Despite its influence in the Dominican Republic, the United States made almost no effort to bring about a compromise solution. No serious thought was given to supporting the return of Bosch, who was then living in Puerto Rico. U.S. leaders felt that he would be opposed by the Dominican military. No other alternatives acceptable to the pro-Bosch forces were discussed. Embassy officials did not actively try to get the contending forces to negotiate some kind of settlement.[53]

[50] Description of developments in the Dominican Republic is taken from Lowenthal, *Dominican Intervention*, Chs. 1-3.

[51] Quoted in Lowenthal, *ibid.*, p. 97.

[52] Johnson, "U.S. Business Interests in Cuba," p. 200.

[53] The discussion in this section draws very heavily on Lowenthal, *Dominican Intervention*, Ch. 3.

Although it is true that there were leftist elements in the forces supporting Bosch's return, American officials almost certainly exaggerated their importance. U.S. information was concentrated on this one aspect of developments in the Dominican Republic. After more well-known pro-Bosch civilian leaders had fled or taken asylum on the second or third day of the rebellion, the only antigovernment activists with whom U.S. officials were familiar were those that had communist connections. The United States had virtually no information about the middle-level military officers and civilians who were actually leading the revolt. The American obsession with the dangers of another communist takeover in the Caribbean had led to a severe distortion of the information that was being received.

There is a nonlogical element to American behavior in the Dominican Republic that is present in a number of the cases of American intervention in the period after 1945. The perception of American leaders was skewed by their fixation on the dangers of a communist takeover. It is true that the situation in Santo Domingo was confused, and that the level of violence during the week of April 24 was unprecedented in Dominican history. Nevertheless, what American policy-makers saw happening was not what a detached observer would have seen. Despite the seriousness of using American troops in Latin America for the first time in thirty years, there was no extensive search for alternative solutions. U.S. central decision-makers felt compelled to send in the marines. There is little evidence of prudent calculation, of an attempt to clearly relate means and ends.[54] Opposition to communism more closely resembles a millennial goal, a religious quest, than a logical or rational strategy.

Chile under Salvador Allende

During the 1960s the fundamental objective of America's policy toward Chile was to prevent Salvador Allende, the leader of

[54] For a discussion of the correspondence between subjective and objective (as perceived by a disinterested third party) situations and means-ends calculations, as a criterion for logical action, see Pareto's analysis in *Sociological Writings*, pp. 143-49, and 183-85, as well as Ch. I of this study.

the Socialist Party, from coming to power. In 1970 this effort failed. Allende won a bare plurality in a three-man race; but in accordance with practice, he was elected President by the Chilean Congress in the fall of 1970.

Allende's platform had called for internal reforms and expanded relations with the Communist Bloc. During the campaign he had also announced his intention to fully nationalize the copper industry, which was, next to oil in Venezuela, the largest single U.S. investment in the hemisphere. (Majority ownership and some aspects of managerial control had, as we have seen in Chapter VII, already passed into the hands of the Chilean state before 1970.) Once in power, Allende quickly moved to carry out his promises. In December 1970 the new government introduced a constitutional amendment providing for full state control of the copper industry. This measure also took determination of the compensation to be paid to the companies out of the Chilean judicial system and placed it, in effect, in the hands of the President. It was unanimously passed by the Chilean Congress in July 1971, a body in which the socialists held less than half the seats. Kennecott and Anaconda were nationalized in September. Other major U.S. holdings were also taken. The largest of these was a $153 million investment that the International Telephone and Telegraph Company (ITT) held in Chitelco, Chile's telephone company. Other nationalizations involved Bethlehem Steel, several American banks, and the Ralston Purina Company.[55]

Corporate Response

Virtually all of the American corporations were, for one reason or another, resigned to leaving Chile. The copper companies realized that they had no political support. Chitelco was the last operating telephone company owned by ITT outside of American territory; the company's executives had concluded that public utilities were too sensitive to remain in foreign hands. The American banks generally kept a low profile. Many corporations, like

[55] U.S. Senate, *Covert Action in Chile*, p. 5; Moran, "Transnational Strategies," p. 280; U.S. Senate, Committee on Foreign Relations, Subcommittee on Multinational Corporations, *Multinational Corporations*, Hearings, Part 1, p. 273; *New York Times*, Sept. 21, 1971, 1:3.

Ralston Purina, had insurance from the Overseas Private Investment Company (OPIC), an American government entity, against losses resulting from expropriation.

The value of Chilean investments varied widely among companies. The book value of the two largest copper companies was about $500 million; Anaconda's holdings were larger than Kennecott's. Cerro's investment was under $100 million.[56] ITT claimed $153 million for the 76 percent share of Chitelco that it still held. (The rest had been sold to Chilean public and private entities during the Frei regime.) Bethlehem had an iron ore mine worth less than $50 million. American banks had only very modest equity investments, ranging from $1 to $3 million.

The fate of U.S. companies under Allende also varied. Some were able to reach a satisfactory settlement. All of the banks did, and so did Bethlehem Steel, which received some $20 million for its mine, and Cerro, the third largest copper company, which maintained cordial relations with the Allende regime. (The company continued to provide technical assistance and was not affected by the excess profits tax imposed on Kennecott and Anaconda.) Cerro concluded a preliminary settlement with Chile for $37.6 million in December 1972 and was negotiating a final accord when Allende was overthrown. Ralston Purina, which had a feed mill and a poultry processing plant in Chile worth about $1 million that were taken over by workers in November 1970, received payment from the Overseas Private Investment Corporation in the summer of 1972.[57]

However, the three largest American investors—Anaconda, Kennecott, and ITT—did not fare so well. Chile took a very tough stand with the copper companies. In September 1971 the government levied an excess profits tax of $774 million that exceeded the book value of the companies' investments by $200 million. On October 11, 1971, Chile's Comptroller General announced that there would be no compensation for either firm. Furthermore, by the end of 1971 Chile had defaulted on some of its foreign debts,

[56] *New York Times*, Sept. 21, 1971, 1:3.

[57] *New York Times*, May 21, 1971, 9:1; Charles River Associates, *Copper Market*, p. 16; *Wall St. Journal*, March 13, 1974, 2:3; U.S. Senate, *Multinational Corporations*, Hearings, Part 1, pp. 374, 376, 391.

including $14 million due Anaconda under the 1969 agreement, which gave the state majority ownership of the El Salvador and Chucuicamata mines.[58] The Allende regime did enter into negotiations with ITT after Chitelco was nationalized, but these were broken off in March 1972 when Jack Anderson, the newspaper columnist, published excerpts from purloined company documents showing that ITT had tried to influence Chile's internal affairs.

The reaction of the corporations to Allende's nationalizations varied with their stakes and success in securing compensation. Most were conciliatory. The banks, Cerro, Bethlehem Steel, Ralston Purina, and others were not anxious to have sanctions imposed on Chile, and they did make satisfactory settlements.[59]

Kennecott worked out a strikingly successful strategy for protecting its investments without assistance from the American government. When it exhausted local appeals against the Chilean tax judgment, it brought pressure through third parties. Kennecott filed suits against Chilean copper shipments in France, West Germany, Sweden, and Italy, which affected about 7 percent of Chile's exports. In 1973 sales in France and Sweden were suspended by these legal actions. Kennecott also formed transnational alliances, tying the interests of copper purchasers and financial institutions in the United States, Europe, and Japan to Kennecott's settlement with Chile. After nationalization these third parties also put pressure on Chile. As a result of these tactics and earlier agreements with Chile, Kennecott received more in compensation after 1971 than the net worth of its holdings in 1964 when it was the sole owner of El Teniente.[60]

None of the companies discussed above pressed the American government to take a hard line in Chile. They were able either to work out satisfactory arrangements directly with Chile, as the

[58] *New York Times*, Sept. 29, 1971, 1:3; Chadwin, "Nixon Administration Debates," pp. 97-107; *New York Times*, Jan. 6, 1972, 53:6.

[59] U.S. Senate, *Multinational Corporations*, Hearings, Part 1, pp. 269, 359ff., 374-76, 384, 391.

[60] Charles River Associates, pp. 16, 20; *New York Times*, Sept. 8, 1972, 45:6, and Oct. 5, 1972, 67:3. See Moran, "Transnational Strategies," pp. 281, 282, for an elaboration of transnational alliance strategies.

banks and Cerro did, or to exercise effective power on their own, as Kennecott did, or to avoid financial loss through OPIC insurance, as Ralston Purina did. There were, however, two major American companies—Anaconda and ITT—that were not only dissatisfied with developments in Chile but also sought to enlist official American support.

Anaconda was not in an enviable position. It did not develop alliances with third parties. Chile was a very important part of its operations. With an investment of several hundred million dollars at stake, its executives viewed developments under the Allende regime with alarm, and they turned to the American government for assistance. Anaconda wanted the United States to protest more strongly the constitutional amendment introduced in Chile in December 1970, because it denied access to the regular Chilean courts, which, a company official stated, "we had depended on for over fifty years."[61] Early in 1971 Anaconda executives visited several U.S. policy-makers with a proposal that nationalized American property in Chile be compensated for by a loan from the United States, which would be repaid by the shipment of raw materials. This was rejected, in part because it raised legal problems. The company's Washington representative took the initiative in establishing a committee composed of firms with interests in Chile whose members spoke with Kissinger's assistant for Latin American affairs and lobbied Congress for a tougher stand. However, Anaconda officials testified in 1973 that they were not interested in programs that would economically destabilize Chile, since destabilization would make it more difficult for them to get compensation. During the Allende period Anaconda got very little, and its top management was ultimately fired.[62]

It is impossible to write about American relations with Allende without looking at a company that has little to do with raw materials, the International Telephone and Telegraph Company. ITT pressed more vigorously than any other U.S. corporation for a hard line in Chile. Its major investment was the Chilean Telephone Company. By 1970 ITT had sold 24 percent of the company to private or public Chilean interests; the remaining 76 per-

[61] U.S. Senate, *Multinational Corporations*, Hearings, Part 1, p. 272.

[62] *Ibid.*, Part 1, p. 271; Part 2, pp. 1009, 1052-61; Moran, *Copper in Chile*, p. 151; Moran, "Transnational Strategies," p. 283.

cent, it claimed, was worth $153 million, of which about $90 million was covered by OPIC insurance.[63]

In 1970 ITT began an intensive lobbying effort spearheaded by the corporation's president, Harold Geneen. Geneen met with Attorney General John Mitchell, John Ehrlichman, Charles Colson, and Vice-President Spiro Agnew, among others. The main issue in these meetings was ITT's antitrust problems, but Chile was probably discussed also. On Chile Geneen talked with Alexander Haig and Peter Peterson, the head of the Council on International Economic Policy. On July 16, 1970, Geneen met with William Broe, the head of clandestine services for the western hemisphere division of the Central Intelligence Agency, at a Washington hotel suite maintained by ITT. At this meeting Geneen offered Broe a million dollars to be used by the American government in Chile. The money was refused, but the Agency did suggest ways in which it could be gotten to Jorge Alessandri, Allende's most conservative opponent. ITT eventually put some $350,000 into the Chilean presidential campaign. Other American corporations gave an equal amount. In September 1970 another offer of one million was made to Kissinger and CIA Director Richard Helms by John McCone, a former CIA Director and now an ITT board member. On October 23 ITT sent a letter to Kissinger recommending actions that could be taken against Allende. ITT took the most active part in an ad hoc business group on Chile, which was established in Washington in January 1971 to bring pressure on the American government. During the summer of 1971 company officials drafted letters to key Congressmen asking what was being done to halt expropriations in Latin America and why the Hickenlooper Amendment (which would have automatically cut American foreign aid) was not being applied. Both before and after the 1970 elections ITT pressed American news media to publish unsympathetic stories about Allende.[64] A letter written by an ITT official in July 1971 to Kennecott and Anaconda admonished them for not "raising more hell publically [*sic*] about the hosing they are about to get in Chile."[65]

[63] U.S. Senate, *Multinational Corporations*, Hearings, Part 1, pp. 44-45.

[64] *Ibid.*, Part 1, pp. 33, 182-83, 246, 431-32, 448; Part 2, pp. 1040, 1046; U.S. Senate, *Covert Action in Chile*, pp. 12-13.

[65] U.S. Senate, *Multinational Corporations*, Hearings, Part 2, p. 1037.

Precisely why ITT took such a hard line, and lobbied so strenuously, is a question too fascinating to pass over without comment; it offers an opportunity to speculate, if not come to firm conclusions, about the motivations of corporate behavior. The simplest explanation is one offered by Geneen himself when he testified before the Senate Subcommittee on Multinational Corporations. He argued that he acted to protect ITT's potential equity losses of some $50 million, which were not covered by OPIC insurance. In 1971 ITT did make provisions for losses of $70 million on its Chilean operations. This sum amounted to 60¢ per common share and reduced the company's earnings per share from $3.14 in 1970 to $2.85 in 1971. But part of this loss could be counted against tax liabilities when Chitelco was taken off the company's books. In 1970 ITT had gotten about 4 percent of its sales and revenues and 10 percent of net income from utility operations, most of which were attributable to Chile.[66] While potential losses in Chile were not insignificant, they were hardly a make-or-break proposition for the company. Its more dynamic operations were not associated with operating telephone companies. Its long-term growth was not affected. Anaconda, which had more to lose, took a more conciliatory attitude.

A second explanation is that ITT, unlike the copper companies, was not resigned to losing access to Chile. It was not Chitelco per se that was important, for corporate officials realized that public utilities were too politically salient to remain in foreign hands, but rather the desire to keep the world open for the diversified services and products offered by a multinational conglomerate.[67] However, the banks were in a similar position, also anxious to maintain their global position. Yet they took a much lower profile, acting on the assumption that sooner or later they would be back. For a company with many foreign interests, political intrigue, if it is discovered, can be costly.

In the end, it is difficult to understand ITT's behavior except by understanding Geneen himself. The offer of one million dollars was first made privately by Geneen to William Broe of the CIA; it was made again to State Department officials and members

[66] ITT, *Annual Report*, 1971, pp. 2, 21, 25; 1970, p. 3.

[67] U.S. Senate, *Multinational Corporations*, Hearings, Part 1, p. 211.

of Kissinger's staff in September 1970 at Geneen's instructions. The money was never discussed with the company's board of directors.[68]

Geneen's position was closer to that of the founding father of an enterprise than the chief executive of an old and established firm. In a modern industrial corporate economy it is not easy to find circumstances where one would expect entrepreneurial rather than managerial behavior. Few large companies are run by the men who founded them. Most business executives are caretakers, not creators. The range of choices open to them has been circumscribed by technological, economic, and political boundaries. During the 1960s, however, creativity manifested itself in the building of conglomerates, which involved financial manipulation and managerial skill rather than the development of new products. It is not coincidental that Geneen began his career as an accountant. ITT was old, but it was in the process of transforming itself. Under Geneen's leadership it had become one of the most successful modern conglomerates. It had moved out of its original base in communications to a wide variety of activities including hotels, car rentals, and insurance. The company was in many ways Geneen's creation. He was given considerable discretion by the board of directors. He was in a position to impose his views on corporate policies, and he obviously found developments in Chile very distasteful.

Public Response

While the reaction of the private sector to developments in Chile varied, the response of the American government was firm. The United States did virtually all that it could, short of overt military intervention, first to prevent Allende from coming to office and then to foster his downfall. This effort involved both overt and covert economic and political pressure.

American officials may have been taken by surprise by Allende's narrow election victory. The CIA had public opinion polls showing that Alessandri would win in 1970 with 40 percent of the vote.[69] The United States had put large amounts of resources into

[68] *Ibid.*, pp. 214, 438-39.

[69] *Ibid.*, p. 290.

Chile during the Frei period. It would not have been easy to admit that the specific aim of this policy, which was to prevent Allende from becoming President, had not been achieved.

Once the election had been held, however, the reaction from the White House was ferocious. The United States followed two institutionally distinct paths, known as Track I and Track II, to prevent Allende from taking office. Track I involved measures taken by the 40 Committee, the interagency group that approved foreign covert activities. It included an effort to bribe members of the Chilean Congress to vote against Allende. When a candidate received less than a majority of the popular vote, the Chilean constitution required that the president be elected by the legislature. In practice, the legislature had always selected the candidate with a plurality. Contacts were made with Frei, through the American embassy in Santiago, to try to enlist his support. Frei was prevented by law from succeeding himself, and one scenario called for the legislature to elect Alessandri, who would then resign, opening the way for a new popular election that would return Frei to office. But the plan came to naught, it was judged to be too dangerous given its low chance of success, and the bribes were not made. The members of the 40 Committee then began to look at the prospect for a military coup.

Such possibilities were already under consideration in what came to be known as Track II, which involved direct contacts between the CIA and the Chilean military. Track II began on September 15 when Richard Nixon instructed CIA Director Richard Helms to foment a military coup in Chile. The 40 Committee was not informed, nor was the American embassy. Rene Schneider, the commander-in-chief of the Chilean army, opposed a coup. On October 22 the CIA passed machine guns and ammunition to a group that had tried unsuccessfully to kidnap Schneider on October 19. On the same day Schneider was killed in a bungled kidnapping effort by another group of officers. The CIA had been in contact with the men who were later convicted of involvement in this plot. However, these stratagems did not prevent Allende from becoming President. On October 24 he was endorsed by Chile's Congress.[70]

[70] Information on U.S. foreign policy is taken from U.S. Senate, *Alleged Assassination Plots*, pp. 225-33, and *Covert Action in Chile, passim*.

With Allende in power, covert political intervention continued. In addition, a wide variety of economic pressures were brought against Chile. This policy was initiated at the highest levels of the American government and elaborated in National Security Decision Memorandum 93 (NSDM 93), which was issued in early November 1970. Bilateral assistance was virtually stopped. Aid grants dropped from $35 million in 1969 to $1.5 million in 1971, although funds already in the pipeline were allowed to go through. Export-Import Bank credits, which were $234 million in 1967 and $29 million in 1969, fell to nothing in 1971. The United States also opposed loans to Chile from international lending organizations: credits from the Inter-American Development Bank went from $46 million in 1970 to $2 million in 1971; the World Bank provided no new loans to Chile between 1970 and 1973. The only significant source of public external finance was the International Monetary Fund, which extended some $90 million through its special facility for compensating countries for fluctuations in their export earnings. Financing from private sources dried up too: short-term U.S. commercial credits dropped from about $300 million under Frei to $30 million while Allende was in office. The United States also made sales from its copper stockpile, which contributed to depressing international prices, lowering Chile's foreign exchange earnings.[71]

These economic sanctions were telling. Chile was heavily in debt. It needed foreign capital to meet its import needs. No matter how judiciously Allende's socialist reforms had been implemented, there would invariably have been some economic disruption. The price of copper, Chile's major export, was falling. The loss of commercial credits was particularly painful because so much of Chile's capital stock was American, and spare parts were most easily obtainable from the United States. The lack of spare parts may have contributed to the truckers' strike, which touched off the chain of events that led to the military overthrow of Allende in 1973.[72]

American policy-makers did not limit pressure to economic measures. An extensive covert political program was also carried

[71] U.S. Senate, *Covert Action in Chile*, pp. 27, 32, 33; *Washington Post*, Jan. 30, 1974, A19:1; Farnsworth, "Chile," p. 132.

[72] Farnsworth, p. 137.

out. American penetration of the Chilean political system was, as we have seen, nothing new. Strong U.S. backing had secretly been given to Frei while he was President, but the scale increased after 1970. Between 1964 and 1970 the CIA spent some $3 million in Chile. Between 1970 and Allende's overthrow in September 1973 it spent $8 million. This money was used to support the National and Christian Democratic parties, to place stories in the mass media, and occasionally to finance private interest groups. The CIA also maintained covert contacts with members of the Chilean army. Even under Allende, aid to the armed forces was continued.[73]

These efforts had some impact, although domestic factors were probably more important. After internal turmoil, including a crippling truckers' strike, Allende was overthrown in a bloody military insurrection in 1973. The CIA was aware of military plotting, although it did not directly participate in the coup.[74]

One cannot deny that the United States made an extraordinary effort in Chile. What motivated American policy-makers? On the face of it, corporate interests and corporate pressure seem a plausible explanation. ITT, after all, showed its seriousness by offering a million dollars. Anaconda was clearly very concerned, even though it did not push for economic destabilization in Chile. The new military regime did give generous compensation for American properties. The United States had strongly backed private demands for adequate payments. And economic pressure was justified by Chile's expropriation of U.S. property.[75]

All the same, the protection of corporate interests is not a convincing explanation for American policy. Prompt and adequate compensation was a flexible guide, not a firm dictum. Often in the past the U.S. Treasury had indirectly shouldered the burden of payments to companies to lubricate political relations between the

[73] U.S. Senate, *Covert Action in Chile*, pp. 1, 2, 6, 10; *New York Times*, Jan. 16, 1974, 34:2.

[74] U.S. Senate, *Covert Action in Chile*, pp. 37-39. For a discussion of domestic causes of Allende's downfall see Landsberger and McDaniel, "Hypermobilization in Chile."

[75] *Wall St. Journal*, July 25, 1974, 8:3; *New York Times*, Feb. 20, 1976, 47:6, and Oct. 14, 1971, 1:2.

United States and host-country governments. American policy-makers had decided on a tough line in Chile before compensation became an issue. It was not clear when Allende came to office what level of payments he would authorize for nationalized property. During his early months as President, Chile took a conciliatory posture. Cerro maintained cordial relations with the new regime. Bethlehem Steel and American banks concluded satisfactory agreements. Even ITT was still negotiating when Jack Anderson published documents implicating the company in Chile's internal affairs. As we have seen, however, the basic American decisions to oppose Allende were taken by Nixon and the 40 Committee in September 1970, and by the National Security Council as articulated in NSDM 93 in November 1970. This was well before it became clear that Allende would not compensate Anaconda and ITT, the two companies with the most to lose in Chile.

American public officials, rather than being pressured and used by corporate managers, kept the private sector in the dark about the full extent of efforts to change Chile's government. At a meeting with businessmen on October 9, 1970, the American Ambassador in Santiago said that he expected Allende to be elected by the Congress and was relatively positive about prospects for the new regime. An Anaconda official reported to his superiors that "the Ambassador states that he expects the policy of the U.S. government in regard to nationalization will be that a U.S. company nationalized will receive adequate, just and timely compensation. To questions as to what was adequate and what was timely the Ambassador was very evasive."[76] In Washington U.S. companies were not informed about the full range of American actions. When John McCone offered ITT's one million to Kissinger, he was told that he would be called if the government developed a plan; Kissinger never got in touch with him. An ITT official in Santiago did learn of Track I, however. Whether this information was passed to high corporate officials is not known.[77] Geneen testified before the Senate Subcommittee on Multinational Corporations that the "U.S. Government for its own reasons took no ac-

[76] U.S. Senate, *Multinational Corporations*, Hearings, Part 2, p. 1051.

[77] *Ibid.*, Part 1, pp. 102, 130.

tion," implying that he was ignorant of official initiatives.[78] But he may have been lying.[79]

While American public officials kept private corporations at some distance, they also tried to use them. A close examination of the circumstances surrounding ITT's offer of one million dollars suggests that it was the government that was trying to manipulate the corporation, and not the other way around. Harold Geneen's contact with the CIA was arranged by John McCone. McCone, a member of the company's board of directors, was a former head of the CIA. He was a close friend of Richard Helms, who was directing the Agency in 1970. During the summer of 1970 McCone and Helms had several conversations about developments in Chile, and it was then that McCone asked Helms to arrange a meeting for Geneen. It was McCone who informed Geneen of the contributions that American companies had made during the 1964 Chilean elections. In all of this intrigue McCone's actions are more easily explained by his former government position than by his corporate one. Despite the comforts of a corporate directorship, it would be surprising if being head of the CIA had not left a deeper mark. Geneen's meeting in July 1970 was not with someone from the intelligence-gathering branch of the CIA, but with the director of clandestine operations for the western hemisphere. The Agency must have been interested in doing something other than having a friendly chat with a company president, or even passing on tidbits of information; officials from the Agency's intelligence-gathering side could have been used for that purpose. The CIA approved ITT's efforts to promote Alessandri's election by placing anti-Allende stories and editorials in Chile's mass media and giving the antisocialist paper *El Mercurio* financial support. On September 29 Geneen's contact (Broe) flew to New York to discuss schemes for economic de-

[78] *Ibid.*, p. 461.

[79] He would not have been the only witness at the hearings who did not give the whole truth. All of the corporate witnesses testified that they maintained a policy of neutrality, yet private money was funneled to Alessandri during the 1970 campaign. Both Ambassador Korry and Assistant Secretary of State for Latin America, Charles Meyer, testified that the United States was following a policy of nonintervention, although the investigations of the Senate Select Committee on Intelligence Activities indicate that they both knew about Track I. See U.S. Senate, *Alleged Assassination Plots*, pp. 225-54.

stabilization, such as restricting bank credit and limiting corporate expenditures. He also asked ITT to make contact with other American companies, and provided a list of likely prospects. ITT executives were not impressed, however, and did not follow up Broe's recommendations. All of this suggests more a CIA effort to use ITT as an instrument of state policy than corporate perversion of the foreign policy process. This tactic failed because ITT did not go along. After Allende's victory the 40 Committee directed the State Department to get corporations to bring economic pressure on Chile.[80]

The ITT episode has generally been interpreted as an example of the way in which private interests pervert public policy—an argument very much in conformity with an instrumental Marxist or interest-group interpretation of politics. The evidence presented here, however, suggests that the direction of influence was very different. It was not the corporation that used the state, but the state that used the corporation. The CIA was able to take advantage of Geneen's predispositions. The possibility of funneling corporate money into Chile appears to have come initially from the state. This is the kind of relationship suggested by a vision of politics that regards central decision-makers as not only having autonomy from societal pressures but also being able to manipulate the behavior of private actors.

American policy cannot be explained by corporate pressure. Most American firms had worked out a satisfactory solution with Allende. Of those that had not, Anaconda feared that economic disruption would make it more difficult to get compensation. ITT's action must at least in part be explained by manipulation of the company by state actors, rather than the other way around.

If American policy cannot be interpreted as a response to corporate pressure, what of general economic objectives? Security of supply is not very convincing. The United States is largely self-sufficient in copper. In 1970 imports from Chile amounted to only about 4 percent of U.S. use, total imports only to 13 percent.[81] Furthermore, American officials had been quite willing to see the

[80] U.S. Senate, *Multinational Corporations*, Hearings, Part 1, pp. 93ff., 245, 250-56, 465; *Covert Action in Chile*, pp. 12, 13.

[81] Metallgesellschaft Aktiengesellschaft, *Metal Statistics 1962-1972*, Frankfurt-am-Main, 1973, pp. 208, 210, 213.

nationality and even effective control of production pass from American companies into the hands of the Chilean government. This process was already far advanced under the Frei regime, which was strongly supported by the United States. American officials had pressured Anaconda to sell a majority interest to Chile. Policy-makers were resigned to the loss of the copper mines, regardless of who won the 1970 election.[82]

American behavior in Chile cannot be explained in terms of economic interests, whether defined by corporate profits or security of raw materials supplies. The answer lies rather in the direction of the broader political concerns at stake. As in all other cases of covert or overt intervention, these concerns were catalyzed by the fear that a communist regime would come to power. In a background briefing on September 16, 1970, Kissinger described Allende as a "man backed by the Communists and probably a Communist himself. . . ." He went on to say that if the Chilean Congress affirmed Allende, it would present problems in the entire hemisphere.[83] After Allende's victory on September 4 the CIA's Directorate of Intelligence circulated the following assessment:

> Regarding threats to U.S. interests, we conclude that:
>
> 1. The U.S. has no vital national interests within Chile. There would, however, be tangible economic losses.
>
> 2. The world military balance of power would not be significantly altered by an Allende government.
>
> 3. An Allende victory would, however, create considerable political and psychological costs:
>
> a. Hemispheric cohesion would be threatened by the challenge that an Allende government would pose to the OAS and by the reactions that it would create in other countries. We do not see, however, any likely threat to the peace of the region.
>
> b. An Allende victory would represent a definite psychological advance for the Marxist idea.[84]

[82] U.S. Senate, *Covert Action in Chile*, p. 45.

[83] Quoted in Fagen, "The United States and Chile," p. 297.

[84] U.S. Senate, *Alleged Assassination Plots*, p. 229.

Conclusion

This is as good a summary as any of American concerns, not only in Chile but elsewhere. Policy-makers did not ignore economic considerations, but their attention was focussed on other matters: more precisely, the possibility of regimes that called themselves communist securing power in Third World states. The overt and covert use of force by the United States after the Second World War was not closely identified with tangible economic gain or the protection of territorial and political integrity. If it had been, American foreign policy would be much easier to understand. Fear about "a definite psychological advance for the Marxist idea," effervescent though it may be, comes much closer to providing at least a decision rule that can retrodictively predict when American leaders were willing to use force.

A decision rule is not a fully satisfying formulation, however, for it avoids the question of why this pattern of behavior developed, of how it can best be placed in some broader conception of national motivations. As the cases in the preceding two chapters reveal, the argument that state policy was determined by corporate preferences is not convincing. There are too many deviations between the desires of private managers and the actions, or lack of them, of government officials. But three kinds of arguments remain to be considered: strategic, economic, and ideological. Which of these best explains the salience that communist-dominated regimes assumed for American central decision-makers?

Let us begin with strategic considerations. The notion of strategic interests has become very malleable. Analytic clarity requires that its definition be limited. Strategic goals can be understood as referring to the preservation of a country's territorial and political integrity. This is not just a semantic sleight of hand. It does conform with common usage: in balance-of-power or realist theories, predictions and explanations about the behavior of states are based on defining goals in this way. For the superpowers, one of which is the subject of this study, the protection of territorial integrity (or of the population from nuclear holocaust) is a function of the nuclear balance. Deterrence rather than defense has become the key issue. Since the late 1950s an erudite body of literature has been developed defining the conditions for stability in a nuclear world. Of all of the cases of overt and covert American intervention since the Second World War, the *only* one that may have affected the strategic balance was Cuba. The Soviet attempt to place intermediate-range missiles on Cuba during the early 1960s can plausibly (although not necessarily) be seen as a development that altered the nuclear balance because the Soviet arsenal was, at that time, far inferior to the American. Other overt and covert interventions were not related to core objectives. Strategic goals defined as preserving a state's territory from invasion, or its population from annihilation, do not provide an adequate explanation for American intervention in the period after the Second World War.

Strategic goals related to preserving political integrity present a more complicated problem. Here developments in third countries could affect the basic nature of the polity in the United States and the Soviet Union. The Russian invasions of Hungary and Czechoslovakia were precipitated by events that undermined the primacy of the Communist Party in those countries. The United States has not been confronted with a similar situation. But if Europe and Japan were to adopt militant communist regimes, there would be unavoidable political repercussions in the United States. It is far from certain that a liberal democratic polity could survive under such circumstances.

Regime changes in Asia, Latin America, and especially Africa, however, could not have an impact on American domestic politics comparable to those in Europe and perhaps Japan. This is not to say that such developments are irrelevant, but their effect has been limited to electoral politics rather than the basic nature of the U.S. political system. Even in the electoral arena the issue is not straightforward. The contention that interventions have been based on the fear of losing office must be made by reference to perceptions rather than actual results, for continued involvement can, as Lyndon Johnson showed us in 1968, lead to the loss of office as surely as the assumption of power by a communist regime. At any rate, being voted out of office is not a change in the basic nature of a country's political system. Electoral outcomes are not strategic goals. After Cuba, Vietnam, and Cambodia it is difficult to argue that communist takeovers, not to mention various mutations of socialism that are now prominent in Asia, Africa, and Latin America, affect the strategic interests of the United States understood as the preservation of territorial and political integrity.

Even if such a connection could be demonstrated, it would not offer much guidance in choosing between a statist and structural Marxist interpretation of American policy. Although the goal of defending a country's territory and polity is usually associated with a balance-of-power or statist approach, it does not contradict the logic of a structural Marxist position. To preserve the coherence of any society, elemental strategic aims must be satisfied. In sum, it is difficult to understand American intervention after World War II in strategic terms, and even if one could, it would not contribute much to delineating the differences between statist and structural Marxist arguments.

Economic goals offer a second explanation for why American central decision-makers used overt or covert force to oppose communist regimes in Third World countries. As we have seen, it is very difficult to explain American behavior in terms of specific and narrowly defined economic objectives. U.S. policy has often deviated from the expressed preferences of major American corporations. As Table VIII-1 indicates, there is no clear correlation between American investment and countries where intervention has taken place. Various kinds of instrumental Marxist arguments are not very compelling.

However, structural Marxist contentions must be carefully considered. Here opposition to communist regimes is related to preserving the structure of the world capitalist system as a whole. In his *Age of Imperialism* Harry Magdoff makes such a case:

> But the reality of imperialism goes far beyond the immediate interest of this or that investor: the underlying purpose is nothing less than keeping as much as possible of the world open for trade and investment by the giant multinational corporations.[85]

What matters to the business community, and to the business

[85] Magdoff, *Age of Imperialism*, p. 14.

> system as a whole, is that the option of foreign investment (and foreign trade) should remain available. For this to be meaningful, the business system requires, as a minimum, that the political and economic principles of capitalism should prevail and that the door be fully open for foreign capital at all times. How much or how little an open door may be exploited is not the issue.[86]

For Magdoff, and for other structural Marxists, state action is not limited to the protection of specific economic aims. Its purpose in foreign affairs is to maintain a system in which capitalism's need for expansion can be satisfied. A closed international environment, one in which foreign markets, investment opportunities, and raw materials were not available, would eliminate one of the important mechanisms through which a capitalist system deals with its inherent contradictions.

There are three problems with this interpretation. First, it does not account for the relatively passive American response to the dangers posed by economic nationalism. Second, it assumes that socialist or communist regimes would foreclose opportunities for multinational corporations. Third, it cannot adequately deal with the nonlogical aspects of American interventionism, particularly as they were finally manifest in Vietnam. This third argument is the most important. A structural Marxist analysis assumes calculations based on interests. In coping with falling rates of profit and the tension between the socialization of labor and the private appropriation of profits, the capitalist state strives to act rationally. It tries to find the course that will best preserve the coherence of its society. State behavior that undermines coherence defies the epistemological foundations of a structural Marxist position, particularly if such policies are nonlogical.

A structural Marxist argument cannot adequately explain the rapidity with which American central decision-makers accepted economic nationalism, particularly when this is contrasted with their adamant reaction against regimes that were perceived as being communist. As we have seen, nationalist sentiments in Third World countries provided a powerful motivation for taking

[86] *Ibid*., p. 20.

over foreign companies. New rulers could legitimate themselves by attacking salient foreign investments. This possibility existed for a fairly wide range of regime types: it was not just limited to those that explicitly identified themselves as communist. Until the late 1960s U.S. leaders were willing to use diplomatic and economic pressure to counter economic nationalism. But when they did not fear that a communist regime might come to power, they were unwilling to use force. As they learned, mainly from their experience in Peru, that pressure only tended to aggravate relations, they moved towards a genuinely conciliatory position.

I do not mean to argue that economic nationalism has meant the end of foreign investment. Clearly, it has not. While some industries, particularly those producing raw materials, have been subject to considerable pressure, others have been able to expand their activities. Multinational banks extended large loans to some less developed countries during the 1970s. However, on the spectrum ranging from societies fully open to foreign investments to those completely closed, economic nationalism has pushed things toward the latter pole. The discretion of corporate managers has been circumscribed by the controls imposed by host-country governments over the movement of goods, capital, and labor (managerial talent). American companies and American central decision-makers have adapted to these difficulties with considerable flexibility, but this adjustment should not obscure the fact that some opportunities for foreign economic activities have been closed or limited.

The situation is also more complicated on the other side of the spectrum. Assumption of power by a communist regime does not necessarily mean that the opportunities for American corporations will be completely eliminated. This fact is brought out by the recent growth of American economic relations with the Communist Bloc. From 1970 to 1976 American exports to socialist areas in Europe and Asia increased by a factor of ten, accounting for about 3 percent of foreign shipments in 1976. Continued growth is expected. Soviet trade with West Germany and Japan, also capitalist countries, is considerably higher than exchanges with the United States. Financial transactions with the Eastern Bloc have also increased substantially. Poland, Bulgaria, Rumania, and the Soviet

Union have been heavy borrowers. By the middle of 1977 estimates of the amount borrowed by the Soviet Bloc ranged up to $40 billion.[87]

Despite socialism, economic relations have not been limited to trade and finance; American industrial companies have also been involved with communist countries. By the mid-1970s the Soviet Union had 31 turnkey projects with Western corporations, the largest costing $1.5 billion for a large diameter pipe plant built by West German interests. Industrial cooperation agreements have been signed with the Russians by 96 American firms, of which 58 are among the 500 largest U.S. corporations. A number of Eastern Europe states including Yugoslavia, Rumania, and Hungary have provided for direct investment from foreign corporations in the form of joint ventures with state-owned enterprises. U.S. businessmen have even been pressing Washington to improve relations with Hanoi, which has given European and Japanese companies very favorable terms.[88]

All of this is not to say that the coming to power of communist regimes offers great economic opportunities for world capitalism. But it does indicate that the situation is not entirely negative. Furthermore, assuming that socialist regimes in the Third World would be interested in maintaining their independence, it is not likely that they would close themselves off economically from the West. Castro is reported to have told Allende that it would be a mistake to break ties with the United States. At least to some extent, the low level of American economic activity with the Eastern Bloc reflects U.S. policy. Most favored nation treatment has still been denied a number of communist countries including the Soviet Union. The Eastern Bloc is subject to various embargoes and quotas. The resources that American leaders were willing to

[87] U.S., Economic Report of the President, Jan. 1977, p. 299; *Wall St. Journal*, March, 16, 1977, 14:3; U.S. Congress, Joint Economic Committee, *Soviet Economy*, p. 694; Marshall Goldman, "Soviet Bloc Moves to Reduce Deficit," *Wall St. Journal*, March 16, 1977, p. 22. This compares with as much as $75 billion owed by non-oil LDCs.

[88] U.S. Congress, *Soviet Economy*, pp. 748, 773, 777; Nichols, "Western Investment in Eastern Europe: The Yugoslav Example," in U.S. Congress, Joint Economic Committee, *Economies of Eastern Europe*, p. 725; *Wall St. Journal*, March 11, 1977, 1:1, and July 7, 1977, 16:2.

expend to prevent a country from going communist cannot be adequately understood from a structural Marxist perspective. Communist regimes have not necessarily brought an end to economic opportunity. In sum, the extent to which the United States has ignored economic nationalism, while using force to oppose communism in the Third World, does not necessarily conform with the structural needs of advanced capitalism.

If there are problems with both strategic and economic arguments, can a stronger case be made for an ideological interpretation of American policy? As I argued in Part One of this study, an ideological foreign policy is characterized by two basic considerations: First, it is specifically directed toward affecting the political characteristics of foreign regimes; and second, it has a strong nonlogical component reflected in misperception or a lack of means–ends calculations. I do not mean to say that the policy is illogical or irrational—that there is *no* relationship between means and ends; all I am suggesting is that there is no clear calculation, little evidence of prudence, in the behavior of the state.

Two of the cases discussed in this chapter, Guatemala and the Dominican Republic, are examples of an ideological foreign policy. In both American intervention was precipitated by opposition to communist regimes. In Guatemala U.S. central decision-makers concluded that the government was becoming dominated by communists and was a potential entry point for Soviet penetration in the western hemisphere. In the Dominican Republic American intervention was precipitated by the fear that communists might seize control of the government. In both countries these perceptions were, at least to some extent, incorrect. Communists were influential in Guatemala, but they did not control the regime. In the Dominican Republic the obsession with the dangers of another Castro skewed the flow of information in a way that exaggerated the importance of communists in the pro-Bosch forces. While the covert intervention in Guatemala does not suggest an absence of means–ends calculations (the costs involved for the United States were not very high), American behavior in the Dominican Republic involved not only misperception but also imprudence. The landing of 23,000 marines was a sharp break with American policy of the previous thirty years. It flew in the face of American protestations about respect for the integrity of Latin American states. It ungloved the hegemonic fist in a setting where control might best have been exercised by more subtle means.

Nevertheless, these two cases were not failures. American central decision-makers got what they wanted. Neither Guatemala nor the Dominican Republic had any substantial negative impact on the coherence of American society. If these cases were all the evidence that could be brought to bear to distinguish between a statist and structural Marxist interpretation, it would not be possible to give a decisive defense of either position.

Unhappily, the cases discussed in detail in this chapter (limited to countries that had U.S. raw materials investments) are not the only examples of U.S. intervention. One stands out above all the others—Vietnam. In Vietnam there was an absence of any clear and direct American interests, either economic or strategic. The costs incurred were enormous in both political and economic terms. Polling data indicate that the conduct of the war was one factor contributing to a sharp decline in popular trust in government: between 1958 and 1964 responses to survey questions showed that there had been a 2 percent drop in trust; between 1964 and 1970 the drop was 17 percent. Although the empirical evidence is weak, this change in attitude probably means that the legitimacy of the regime has declined.[89] When the legitimacy of the regime is suspect, it is more difficult for central decision-makers to effectively maintain the coherence of the system as a whole. One legacy of Vietnam, and the other contentious issues of the 1960s, may be the general ho-hum that greeted President Carter's spring 1977 statement that the energy crisis was the moral equivalent of war. Whatever faults the administration's program itself might have had, the President was unable to generate the popular pressure needed to overcome particularistic interests represented in Congress. In addition, the Vietnam War contributed to the American balance-of-payments deficit during the late 1960s, and thus to the demise of the Bretton Woods monetary system in August 1971 and to the pressures that precipitated

[89] For a discussion of decline in trust see Miller "Political Issues and Trust" and "Rejoinder," and Citrin, "Comment."

double-digit inflation during the early 1970s. It forced one President to relinquish hopes of seeking a second elected term. It caused substantial domestic disorder. It weakened one major institution—the universities. It lessened the confidence of American allies. In sum, it damaged the coherence of society in the United States, precisely the opposite of the result that a structural Marxist argument would expect from state policy.

For those of us who listened to some ten years of rationales for U.S. intervention in Vietnam there is one gnawing thought: they just do not make any sense. This is not for want of trying. The Gravel edition of the Pentagon Papers has a section in each of its four volumes entitled "Justifications for the War."[90] One hundred and forty-five separate statements are listed. The fourth volume, which covers the period from 1965 to 1967, includes the following rationales: resisting wars of national liberation; opposing aggression; countering a strategic threat; honoring bilateral and multilateral commitments; protecting healthy national entities; pursuing freedom; limiting Communist Chinese expansion; ensuring the availability of natural resources in Southeast Asia; shielding the weak; maintaining allied confidence in the United States. I am sure that further plowing through these massive volumes would reward the studious with a statement defending any proposition that one cared to make about why the United States intervened in Vietnam. I would also suggest that no one of them, or all of them put together for that matter, would leave any more satisfied feeling.

To demonstrate the nonlogical character of American behavior in Vietnam, the absence of means–ends calculations, it is worth reflecting further on the dominant rationale for U.S. intervention—the domino theory. The domino theory was a statement of American goals, of what the use of troops was supposed to achieve. But what is striking is the amorphousness, the lack of precision, that typified even the most thorough and most secret internal documents. It was not clear how many dominoes would fall, or what would push them. Would it be Cambodia? Laos?

[90] The Senator Gravel Edition of the Pentagon Papers, *The Defense Department History of United States Decision Making on Vietnam*, Boston, n.d., Vol. 1, pp. 584-87; Vol. 2, pp. 794-97; Vol. 3, pp. 707-10; Vol. 4, pp. 626-30.

Thailand? The Indian subcontinent? Or even Japan? Would they be toppled by military conquest or covert aid to indigenous guerrillas; or would they be undermined by internal subversion bolstered by a renewed communist ideology? None of these questions was precisely answered.

The lack of a clear definition of American goals has been recognized by commentators with very different perspectives. Noam Chomsky writes: "It is an interesting and important fact that the planners are generally so vague and imprecise about the mechanism by which the rot will spread in the wake of a communist victory in Vietnam, or about just what is entailed by an 'accommodation' to Communist China."[91] In a detailed review of various editions of the Pentagon Papers, H. Bradford Westerfield calls dominoes "the very icons of *faith*" (my italics).[92] Leslie Gelb, who headed the team that wrote and compiled the Pentagon Papers, says that "no systematic or serious examination of Vietnam's importance to the United States was ever undertaken within the American government. Endless assertions passed for analysis."[93] It is not surprising, then, that explanations for American intervention in Vietnam are unsatisfactory.

The reason is not just that the goals were vaguely formulated; it is that there seems so little relationship between means and ends. The costs of intervention were palpable and high, particularly by 1967, measured in both lives and the stability of American society. The benefits were remote and vague. If the United States had been able to maintain South Vietnam as a viable noncommunist political entity through the use of diplomacy, economic coercion, covert intervention, or even a short-lived overt use of troops akin to the Dominican or Lebanese expeditions, then the failure to clearly state goals could be passed over: it would be more difficult to argue that American behavior in Vietnam was nonlogical. As we know, there was no simple and low-cost solution. Yet, when the communists finally won, none of the dire consequences suggested by American policy-makers came to pass.

What, then, are we left with? We confront a situation in which

[91] Chomsky, "The Pentagon Papers," p. 8.
[92] Westerfield, "Three Versions of the Pentagon Papers," p. 690.
[93] Gelb, "Vietnam," p. 146.

U.S. leaders intervened in Vietnam, as they had in every other case involving the covert or overt use of force, because they perceived the threat of a communist regime. In some cases, including Vietnam, as well as Korea, Cuba, and Chile, this perception was accurate. In others, including the Dominican Republic, Guatemala, Iran, and the Congo, it was questionable. In Lebanon it was clearly incorrect. However, in Vietnam, more than in any of the other cases in which American leaders resorted to force, the absence of prudent calculation is evident. The impact of quadrupled oil prices has been far worse than any consequences of the North Vietnamese victory; yet, as we have seen, U.S. reaction to OPEC has hardly been extreme. There was frequently no clear relationship between benefits and costs, between ends and means. This nonlogical behavior, along with a goal directly related to the political structures of other countries, is the hallmark of an ideological foreign policy.

This is a form of behavior that cannot be easily apprehended from a structural Marxist perspective. For structural Marxists, the central purpose of the state is to preserve the coherence of the society; the state strives to act rationally. This is not to say, however, that it will always succeed. The state may confront contradictions that it cannot overcome. Habermas, for instance, argues that bourgeois states face a "rationalization crisis" because the philosophical tenets of capitalism prevent the state from effectively intervening in the economy.[94] The title of O'Connor's book, *The Fiscal Crisis of the State*, refers to the growing gap between public expenditures and public revenues caused by the need to support the monopoly sector of the economy. This gap can lead to economic and political difficulties that the state may be unable to overcome. Gough argues that the rising power of the labor movement makes it impossible for the state to check inflation effectively.[95] In these circumstances, which are manifestations of basic contradictions in capitalist society, the state may fail to formulate a coherent and consistent set of goals. It may be unable to fulfill its basic task of preserving societal cohesion because the social fissures that it must try to cover over are too deep. Hence,

[94] Habermas, *Legitimation Crisis*, pp. 61-68.

[95] Gough, "State Expenditure in Advanced Capitalism," pp. 86ff.

structural Marxism does point to the possibility of irrational state behavior, behavior that might fail to preserve the cohesion of capitalist society—but only if the state faces fundamental and irresolvable social and economic contradictions.

No credible case can be made for the position that Vietnam was a manifestation of such deep contradictions. Vietnam cannot be understood in relation to direct economic interests; there were none. It is hard to make a case for indirect interests. Chomsky has argued that the war was important because it benefitted certain sectors of the American economy.[96] However, these same sectors could have been supported in other ways. Rationalizing high levels of military expenditure would have been easier for the U.S. government to accomplish by picturing the Soviet Union and China as implacable enemies than by engaging in a land war in Southeast Asia. Superpower conflict offers the opportunity for virtually limitless expenditures, with no clear way of measuring what is really needed. How many Trident submarines do we need: none? ten? twenty? fifty? more? At over one and a half billion dollars apiece, making one determination rather than another is not a trivial matter. A strategic weapons program is more flexible than overt military intervention: the financial benefits can be channelled more precisely, and the adverse consequences, such as inflation, can be better controlled.

But what of less concrete concerns? What of ideology? I will try to show in the following chapter that ideology was the key to American action. Can a structural Marxist position rest its case upon the same variable?

Structural Marxists have been concerned with ideology. They see it in much the same position, and serving the same function, as the state. Ideology is ultimately related to underlying social structures, but it is not merely the handmaiden of the capitalist class, something that can be manipulated to serve narrow and specific interests. On the contrary, to be effective, ideology must appear to be remote from the dominant class. Only then can it fulfill its basic function of preserving societal cohesion by obfus-

[96] Chomsky, "The Pentagon Papers."

cating and masking the underlying reality of economic exploitation. In bourgeois capitalist systems the dominant liberal ideology maintains that all men are equal. It banishes notions of class from its vocabulary. It views individuals as autonomous willing beings selling their services in a free market.[97]

Can Vietnam be understood from a structural Marxist perspective that emphasizes ideology? Such an argument would be difficult, for American intervention in Vietnam undermined the very coherence that the dominant ideology is supposed to preserve. It made maintaining domestic stability a problem. Furthermore, American liberalism has clearly been compatible with a noninterventionist foreign policy. Throughout the nineteenth century and much of the twentieth the dominant theme of American foreign policy was isolationism, at least with respect to distant and remote areas where explicit American interests were not threatened. Other capitalist states, moreover, did not find it necessary to follow the United States into Vietnam. On the contrary, America's closest allies became increasingly uncomfortable with U.S. policy. In sum, an ideological policy that ultimately weakened domestic social coherence cannot be easily understood from a structural Marxist perspective, especially when American beliefs have been compatible with nonintervention.[98]

Vietnam has taken us rather far afield from raw materials. Unfortunately, international relations is not like survey research: its sample size is very small. Nonlogical behavior is reflected in some of the American interventions that are associated with raw materials, but the costs of using force in these cases were not very high. A structural Marxist position could explain them away. But

[97] See Poulantzas, *Political Power and Social Classes*, Ch. 3, for an example of this mode of analysis.

[98] There is a formulation offered by some working in a Marxist tradition that cannot be distinguished from the arguments offered here. Habermas, for instance, sees ideology not simply as a manifestation of a particular class structure (the position taken by Poulantzas) but as a phenomenon that can take on a life of its own. In *Legitimation Crisis* he writes that the "evolution of morality, like the evolution of science, is dependent on truth" (p. 88). Once ideology is accorded such an autonomous role, there is no empirical evidence that can distinguish this position from a statist one.

it cannot explain away Vietnam. Here there was not only a clear absence of means–ends calculation, as well as some misperception, but also a great strain on domestic social cohesion. This outcome is the very opposite of what a structural Marxist expects from the state or the dominant ideology. I will try to show in the next chapter that such behavior can be understood from a statist perspective.

PART FOUR

CHAPTER IX

Conclusions and Prospects

For at least a decade students of foreign policy have had to deal with a discomforting problem: most used a conceptual approach that treated the state as a unified rational actor, yet many felt uncomfortable with its assumptions. While the conventional model yielded many interesting findings, its analytic categories did not appear to represent actual institutions faithfully. The notion of the state seemed merely a shorthand for a complex set of bureaucratic institutions and roles. No modern country is run by a prince. Officials in Washington, who spend a good part of their time at interdepartmental meetings, play bureaucratic politics even if they do not know the proper label, just as Molière's Monsieur Jourdan spoke prose. It has become commonplace to think of the American government as a large blundering bureaucratic mass incapable of sustained action and rational behavior. The greatest problems of public policy are described not in terms of goals but in terms of management skills. Decision-making is seen as a morass of conflicting interests extending from the society through the ostensibly hierarchically ordered central bureaucracy of the state.

In addition, the state-centric model used in international relations has seemed at odds with the most prevalent approaches to domestic politics. At least in the United States, a pluralist image has dominated the analysis of politics. The behavior of the state is seen as a product of societal pressures. A liberal perspective may grant that the state is one interest among many (indeed, the bureaucratic politics model extends interest-group politics into the bureaucracy), but it rejects the notion of a national interest that is not a product of the aggregation of particularistic societal goals. Interest-group analysis has not been applied to high politics because it could be assumed that all groups in the society would support the preservation of territorial and political integrity; but in the area of international economic relations there is, *a priori*, no such clear societal consensus. Tariff levels, exchange rates, and foreign investment all benefit some groups and harm others.

Marxist theories have offered a clear alternative to the realist model. This approach has an integrated view of domestic and international politics. In both spheres state behavior is seen as a product of societal needs. For instrumental Marxists, government officials are the handmaiden of particular societal groups. This is probably still the dominant perspective from the left.[1] There is a more sophisticated version of the Marxist position, structural Marxism, which views the state as an autonomous institution whose task is to preserve the coherence of capitalist society as a whole. This may mean acting against the preferences voiced by particular capitalist groups. For both liberals and Marxists, however, the state is, in the final analysis, an epiphenomenon: its behavior reflects disaggregated societal needs, either directly for interest-group and instrumental Marxist analyses or more circumspectly for structural Marxist ones. The concept of the national interest has no meaning except as a summation of particularistic preferences.

This study has tried to demonstrate that neither a liberal nor a Marxist conception is adequate. Its micro-theoretic task has been to elaborate a statist approach by inductively investigating the national interest and policy-making processes in the United States. This investigation has shown that the state has purposes of its own. The national interest does have empirical reality if it is defined as a consistent set of objectives sought by central decision-makers. The cases analyzed in this book suggest that there has been a clear rank-ordering of goals for American policy related to foreign raw material investments. In order of increasing impor-

[1] E.g., see Engler, *Brotherhood of Oil*. In the third chapter Engler states that Eisenhower's farm at Gettysburg was paid for by several oil men and the Eisenhower administration showed "complete deference to private enterprise and profit." Kennedy's Treasury Secretary, Douglas Dillon, was a director of Chase Manhattan Bank and thus tied to the Rockefellers and big oil. Nixon's campaigns were partly financed by oil money, and his Secretary of the Interior, Walter Hickel, was an avid developer. Nixon's law firm, from which he took his Attorney General, John Mitchell, represented El Paso Natural Gas.

tance the ranking has been: 1) maximize the competitive structure of the market and thereby reduce prices; 2) increase security of supply; 3) secure general foreign policy objectives.

This is not to say that the policies actually implemented by the United States have been coherent. Looking at what the American government actually did, as opposed to what central decision-makers preferred, presents a complicated picture. The fragmentation of power in the political system has allowed powerful private groups to block many state initiatives. This has been most evident when achieving state aims required positive action from private firms. This situation existed in all of the cases involving the promotion of foreign investment. To get oil investment in Iraq in the 1920s and Iran in the 1950s, central decision-makers had to compromise their desire for greater competition by sanctioning the Red Line Agreement and downgrading the oil antitrust suit from a criminal to a civil action. While government officials were successful in getting Firestone into Liberia during the 1920s, other U.S. rubber firms were not responsive to the government's call for new investments in non-British areas. Private actors were also able to block public initiatives when decisions could not be held within the executive branch. During the 1940s efforts to buy Aramco, construct an oil pipeline, and sign an agreement with the United Kingdom were frustrated because they needed Congressional approval.

In contrast, cases requiring positive action by the state rather than the private sector present a different picture of power relationships. This category includes almost all issues concerning the protection of foreign investment. Companies usually wanted more support than central decision-makers were willing to give. Government officials did assuage private dissatisfaction with monetary payments: loans and trading arrangements made it easier for Bolivia and Mexico to compensate U.S. oil firms in the early 1940s; OPIC insurance took the sting out of some nationalizations in the 1960s and 1970s; part of the loss from foreign takeovers could always be written off against U.S. tax liabilities. All of these devices were essentially transfers among American actors. Even the largest and most powerful private corporations were not able to turn instruments of state power to private purposes when this would violate the national interest, the aims sought by central decision-makers. Such instruments, particularly the use of force, were controlled by public institutions that have been well insulated from private pressures. The White House and the State Department were concerned with broader foreign policy goals.

The cases are not equally useful in contributing to the macrotheoretic aim of this study—distinguishing among statist, Marxist, and liberal interpretations of foreign policy. Some are more or less compatible with all three theories. These include all of the examples of investments actively promoted by the state—rubber in Liberia, oil in the Middle East and the Dutch East Indies during the 1920s, and oil in Iran in the 1950s. In these instances public and private preferences were fairly closely aligned and were associated with general societal goals. Although the assertive role played by the state here cannot be as readily understood from a pluralist or instrumental Marxist position, nevertheless the evidence these cases provide for preferring one competing interpretation over another is not very decisive.

Cases that show a clear divergence between corporate and state preferences are more analytically useful; they support statist and structural Marxist positions over interest-group and instrumental Marxist ones. Such divergences arose most frequently from disputes involving the takeover of U.S. firms. In 1919 Woodrow Wilson rejected private appeals that troops be used to protect American interests in Mexico. Before World War II American central decision-makers turned a deaf ear to oil company entreaties for more vigorous official backing in Peru and Mexico. In 1966 Assistant Secretary of State Lincoln Gordon relaxed economic sanctions against Peru while Exxon officials continued to prefer strong pressure. At the Teheran negotiations in January 1971 U.S. policy-makers undermined oil company bargaining strategy by endorsing separate negotiations for the Persian Gulf, the procedure favored by Saudi Arabia and Iran. Examples such as these weigh heavily against any interpretation that views state behavior as a function of direct private pressure. The strongest conclusion that emerges from the evidence presented in the case studies is that instrumental Marxist and liberal arguments are inadequate.

The two approaches whose relative merits are most difficult to assess are structural Marxism and statism. Both see the state as an autonomous actor concerned with long-term objectives. The difference lies in the type of aims that are sought. For a statist paradigm, the state has its own needs and goals, which cannot be reduced to specific societal interests. For a structural Marxist paradigm, state behavior is ultimately related to preserving a set of exploitative economic relationships that benefit a particular class. It is not easy to find empirical evidence that can separate the two. Here the argument that a statist paradigm is more powerful rests upon two examples. The first is the effort of the American government to buy Aramco during the Second World War. A violation of the basic norm of capitalism—private property—in a situation in which there was neither immediate pressure from the working class nor a clearly demonstrable long-term need cannot fit easily with a structural Marxist interpretation. Nevertheless, the state failed, and this case could be explained away, albeit with some sacrifice of elegance, as an aberration based upon individual peculiarities. The second set of empirical cases that support a statist perspective are drawn from instances where the United States was prepared to use either covert or overt force. After 1945 all of these were clearly associated with the goal of preventing communist regimes from assuming or holding power. This aim can be comprehended from a structural Marxist perspective: communism does not enhance capitalism's long-term prospects. It can also be understood from a statist perspective: the United States wanted to remake the world in its own Lockean liberal image. However, the nonlogical manner in which American leaders pursued their anticommunism is not compatible with a structural Marxist position. The absence of means–ends calculations, coupled with misperception, led to policies that undermined the coherence of American domestic society, particularly in Vietnam. This is the very opposite result from the one predicted by a structural Marxist argument, but it is compatible with a statist view that sees the state as capable of defining its own autonomous goals.

Interest and Ideology in U.S. Foreign Policy

The final piece of the puzzle that must be fit into place is to relate more precisely the broad foreign policy goals pursued by

U.S. leaders to a statist interpretation of American foreign policy. It is all well and good to create a catchall category for any apparently noneconomic objective sought by policy-makers, but this is hardly a convincing defense of a statist interpretation of American behavior. If these aims changed from one day to the next, or even from one year to the next, because of bureaucratic battles, or private pressures, or the transitory moods of presidents, then a statist approach would not be adequate. This study has not tried to identify the national interest with some divinely or logically ordained goal for the state, nor has it viewed it as an analytic assumption that can be used to derive propositions about the international system. Instead, this has been an inductive enterprise. Chapter II, which reviews the stated aims of American raw materials policy, offers some clues by indicating what kinds of objectives are likely to be important. The case studies themselves show which aims have actually been most emphasized. What they reveal is that the general aims of American policy have moved from a concern with territorial and political integrity and with security of supply before World War II (with the exception of Woodrow Wilson's presidency) to an emphasis on ideological goals after 1945.

In *The Logic of World Order* Franz Schurmann posits a fundamental distinction between interests and ideology, between expansionism on the one hand and imperialism on the other. Interests involve *material* aims and the social and physical quality of life. Ideology is concerned with order, security, and justice. Imperialism is a manifestation of ideology, a vision of how the world should be ordered on a global basis. It has a "total world-wide quality," whereas expansionism is incremental and concerned with material interests.[2]

The broad foreign policy aims implicit in U.S. policy toward foreign raw materials investments must be seen as both expansionist and imperialist. The division between the two is largely chronological. Before the Second World War the United States was an expansionist but not an imperialist nation. With the excep-

[2] Schurmann, *Logic of World Power*, p. 6. For discussions of the concept of ideology that emphasize its functions as a map or guide in an uncertain world see Sartori, "Politics, Ideology, and Belief Systems"; Geertz, "Ideology as a Cultural System."

tion of Wilson's policies in Mexico, American behavior can be understood in terms of interests—that is, specific economic aims or the preservation of territorial and political integrity (the core goals of any state). U.S. policy after the Second World War must be understood in terms of ideology: leaders were driven by a vision of what the global order should be like. Covert or overt force was used only when policy-makers saw their vision threatened. This politics of vision had been foreshadowed by Woodrow Wilson's actions toward Mexico. The vision itself was a manifestation of American liberalism, what Louis Hartz has called the totalitarian hold of a Lockean world view on American life.[3]

The Politics of Interest

The preceding chapters examine several cases of raw materials policy before the Second World War. They are: the promotion of rubber investment in Liberia and of oil in the Middle East and East Indies, the reaction to Mexican developments during the first decade of the revolution and to oil nationalizations in Bolivia and Mexico in the late 1930s. The two cases related to the promotion of new investment involved interests, specifically, promoting security of supply by developing resources that were controlled by American rather than British or Dutch corporations. The response to Mexico's and Bolivia's takeovers was also related to interests, although these were political rather than economic. American policy-makers feared German encroachment in the western hemisphere. In retrospect these perceptions appear exaggerated. However, the Germans were active in the late 1930s. They owned airlines, including one in Colombia, that was in striking distance of the Panama Canal. Regimes in important Latin American countries such as Argentina and Brazil had taken the trappings of fascism; Peron did not declare war on Germany until 1945. There were large German communities in a number of South and Central American nations. Trade ties with Germany increased during the 1930s. In fact, Mexico had been able to mitigate the impact of the embargo imposed by the oil companies in 1938 by making sales to Germany. The decision to settle the Bolivian and Mexican oil na-

[3] Hartz, *The Liberal Tradition*.

tionalization disputes, despite the protests of the companies, was but one of many actions taken to cement ties in the western hemisphere. Others included increased loans from the Export-Import Bank, special raw materials purchases, the signing of the Inter-American Coffee Agreement, and closer military cooperation and planning.

After World War II the many cases involving the protection of raw materials investments, where the American government did not use force, are also explicable in terms of interests. The takeover of American companies in Zambia, Peru, Chile, the OPEC states, and many others did constitute a threat to security of supply. This was graphically illustrated by the production cutback imposed by Arab oil producers after the October War. When multinationals controlled production, they limited output to maintain specified price targets (posted prices), but they never threatened the basic economic interests of consuming nations. Such action would have been folly. As OPEC has so amply demonstrated, there were monopoly profits in the oil industry that the companies had not exploited. But tapping these monopoly rents would have undermined the political position of the corporations within the United States. Corporate managers are not wont to follow such risky policies.

There is also a less direct, but probably more serious, long-term supply problem. Less developed countries may not be able to generate the capital necessary to develop new mines and oil fields. Private companies have shunned most large new outlays because they are too risky. Many nonoil producing countries are heavily in debt to private as well as public financial institutions. If new investments cannot be made, then security of supply in the future will be threatened.

While American central decision-makers were willing to use diplomatic and economic pressure to protect American firms, they were not prepared to use force. The use of force would have been imprudent: with the exception of oil, the application of overt military action would have been incommensurate with the interests at stake. None of the other takeovers posed an immediate threat to the economic security of the United States or its close allies. Vietnam had demonstrated the difficulty of fighting a war in an environment in which the local population was hostile. As U.S. policy-makers became increasingly aware of the depths of nationalist sentiments, particularly through their experience in Peru, they moved toward a policy of accommodation. Furthermore, while raw materials investments were being nationalized, U.S. firms engaged in manufacturing were expanding their activities in many Third World countries.[4]

In sum, American policies associated with settling the Bolivian and Mexican disputes before the Second World War and those dealing with nationalizations in the last decade can be understood in the terms of a politics of interest. In the late 1930s insuring political solidarity in the hemisphere was more important than protecting the prerogatives of the oil companies. During the 1960s and 1970s the risks of using force to protect U.S. firms from takeovers were too great given the potential benefits, except for oil.[5] Only oil-exporting countries have been able to establish an effective cartel involving production controls by at least some countries. In the longer term there are possibilities for substitution and the development of new supplies. The action of the United States in postwar cases of nationalization where force was not used reflected prudent calculation. These cases can be seen as exemplifying a politics of interest where action was directed toward material goals and the behavior of the state was logical or rational—in other words, where there was a clear association between means and ends.

The Politics of Ideology

However, there are a set of cases that cannot be explained in terms of interests. These include almost all of the instances in which the American government used force: in Mexico in 1914, in Iran in 1953, in Guatemala in 1954, in Cuba and the Dominican Republic during the early 1960s, and in Chile after 1970. As

[4] Vernon, *Storm over the Multinationals*, pp. 146-47.

[5] In the case of petroleum, the use of force would be compatible with a politics of interest because the economic stakes are so great. However, the uncertainties involved in occupying the Arabian fields also make a more cautious policy explicable from the same perspective. For the case for intervention see Tucker, "Oil: The Issue of American Intervention."

Table VIII-1 indicates, there is no clear relationship between economic stakes and the use of force. What, then, impelled American decision-makers?

After the Second World War the one thing that all of the cases associated with the use of force shared was that policy-makers feared a communist takeover. But why was this in itself enough to prompt such an extreme response? The realm of interests offers no answer. Although none of the cases we have examined involved great sacrifices, at least one, Cuba, was humiliating and unsuccessful. Moreover, if we cast our net wider and include Vietnam and even Korea, it is clear that American policy-makers were willing to bear heavy costs to prevent communist regimes from coming to power. It is not possible to explain this behavior in terms of strategic interests, that is, protecting the territorial and political integrity of the United States. It is not possible to explain it in terms of the goal of strengthening ties with major allies, the Western European states and Japan, with the possible exception of the relationship between Japanese concerns and Korea. It is not possible to explain these interventions in terms of economic interests: such stakes were present in the cases investigated in Chapter VIII but not in Korea, Lebanon, or Vietnam. Furthermore, American officials were willing to allow major holdings to be nationalized in many countries, most importantly those exporting oil, with barely a murmur of protest, and they tacitly supported Chilean copper takeovers before 1970.

One must look to the realm of ideology, of vision, for a persuasive explanation of American policy. American revulsion toward communism was intense and long-standing. The American reaction to the Bolshevik revolution was peculiarly hysterical. The red scare after the First World War and McCarthyism in the late 1940s were precipitated by foreign developments. When Castro visited the United States in 1959, his entourage was irked by the obsessive concern with communism. "It was as if the U.S. did not care what Cuba was, provided it was not Communist."[6] It was opposition to communism that led the United States into two extended and bloody land wars in Asia.

[6] Thomas, *Cuba*, p. 1211.

As Louis Hartz has argued, the intensity of this reaction is best understood as a result of the exclusive dominance of Lockean liberalism within the United States. In the United States this political vision has never been effectively challenged from either the left or the right. The application of America's world view to the Third World has been most fully articulated by Robert Packenham. Packenham argues that the attitudes of American policy-makers were dominated by four basic assumptions: change and development are easy, all good things go together, radicalism and revolution are bad, and distributing power is more important than accumulating power. All of these assumptions reflect liberal commitments to individualism and democracy, or the American historical experience of rapid growth without revolutionary upheaval.[7]

Communism was antithetical to this set of beliefs. It had grown out of a socialist perspective that had never taken root in the United States. It emphasized basic disharmonies within society. It advocated violent change. It rejected individualism. In practice, communist societies had given the state great power. Communism was more threatening to U.S. leaders than any other ideology they encountered.

I do not mean to argue that American policy-makers were immaculate liberals who sought nothing but Lockean ideals. In the period after the Second World War the United States supported many authoritarian regimes of the right. In part this practice resulted from constrained choice. U.S. leaders in the 1950s and 1960s were not quite as naive as Woodrow Wilson about the prospects for instant democracy; to paraphrase President Kennedy, the United States preferred democratic regimes, but when this alternative was unrealistic, they favored right-wing over left-wing dictatorships. This choice is consistent with a Lockean belief structure. First, right-wing regimes were more prone to recognize the legitimacy of a private sphere of action; they rarely made the same totalitarian, that is total, state claims on the society that were typical of the left. In addition, the right was less of a threat because it lacked the external support that a communist regime might be able

[7] Packenham, *Liberal America and the Third World*, esp. Ch. 3.

to draw from the Soviet Bloc. Soviet assistance could bolster such regimes, making it less likely that they could be transformed along lines that more closely followed the contours of America's vision.

But why has ideology only become important at a certain period in the nation's history? Basic beliefs are not variable: they are constant over time. Why do they affect policy during some periods but not others? The answer is basically found in the international distribution of power among states. Ideological goals can be pursued only by the very powerful and perhaps also the very weak, by those who can make things happen and those who cannot change what happens. For most states it must be interests, and not visions, that count. A state whose core objectives are threatened can rarely engage in creating a global order. Political culture or ideology will affect perceptions and therefore policy, but the objectives of policy will be in the realm of interests. Even when core objectives are not at stake, most states are likely to seek identifiable, usually material, objectives. Small and medium-size states do not have the resources to change domestic regimes in other countries or create new international structures. Even quite large states are likely to be expansionist rather than imperialist, to impose their will on others to secure specific goals, to act in terms of a calculus in which costs are weighed against benefits. Only states whose resources are very large, both absolutely and relatively, can engage in imperial policies, can attempt to impose their vision on other countries and the global system. And it is only here that ideology becomes a critical determinant of the objectives of foreign policy. Great power removes the usual restraints on central decision-makers. Very powerful states escape some of the consequences of the inherently anarchic nature of the international system. For them it is not a Hobbesian world because there is no opponent that can threaten their core interests. Policy-makers have at their disposal resources that are not committed to preserving identifiable economic aims or territorial and political integrity. They can enter the realm of vision (although it has rarely turned out to be the kingdom of God).

Perhaps two analogies will make this argument clearer. The association of an ideological foreign policy with a hegemonic state is based implicitly upon an assumption of a hierarchy of goals. The state can only move on to higher things (structuring foreign regimes and the international system in its own image) if more fundamental aims (protecting territorial and political integrity) have been satisfied. In *Sociobiology* Edward O. Wilson offers a similar explanation for the diversity of human cultures. He argues that humans display an extremely wide set of cultural variations. The behavioral range of other animals is much narrower. Humans are able to establish more diverse social habits only because they have so thoroughly dominated their environment. Basic needs are no longer the determinant of social organization. "No species of ant or termite enjoys such freedom. . . . In short, animal species tend to be tightly packed in the ecosystem with little room for experimentation or play. Man has temporarily escaped the constant or interspecific competition."[8] Just as man in the biosphere can engage in many activities not directly related to the survival of the species, hegemonic states can pursue ideological goals because more basic needs are not threatened.

A second analogy is offered in the work of the psychologist Abraham Maslow, who makes an argument explicitly based on a hierarchy of needs. When more basic individual needs are satisfied, he sees new ones emerging to motivate human activity. Physiological necessities are the most fundamental. If food, clothing, and shelter are available, then safety, love and affection, esteem (including freedom, competence, prestige, recognition, and dominance), and finally self-actualization become, in that order, the most important driving forces. An individual only moves on to a higher need when more basic ones are satisfied. Maslow summarizes his argument in the following terms: "We have seen that the chief principle of organization in human motivational life is the arrangement of needs in a hierarchy of lesser or greater priority or potency. The chief dynamic principle animating this organization is the emergence of less potent needs upon the gratification of more potent ones."[9] Just as the human species in the biosphere, and individual men in their quest for fulfillment, can move on to

[8] Wilson, *Sociobiology*, p. 550.

[9] Maslow, *Motivation and Personality*, p. 107.

less pressing goals only after more basic ones (the survival of the species or the individual) have been satisfied, so hegemonic states can indulge in ideological foreign policies because their core objectives are not in jeopardy.

The Historical Evolution of U.S. Policy

Writers who have emphasized the importance of ideology have generally argued that there has been a cyclical tendency in American foreign policy.[10] Periods of external expansion have alternated with periods of insularity. Americans move in one generation to remake the outside world, encounter failure and frustration, and turn away from external involvement in the next generation. The argument here suggests that there has been a more linear development in American foreign policy. The basic determinant of the goals sought by American central decision-makers has not been generational experience but America's place in the international political system—that is, its power in relation to other states.

Until the last decade of the nineteenth century the country was insular and isolationist. The Monroe Doctrine was a symbol, not a guide to action. The resources of the nation were devoted to internal development. The United States still relied on European capital. It was British naval power that limited European incursions into the western hemisphere. American leaders did voice support for various bourgeois revolutions in Europe, but the resources they were willing to expend on such activities were quite small. Lockean liberalism did have an impact, but the distribution of power in the international system, and America's place in it, precluded ideological goals from dominating American actions.

With the exception of Wilson's tenure, the United States moved to an expansionist policy between 1896 and 1941. It translated its power resources derived from its size and technological capabilities into a more aggressive foreign policy. But its actions were directed to material goals, strategic or economic. This kind of behavior was first manifest in the Caribbean and the Pacific. No longer were U.S. central decision-makers content to rely on Brit-

[10] Hartz, Ch. 11; Roskin, "From Pearl Harbor to Vietnam."

ain to limit European penetration of the western hemisphere. In Cuba, the Dominican Republic, Haiti, Venezuela, Nicaragua, and elsewhere, American policy-makers intervened both diplomatically and militarily. Regardless of whether American expansionism is viewed as aimed at economic exploitation or limiting strategic vulnerability, it can still be seen as a manifestation of a politics of interest: specific, identifiable goals related to material or political well-being were at stake.

During the interwar years the United States remained expansionist but nonimperial. America turned against Wilson's attempt to create a new international order after the First World War. The Senate rejected the League of Nations. During the 1920s the United States insisted on the repayment of war debts regardless of German reparation payments, even though capital movements from America's allies depended on transfers to them from Germany. Decisions taken by American policy-makers in the late 1920s and early 1930s helped precipitate and exacerbate the Great Depression, because Hoover and Roosevelt paid most attention to domestic economic problems and failed to perceive the relationship between American welfare and the health of the global system. In the area of raw materials American policy-makers were primarily concerned with security of supply. As we have seen, they actively promoted rubber investment in Liberia and oil investment in the Middle East and Dutch East Indies. They opposed efforts to establish cartels in natural rubber, coffee, and other materials. They supported new raw materials investments in Latin America.

All of these activities can be understood in terms of a calculus of interests. There was a direct payoff, usually economic, in the repayment of war debts, concentration on domestic economic problems, opposition to cartels, and new raw materials investments. In retrospect some of these actions appear shortsighted. American leadership might have mitigated the Depression of the 1930s, but only by adopting policies that broke radically with past behavior. Moreover, it is not clear that during the interwar years the United States had the power to construct a new global order. London was still the world's financial center. The British pound remained the world's leading international currency. Until the

Second World War the United States was an expansionist, not an imperial state.

Only after 1945 did American leaders move consistently to a politics of ideology, although such behavior had been foreshadowed by Woodrow Wilson. Wilson was a man whose time had not come. By 1914 the United States was, in economic strength, the most powerful nation on earth. But it had near rivals in Russia, Germany, and Britain. The beliefs of its citizens and many of its institutions were still attuned to the insularity of the nineteenth century, or at best the expansionism of McKinley and Roosevelt. Wilson had at his disposal substantial resources, but these were not sufficient to implement and carry through a politics of vision, although a visionary he certainly was. Probably no American leader has ever so clearly articulated the ideals of liberalism. His policy toward the Mexican Revolution was but one manifestation of his more general attitudes. He eschewed acting for the sake of interests. He castigated American corporations. He helped bring down Huerta, the Mexican leader most favorably disposed toward American investors during the first decade of the revolution. For Wilson, democracy was more important than oil, silver, or copper, especially if it triumphed through his efforts.

Although Wilson failed in his more global goals, they were resurrected after World War II. The United States emerged from the war in an extraordinarily powerful position. The economies of all of the other major industrial states had been shattered. Great Britain, a rival of the United States in the interwar years, was starving and freezing by the winter of 1946-1947. The United States controlled almost all of the world's gold reserve. Its economy was several times larger than that of its nearest rival. It was the only possible source of capital and equipment for postwar reconstruction. Although the United States had disbanded most of its army, it did have a monopoly of atomic weapons until 1949.

In this setting American leaders were not content to pursue only interests; they wanted to impose their vision on the world. This imperative was all the stronger because of the experience of the previous fifteen years: the Depression and the Second World War had almost shattered capitalist societies. The vision American leaders drew on, Lockean liberalism, was their own; it was particularly intense because of its totalitarian hold on the American psyche. The greatest challenge to that vision came from communism, a challenge all the more severe because it had the support of another powerful state, the Soviet Union. Until the late 1960s American leaders had little sensitivity to the possibility of indigenous socialism or radicalism in the Third World.

The ideological goals pursued by U.S. central decision-makers cannot be relegated to the realm of interests, as Marxist analysts are wont to do. For Marxism, ideology is a mask or a weapon used to further underlying class interests. Ideas do not have a life of their own. They do not play an independent part in organizing social and political behavior. In the American interventions after the Second World War, however, economic goals and the stability of the social system in general were, ultimately in Vietnam, sacrificed to an ideological vision. American behavior lacked the central hallmark of a politics of interest—rational calculation. Relationships between means and ends were unclear. There was a persistent tendency to misperceive. A belief in how society ought to be ordered was more powerful than material concerns. In Pareto's terminology, American policy was nonlogical.

It is not surprising that an imperial country's foreign policy should assume an ideological cast in which objectives are associated with basic social values and behavior is nonlogical. Clifford Geertz has argued that ideologies become important when the existing body of tradition or belief that guides political action breaks down. "It is a loss of orientation that most directly gives rise to ideological activity. . . ."[11] In international relations the functional equivalent for the state of traditional guides to action are the imperatives imposed by the anarchy of the international system. Normal states cannot follow policies that endanger their territorial and political integrity. However, such constraints do not exist for an imperial state. Like the society that has lost its bearings, it is in a world that lacks clear markers. It has power that can be used for objectives that are not associated with clearly definable needs. It can try to remake the world. World makers are not guided by prudence, for they see their objectives as consum-

[11] Geertz, p. 64.

matory goals that are worth virtually any sacrifice. Although the form of expansionism varies, depending upon the dominant ideology of the state, countries with enough power to ignore specific foreign policy goals have virtually always become imperialists.[12]

Ideology and the Statist Paradigm

An ideological foreign policy is best understood from a statist perspective for two reasons. First, the central characteristic of such a policy is that it does not offer benefits for any specific societal groups. Neither interest-group nor instrumental Marxist approaches can offer a very satisfactory explanation for such behavior: for both, government action is understood to result from particular societal pressures. A structural Marxist approach also fails to give an adequate understanding of American behavior after World War II. It would be possible for this paradigm to deal with the pursuit of ideological ends if this were necessary to preserve the coherence of capitalist society. However, in a number of cases, particularly Vietnam, efforts to remake political and economic structures in other countries weakened the social fabric of the United States itself. Central decision-makers did not act in the prudential and calculating way that one would expect from a structural Marxist approach. Ideological goals became an end in themselves. Only the state, viewed as an autonomous institution, can make such goals the primary objectives of policy; for the state is the only institution that can formulate aims that either have very diffuse benefits or impose costs on specific societal groups or the society as a whole. Such behavior can be understood from a statist perspective whose basic assumption is that the state is autonomous. The independence of central decision-makers from particular pressures allows them to formulate objectives that could not be effectively articulated by any nonstate actors. The state is not one interest group among many, or the servant of general societal needs; it is an institution with purposes and powers of its own.

[12] The argument here should be contrasted with Schumpeter's assertion that mindless expansionism (imperialism) was associated with an atavistic aristocratic social structure. There is a certain mindless aspect to the foreign policy of an imperial state in that its actions are nonlogical and oriented toward nonmaterial goals.

The second aspect of an ideological foreign policy that suggests the power of a statist approach is that the ability to carry out such a policy is intimately related to a nation's place in the international system. To understand an ideological foreign policy, it is necessary to begin at the basic starting point for a realist approach to international politics: the distribution of power among states. An ideological foreign policy can be associated with a hegemonic state, because such a state can ignore interests. A state acting in an imperial role, as an orderer of the global system, is not sensitized to material limitations.

Neither a liberal nor a Marxist perspective can deal with the importance of the international distribution of power in explaining American foreign policy. Both of these perspectives begin with internal pressures on the state emanating from either particular or general societal needs. Policy comes from the bottom up. A statist or realist perspective begins with the distribution of power among states. Policy comes from the top down. Under normal circumstances states will act on the basis of interests. However, a state that is so powerful that it no longer need be concerned with its territorial and political integrity, and all of the ancillary policies that follow from these basic goals, such as preserving the security of raw materials supplies, can make ideological goals the most important aspect of its foreign policy. For two and a half decades after the Second World War Lockean liberalism was the key to American foreign policy; it was the desire to create a world order in America's image that led to the use of force.

Prospects

Despite the domestic weakness of the American state, raw materials have rarely been an impediment to economic growth. Until the early 1970s the enormous increase in demand for unprocessed goods following World War II was met with relatively stable prices. New supplies were smoothly integrated into the global economy. In large measure this success must be attributed to multinational corporations. These institutions were able to accumulate capital, project demand, undertake large new projects, generate new technology, and efficiently distribute their products. Most of these companies had their home office in the United States. Their accomplishments cannot be gainsayed.[13]

Yet it is also necessary to recognize that private actors operated within a larger international economic structure created and sustained by state power. After the Second World War the United States ordered the international economic environment. It pressed for a set of rules that facilitated the operations of multinational corporations. The United States helped establish a stable international monetary system that made it easy to transfer capital from one country to another. It supported an open trading system that allowed multinationals to move their products around the world. American officials insisted that the treatment of the foreign subsidiaries of multinational firms should be nondiscriminatory—that is, that the rules governing their activities should be the same as those applied to domestic firms. The United States had the economic, ideological, and military power to maintain these practices over a wide geographic area for some twenty-five years.[14] This structure created a stable environment within which the managers of multinational raw materials firms were able to act with efficiency and dispatch. They could make commitments to large new projects with the confidence that they would be able to transfer capital and technology, and that there would be a market for their products.

[13] In the oil industry, in particular, multinationals have been subject to much criticism. See, e.g., Engler, *Brotherhood of Oil*, and Blair, *Control of Oil*. The fact remains that the international oil companies were able to meet dramatic increases in oil demand from the late 1940s until the early 1970s with prices that were virtually stable in nominal terms and declining in real terms. The era of "cheap energy" was the period when the international oligopoly of private companies was able to run the industry. The consequence of greater competition in crude petroleum was to give oil-exporting states more money, not to lower prices for consumers.

[14] I have elaborated this argument in "State Power and the Structure of International Trade." It is important to recognize that this structuring of the international economic system cannot easily be explained by narrow American economic interests. U.S. decision-makers were willing to tolerate many deviations from a liberal world order of which the most important were probably the Common Agricultural Policy of the EEC and Japanese protectionism. In this issue area, as well as the ones discussed in this study, American foreign policy cannot be adequately understood without considering the impact of Lockean visions on decision-makers.

While the multinationals still possess an extraordinary bundle of financial, technological, market, and service skills, the international environment in which they must act is changing dramatically. The signs of this transformation are manifest in many areas. The international monetary system is confused. Since 1973 exchange-rate fluctuations have been severe enough to present problems for multinational corporations despite their own financial sophistication and access to international banks.[15] There have been increasing signs of protectionism. The Trade Act enacted in 1974 imposes more stringent requirements on the Treasury Department for carrying out investigations related to dumping and other violations of American law, mandates that changes in nontariff barriers be approved by the Congress, and makes it easier to invoke the escape clause. Multinationals are under attack, particularly raw materials operations in Third World countries. Such developments will make it harder for multinationals to be truly multinational, that is, to transact business across national boundaries with the same discretion that they can within one country.

There has also been growing dissatisfaction in the United States with the operations of multinationals. American labor unions have called for restrictions on international operations. Although the clearest legislative manifestation of these sentiments, the Burke–Hartke Bill, was defeated, it has not been without effect. The 1975 Tax Act denies depletion allowances to large firms while keeping them for smaller ones. The 1974 Trade Act made it easier for unions to get action on charges of unfair trade practices. The revelations of illegal foreign corporate payoffs have led to demands for tighter regulations.

All of these developments will make it more difficult for multinational corporations to operate as effectively in the future as they have in the past. With respect to issues discussed here, they are unlikely to maintain the level of security of raw materials supply that they provided in the past. This security was based in large part on corporate ability to predict demand and develop new mines and oil fields. At least the latter part of this exercise is becoming more treacherous for two reasons. First, while there may not be any

[15] *Wall St. Journal*, June 7, 1976, 1:6.

exhaustion of raw materials in a physical sense, it is becoming more costly to develop new mineral deposits. The most accessible areas, particularly in politically safe countries, have already been exploited. New projects are very expensive. The outlay for the Cuajone copper mine in southern Peru, an enterprise involving the Export-Import Bank, the World Bank, a consortium of fifty-four private financial institutions as well as Asarco, Cerro, Phelps Dodge, Newmont, and Royal Dutch Shell, has been estimated at $656 million. Estimated costs for new nickel mines in Guatemala and Indonesia are $250 million and $800 million. More than $7 billion has been invested in the Alaskan pipeline. The first project for producing oil from shale in the United States was abandoned in 1974 because of skyrocketing expenses, including an estimated 40 percent increase in construction costs during one six-month period; $40 million had already been spent when the project was halted. Efforts to derive natural gas from coal in the United States have also been delayed because of rising costs. The expenses of drilling for oil are likewise rising rapidly. In 1976 a number of major corporations abandoned exploration in the Peruvian interior after losing about $750 million.[16]

Second, unpredictable market conditions have made private corporations more reluctant to make such large and long-term capital outlays. One source of uncertainty has been the political attitudes of Third World countries. Foreign capital expenditures in mining and smelting by majority-owned affiliates of U.S. companies have fallen markedly in recent years. Measured in current dollars, they were $7.1 billion in 1966, $9.4 billion in 1971, $4.2 billion in 1975, and about $3.6 billion in 1976. The slide in Latin America was particularly steep.[17] Because of higher oil prices, many less developed states have had to borrow heavily from private international capital markets. It will not be easy for them to generate capital to increase raw materials output. A proposal for an International Resources Bank (first made by the United States

[16] *Wall St. Journal*, June 24, 1976, 21:1, and Oct. 7, 1974, 7:1; *New York Times*, Feb. 5, 1975, 43:1; *Los Angeles Times*, July 8, 1976, 1:1; IMF, *Survey*, Feb. 7, 1977, p. 35; Vernon, *Storm over the Multinationals*, pp. 150-51.

[17] U.S., National Commission on Supplies and Shortages, *Government and the Nation's Resources*, p. 37.

at the 1976 UNCTAD conference), which would be a vehicle for directly or indirectly providing additional capital for resource development in Asia, Africa, and Latin America, has not won international endorsement. Less developed countries have become suspicious of initiatives coming from the industrialized world. In the period 1970 through 1975, 80 percent of exploration for major nonfuel minerals was in the United States, Canada, Australia, and South Africa.

Uncertainty has also come from changing conditions in world markets. The United States could spend billions of dollars to develop new sources of energy, but there are still many years of reserves under the Arabian sands that can be extracted at less than 20¢ per barrel. The OPEC cartel will not last forever. If it collapses and prices erode, a corporation that had invested large sums in new projects could find itself unable to compete. Under such circumstances there would be great pressure for protective legislation and other forms of government intervention. But given the fragmentation of power in the American political system, there is no sure guarantee that such demands would be satisfied. A similar problem exists in the aluminum industry. Exporting states have recently been able to increase their taxes on bauxite severalfold. Aluminum is the most abundant metal in the earth's crust and can be extracted from clays widely distributed in several areas of the United States. However, the costs are much higher. The aluminum companies are not likely to make such large investments unless they have guarantees that their products will be protected from foreign competition. Given the structure of the American political system, however, it is difficult to make such guarantees credible.

The uncertainty inherent in raw materials markets has driven many corporations to diversify. This trend is very apparent in the oil industry. Much activity is in energy-related areas: Exxon, Conoco, and Occidental are major coal-producing companies. Oil companies have also invested in other raw materials sectors: Standard Oil of California acquired 20 percent of the stock of AMAX in 1975, Atlantic Richfield secured 27 percent of Anaconda's stock in 1976. New activities have been taken on even further afield. The most publicized has been Mobil's merger with Marcor, the parent holding company of Montgomery-Ward and the Container Corporation of America. At the same time, the major petroleum firms have become more reluctant to commit large new sums to exploration because of the uncertainty of the market. In 1976 most companies trimmed their exploration expenditures; seismic exploration off the American coast, an indicator of future activity, has been declining since 1974.[18] All of these developments make perfect sense when viewed from the standpoint of corporate objectives: diversification is an excellent hedge against the risks inherent in concentrating all of a firm's activities in an economic sector beset by uncertainties. Unfortunately, the incentive for private actors not to make commitments to new exploration will make it more difficult for the United States to guarantee secure sources of raw material.

It is not the limits to growth in a technological or geological sense, but in a political one, that will present problems in the future that have been muted in the past. Despite its internal fragmentation, the external power of the United States allowed it to create a stable international economic environment. Within this environment multinational corporations were able to put together and apply effectively an extraordinary bundle of human and material skills. The resources available to the United States are no longer as relatively large as they were in the period after the Second World War. Domestic support for the unrestricted movement of capital and goods is waning. Disaffection in other countries, particularly in the Third World, is growing. As the slack provided by America's hegemonic position dissipates, the costs of domestic political fragmentation will become more severe. Corporations cannot operate effectively without a stable environment, but the state may not be able to provide one. The deficiencies of a weak political system may become more apparent.

[18] *Wall St. Journal*, March 29, 1976, 2:1; May 17, 1976, 8:1; June 23, 1976, 34:1.

APPENDIX

The Evolution of Foreign Raw Materials Investments

By the end of the nineteenth century American companies had already begun to search for foreign raw materials supplies. They looked first to the neighboring countries to the south, particularly Mexico, which was the largest single recipient of U.S. direct investment in mining and petroleum before the First World War, and to the Caribbean, where almost half of all agricultural investments were placed. World War I was followed by a great spurt in supply-oriented investments. Between 1919 and 1929 the book value of American petroleum investments increased from $604 million to $1,341 million, and those of mining from $876 million to $1,127 million. Canada and Chile were the largest new targets for mining investment, Venezuela for oil. Agricultural holdings, particularly in Cuban sugar, also increased dramatically during the 1920s. Outside the western hemisphere activity was modest before 1930. During the Depression there was a contraction in the value of mining, petroleum, and agriculture in almost all parts of the world. The conclusion of the Second World War brought new activity. Although the only major new commodities sought overseas were iron ore and uranium, the former prompted by the decline of American reserves and the latter by the development of atomic energy, there was a great expansion in areas other than agriculture where the foundations had been layed in earlier decades. Between 1950 and 1970 the book value of American petroleum and mining investments (excluding European petroleum holdings, which were in processing and distribution) both grew more than fivefold. Increases took place in almost all parts of the world.

The pattern for petroleum is shown in Table A-1. These figures include refining and distribution as well as exploration and production. Before the First World War the amount of overseas petroleum production was minimal. Jersey Standard had minor operations in Rumania and the Dutch East Indies, and Doheny and others had begun to open up Mexico, but most of the value shown for early years was in refining and particularly distribution. After World War I activities in less developed areas generally involved crude oil production, those in Europe the distribution of finished products, and those in Canada and Oceania both production and distribution.

The value of U.S. mining investments is shown in Table A-2. These figures include smelting as well as mining. The contrast with petroleum in terms of growth is striking. Mining reached its highest relative importance before the First World War, whereas petroleum did not reach its peak until 1960.

As Table A-3 shows, the impact of the Depression on American agricultural investments was sharper than for either mining or petroleum. Land investments encountered political opposition in host countries before extractive industries. Although figures are not included for the period after 1940, the Cuban nationalizations of the 1960s reduced the importance of foreign investment in agriculture to very modest levels.

Table A-1

U.S. Direct Foreign Investment in Petroleum

(book value in millions of dollars)

	1897	1908	1914	1919	1929	1940	1950	1960	1970
Latin America	8	70	133	331	784	564	1310	3120	3940
Mexico	1	50	85	200	206	42			
Caribbean	2	5	6	15	62	65			
Central America				3	4				
South America	5	15	42	113	512	457			
Canada & Newfoundland	6	15	25	30	55	120	420	2660	4810
Europe	55	99	138	158	239	306	430	1760	5470
Asia	14	36	40	50	151	177	780	1660	3020
Africa	1	2	5	10	32	50	120	410	2090
Oceania	1	2	2	25	81	49	110	370	740
Total Petroleum	85	224	343	604	1341	1277	3390	10810	21710
Petroleum as a Percentage of Total U.S. Direct Investment	13%	14%	13%	16%	18%	18%	29%	34%	28%

Sources: Wilkins, *Emergence of Multinational Enterprise*, p. 110, and *Maturing of Multinational Enterprise*, pp. 31, 55, 182, 330.

TABLE A-2

U.S. Direct Foreign Investment in Mining
(book value in millions of dollars)

	1897	1908	1914	1919	1929	1940	1950	1960	1970
Latin America	79	303	549	661	802	513	670	1270	2070
Mexico	68	234	302	222	248	168			
Caribbean	3	6	15	21	18	8			
Central America	2	10	11	14	8	7			
South America	6	53	221	404	528	330			
Canada & Newfoundland	55	136	159	200	318	187	330	1320	2990
Europe		3	5		37	53	30	50	80
Asia		1	3	4	10	8	20	20	90
Africa			4	11	54	22	60	250	450
Oceania					6	n.a.	10	30	490
Total Mining	134	445	720	876	1227	783	1130	2950	6170
Mining as a Percentage of Total U.S. Direct Investment	21%	27%	27%	23%	16%	11%	10%	9%	8%

Source: Same as Table A-1.

Table A-3

U.S. Direct Foreign Investment in Agriculture
(book value in millions of dollars)

	1897	1908	1914	1919	1929	1940	1950	1960	1970
Latin America	59	161	246	503	884	359			
Mexico	12	40	70	48	58	10			
Caribbean	34	92	114	382	652	286			
Central America	4	18	37	44	130	51			
South America	9	11	25	29	44	12			
Canada & Newfoundland	18	25	101	50	30	10			
Europe									
Asia			12	32	63	63			
Oceania									
Total Agriculture	77	186	356	587	986	432			
Agriculture as a Percentage of Total U.S. Direct Investment	12%	11%	13%	15%	13%	6%			

Source: Same as Table A-1.

Bibliography

Acheson, Dean. *Present at the Creation*. New York: Norton, 1969.

Adelman, M. A. *The World Petroleum Market*. Baltimore: Johns Hopkins University Press, 1972.

Alexander, Robert J. *The Bolivian National Revolution*. New Brunswick: Rutgers University Press, 1958.

Allison, Graham. *Essence of Decision: Explaining the Cuban Missile Crisis*. Boston: Little, Brown, 1971.

Almond, Gabriel A., and Sidney Verba. *The Civic Culture*. Boston: Little, Brown, 1965.

Anderson, Irvine, Jr. *The Standard-Vacuum Oil Company and United States East Asian Policy, 1933-1941*. Princeton: Princeton University Press, 1975.

Aron, Raymond. *The Imperial Republic*. Englewood Cliffs: Prentice-Hall, 1974.

Art, Robert. "Bureaucratic Politics and American Foreign Policy: A Critique," *Policy Sciences* 4. December 1973.

Atkins, G. Pope, and Larman C. Wilson. *The United States and the Trujillo Regime*. New Brunswick: Rutgers University Press, 1972.

Bachrach, Peter, and Morton Baratz. "The Two Faces of Power," *American Political Science Review* 56. December 1962.

Bailey, Stephen K. "The Public Interest: Some Operational Dilemmas," in *Nomos V: The Public Interest*, ed. Carl J. Friedrich. New York: Atherton, 1962.

Baker, Ray Stannard. *Woodrow Wilson, Life and Letters, Vol. 4*. New York: Doubleday, Doran, 1931.

Baklanoff, Eric N. *Expropriation of U.S. Investments in Cuba, Mexico and Chile*. New York: Praeger, 1975.

———. "International Economic Relations," in Carmelo Mesa-Lago, ed., *Revolutionary Change in Cuba*. Pittsburgh: University of Pittsburgh Press, 1971.

Baran, Paul, and Paul Sweezy. *Monopoly Capitalism*. London: Penguin, 1966.

Barnard, Chester I. *The Functions of the Executive*. Cambridge: Harvard University Press, 1950.

Barratt Brown, Michael. "A Critique of Marxist Theories of Imperialism," in Roger Owen and Bob Sutcliffe, eds., *Studies in the Theory of Imperialism*. London: Longman, 1972.

Barry, Brian M. "The Economic Approach to the Analysis of Power and Conflict," *Government and Opposition* 9. Spring 1974.

———. "The Use and Abuse of the Public Interest," in *Nomos V: The Public Interest*, ed. Carl J. Friedrich. New York: Atherton, 1972.

Bauer, Raymond, Ithiel de Sola Pool, and Lewis Anthony Dexter. *American Business and Public Policy*. New York: Atherton, 1967.

Beard, Charles A. *The Idea of National Interest: An Analytical Study in American Foreign Policy*. Chicago: Quadrangle, 1966.

Bemis, Samuel Flagg. *The Latin American Policy of the United States: An Historical Interpretation*. New York: Harcourt, Brace, 1943.

Berman, Daniel M., and Robert A. Heineman. "Lobbying by Foreign Governments on the Sugar Act Amendments of 1962," *Law and Contemporary Problems* 28. Spring 1963.

Bernstein, Marvin D. *The Mexican Mining Industry, 1890-1950*. Albany: State University of New York Press, 1964.

Bidwell, Percy W. *Raw Materials: A Study of American Policy*. New York: Harper & Brothers, 1958.

Billet, Leonard. "The Just Economy: The Moral Basis of the Wealth of Nations," *Review of Social Economy* 24. December 1976.

———. "Political Order and Economic Development: Reflections on Adam Smith's Wealth of Nations," *Political Studies* 23. December 1975.

Blair, John M. *The Control of Oil*. New York: Pantheon, 1976.

Blasier, Cole. "The Elimination of United States Influence," in Carmelo Mesa-Lago, ed., *Revolutionary Change in Cuba*. Pittsburgh: University of Pittsburgh Press, 1971.

———. *The Hovering Giant: U.S. Responses to Revolutionary Change in Latin America*. Pittsburgh: University of Pittsburgh Press, 1976.

———. "The United States and the Revolution," in James M. Malloy and Richard S. Thorn, eds., *Beyond the Revolution: Bolivia Since 1952*. Pittsburgh: University of Pittsburgh Press, 1971.

Bloom, Howard S., and H. Douglas Price. "Voter Response to Short-Run Economic Conditions: The Asymmetric Effect of Prosperity and Recession," *American Political Science Review* 68. December 1975.

Bonsal, Philip W. *Cuba, Castro and the United States*. Pittsburgh: University of Pittsburgh Press, 1971.

Boyd, James. "Historical Background for a National Materials Policy," in U.S., Congress, Senate, Committee on Public Works, *Problems and Issues of a National Materials Policy*. Papers, 91st Congress, 2nd session, 1970.

Brandes, Joseph. *Herbert Hoover and Economic Diplomacy*. Pittsburgh: University of Pittsburgh Press, 1962.

Bridges, Amy Beth. "Nicos Poulantzas and the Marxist Theory of the State," *Politics and Society* 4. Winter 1974.

Burnham, Walter Dean. *Critical Elections and the Mainsprings of American Politics*. New York: Norton, 1970.

Butterfield, Herbert. "The Balance of Power," in Herbert Butterfield and Martin Wight, eds., *Diplomatic Investigations: Essays in the Theory of International Politics*. Cambridge: Harvard University Press, 1968.

Calleo, David P., and Benjamin M. Rowland. *America and the World Political Economy: Atlantic Dreams and National Realities*. Bloomington: Indiana University Press, 1973.

Carey, James C. *Peru and the United States, 1900-1962*. Notre Dame: University of Notre Dame Press, 1964.

Chadwin, Mark L. "Foreign Policy Report: Nixon Administration Debates New Position Paper on Latin America," *National Journal*. January 15, 1972.

———. "Foreign Policy Report: Nixon's Expropriation Policy Seeks to Soothe Angry Congress," *National Journal*. January 22, 1972.

Chandler, Alfred D., Jr. *Strategy and Structure: Chapters in the*

History of the American Industrial Enterprise. Cambridge: MIT Press, 1962.

Charles River Associates. *Forecasts and Analysis of the Copper Market*. Cambridge, Mass., May 1973.

Chomsky, Noam. "The Pentagon Papers and U.S. Imperialism in South East Asia," in *Spheres of Influence in the Age of Imperialism*. London: Spokesman, 1972.

Church, Frank. "The Impotence of the Oil Companies," *Foreign Policy* 27. Summer 1977.

Citrin, Jack. "Comment," *American Political Science Review* 68. September 1974.

Clendenen, Clarence C. *Blood on the Border: The United States Army and the Mexican Irregulars*. New York: Macmillan, 1969.

Cline, Howard F. *The United States and Mexico*. Cambridge: Harvard University Press, 1963.

Cohen, Benjamin J. *The Question of Imperialism*. New York: Basic Books, 1973.

Coleman, D.C. *Revisions in Mercantilism*. London: Methuen, 1969.

Colm, Gerhard. "The Public Interest: Essential Key to Public Policy," in *Nomos V: The Public Interest*, ed. Carl J. Friedrich. New York: Atherton, 1962.

Cooper, Richard N., and Robert Z. Lawrence. "The 1972-75 Commodity Boom," *Brookings Papers on Economic Activity* 3. 1975.

Cronon, E. David. *Josephus Daniels in Mexico*. Madison: University of Wisconsin Press, 1960.

Cumberland, Charles C. *Mexican Revolution: The Constitutionalist Years*. Austin: University of Texas Press, 1972.

Cyert, Richard M., and James G. March. *A Behavioral Theory of the Firm*. Englewood Cliffs: Prentice-Hall, 1963.

Dahl, Robert A. *Pluralist Democracy in the United States*. Chicago: Rand McNally, 1967.

———. *Who Governs?* New Haven: Yale University Press, 1961.

Daniels, Josephus. *The Wilson Era: Years of Peace, 1910-1917*. Chapel Hill: University of North Carolina Press, 1944.

Dean, Heather. "Scarce Resources: The Dynamic of American Imperialism," in K. T. Fann and Donald C. Hodges, eds., *Readings in U.S. Imperialism.* Boston: Porter Sargent, 1971.

DeNovo, John A. *American Interests and Policies in the Middle East, 1900-1939.* Minneapolis: University of Minnesota Press, 1963.

———. "The Movement for an Aggressive American Oil Policy Abroad, 1918-1920," *The American Historical Review* 61. July 1956.

Destler, I. M. et al. *Managing an Alliance: The Politics of U.S.–Japan Relations.* Washington: The Brookings Institution, 1976.

Diamond, William. *The Economic Thought of Woodrow Wilson.* Baltimore: Johns Hopkins University Press, 1943.

Dunn, Frederick Sherwood. *The Diplomatic Protection of Americans in Mexico.* New York: Columbia University Press, 1933.

Easton, David. *The Political System: An Inquiry into the State of Political Science.* New York: Knopf, 1971.

Edwards, Gertrud G. "Foreign Petroleum Companies and the State in Venezuela," in Raymond F. Mikesell, ed., *Foreign Investment in the Petroleum and Mineral Industries.* Baltimore: Johns Hopkins University Press, 1971.

Einhorn, Jessica Pernitz. *Expropriation Politics.* Lexington: D.C. Heath, 1974.

Eisenhower, Dwight D. *Mandate for Change, 1953-1956.* Garden City: Doubleday, 1963.

Eisenhower, Milton S. *The Wine is Bitter.* Garden City: Doubleday, 1963.

Engler, Robert. *The Brotherhood of Oil: Energy Policy and the Public Interest.* Chicago: University of Chicago Press, 1977.

———. *The Politics of Oil.* Chicago: University of Chicago Press, 1961.

Fagen, Richard R. "The United States and Chile: Roots and Branches," *Foreign Affairs* 53. January 1975.

Farnsworth, Elizabeth. "Chile: What Was the U.S. Role: More Than Admitted," *Foreign Policy* 16. Fall 1974.

Feis, Herbert. *The Diplomacy of the Dollar, 1919-1932.* New York: Norton, 1950.

Feis, Herbert. *Europe, The World's Banker, 1870-1914*. New York: Norton, 1965.

———. *Three International Episodes Seen From E.A.* New York: Norton, 1966.

Fenno, Richard F., Jr. "The Internal Distribution of Influence: The House," in David B. Truman, ed., *The Congress and America's Future*, 2nd edn. Englewood Cliffs: Prentice-Hall, 1973.

Fieldhouse, D. K. "Imperialism: An Historiographical Revision," *Economic History Review*, 2nd series, 14. December 1961.

First National City Bank v. Banco Nacional de Cuba, "Brief for Respondent," in *International Legal Materials* 2. January 1972.

Flathman, Richard E. *The Public Interest: An Essay Concerning the Normative Discourse of Politics*. New York: Wiley, 1966.

Ford, Alan W. *The Anglo-Iranian Oil Dispute of 1951-1952*. Berkeley: University of California Press, 1954.

Franck, Thomas, and Edward Weisband. *Word Politics*. New York: Oxford University Press, 1972.

Frey, John W., and H. Chandler Ide. *A History of the Petroleum Administration for War*. Washington: Petroleum Administration for War, 1946.

Furnish, Dale B. "Days of Revindication and National Dignity: Petroleum Expropriations in Peru and Bolivia," in Richard B. Lillich, ed., *The Valuation of Nationalized Property in International Law,* Vol. II. Charlottesville: University Press of Virginia, 1973.

Gardner, Lloyd C. *Economic Aspects of New Deal Diplomacy*. Madison: University of Wisconsin Press, 1964.

Geertz, Clifford. "Ideology as a Cultural System," in David E. Apter, ed., *Ideology and Discontent*. New York: Free Press, 1964.

Gelb, Leslie H. "Vietnam: The System Worked," *Foreign Policy* 3. Summer 1971.

George, Alexander and Juliette. *Woodrow Wilson and Colonel House*. New York: John Day, 1956.

Gerschenkron, Alexander. *Economic Backwardness in Historical Perspective*. Cambridge: Harvard University Press, 1962.

Gibb, George Sweet, and Evelyn H. Knowlton. *History of the Standard Oil Company (New Jersey): The Resurgent Years, 1911-1927*. New York: Harper & Brothers, 1956.

Gilpin, Robert. *U.S. Power and the Multinational Corporation*. New York: Basic Books, 1975.

Girvan, Norman. *Foreign Capital and Economic Underdevelopment in Jamaica*. Kingston, Jamaica: Institute of Social and Economic Research, University of the West Indies, 1971.

Gough, Ian. "State Expenditure in Advanced Capitalism," *New Left Review* 92. July/August 1975.

Gould, Charles A. *The Last Titan: Percival Farquhar*. Stanford: Institute of Hispanic American and Luso-Brazilian Studies, Stanford University, 1964.

Goals for Americans. Englewood Cliffs: Prentice-Hall, 1960.

Goff, Fred, and Michael Locker. "The Violence of Domination: U.S. Power and the Dominican Republic," in Irving Louis Horowitz, Josue de Castro, and John Gerassi, eds., *Latin American Radicalism*. New York: Vintage, 1969.

Gold, David A., Clarence Y. H. Lo, and Erik Olin Wright. "Recent Developments in Marxist Theories of the Capitalist State," *Monthly Review* 27. October/November 1975.

Gonzalez, Edward. "Partners in Deadlock: The United States and Castro, 1959-1972." Los Angeles: Southern California Arms Control and Foreign Policy Seminar, 1972.

Goodsell, Charles T. *American Corporations and Peruvian Politics*. Cambridge: Harvard University Press, 1974.

———. "Diplomatic Protection of U.S. Business in Peru," in Daniel A. Sharp, ed., *U.S. Foreign Policy and Peru*. Austin: University of Texas Press, 1972.

Gordon, Robert A. *Business Leadership in the Large Corporation*. Berkeley: University of California Press, 1961.

Green, David. *The Containment of Latin America*. Chicago: Quadrangle, 1971.

Grew, Joseph C. *Turbulent Era: A Diplomatic Record of Forty Years*. Boston: Houghton Mifflin, 1952.

Habermas, Jurgen. *Legitimation Crisis*. Boston: Beacon Press, 1975.

Haley, P. Edward. *The Diplomacy of Taft and Wilson with Mexico, 1910-1917*. Cambridge: MIT Press, 1970.

Halperin, Morton H., with the assistance of Priscilla Clapp and Arnold Kanter. *Bureaucratic Politics and Foreign Policy*. Washington: The Brookings Institution, 1974.

Harbaugh, William Henry. *Power and Responsibility: The Life and Times of Theodore Roosevelt*. New York: Farrar, Straus & Cudahy, 1961.

Hartz, Louis. *The Liberal Tradition in America*. New York: Harcourt, Brace, 1955.

Hays, Samuel P. *Conservation and the Gospel of Efficiency*. Cambridge: Harvard University Press, 1959.

Heckscher, August F., ed. *The Politics of Woodrow Wilson: Selections from His Speeches and Writings*. New York: Harper & Row, 1956.

Heckscher, Eli. *Mercantilism*. New York: Macmillan, 1955.

Herzog, Jesus Silva. "Mexico's Case in the Oil Controversy," *International Conciliation* 345. December 1938.

Hinrichs, Harley H. *A General Theory of Tax Structure Change During Economic Development*. Cambridge: Harvard Law School, 1966.

Hirschman, Albert O. *National Power and the Structure of Foreign Trade*. Berkeley: University of California Press, 1945.

Hoover, Herbert. *The Memoirs of Herbert Hoover, Volume II: The Cabinet and the Presidency, 1920-1933*. New York: Macmillan, 1952.

Huddle, Franklin P. "The Evolving National Policy for Materials," *Science*. February 20, 1976.

Hughes, Charles Evans. *The Autobiographical Notes of Charles Evans Hughes*, ed. David J. Danelski and Joseph S. Tulchin. Cambridge: Harvard University Press, 1973.

Huitt, Ralph K. "The Internal Distribution of Power: The Senate," in David B. Truman, ed., *The Congress and America's Future*, 2nd edn. Englewood Cliffs: Prentice-Hall, 1973.

Hull, Cordell. *The Memoirs of Cordell Hull*. New York: Macmillan, 1948.

Huntington, Samuel P. "Congressional Responses to the Twentieth Century," in David B. Truman, ed., *The Congress and America's Future*, 2nd edn. Englewood Cliffs: Prentice-Hall, 1973.

———. *Political Order in Changing Societies*. New Haven: Yale University Press, 1968.

Ingram, George M. *Expropriation of U.S. Property in South America: Nationalization of Oil and Copper Companies in Peru, Bolivia and Chile*. New York: Praeger, 1974.

Johnson, Leland L. "U.S. Business Interests in Cuba and the Rise of Castro," *World Politics* 17. April 1965.

Johnson, Lyndon Baines. *The Vantage Point: Perspectives on the Presidency, 1963-1969*. New York: Holt, Rinehart and Winston, 1971.

Jones, Charles O. "Representation in Congress: The Case of the House Agriculture Committee," *American Political Science Review* 55. June 1961.

Kane, N. Stephen. "American Business and Foreign Policy: The Recognition of Mexico, 1920-1923," *Political Science Quarterly* 90. Summer 1975.

Kantor, Harry. "The Development of Acción Democratica de Venezuela," *Journal of Inter-American Studies* 1. April 1959.

Kaplan, Eugene J. *Japan: The Government-Business Relationship: A Guide for the American Businessman*. Washington: Department of Commerce, 1972.

Kaplan, Morton A. *System and Process in International Politics*. New York: Wiley, 1957.

Katzenstein, Peter J. "International Relations and Domestic Structures: Foreign Economic Policies of Advanced Industrial States," *International Organization* 30. Winter 1976.

———. "Introduction: Domestic and International Forces and Strategies of Foreign Economic Policy," and "Conclusion: Domestic Structures and Strategies of Foreign Economic Policy," in Peter J. Katzenstein, ed., *Between Power and Plenty: Foreign Economic Policies of Advanced Industrial States*, special issue of *International Organization* 31. Autumn 1977. Also published in book form by the University of Wisconsin Press, 1978.

Kemp, Tom. "The Marxist Theory of Imperialism," in Roger Owen and Bob Sutcliffe, eds., *Studies in the Theory of Imperialism*. London: Longman, 1972.

Kendall, Willmoore. "The Two Majorities," *Midwest Journal of Political Science* 4. November 1960.

Klein, Herbert S. "American Oil Companies in Latin America: The Bolivian Experience," *Inter-American Economic Affairs* 18. Autumn 1964.

Knorr, Klaus E. *World Rubber and Its Regulation*. Stanford: Stanford University Press, 1945.

Kolko, Gabriel, *The Roots of American Foreign Policy*. Boston: Beacon Press, 1969.

Kolko, Joyce and Gabriel. *The Limits of Power: The World and United States Foreign Policy, 1945-1954*. New York: Harper & Row, 1972.

Krasner, Stephen. "Are Bureaucracies Important?" *Foreign Policy* 7. Summer 1972.

———. "The Search for Stable Resource Flows: Structuring International Raw Materials Markets," in Gerald and Louann Garvey, eds., *The Political Economy of International Resource Flows*. Lexington: D.C. Heath, 1977.

———. "State Power and the Structure of International Trade," *World Politics* 28. April 1976.

Kronstein, Heinrich, and John T. Miller, Jr., in cooperation with Ira E. Schwartz. *Modern American Antitrust Law: A Guide to its Domestic and Foreign Application*. Dobbs Ferry, N.Y.: Oceania, 1958.

Krueger, Robert B. *The United States and International Oil: A Report for the Federal Energy Administration on U.S. Firms and Government Policy*. New York: Praeger, 1975.

Kurth, James R. "Testing Theories of Economic Imperialism," in Steven J. Rosen and James R. Kurth, eds., *Testing Theories of Economic Imperialism*. Lexington: D.C. Heath, 1974.

LaFeber, Walter. *America, Russia and the Cold War, 1945-1966*, 2nd edn. New York: Wiley, 1972.

Landsberger, Henry A., and Tim McDaniel. "Hypermobilization in Chile, 1970-1973," *World Politics* 28. July 1976.

Lane, Robert E. *The Regulation of Business: Social Conditions of*

Government Economic Control. New Haven: Yale University Press, 1954.

Larson, Henrietta M., Evelyn H. Knowlton, and Charles S. Popple. *History of the Standard Oil Company (New Jersey): New Horizons, 1927-1950.* New York: Harper & Row, 1971.

Laski, Harold J. *The Foundations of Sovereignty and Other Essays.* New York: Harcourt, Brace, 1921.

———. *The State in Theory and Practice.* New York: Viking Press, 1935.

League of Nations. *Industrialization and Foreign Trade.* Geneva, 1945.

Leeman, Wayne. *The Price of Middle East Oil.* Ithaca: Cornell University Press, 1962.

Lenin, V. I. *Imperialism: The Highest Stage of Capitalism.* New York: International Publishers, 1939.

Lenczowski, George. *The Middle East in World Affairs.* Ithaca: Cornell University Press, 1956.

Leonhard, Wolfgang. "The Domestic Politics of the New Soviet Foreign Policy," *Foreign Affairs* 52. October 1973.

Levinson, Jerome, and Juan de Onis. *The Alliance that Lost Its Way.* Chicago: Quadrangle, 1970.

Leys, Wayne A.R. "The Relevance and Generality of 'The Public Interest,' " in *Nomos V: The Public Interest*, ed. Carl J. Friedrich. New York: Atherton, 1962.

Lief, Alfred. *Harvey Firestone: Free Man of Enterprise.* New York: McGraw-Hill, 1951.

Lieuwen, Edwin. *Petroleum in Venezuela, A History.* Berkeley: University of California Press, 1954.

———. *Venezuela*, 2nd edn. London: Oxford University Press, 1965.

Link, Arthur S. *Woodrow Wilson and the Progressive Era, 1910-1917.* New York: Harper & Row, 1954.

Lippmann, Walter. "Vested Rights and Nationalism in Latin America," *Foreign Affairs* 5. April 1927.

Lipson, Charles H. "Corporate Preferences and Public Policies: Foreign Aid Sanctions and Investment Protection," *World Politics* 28. April 1976.

Lipson, Charles. H. *Standing Guard: The Protection of U.S. Foreign Investment*. Berkeley: University of California Press, 1978.

Litvak, Isaiah A., and Christopher J. Maule. "Nationalisation in the Caribbean Bauxite Industry," *International Affairs* 51. January 1975.

Longrigg, Stephen Hemsley. *Oil in the Middle East: Its Discovery and Development*. 2nd and 3rd edn. London: Oxford University Press, 1961, 1968.

Lowenthal, Abraham F. *The Dominican Intervention*. Cambridge: Harvard University Press, 1972.

———. "Peru's Ambiguous Revolution," *Foreign Affairs* 52. July 1974.

Lowi, Theodore J. "American Business, Public Policy, Case-Studies, and Political Theory," *World Politics* 16. July 1964.

———. "Decision Making vs. Policy Making: Toward an Antidote for Technocracy," *Public Administration Review* 30. May/June 1970.

———. "Four Systems of Policy, Politics and Choice," *Public Administration Review* 32. July/August 1972.

———. "Making Democracy Safe for the World: National Politics and Foreign Policy," in James Rosenau, ed., *Domestic Sources of Foreign Policy*. New York: Free Press, 1967.

Mack, Andrew. "Comparing Theories of Economic Imperialism," in Steven J. Rosen and James R. Kurth, eds., *Testing Theories of Economic Imperialism*. Lexington: D.C. Heath, 1974.

Magdoff, Harry. *The Age of Imperialism*. New York: Monthly Review Press, 1969.

———. "Comments," in Stephen J. Rosen and James R. Kurth, eds., *Testing Theories of Economic Imperialism*. Lexington: D.C. Heath, 1974.

———. "Imperialism Without Colonies," in Roger Owen and Bob Sutcliffe, eds., *Studies in the Theory of Imperialism*. London: Longman, 1972.

Mansfield, Harvey C., Sr. "The Congress and Economic Policy," in David B. Truman, ed., *The Congress and America's Future*, 2nd edn. Englewood Cliffs: Prentice-Hall, 1973.

———. "The Dispersion of Authority in Congress," in Harvey

C. Mansfield, Sr., ed., *Congress Against the President*. New York: Praeger, 1975.

Marcosson, Isaac F. *Metal Magic: The Story of the American Smelting and Refining Company*. New York: Farrar, Straus, 1949.

Martz, John D. *Acción Democratica: Evolution of a Modern Political Party in Venezuela*. Princeton: Princeton University Press, 1966.

———. "Venezuela's 'Generation of '28': The Genesis of Political Democracy," *Journal of Inter-American Studies* 6. January 1964.

Maslow, Abraham H. *Motivation and Personality*. New York: Harper & Row, 1954.

Mason, Edward S. "American Security and Access to Raw Materials," *World Politics* 1. January 1949.

Mayhew, David R. *Congress: The Electoral Connection*. New Haven: Yale University Press, 1974.

McKie, James W. "Changing Views," in James W. McKie, ed., *Social Responsibility and the Business Predicament*. Washington: The Brookings Institution, 1974.

Meade, Edward Earle. "The Turkish Petroleum Company—A Study of Oleaginous Diplomacy," *Political Science Quarterly* 39. June 1924.

Meinecke, Friedrich. *Machiavellism*. New Haven: Yale University Press, 1957.

Meyer, Lorenzo. *Mexico y Estados Unidos en el conflicto petrolero (1917-1942)*. Mexico City: El Colegio de Mexico, 1968.

Michalet, Charles-Albert. "France," in Raymond Vernon, ed., *Big Business and the State: Changing Relations in Western Europe*. Cambridge: Harvard University Press, 1974.

Mikdashi, Zuhayr. *The Community of Oil Exporting Countries: A Study in Governmental Co-operation*. London: George Allen and Unwin Ltd., 1972.

Milbrath, Lester W. "Interest Groups and Foreign Policy," in James N. Rosenau, ed., *Domestic Sources of Foreign Policy*. New York: Free Press, 1967.

Miliband, Ralph. *The State in Capitalist Society*. New York: Basic Books, 1969.

Miller, Arthur H. "Political Issues and Trust in Government: 1964-1970," *American Political Science Review* 68. September 1974.

———. "Rejoinder," *American Political Science Review* 68. September 1974.

Monson, Joseph R., and Anthony Downs. "A Theory of Large Managerial Firms," in Bruce Russett, ed., *Economic Theories of International Relations*. Chicago: Markham, 1968.

Moran, Theodore H. "The Alliance for Progress and the Foreign Copper Companies and Their Local Conservative Allies in Chile, 1955-1970," *Inter-American Economic Affairs* 25. Spring 1972.

———. "The Future: OPEC Wants Them," *Foreign Policy* 25. Winter 1976-1977.

———. *Multinational Corporations and the Politics of Dependence: Copper in Chile*. Princeton: Princeton University Press, 1974.

———. "Transnational Strategies of Protection and Defense by Multinational Corporations: Spreading the Risk and Raising the Cost for Nationalization in Natural Resources," *International Organization* 27. Spring 1973.

Morgenthau, Hans J. *Politics Among Nations: The Struggle for Power and Peace*, 4th edn. New York: Knopf, 1967.

———. "Comments," *Foreign Policy* 18. Spring 1975.

Munro, Dana. *Intervention and Dollar Diplomacy in the Caribbean, 1900-1921*. Princeton: Princeton University Press, 1964.

———. *The United States and the Caribbean Republics, 1921-1923*. Princeton: Princeton University Press, 1974.

Nash, Gerald D. *United States Oil Policy, 1890-1964*. Pittsburgh: University of Pittsburgh Press, 1968.

Nettl, J. P. "The State as a Conceptual Variable," *World Politics* 20. July 1968.

Neustadt, Richard E. *Presidential Power: The Politics of Leadership*. New York: Wiley, 1960.

Nixon, Richard M. *Six Crises*. New York: Doubleday, 1962.

O'Connor, James. *The Fiscal Crisis of the State*. New York: St. Martin's Press, 1972.

Oil and Gas Journal (Tulsa).

O'Leary, James P. "Systems Theory and Regional Integration: The Market Model of International Relations." Unpub. Ph.D. diss., The Johns Hopkins University, 1976.

Oppenheim, V. H. "The Past: We Pushed Them," *Foreign Policy* 25. Winter 1976-1977.

Paarlberg, Robert L. "Domesticating Global Management," *Foreign Affairs* 54. April 1976.

———. "United States Attention to the Third World, 1945-1974: The Logic of Foreign Policy Agenda Formation." Unpub. Ph.D. diss., Harvard University, 1975.

Packenham, Robert A. *Liberal America and the Third World*. Princeton: Princeton University Press, 1973.

Padgett, L. Vincent. *The Mexican Political System*. Boston: Houghton Mifflin, 1966.

Pareto, Vilfredo. *The Mind and Society: A Treatise on General Sociology*. New York: Dutton, 1963.

———. *Sociological Writings*, selected and introduced by S. E. Finer. New York: Praeger, 1966.

Parrini, Carl P. *Heir to Empire: United States Economic Diplomacy, 1916-1923*. Pittsburgh: University of Pittsburgh Press, 1969.

Patch, Richard W. "Bolivia: U.S. Assistance in a Revolutionary Setting," in Richard N. Adams et al., *Social Change in Latin America Today: Its Implications for United States Policy*. New York: Harper & Row, 1960.

Patrick, Hugh, and Henry Rosovsky, eds. *Asia's New Giant: How the Japanese Economy Works*. Washington: The Brookings Institution, 1976.

Penrose, Edith T. *The Large International Firm in Developing Countries: The International Petroleum Industry*. London: George Allen and Unwin Ltd., 1968.

Perroux, F. "The Domination Effect and Modern Economic Theory," in W. F. Rothschild, ed., *Power in Economics*. Baltimore: Penguin, 1971.

Polsby, Nelson W. *Congress and the Presidency*, 2nd edn. Englewood Cliffs: Prentice-Hall, 1971.

Potter, David. *People of Plenty*. Chicago: Chicago University Press, 1954.

Poulantzas, Nicos. "The Capitalist State: A Reply to Miliband and Laclau," *New Left Review* 95. January/February 1976.

———. *Political Power and Social Classes*. London: New Left Books, 1975.

Powell, J. Richard. *The Mexican Petroleum Industry, 1938-1950*. Berkeley: University of California Press, 1956.

Powelson, John P. "International Lending Agencies," in Daniel A. Sharp, ed., *U.S. Foreign Policy and Peru*. Austin: University of Texas Press, 1972.

Prain, Ronald. *Copper: The Anatomy of an Industry*. London: Mining Journal Books, 1975.

Preston, Anthony, and John Major. *Send a Gunboat! A Study of the Gunboat and Its Role in British Policy, 1854-1904*. London: Longmans, Green, 1967.

Preston, Lee E. "Corporation and Society: The Search for a Paradigm," *The Journal of Economic Literature* 13. June 1975.

Price, David E. "The Politics of Sugar," *Review of Politics* 33. April 1971.

Rausch, George J., Jr. "The Exile and Death of Victoriano Huerta," *Hispanic-American Historical Review* 42. May 1962.

Rippy, Merrill. *Oil and the Mexican Revolution*. Leiden: Brill, 1972.

Rosenau, James N. "National Interest," *International Encyclopedia of the Social Sciences*, Vol. 11. New York: Macmillan, 1968.

Roskin, Michael. "From Pearl Harbor to Vietnam: Shifting Generational Paradigms," *Political Science Quarterly* 89. Fall 1974.

Rourke, Thomas. *Gomez, Tyrant of the Andes*. New York: William Morrow, 1936.

Russett, Bruce M., and Elizabeth C. Hanson. *Interest and Ideology: The Foreign Policy Beliefs of American Businessmen*. San Francisco: Freeman, 1975.

Sartori, Giovanni. "Politics, Ideology, and Belief Systems," *American Political Science Review* 63. June 1969.

Schattschneider, E. E. *Politics, Pressures and the Tariff: A Study of Free Enterprise in Pressure Politics, as Shown in the 1929-1930 Revision of the Tariff.* New York: Prentice-Hall, 1935.

———. *The Semisovereign People: A Realist's View of Democracy in America.* New York: Holt, Rinehart and Winston, 1960.

Schelling, Thomas C. "Command and Control," in James W. McKie, ed., *Social Responsibility and the Business Predicament.* Washington: The Brookings Institution, 1974.

Schneider, Ronald M. "Guatemala: An Aborted Communist Takeover," in Thomas T. Hammond, ed., *The Anatomy of Communist Takeovers.* New Haven: Yale University Press, 1975.

Schubert, Glendon. "Is There a Public Interest Theory?" in *Nomos V: The Public Interest*, ed. Carl J. Friedrich. New York: Atherton, 1962.

Schurmann, Franz. *The Logic of World Power.* New York: Pantheon, 1974.

Seidman, Harold. *Politics, Position and Power: The Dynamics of Federal Organization.* New York: Oxford University Press, 1970.

Shonfield, Andrew. *Modern Capitalism: The Changing Balance of Public and Private Power.* London: Oxford University Press, 1965.

Shwadran, Benjamin. *The Middle East, Oil and the Great Powers.* New York: Wiley, 1973.

Sigmund, Paul E. "The 'Invisible Blockade' and the Overthrow of Allende," *Foreign Affairs* 52. January 1974.

Simon, Herbert A. *Models of Man.* New York: Wiley, 1957.

Sklar, Richard L. *Corporate Power in an African State: The Political Impact of Multinational Mining Companies in Zambia.* Berkeley: University of California Press, 1975.

Smith, David N., and Louis T. Wells, Jr. *Negotiating Third World Mineral Agreements: Promises as Prologue.* Cambridge, Mass.: Ballinger, 1976.

Smith, Robert Freeman. "The Formation and Development of the International Bankers Committee on Mexico," *The Journal of Economic History* 23. December 1963.

Smith, Robert Freeman. *The United States and Cuba*. New York; Bookman Associates, 1960.

———. *The United States and Revolutionary Nationalism in Mexico, 1916-1932*. Chicago: University of Chicago Press, 1972.

Smith, Tony. "Changing Configurations of Power in North–South Relations," *International Organization* 31. Winter 1977.

Sorauf, Frank J. "The Conceptual Muddle," in *Nomos V: The Public Interest*, ed. Carl J. Friedrich. New York: Atherton, 1962.

Staley, Eugene. *War and the Private Investor: A Study in the Relations of International Politics and International Private Investment*. Garden City: Doubleday, Doran, 1935.

Steinbrunner, John. "Beyond Rational Deterrence: The Struggle for New Conceptions," *World Politics* 28. January 1976.

Stobaugh, Robert. "The Oil Companies in the Crisis," *Daedalus* 104. Fall 1975.

Suleiman, Ezra N. *Politics, Power and Bureaucracy in France: The Administrative Elite*. Princeton: Princeton University Press, 1974.

Tanzer, Michael. *The Political Economy of International Oil and the Underdeveloped Countries*. Boston: Beacon Press, 1969.

Thatcher, Harold W. *Planning for Industrial Mobilization, 1920-1940*. Office of the Quartermaster General, Historical Section, Q.M.C. Historical Studies, No. 4, August 1943.

Thomas, Hugh. *Cuba: The Pursuit of Freedom*. New York: Harper & Row, 1971.

Tillema, Herbert K. *Appeal to Force: American Military Intervention in the Era of Containment*. New York: Crowell, 1973.

Treverton, Gregory F. "United States Policy Making in the IPC Case." Unpublished paper, Harvard University, 1974.

Trow, Clifford W. "Woodrow Wilson and the Mexican Interventionist Movement of 1919," *Journal of American History* 58. June 1971.

Truman, David B. *The Governmental Process: Political Interests and Public Opinion*, 2nd edn. New York: Knopf, 1971.

Tucker, Robert W. "Oil: The Issue of American Intervention," *Commentary* 59. January 1975.

Tugwell, Franklin. *The Politics of Oil in Venezuela*. Stanford: Stanford University Press, 1976.

Tulchin, Joseph S. *The Aftermath of War: World War I and U.S. Policy toward Latin America*. New York: New York University Press, 1971.

U.N. Economic and Social Council. *Permanent Sovereignty over Natural Resources*. A/9716. September 20, 1974.

U.N. Economic and Social Council, Committee on Natural Resources. *Permanent Sovereignty over Natural Resources*. E/C.7/53. January 31, 1975.

U.S., Congress, House, Agriculture Committee. *Extension of the Sugar Act of 1948*. Hearings, 86th Congress, 2nd session, 1960.

U.S., Congress, House, Committee on Foreign Affairs. *Expropriation of American-Owned Property by Foreign Governments in the Twentieth Century*. Committee Print, 88th Congress, 1st session, 1963.

U.S., Congress, Joint Economic Committee. *Reorientation and Commerical Relations of the Economies of Eastern Europe*. 93rd Congress, 2nd session, 1974.

U.S., Congress, Joint Economic Committee. *Soviet Economy in a New Perspective*. 94th Congress, 2nd session, 1976.

U.S., Congress, Senate. *Correspondence Relating to Wrongs Done to American Citizens by the Government of Venezuela*. Document No. 413, 60th Congress, 1st session, 1908.

U.S., Congress, Senate. *Restrictions on American Petroleum Prospectors in Certain Foreign Countries*. Document No. 272, May 1960.

U.S., Congress, Senate, Committee on Foreign Relations. *Investigation of Mexican Affairs*. Hearings, Document No. 285, 66th Congress, 2nd session, 1920.

U.S., Congress, Senate, Committee on Foreigns Relations. *Major Instances of Expropriation of Property Belonging to U.S. Nationals Since World War II*. Report No. 1535, 87th Congress, 2nd session, 1962.

U.S., Congress, Senate, Committee on Foreign Relations. *Petroleum Agreement with Great Britain and Northern Ireland*. Hearings, 80th Congress, 1st session, 1947.

U.S., Congress, Senate, Committee on Foreign Relations, Subcommittee on Multinational Corporations. *A Documentary History of the Petroleum Reserve Corporation 1943-1944*. Committee Print, 93rd Congress, 2nd session, May 8, 1974.

U.S., Congress, Senate, Committee on Foreign Relations, Subcommittee on Multinational Corporations. *The International Petroleum Cartel, The Iranian Consortium and U.S. National Security*. Committee Print, 93rd Congress, 2nd session, February 21, 1974.

U.S., Congress, Senate, Committee on Foreign Relations, Subcommittee on Multinational Corporations. *Multinational Corporations and U.S. Foreign Policy*. Hearings, Parts 1 through 9, 93rd Congress, 1973-1975.

U.S., Congress, Senate, Committee on Foreign Relations, Subcommittee on Multinational Corporations. *Multinational Oil Corporations and U.S. Foreign Policy*. Report, 93rd Congress, 2nd session, January 2, 1975.

U.S., Congress, Senate, Committee on Foreign Relations, Subcommittee on Western Hemisphere Affairs. *United States Relations With Peru*. Hearings, 91st Congress, 1st session, 1969.

U.S., Congress, Senate, Committee on Public Works. *Toward A National Materials Policy*. Committee Print, 91st Congress, 1st session, 1969.

U.S., Congress, Senate, Select Committee to Study Governmental Operations with Respect to Intelligence Activities. *Alleged Assassination Plots Involving Foreign Leaders*. Interim Report, Report No. 94-95, 94th Congress, 1st session, 1975.

U.S., Congress, Senate, Select Committee to Study Governmental Operations with Respect to Intelligence Activities. *Covert Action in Chile, 1963-1973*. Committee Print, 94th Congress, 1st session, 1975.

U.S., Congress, Senate, Special Committee Investigating the National Defense Program. *Petroleum Arrangements with Saudi Arabia*. Hearings, Part 41, 80th Congress, 2nd session, 1948.

U.S., Congress, Senate, Special Committee Investigating Petroleum Resources. *American Petroleum Interests in Foreign Countries*. Hearings, 79th Congress, 1st session, 1945.

U.S., Congress, Senate, Special Committee Investigating Petroleum Resources. *Diplomatic Protection of American Petroleum Interests in Mesopotamia, Netherlands, East Indies, and Mexico*. Senate Document 43, 79th Congress, 1st session, 1945.

U.S., Congress, Senate, Special Committee Investigating Petroleum Resources. *Investigation of Petroleum Resources in Relation to the Natural Welfare*. Report No. 179, 79th Congress, 1st session, 1945.

U.S., Congress, Senate, Special Committee Investigating Petroleum Resources. *Investigation of Petroleum Resources in Relation to the National Welfare*. Report No. 9, 80th Congress, 1st session, 1947.

U.S., Council on International Economic Policy. *Critical Imported Materials*. Special Report, December 1974.

U.S., Department of Commerce, *Survey of Current Business*.

U.S., Department of Commerce, *U.S. Balance of Payments, Statistical Supplement, 1963*.

U.S., Department of Commerce, Bureau of the Census. *Concentration Ratios in Manufacturing*. 1972 Census of Manufactures, Special Report Series, MC 72 (SR)-2. 1975.

U.S., Department of Commerce, Bureau of the Census. *Historical Statistics of the United States, Colonial Times to 1970*. 1975.

U.S., Department of State. *Foreign Relations of the United States*.

U.S., Department of State. *Bulletin*.

U.S., Department of State, Bureau of Intelligence and Research. "Disputes Involving U.S. Foreign Direct Investment July 1, 1971 through July 31, 1973." Research Study RECS-6 (mimeo), February 1974.

U.S., Department of State, Bureau of Intelligence and Research. "Nationalization, Expropriation and Other Takings of United States and Certain Foreign Property Since 1960." Research Study RECS-14 (mimeo), December 1971.

U.S., Federal Trade Commission. *The International Petroleum Cartel*. 1952.

U.S., National Commission on Materials Policy. *Material Needs and the Environment Today and Tomorrow*. Final Report, June 1973.

U.S., National Commission on Materials Policy. "National Materials Policies as Reflected in the Laws of the United States." Report prepared by the Arctic Institute of North America (mimeo), September 1972.

U.S., National Commission on Supplies and Shortages. *Government and the Nation's Resources*. Report, December 1976.

U.S., National Resources Board. *A Report on National Planning and Public Works in Relation to Natural Resources and Including Land Use and Water Resources with Final Recommendations*. December 1934.

U.S., National Resources Committee, Report of the Energy Resources Committee. *Energy Resources and National Policy*. January 1939.

U.S., President's Cabinet Committee on Minerals Policy. *Report of the President's Cabinet Committee on Minerals Policy* (mimeo). November 1954.

U.S., President's Materials Policy Commission (Paley Commission). *Resources for Freedom*. Report, June 1952.

Van Alstyne, R. W. *The Rising American Empire*. New York: Oxford University Press, 1960.

Verba, Sidney. "Assumptions of Rationality and Non-Rationality in Models of the International System," in Klaus Knorr and Sidney Verba, eds., *The International System: Theoretical Essays*. Princeton: Princeton University Press, 1961.

Vernon, Raymond. "The Distribution of Power," *Daedalus* 104. Fall 1975.

———. "Enterprise and Government in Western Europe," in Raymond Vernon, ed., *Big Business and the State: Changing Relations in Western Europe*. Cambridge: Harvard University Press, 1974.

———. "An Interpretation," *Daedalus* 104. Fall 1975.

———. *Sovereignty at Bay*. New York: Basic Books, 1971.

———. *Storm over the Multinationals: The Real Issues*. Cambridge: Harvard University Press, 1977.

Viner, Jacob. "Power Versus Plenty as Objectives of Foreign Policy in the Seventeenth and Eighteenth Centuries," *World Politics* 1. October 1948.

Vogel, David A. "Why Businessmen Distrust Their State: The Political Consciousness of American Corporate Executives," *British Journal of Political Science* 7. October 1977.

Wallace, Benjamin Bruce, and Lynn Ramsay Edminister. *International Control of Raw Materials*. Washington: The Brookings Institution, 1930.

Waltz, Kenneth N. *Foreign Policy and Democratic Politics: The American and British Experience*. Boston: Little, Brown, 1967.

———. "The Myth of National Interdependence," in Charles Kindleberger, ed., *The International Corporation*. Cambridge: MIT Press, 1970.

———. "Theory of International Relations," in Nelson Polsby and Fred I. Greenstein, eds., *Handbook of Political Science*, Vol. VIII. Menlo Park: Addison-Wesley, 1975.

Ward, George W. "The Mexican Oil Problem," *International Conciliation* 345. December 1938.

Weber, Max. *Economy and Society: An Outline of Interpretive Sociology*, ed. Guenther Roth and Claus Wittich. New York: Bedminster Press, 1968.

Weisberg, Richard C. *The Politics of Crude Oil Pricing in the Middle East, 1970-1975*. Berkeley: Institute of International Studies, 1977.

Wells, Louis T., Jr. "The Evolution of Concession Agreements." Development Report No. 117 (mimeo). Cambridge: Development Advisory Service, Harvard University, 1968.

Westerfield, H. Bradford. "What Use Are Three Versions of the Pentagon Papers?" *American Political Science Review* 69. June 1975.

Whittlesey, Charles R. *Governmental Control of Crude Rubber: The Stevenson Plan*. Princeton: Princeton University Press, 1931.

Wilkins, Mira. *The Emergence of Multinational Enterprise: American Business Abroad from the Colonial Era to 1914*. Cambridge: Harvard University Press, 1970.

———. *The Maturing of Multinational Enterprise: American*

Business Abroad from 1914 to 1970. Cambridge: Harvard University Press, 1974.

Williams, Benjamin H. *Economic Foreign Policy of the United States*. New York: McGraw-Hill, 1929.

Williamson, Oliver E. *The Economics of Discretionary Behavior: Managerial Objectives in a Theory of the Firm*. Englewood Cliffs: Prentice-Hall, 1964.

Wilson, Charles Morrow. *Liberia*. New York: William Sloan, 1947.

Wilson, Edward O. *Sociobiology: The New Synthesis*. Cambridge: Harvard University Press, 1975.

Wilson, James Q. *Political Organizations*. New York: Basic Books, 1973.

———. "The Politics of Regulation," in James W. McKie, ed., *Social Responsibility and the Business Predicament*. Washington: The Brookings Institution, 1974.

Wilson, Joan Hoff. *American Business and Foreign Policy*. Lexington: University Press of Kentucky, 1971.

Wise, David, and Thomas B. Ross. *The Invisible Government*. New York: Random House, 1964.

Wolfe, Alan. "New Directions in the Marxist Theory of Politics," *Politics and Society* 4. Winter 1974.

Wood, Bryce. *The Making of the Good Neighbor Policy*. New York: Columbia University Press, 1961.

Zysman, John. *Political Strategies for Industrial Order: State, Market and Industry in France*. Berkeley: University of California Press, 1977.

Index

RELATED BOOKS WRITTEN UNDER THE AUSPICES OF THE CENTER FOR INTERNATIONAL AFFAIRS, HARVARD UNIVERSITY

United States Manufacturing Investment in Brazil, by Lincoln Gordon and Engelbert L. Grommers, 1962. Harvard Business School.

The Economy of Cyprus, by A. J. Meyer, with Simos Vassiliou (sponsored jointly with the Center for Middle Eastern Studies), 1962. Harvard University Press.

Entrepreneurs of Lebanon, by Yusif A. Sayigh (sponsored jointly with the Center for Middle Eastern Studies), 1962. Harvard University Press.

The Dilemma of Mexico's Development, by Raymond Vernon, 1963. Harvard University Press.

Foreign Aid and Foreign Policy, by Edward S. Mason (sponsored jointly with the Council on Foreign Relations), 1964. Harper & Row.

Public Policy and Private Enterprise in Mexico, edited by Raymond Vernon, 1964. Harvard University Press.

Export Instability and Economic Development, by Alasdair I. MacBean. 1966. Harvard University Press.

Europe's Postwar Growth, by Charles P. Kindleberger, 1967. Harvard University Press.

Aid, Influence, and Foreign Policy, by Joan M. Nelson, 1968. The Macmillan Company.

The Brazilian Capital Goods Industry, 1929-1964, by Nathaniel H. Leff (sponsored jointly with the Center for Studies in Education and Development), 1968. Harvard University Press.

Economic Policy-Making and Development in Brazil, 1947-1964, by Nathaniel H. Leff, 1968. John Wiley & Sons.

Taxation and Development: Lessons from Colombian Experience, by Richard M. Bird, 1970. Harvard University Press.

The Kennedy Round in American Trade Policy: The Twilight of the GATT? by John W. Evans, 1971. Harvard University Press.

Korean Development: The Interplay of Politics and Economics, by David C. Cole and Princeton N. Lyman, 1971. Harvard University Press.

Sovereignty at Bay: The Multinational Spread of U.S. Enterprise, by Raymond Vernon, 1971. Basic Books.

Organizing the Transnational: The Experience with Transnational Enterprise in Advanced Technology, by M. S. Hochmuth, 1974. Sijthoff (Leiden).

Multinational Corporations and the Politics of Dependence: The Case of Copper in Chile, by Theodore Moran, 1974. Princeton University Press.

The Andean Group: A Case Study in Economic Integration among Developing Countries, by David Morawetz, 1974. M.I.T. Press.

Big Business and the State: Changing Relations in Western Europe, edited by Raymond Vernon, 1974. Harvard University Press.

Economic Policymaking in a Conflict Society: The Argentine Case, by Richard D. Mallon and Juan V. Sourrouille, 1975. Harvard University Press.

The Politics of International Monetary Reform—The Exchange Crisis, by Michael J. Brenner, 1976. Cornell University Press.

The Oil Crisis, edited by Raymond Vernon, 1976. W. W. Norton & Co.

Bankers and Borders: The Case of the American Banks in Britain, by Janet Kelly, 1977. Ballinger Publishing Co.

Storm Over the Multinationals: The Real Issues, by Raymond Vernon, 1977. Harvard Univerity Press.

Commodity Conflict: The Political Economy of International Commodity Negotiations, by L. N. Rangarajan, 1978. Cornell University Press and Croom Helm (London).

Money and Power, by Jonathan Aronson, 1978. Sage Publications.

LIBRARY OF CONGRESS CATALOGING
IN PUBLICATION DATA

Krasner, Stephen D. 1942-
Defending the national interest.

"Written under the auspices of the Center for International Affairs, Harvard University."
Bibliography: p.
Includes index.
1. United States—Foreign economic relations.
2. United States—Foreign relations. 3. Investments, American. 4. Raw materials. I. Harvard University. Center for International Affairs. II. Title.
HF1455.K77 332.6'7373 78-51175
ISBN 0-691-07600-6
ISBN 0-691-02182-1 pbk.